D1760804

LIVERPOOL INSTITUTE
OF HIGHER EDUCATION

L I B R A R Y

WOOLTON ROAD,
LIVERPOOL, L16 8ND

From Garden Cities to New Towns

STUDIES IN HISTORY, PLANNING AND THE ENVIRONMENT

Series editors   **Professor Gordon E. Cherry,**
University of Birmingham

Professor Anthony Sutcliffe,
University of Leicester

To Colin Ward

From Garden Cities to New Towns

Campaigning for town and
country planning, 1899 - 1946

Dennis Hardy

E & FN SPON
An Imprint of Chapman & Hall

London · New York · Tokyo · Melbourne · Madras

UK	Chapman & Hall, 2–6 Boundary Row, London SE1 8HN
USA	Chapman & Hall, 29 West 35th Street, New York NY 10001
JAPAN	Chapman & Hall Japan, Thomson Publishing Japan, Hirakawacho Nemoto Building, 7F, 1-7-11 Hirakawa-cho, Chiyoda-ku, Tokyo 102
AUSTRALIA	Chapman & Hall Australia, Thomas Nelson Australia, 102 Dodds Street, South Melbourne, Victoria 3000
INDIA	Chapman & Hall India, R. Seshadri, 32 Second Main Road, CIT East, Madras 600 035

First edition 1991

© 1991 Dennis Hardy

Typeset in 11/12pt Times by Rowland Phototypesetting Ltd
Bury St Edmunds, Suffolk
Printed in Great Britain by St Edmundsbury Press Ltd
Bury St Edmunds, Suffolk

This book was commissioned and edited by
Alexandrine Press, Oxford

ISBN 0 419 15570 8

Apart from any fair dealing for the purposes of research or private study, or criticism or review, as permitted under the UK Copyright Designs and Patents Act, 1988, this publication may not be reproduced, stored, or transmitted, in any form or by any means, without the prior permission in writing of the publishers, or in the case of reprographic reproduction only in accordance with the terms of the licences issued by the Copyright Licensing Agency in the UK, or in accordance with the terms of licences issued by the appropriate Reproduction Rights Organization outside the UK. Enquiries concerning reproduction outside the terms stated here should be sent to the publishers at the UK address printed on this page.

The publisher makes no representation, express or implied, with regard to the accuracy of the information contained in this book and cannot accept any legal responsibility or liability for any errors or omissions that may be made.

British Library Cataloguing in Publication Data

Hardy, Dennis
From garden cities to new towns.
1. Great Britain. New towns
I. Title
307.7680941

ISBN 0 419 15570 8

Library of Congress Cataloging-in-Publication Data

Hardy, Dennis.
From garden cities to new towns/Dennis Hardy. – 1st ed.
p.   cm. – (Studies in history of planning in the environment)
Includes bibliographical references (p.   ) and index.
ISBN 0 419 15570 8
1. Town and Country Planning Association (Great Britain)—History.
2. City planning—Great Britain—History.
I. Title   II. Series.
HT169.G7H37   1991
307.1′216′0941—dc20   90-49769
                                                        CIP

LIVERPOOL INSTITUTE
OF HIGHER EDUCATION

Order No. / Invoice No. 762-80
L5023/5704756

Accession No.
175781

Class No.
914·202 HAR

Control No.
0419172270X

Catal.
✗ 4/05

CONTENTS

L. I. H. E.
THE BECK LIBRARY
WOOLTON RD. LIVERPOOL, L16 8ND

PREFACE

Over nearly half a century (more when one takes account of the various antecedents) a campaign was mounted to persuade the rest of society of the merits of creating new settlements as a key to wider reforms. Each new settlement, originally conceived as a garden city, would blossom like a flower in the desert. It was a campaign rooted in idealism, though compromises and changes were necessarily made along the way. From an original preoccupation with privately-sponsored garden cities the path of the campaign takes us into the arena of State planning and the introduction of a governmental new towns programme.

The course of this path, from garden cities to new towns, can be traced back to a setting of radical politics in late-Victorian Britain. For it was then, in 1899, that the Garden City Association was formed, with the aims of promoting the idea of the garden city and of initiating a practical scheme. The philosophy of the organization was based on the contents of a book by Ebenezer Howard, *To-morrow: A Peaceful Path to Real Reform*, published in the previous year.

From its Victorian origins, the campaign of the Association (re-named the Garden Cities and Town Planning Association in 1909, and, then, the Town and Country Planning Association in 1941) was constantly updated in the light of wider changes in Britain in the first half of the twentieth century. Political, social and geographical factors in this period provide an evolving context for what was widely known as the garden city movement. Although, in a different form, the campaign continues to this day, a natural watershed is reached with the passing of the New Towns Act in 1946. It is this date that marks the limits of this book.

For the period 1899 to 1946, an attempt is made to disentangle three themes. The first is simply to record the history of the campaign, piecing together the various fragments of evidence and interpretation; the second theme, from a more detached standpoint, is to see this as a case study of pressure group politics; and the third is to locate the campaign within a wider context of modern town planning history.

The evidence leads me to the qualified conclusion that the campaign achieved some of its original objectives and was an important source of influence on planning thought and legislation. Yet it is also concluded that the effectiveness of a single pressure group cannot be assessed in isolation from a wider context of constraints and opportunities. The 1946 New Towns Acts was by no means solely due to the persistence of this one campaign.

Beyond 1946 the story continues but with a different theme. With a new towns programme underway and a system of planning in place, the campaign is redirected towards one of seeking to ensure that the promise of the New Jerusalem is fulfilled. Idealism remains the power that fires the campaign; it is the agenda that changes. That, however, is the subject of the sequel to this volume, *From New Towns to Green Politics*.

Dennis Hardy
London, 1990

Acknowledgements

This book has its origins in a project to write the official history of the Town and Country Planning Association, from its late-Victorian origins through to the present. My first debt, therefore, is to the Director, David Hall and to other staff of the Association for accepting the idea and for so willingly opening the doors of the archive. Elsewhere, I have enjoyed similar access to important collections: notably, those of the Garden City Museum at Letchworth, the Howard Papers at Hertfordshire Record Office, the Osborn Papers at Welwyn, the National Housing and Town Planning Council, the Libraries of the Royal Town Planning Institute and the Royal Institute of British Architects, and the John Johnson Collection of Printed Ephemera at the Bodleian Library, Oxford.

I am also indebted to my colleagues at Middlesex Polytechnic for supporting this work in a variety of ways, not least of all through enabling me to spend a sabbatical term in Spring 1987. I wish to thank, especially, Sandy Weeks for cheerfully and efficiently typing the work through its various drafts to the present version.

This particular part of the project was initially presented as a doctoral thesis under the supervision of Michael Hebbert at the London School of Economics. His consistent enthusiasm and deep sense of history provided just the right balance of impetus and advice to assist the research, and his role is warmly acknowledged.

In the end, of course, a work of this sort is inevitably judgemental, and responsibility for how the material has been interpreted rests with me.

Abbreviations

GCA	Garden City Association
GCTPA	Garden Cities and Town Planning Association
TCPA	Town and Country Planning Association
Association	References to the Association are to one of the above at a particular period, or to the organization over the entire period, 1899–1946
CPRE	Council for the Preservation of Rural England
IGCTPA	International Garden Cities and Town Planning Association
IGCTPF	International Garden Cities and Town Planning Federation
IFHTP	International Federation for Housing and Town Planning
LCC	London County Council
LNS	Land Nationalisation Society
MARS	Modern Architectural Research Group
NCSS	National Council for Social Service
NHRC	National Housing Reform Council
NHTPC	National Housing and Town Planning Council
NLS	Nationalisation of Labour Society
PEP	Political and Economic Planning
RIBA	Royal Institute of British Architects
TPI	Town Planning Institute

1

INTRODUCTION

There is a general consensus of opinion that the continual growth
of our large cities and the decline of population in country
districts is an unhealthy sign . . . The only remedy – setting on
one side as contrary to English institutions, anything in the nature
of enforced migration – must therefore be through the discovery
of a form of life possessing greater attraction than our present
cities possess. (GCA Tract No. 1, September 1899)

Towards the close of the last century, in June 1899, a new organization was formed, with the basic aim of campaigning for the adoption
of garden cities. Along this road, believed the founders of the
organization, lay the route to the new form of life called for in its first
public circular [1]. True to its beliefs, the Garden City Association
(which changed its name in 1909 to the Garden Cities and Town
Planning Association, and, again, in 1941, to the Town and Country
Planning Association) achieved its first success with the foundation of
Letchworth Garden City in 1903; and, immediately after the First
World War, a second garden city was established at Welwyn.

Although the Association's campaigning took it well beyond its
initial focus on garden cities as such, undoubtedly a major landmark
in the history of the Association was the passing in 1946 of legislation
that ushered in a State programme of new town building. This
legislation, the New Towns Act, effectively closes the first chapter in
the Association's history; from the eccentric cause of a small organization challenging conventional wisdom, the building of new communities had become an accepted aspect of national policy. From
1946 the Association has continued as an active body, but the
nature of its campaigning (as compared with that of the garden city
pioneers) has taken a markedly different course [2].

In the light of the above course of events, this book opens with the
formation of the Garden City Association in 1899 and ends with the
passing of the New Towns Act in 1946.

Within this time span, there are three objectives. A central objective is simply to write a history of the campaign, attempting to make sense of the extensive archives and scattered records over what is nearly a fifty-year period; and, in particular, seeking to show how the campaign was organized, who participated and why. A second objective is to acknowledge the campaigning body in political terms as a pressure group, evaluating the methods it used to further its cause, and the effectiveness of the campaign in terms of what it achieved. Finally, a third objective is to locate the campaign and the work of the Association within a wider context of environmental planning history, assessing the contribution and importance of the garden city campaign in what was a formative period for planning as a whole.

The story, then, centres on the work of a particular organization in a particular period, effectively the first half of the twentieth century. It is this period which provides the context for the detailed history that follows; the specifics of the campaign are closely enmeshed within a broader network of national and, indeed, world events. The complex relationship between the details of the campaign and this wider context, traced chronologically in subsequent chapters, represents an important theme throughout the book. Initially, in this chapter, the context is mapped out, and issues that have a particular bearing on the campaign are introduced.

A CONTEXT OF CHANGE

The context for understanding the Association's own history is one of change, with three themes in particular having a direct bearing on the fortunes of the garden city campaign. One such theme is that of the development of an ideology of reform in Britain, and associated progress on a variety of policy fronts (including that of town and country planning). The political context became distinctly more receptive to the idea of environmental reform at the end of the period in question than at the beginning. A second contextural theme (not unrelated to the above) is the growth of an environmental lobby, with the Association acting at times in unison with other organizations – professions as well as pressure groups – that were committed to at least some its own ideals and aspirations. Finally, as a third theme, it will be shown that radical transformations in the socio-geographical landscape in this period had a fundamental impact on the Association's own campaign. The changing map of Britain, reflecting a largely unplanned process of urban dispersal coupled with evidence of widening regional inequalities, provided both a setback (in the sense of adding to the problems that garden cities were designed to overcome), and a spur (in raising the issues higher on the political agenda) for the Association's own attempts to secure a more rational pattern of settlement.

Ideology of Reform

To take the first of these broad themes of contextual change, that of the development of an ideology of reform, it has to be noted that the period in question begins in the twilight years of Victorian liberalism and ends in the shining dawn of welfare socialism. By the 1940s the idea of reform had come to mean something quite different from what it had meant in the 1890s, recast, as it was, from a marginal concept to benefit the underprivileged to a universal concept embracing a wide spectrum of social policy. Significantly, too, the idea of public intervention and the associated role of the State was to be transformed from something to be resisted, or at least restrained, to a position that became fundamental to the whole idea of social improvement. Adam Smith and Samuel Smiles, lingering ghosts from a different age, were replaced as sources of ideas and inspiration by the likes of John Maynard Keynes and William Beveridge; the Victorian voluntary movement, in the form, for instance, of the Charity Organisation Society and a host of philanthropic trusts, lost ground to new custodians of social welfare in Whitehall offices; and the Labour Party, playing a novice's role in the early years of the century, in the shadows of both Conservatives and Liberals, emerged in 1945 as the party of government and championing a new era of collectivism.

To generalize in this way, categorizing periods and transitions in such broad terms, has to be tempered with a note of caution. Not only is the reality at any one time inevitably more complex than such generalizations suggest (with a whole range of experience encountered amongst different groups and in different places), but the very idea of an uninterrupted view of social progress is questionable. A 'Whig view of history', resting on a perception of the onward march of liberal values and social improvement, cannot be left unchallenged. Alternative interpretations of events are well-founded, and (apart from being identified below) will form an important part of the subsequent analysis [3]. Yet, in spite of contention as to the motives for reform, and whether or not progress is inevitable, the incidence of change itself is not in dispute. Progress in promoting social reforms by no means followed a smooth course across a tranquil ocean of political acceptance; the voyage was marked by setbacks, when the ship of reform was blown off course or pulled by currents which constantly tried to drag it back into what some regarded as safer waters. But if one simply charts the place of reform at the end of the nineteenth century, and compares it with the position in the 1940s, that alone provides strong empirical grounds for mapping out the course of change in terms of a progression.

Thus, in 1899, when the small group of garden city enthusiasts first hatched their plans, they worked in the knowledge that the powers of public agencies (in all aspects of social policy) were still very limited. In the last quarter of the nineteenth century the range of State activity had been broadened, with new measures introduced on a variety of fronts, but the approach was piecemeal and the effects muted in relation to the scale of problems bequeathed by more than a century of relative neglect [4]. Significantly for the Association, the first concerted programme of social reforms came between 1906 and 1914 (within the first decade of its existence, after the establishment of the first garden city, and at a time of reviewing its role) when successive Liberal Administrations laid what is commonly regarded as the foundations of the modern Welfare State. A second landmark in the history of twentieth-century reforms was flagged in the immediate aftermath of the First World War. Promises were made and hopes raised, but, in the event, little of immediate benefit materialized. It was not, in fact, until after the end of the Second World War that a real breakthrough was achieved, with the first majority Labour Administration pushing back the frontiers of social reform and economic management. By then, the pendulum of presumption had swung indisputably away from the market as the arbiter of change and towards the State and its various agencies as the only rational way ahead [5]. The creation of a Welfare State, in particular, provided a totally different context for the Association to that in which it had been conceived at the end of the past century.

This general pattern of progress is mirrored in the specific area of town and country planning, where the first half of the twentieth century saw the introduction of a variety of measures designed to counter the market as the main arbiter of environmental standards [6]. From the first town planning legislation in 1909, through sub-sequent Acts in 1919, 1925 and 1932, prior to the wide-ranging measures of the 1945 Labour Administration (including the 1946 New Towns Act), the history of the garden city movement is intimately interwoven with this wider movement. Constantly campaigning for the means to promote its own ideals, the Association was gratified at each new legislative step forward, yet at times despondent that the steps were not always sufficiently far-reaching nor even necessarily in the right direction. The early legislation, especially, favoured the extension of metropolitan growth through garden suburbs rather than the creation of new garden cities beyond the old boundaries. For all the reservations of the Association, though, the emergence by the second half of the 1940s of a relatively comprehensive planning system was fundamental to the garden city movement's own history.

Although different writers interpret the changing reform scene in different ways, there is at least agreement on the radical extent of change. Stuart Hall, for instance (who is by no means subscribing to a Whig view of history) writes of the rise of the 'representative/ interventionist state' in the period from the 1880s to the 1920s. During this period, 'old laissez-faire conceptions began to be challenged, new philosophies of state action took shape, the scale of state activity enlarged and the state did begin to pioneer new modes of action of a more interventionist kind.' [7]

What this process of intervention really meant, however, and the true motives for reform that underpinned it, raises questions that will be returned to in the final chapter. Was reform motivated by relentless pressures for social improvement, articulated by politicians and pressure groups, and reflecting a spirit of humanitarianism that has its origins in the nineteenth century? Or was reform a product of political and economic necessity, conceded less on the grounds of altruism and more because the capitalist system in Britain, increasingly vulnerable to world competition, was forced to introduce measures that would enhance both its productive and reproductive capacity? These questions are central to an understanding of the effectiveness of the Association, campaigning for reform on a particular front, in that each casts a different role for pressure groups in the political process. The one view would explain the role of the Association as a potentially important part of the democratic process, capable through its own actions of influencing decisions; while the other view would see the Association, along with other pressure groups, as being largely irrelevant to the real sources of power and decision making.

Hall's analysis stops at the 1920s, but others have reviewed the reform process over a longer period. A. M. Halsey is one who has taken stock of the longer drift of events from the start of the twentieth century, and who, amongst the many fundamental changes that have taken place, sees the growth of the State and the progress made in terms of social reforms as being crucial [8]. Drawing on the work of T. S. Marshall, Halsey measures the worth of these changes against the yardstick of 'citizenship' – 'a tradition of radical reform in which democracy is both a means and an end which seeks to attain a maximum of equality between individuals in a free society.' [9] Citizenship is a concept which (in the first half of the century at least) rested on the Parliamentary process as a means of securing social improvement. But, as a measure of reform, the concept is not without contention. Is the State necessarily the best source of determining and administering progress? For the garden city campaign this proved to be a fundamental question that shaped the strategy of the Association from the very outset, when the campaign pinned its colours to the mast of voluntarism, to 1946, when the direction of its subsequent history was finally sealed by the State. This issue, of the relative benefits to be gained by voluntarism as opposed to the State, and of how strategies were adapted to reflect the growing importance of the State, will also be traced in the subsequent chapters.

Environmental Lobby

In addition to the context of reform, a second area of change that affects the history of the Association is that of the growth of an environmental lobby. It will be shown in the next chapter that the Garden City Association was heir to a nineteenth-century urban reform lobby and that, at the time the Association was formed, numerous groups were already at work in pursuit of environmental improvements. By contrast, what distinguishes the early half of the twentieth century is the extension of the lobby of special interest groups into countryside matters, and the growing importance and influence of professional bodies. The relationship of the Association to this gathering lobby for environmental improvements is something that will be explored in the following chapters.

At this stage it can be noted that evidence of other groups active in the pursuit of environmental improvements demonstrates that the *modus operandi* of the Association as a pressure group was by no means unique. The Association was to be accused of eccentricity because of what they were campaigning for (with, as will be shown, garden cities acquiring a 'cranky' reputation), but not because of its campaigning methods. Extra-parliamentary activity was increasingly to become a legitimate part of the political process, and it is interesting to locate the history of the Association within this context. Moreover, the development of mass communication systems in the twentieth century was to add to the effectiveness of such groups. At the turn of the century, penny tracts and evening lectures in institute halls were part and parcel of the world of propagandist groups (as they would then have been known); by the 1940s, groups with a national appeal were making effective use of radio broadcasting, propagandist films, and international networks. In this respect, the Association was to benefit not only from a growing legitimacy for the process of lobbying governments and others from the outside, but also from new technologies that underpinned its efforts.

Although different meanings can be attached to the growth of pressure groups and professions in the twentieth century, the incidence of growth as such is not to be denied. Anticipating such events, Durkheim had some years previously offered an explanation of the growth of professional and special interest groupings in terms of the need to fill a new vacuum in industrial society between the individualism of the family in a market-based economy, and the collectivism and bureaucracy of the State. Professional organizations, espousing rationality, were seen by Durkheim as a source of moral order and political consensus, with various interests locked together in a web of interdependence [10].

While a strictly functionalist explanation of this sort has its limitations, there is some merit in locating the Association within a network of linked (and, to an extent, interdependent) groups, lobbying for power but, taken together, also a source of power in its own right. It will be seen in subsequent chapters that the Association is constantly seeking the 'middle ground', and that, from the time of its formation through to the building of a lobby for reconstruction in the Second World War, a search for consensus is a consistent feature of the campaign.

It would be misleading to exaggerate the extent to which the political process was radically altered in the first half of the twentieth century – a period during which the question of the franchise as a central issue of political involvement continued to feature until the end of the First World War. The greater rise in the importance of pressure groups and the influence of the professions on governments came after 1945 rather than before. But it was undoubtedly a watershed period, marking a seminal divide between a political system which rested on a limited form of representative government and an emerging system that became more participatory. A rich variety of groups espousing radical causes before 1914, the solid growth of trade unions, environmental pressure groups making their voices heard in the interwar years, and in the 1930s an influential lobby composed of diverse groups campaigning for more assertive government, are all evidence of a discernible drift towards a more participatory model of politics [11].

Historically, in the environmental field, Lowe and Goyder have pointed to two peak periods for new pressure group formation, the first being from the mid-1880s until the turn of the century, and the second in the middle interwar years [12]. What is more, this increase in the number of pressure groups is matched by a parallel increase in the number and influence of professional bodies. As Gordon Cherry shows, between 1880 and 1910 a dozen new associations in a variety of fields were formed in each decade, prior to the formation of the Town Planning Institute at the end of 1913 [13]. The growing importance of this area of political activity constitutes a supportive context in which the Association was able to develop its own campaign. In turn, it will be interesting in the following chapters to trace the extent to which the activities of the Association are adapted to the changing context of constraints and opportunities inherent in the political process.

On the associated question of alliances, although other groups did not share all of the Association's priorities there were, at different times, important areas of collaboration. With its dual interest in town and country, this collaboration was based on the overlapping interests of a wide range of groups. Alliances were formed around specific campaigns, although it was questionable whether these were always of advantage to the Association. Was there not sometimes a danger, one critic noted with bitterness, of mixing wine with water – of diluting the strong message of garden cities with 'inferior practices' [14]?

Certainly, there was no shortage of potential partners. On the urban side, the Association (especially in its early years) found common ground with a variety of housing organizations. One such organization, the National Housing Reform Council, was formed in the year after the Association, and, while its own priorities were by no means identical – campaigning, with a strong lead from municipal councillors, for better housing (whether or not it was sited in a garden city) – an overlapping membership and collaborative campaigns in a common quest for improvement led to a close relationship between the two groups over the years. Later in its campaign, during the Second World War, the Association cast the net widely to identify some 250 groups sharing an interest in planning and reconstruction [15].

It was a similar story on the rural side, with bodies like the National Trust and, especially, the Council for the Preservation of Rural England (formed in 1926) attracting the interest of the Association in the campaign against uncontrolled development. Such alliances, however, were less than solid, and it will be seen that at times (as in the discussions leading to the Scott Report of 1942) the Association's advocacy of garden cities on greenfield sites would cut across the interests of the preservationists [16].

Additionally, there were close links with professional associations, which were themselves active campaigning bodies in their own right. Before the formation of the Town Planning Institute in 1913, the Royal Institute of British Architects (founded in 1834) played an influential role in the lobby for the introduction and effective application of town planning legislation. As early as 1907, the RIBA had established the Development of Towns and Suburbs Committee, under the chairmanship of Aston Webb, to monitor the progress of impending legislation. Changing the name of the special committee in 1908 to that of Town Planning Committee, and again in 1920 to Town Planning and Housing Committee, it attracted some of the planning pioneers (like Patrick Abercrombie and Raymond Unwin) who were to play significant roles in the Association as well. But, again, the alliance between the two organizations was by no means without its problems and one of the interesting themes to pursue is the tension that surfaces from time to time between 'high density' architects and the 'low density' garden city enthusiasts [17].

There is also a close and interesting relationship between the Association and the Town Planning Institute, the former a propagandist body and the latter the professional arm of planning. Particularly in the early years, an overlap not just of general membership but, significantly, of leadership, contributed to a natural alliance of interests. Later in the period, however, the Institute's concern to stay clear of political controversy led to a sharper division between the two organizations. During the Second World War, for instance, it will be seen that it was the Association that took the lead in pressing for effective planning legislation. If there was a difference in method, though, there was an underlying unity of purpose, with the two organizations located within what Eric Reade terms the mainstream of planning thought – 'essentially physical, visual, anti-metropolitan and anti-political' [18]. The waters from which this mainstream flowed, and the course it followed, is another theme that runs through the following chapters.

Changing Landscapes

As well as reformism and the environmental lobby, a third aspect of twentieth-century change to have a direct bearing on the work of the Association was that of the new patterns of settlement and associated lifestyles that emerged in this period.

For the Association, committed to the achievement of garden cities, planned on an orderly basis, the evidence of what actually occurred was of crucial importance. Instead of planned decentralization, the dominant feature was one of urban sprawl, with both private and public suburbs pushing the old city boundaries further into the countryside. In the language of the day, this outward growth was frequently described in organic terms, the tentacles not only of the city but of a debased society reaching out to engulf a dwindling acreage of sanity and civilization. Reviewing Clough Williams-Ellis's *England and the Octopus*, G. K. Chesterton explained to his readers that what was at stake was more than a question of saving the countryside; rather, the struggle was to save the country 'from the modern anarchy of machinery run mad . . . the struggle between a man and a monster' [19].

While (as will be seen below) not everyone reacted to suburbanization like Williams-Ellis and Chesterton, empirically, at least, the evidence of growth was beyond dispute. All the major cities grew larger and, with what was happening in Britain symptomatic of what was happening elsewhere, it is fair to conclude that the 'early twentieth century might be labelled the first age of the giant metropolis' [20]. Before the term 'conurbation' was coined and fell into common usage, H. G. Wells had rightly predicted the advent of the 'urban region', 'laced all together not only by road and railway and telegraph but . . . by a dense network of telephones, parcels delivery tubes . . . like nervous and arterial connections'. [21] For the garden city campaigners, a London-based organization, such predictions were far from fanciful, as the capital city itself grew inexorably throughout this period. Against all the best advice of the Association, the population of Greater London grew from about six million in 1919 to about eight million in 1939, and, in the same period, the built-up area increased by a factor of five [22].

To those who sought a more orderly form of growth, suburbanization was already seen to be a problem at the turn of the century, taking shape on the ground faster than opinion could be aroused to counter it. Around London, late-Victorian suburban villas lined the roads in Edmonton and Tooting, Ealing and Ilford, offering office workers and artisans an escape from the smoke and overcrowding of the inner city. But, from their inception, such developments were condemned for their 'appalling monotony, ugliness and dullness'. [23] New transport developments forced the pace, with, from 1863, the world's first steam-powered underground service carrying commuters into what, by 1915 (with the help of electricity) had come to be known as 'Metro-Land'. John Betjeman would later look back with affection at the semi-detached world that was created in the countryside of Middlesex and Buckinghamshire – enjoying 'sepia views of leafy lanes in PINNER' and 'rural RAYNER'S LANE' [24] – but this was just the kind of situation deplored by the Association. Suburbs without centres were compared unfavourably with what Letchworth and Welwyn had to offer, while the 'straphanging' that was part and parcel of suburban life was shown to be a far cry from the gentle walk or cycle ride to work that was promised in a garden city.

The Association may have had a strong case, but in the interwar period, especially, its role was one of Canute facing a relentless tide. Four million new homes were built, many at low densities of eight to twelve houses to the acre, and, characteristically, without associated jobs and services. The majority of these new developments were for the private market, this period being marked by a striking increase in home ownership (from 10 per cent of all tenures in 1914 to 31 per cent by 1939) [25]. Settlements were transformed, but the building of the suburbs, in turn, was symptomatic of deeper social and occupational changes. Higher incomes, a growth in consumables, and a shifting balance between manual and office workers all contributed to changes in how and where people lived. For some, the suburbs were a land of opportunity. First-time buyers in Metro-Land, for instance, might have settled for a three-bedroomed semi-detached residence in

Ruislip for £350, and a lifestyle beyond the expectations of their urban-based parents. It was a lifestyle, though, of mixed fortunes. To Betjeman, articulating the prospects for the 'better off', it was all so comfortable – 'a world of fine woodwork and a smell of dinner; a stained glass windmill and a pot of tea . . .' [26] But for others, the lure of a new consumer society, set in a suburban idyll, required too much, and 'Men drawing comfortable salaries were soon tempted to acquire not only their jerry-built villas, but cheap cars, wireless sets, furniture and other amenities on the "never never" system. With each new obligation they became more and more the slaves of their employers.' [27] In this material sense, the reality of suburbia fell far short of the Association's garden city ideals; as, indeed, it did in tenure terms, with private ownership rather than a leasehold system – a central plank in the garden city propaganda – precluding the idea of the community sharing in its own rising fortunes.

As well as private developments, the new suburbs were also a product of municipal house-building; though here, too, the Association was at odds with what was happening. Expansive council estates were built on the peripheries of all the major cities, particularly in the 1920s when government subsidies were at their highest. The London County Council Becontree estate, for instance, started in 1921, eventually accommodated nearly 120,000 people. Typically, such estates were built on 'garden suburb' lines, with cottage-style housing, but although the standard of design was often of a higher standard than that in neighbouring private estates, in other respects they shared the common suburban affliction of an absence of overall planning. Two important interwar studies (of Becontree and of Watling, both London estates) illustrate that many of the residents had to travel long distances to work, and families faced constant financial problems in meeting higher rents than they had been used to, and in furnishing the many rooms compared with cramped tenements that they had often left behind [28]. For the garden city campaign, while the lower densities were to be welcomed, a dual opportunity was missed; the estates were neither separate settlements, nor were they planned in the context of a full range of social needs.

For some, neither the private suburbs nor the new council estates were accessible, but an alternative existed in the form of a third arm of suburban development, the plotlands. Laindon and Pitsea, Peacehaven and Jaywick Sands – makeshift settlements, defying all the known laws of civic planning, yet sometimes even claiming to be built on garden city lines [29] – offered cheap and unconventional outlets for the poor and the Bohemian. Far smaller in extent than the suburbs proper, they nevertheless attracted a disproportionate amount of public attention, contributing (in a perverse and unexpected way) to the growing strength of a planning lobby that called for a system where such 'rural slums' could never again be allowed [30].

In the face of these various suburban developments, questions arise that are central to the Association's own progress in the same period. To what extent was the campaigning body overwhelmed by the sheer volume of development that cut across its own garden city ideals? And to what extent was the Association itself to blame for lending support to the development of garden suburbs, as opposed to garden cities, with a consequent confusion and misuse of the garden city idea in the public mind? These are questions that are raised at various times in the Association's history, especially in relation to the interwar period.

If decentralization was one aspect of settlement change, so, too, was an important regional dimension – a dimension that was to become central to the Association's own campaign. While the seeds of what amounted to a growing North-South divide are to be found in the legacy of nineteenth-century investment and industrial location, and while the 1920s revealed a widening rift, it was not until the 1930s that it became an issue of significant political concern.

In the face of the international recession dating from 1929, evidence of a profile of two nations was projected into sharper focus – one nation of buoyant growth and one of stagnation and decline. Indicative of trends in the early 1930s, nearly 400 new factories opened in Greater London between 1932 and 1935, compared with net closures in each of the traditional industrial regions (with the North West and North East the hardest hit) [31]. More salient were the comparative employment figures, with high unemployment rates in the outlying regions reflecting the consequent social effects throughout whole communities of a long-term shift in investment and occupational patterns.

What is of particular interest in throwing light on the Association's campaign is that each of the 'two nations' attracted its own problems, and both were to have an important bearing on the way the garden city campaign was conducted. While the Association and environmentalists railed against the problems of growth and dispersal across the landscape of Southern England, an influential lobby emerged around the cause of economic recovery in other parts of the country. It will be shown how, in the latter half of the 1930s, these two sources of concern were brought together as two halves of the same problem, and how this process, in turn, proved to be an important step towards the introduction of a national system of planning. It will also be shown how the Association's original and longstanding campaign for garden cities was modified in the face of these developments, with the new Honorary Secretary, Frederic Osborn, seeing in the changing situation an unprecedented opportunity for the Association to advance a wider cause.

ORGANIZATION OF THE BOOK

In the light of this background, the findings are presented in the following chapters on a chronological basis. Indeed, the pursuit of the objectives is framed within a relationship of changes in Britain and of changes within the Association in the same period.

Thus, chapter 2 looks at the origins of the campaign, locating the formation of the Association within the ferment of late-Victorian radical politics and a growing sense of urgency and awareness of problems in town and country. This is followed in chapter 3 with a review of the history of the Association in an active and formative period through to 1914, the year that marks the end of an era for the Association as well as the nation. Developments from 1914 to 1939 are traced in chapter 4 under the heading of 'the long campaign' – a campaign which saw a radical change in the strategy and role of the Association, from that of an essentially garden city movement to a powerful lobby for national planning. In turn, chapter 5 attempts to unravel the role of the Association during the years of the Second World War, when the idea of reconstruction and planning attracted widespread interest and support, and in the immediate postwar years, which saw *inter alia* the passing of the 1946 New Towns Act. In each of these chapters, the Association's own history is related to the history of the period, with consideration given both to the methods of operation and to the policy dimension of the organization.

The final chapter constitutes an evaluation, with the work of the Association over the whole period assessed in terms of the objectives of the study. Questions are raised as to the internal workings of the organization, to the effectiveness of the campaign, and to the relationship of the garden city movement to wider developments and progress in town and country planning. What impact, if any, has the Association had on the pattern of twentieth-century policy and development? Would new towns have been introduced had it not been for the groundwork of a lengthy campaign?

NOTES

1. GCA Tract No. 1, 'The Garden City Project', September 1899.
2. The history of the Association since 1946 has been separately researched by the author, and is published as a separate volume, Hardy (1991).
3. An alternative to a liberal interpretation is best represented by the work of political economists. In relation to the origins of town

L. I. H. E.

THE BECK LIBRARY

WOOLTON RD., LIVERPOOL, L16 8ND

planning from this standpoint, see, for instance, Roweis (1981) and Rees and Lambert (1985), chapter 1.

4. For an assessment of the legacy of Victorian urban reforms, and of how much still needed to be done, see, for instance, Ashworth (1954) and Briggs (1968).

5. For different reasons, both liberals and political economists are agreed as to the necessity for State intervention – the former seeing it as an outcome of a long campaign and a victory for reason, the latter reducing it to a question of satisfying the needs of capital. Compare, for instance, Marshall (1965) with Gough (1979), chapter 4.

6. These measures are detailed in subsequent chapters, but an overview is provided, for instance, in Pepler (1949) and Ashworth (1954).

7. Hall, S. (1984), p. 7.

8. Halsey (1986).

9. *Ibid*, p. 147.

10. Elliott (1972), pp. 6–9.

11. An explanation of the place of pressure groups within a pluralist political system is provided in Dunleavy and O'Leary (1987).

12. Lowe and Goyder (1983), pp. 16–17.

13. Cherry (1974*b*), p. 251.

14. Purdom, C. B., quoted in Ashworth (1954), p. 196.

15. *Planning and Reconstruction Year Book*, 1945. This is discussed in chapter 5.

16. Another illustration of tensions between seemingly like-minded organizations can be seen in the Federation of Progressive Societies and Individuals (Joad, 1934). Although this organization championed, as one of its goals, the cause of town and country planning, one of the contributors to its manifesto, G. M. Boumphrey, condemned the garden city movement as a source of worsening rather than improving conditions: 'the towns are but little better, the country is immeasurably worse' (p. 257).

17. An interesting overview of the various strands of planning thought in this period is provided by Peter Hall (1984).

18. Reade (1987), p. 45.

19. Chesterton, G. K., *Architects Journal*, 15 August, 1928.

20. Hall, P. (1984), p. 19.

21. H. G. Wells, quoted in Hall, P. (1984), p. 32.

22. Hall *et al.* (1973), p. 83.

23. Report in *The Times*, 1904, cited in Gaskell (1981).

24. From John Betjeman, 'The Metropolitan Railway', in Delaney (1985), p. 208.

25. For a statistical analysis of these trends (pursued in chapter 4), see Bowley (1945).

26. Betjeman, *op. cit.*

27. From Goldring, D., *Nineteen Twenties*, 1945, in Barker (1978).

28. The two studies, that of Terence Young of Becontree and Dagenham, published in 1934, and Ruth Durant's study of Watling, are reported in Aldridge (1979), pp. 13–16.

29. Peacehaven, for instance, was publicized by its founder, Charles Neville, as 'the garden city by the sea'.
30. The plotlands story is recounted in Hardy and Ward (1984).
31. Ashworth (1954), p. 220.

2

THE ORIGINS OF A
PRESSURE GROUP

This chapter examines the circumstances in which the Garden City Association was established. What was the rationale for forming a new pressure group, and how sound were the ideas on which its campaign was to be based? Taking a wider view, what was the general climate of reform at the time, and to what extent can the garden city campaign be located as part of a wider thrust for social and environmental improvement?

FORMATION OF THE GARDEN CITY ASSOCIATION

> After a few months of such fitful works as I could undertake, I consulted a friend, Mr F. W. Flear, and we decided it would be well to form an Association with a view to securing supporters in a more systematic manner, and of formulating the scheme more completely, so that, at as early a date as possible, a suitable organisation might be created for carrying it out. (Ebenezer Howard, in his postscript to *Garden Cities of To-morrow*, 1902)

Eight months after the publication of *To-morrow: A Peaceful Path to Real Reform*, the author, Ebenezer Howard, met on the 10th June 1899 with twelve fellow sympathizers of the ideas presented in his book [1]. The meeting, called to discuss ways to promote Howard's ideas, was held at the City office of Alexander Payne, an accountant, who was also Treasurer of the Land Nationalisation Society (and who was, in fact, just one of six members at the meeting who belonged to that organization) [2]. In the chair was Alfred Bishop, another long-standing campaigner for land nationalization. Also in the room was an old acquaintance of Howard, J. Bruce Wallace, who had started a Brotherhood Church some years before, and who was

GARDEN CITIES
AND
TOWN PLANNING

Design by Walter Crane for *Garden Cities of To-morrow*, 1902 and subsequently used for the Association's journal, *Garden Cities and Town Planning*.

Ebenezer Howard, 'inventor' of the garden city.
(By courtesy of the Central Library, Welwyn)

constantly searching for ways to establish a co-operative system in place of capitalism [3].

Howard made a statement to the meeting, in which he dwelt upon the advantages and necessity of forming an Association. He argued that each member should make it his business to enlist associates from his own neighbourhood. There were many difficulties to overcome, and members ready to face these difficulties would be of the greatest use to an Association of this kind. It was a committed gathering, and a formal proposal by Joseph Hyder (seconded by Joseph Johnson) calling for the formation of an Association to promote Howard's ideas, 'by educational and other means', was carried unanimously. Francis W. Steere (a barrister, and already Secretary of the Land Nationalisation Society) became the Association's first Honorary Secretary, and Payne took on the job of Honorary Treasurer [4]. Eleven days later a public meeting was held at the Memorial Hall in Farringdon Street, and at that Mr T. H. W. Idris, an industrialist, was elected as Chairman [5].

The Association was constituted from the outset with a Council and an Executive Committee, the former with a potential membership of 100 and the latter restricted to a membership of twenty-five. Soon after the formation of the Association, in September 1899, a tract was produced to explain to a wider public the rationale for the new organization [6]. Details of its rules included in the tract, and a listing of officers, show that already there had been a change in the Honorary Secretaryship, with C. M. Bailhache (a barrister, like his predecessor) taking on the role. A second tract was produced to describe the work of the Association [7].

Although the early years of the Association were to be marked by various reappraisals of priorities, the initial aims were clear enough. Thus, it went to work with the dual brief of spreading an awareness of Howard's ideas and ultimately of formulating 'a practical scheme on the lines of the project with such modifications as may appear desirable.' [8] The Association appealed to all persons 'desirous of improving by constitutional means, the present physical, social and industrial conditions of life in town and country.' [9] Indeed, three months after the Association was formed, Howard could write that the Association numbered amongst its members 'Manufacturers, Cooperators, Architects, Artists, Medical Men, Financial Experts, Lawyers, Merchants, Ministers of Religion, Members of the LCC, Moderates and Progressives, Socialists and Individuals, Radicals and Conservatives.' [10]

From the start, then, the Association was endowed with a practical, reformist brief, the success or failure of which was initially balanced on the logic or otherwise of a book of less then 200 pages by a previously little-known author (who had, in fact, failed to implement a similar scheme some five years earlier, and who could only get his ideas published in 1898 through private sponsorship) [11]. So what was the special appeal contained in *To-morrow: A Peaceful Path to Real Reform* (revised and republished in 1902 as *Garden Cities of To-morrow*)? How sound was the logic of the case it presented, and why should it appeal to the broad following on which the whole rationale of the Garden City Association depended? The answers to these questions, fundamental to the whole campaign, lie in the book itself.

THE IDEA OF THE GARDEN CITY

'Garden City' – where the most approved modern methods of engineering and sanitary science should be adopted, and the utmost attention should be devoted to the securing of healthy and beautiful homes and conditions for all the people . . . a new hope, a new life, a new civilisation. (GCA Tract No. 1, September 1899)

The logic of the idea of the garden city was simple enough. In essence, it amounted to a plan to build new settlements that would at once resolve those problems of town and country that afflicted late-Victorian society. Within his book, in what has become one of the best-known schematic representations in planning, 'the three magnets', Howard asked the rhetorical question – 'The People: where will they go?' The answer, of course, was that they would go to garden cities as these would offer the very best of town and country while removing the worst. Through the garden city a new magnet would be created, 'in which all the advantages of the most energetic and active town life, with all the beauty and delight of the country, may be secured in perfect combination.' [12] In turn, the new garden cities would act as basic building blocks in the progressive reconstruction of society – the 'peaceful path to real reform' referred to in the title of the first edition of Howard's book.

Howard's scheme has been extensively described and analysed by numerous authors (acknowledging the importance of its influence in the history of modern planning) [13], but a summary of the details is important for what follows [14]. Imagine, asks Howard, an area of about 6000 acres of farmland, purchased at agricultural land values (then about £40 per acre). Within this estate, a garden city would be built on about 1000 acres, leaving the rest as an encircling belt of permanently open and productive farmland (reorganized into new farm units). The main settlement would have a population of about 30,000 with another 2000 in the agricultural belt.

The whole unit would be carefully and comprehensively planned. Within the town (probably circular in form), there would be strict zoning to ensure very much higher environmental standards than were commonplace in traditional, unplanned settlements. In the very centre of the town would be an ornamental garden, surrounded by a spacious layout for the main civic buildings (town hall, concert hall, theatre, library, museum, art gallery and hospital) and beyond that an extensive park. This central complex would, in turn, be bounded by a Crystal Palace, a wide glass arcade with shops and exhibitions. Tree-lined avenues and boulevards were proposed, not simply to provide access, but also to distinguish the different neighbourhoods, and to separate the housing from non-residential uses.

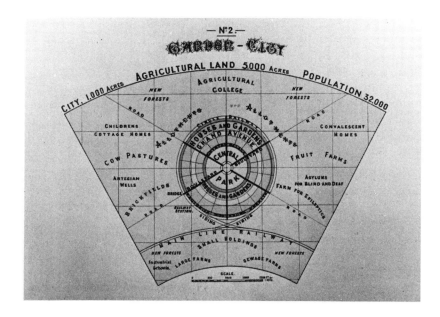

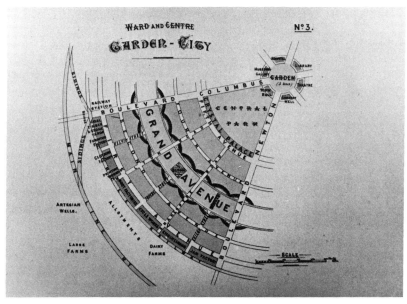

Howard's garden city *in toto* and a section from it. (From *To-morrow: A Peaceful Path to Real Reform*, 1898).

All housing would be built on ample plots (the minimum size being a frontage of twenty feet and a depth of one hundred feet), the essence of the garden city being a city of gardens as well as a city within a garden. Factories (fuelled by electricity), warehouses, dairies, markets, timber and coal yards, and other services would be confined to an outer ring, served by a circular railway which, in turn, would be connected to a main line into the centre of the town and outwards to other parts of the country. Beyond the railway the farmland would begin, a mixture of large farms, smallholdings and allotments, the land fertilized with sewage from the town and, in turn, with much of the produce sold to the local market.

It was, in purely spatial terms, an attractive plan, but what distinguishes it from other model schemes is its unique treatment of land values and tenure arrangements. The sequence envisaged was that, in the first place, capital would be raised by a sponsoring trust, with a rate of return for investors not exceeding 4 per cent. All occupants would pay a rent (referred to as a rate-rent, as there would be no separate general rate levy), and the total income would be used for three purposes – to pay the interest on the initial capital sum, to pay back the capital, and to pay for the general running costs and welfare of the town. Over time, the first two items of expenditure would decrease (it was planned to repay the capital within thirty years), and the Central Council of the municipality would enjoy greater discretion in what could be done to benefit the town. Initially, most of this local expenditure would be spent on building costs and general infrastructure, but the prospect was there for the progressive provision of amenities the like of which was unknown in a traditional local authority. All this was possible, claimed Howard, by keeping the land in common ownership, and by planning the whole exercise from start to finish.

The balance and viability of the scheme depended on restricting the ultimate growth of the town to the planned figure. Expansion, however, could be accommodated by establishing new garden cities beyond the agricultural belt, to form a cluster of 'social cities'. While it might be possible to initiate the first experiment through private negotiation, the subsequent development of the scheme would almost certainly require Parliamentary support (if only to secure the land).

Important components of the scheme had already been suggested by earlier writers, and Howard was the first to acknowledge this debt. As a synthesis, however, the garden city could offer something new. Earlier proposals were drawn upon, but now they were cast in a new mould – 'a unique combination of proposals' [15]. Of those sources that were directly acknowledged, Howard singled out the works of Edward Gibbon Wakefield and Professor Alfred Marshall, who had

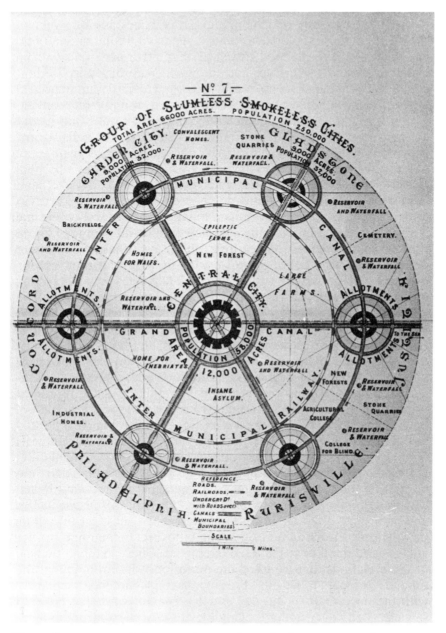

Howard's concept of the social city, formed of separate garden cities. (From *To-morrow: A Peaceful Path to Real Reform*, 1898).

both advocated forms of planned resettlement [16]; the radical land tenure proposals of Thomas Spence, with subsequent revisions by Herbert Spencer [17]; and the model city of James Silk Buckingham [18]. Each of these sets of ideas touched upon vital components of the garden city – the planned dispersal of people and industry, the question of land ownership, and the whole idea of a purpose-built community – but there is no doubt, too, that Howard is influenced by other idealists of his day, with some of whom he was in direct contact.

Of these latter sources of influence, Howard recalls that he was 'carried away' by a reading in about 1888 of *Looking Backward*, Edward Bellamy's utopian vision of American society reorganized on cooperative lines [19]. In Howard's own words, it was this book (published in America in 1888) which helped him 'to realise as never before the splendid possibilities of a new civilisation based on service to the community . . . I determined to take such part, however small it might be, in helping to bring a new civilisation into being.' [20]

Howard also derived 'much inspiration' from the ideas of Henry George [21], first hearing him lecture in 1882 and then reading *Progress and Poverty*. It was the idea of land values properly belonging to the community which appealed to Howard, although he did not share George's enthusiasm for a centralized State system as the right way to appropriate and reallocate the benefits. As with *Looking Backward*, Howard accepted the kernel of the book, but rejected anything that might lead to more centralization, as opposed to basically communal forms of organization.

Additionally, *To-morrow* is peppered with quotes and references to contemporaries of his who shared a belief that society would be a better place if it were to be decentralized – John Ruskin, Leo Tolstoy, the Topolobampo communitarians, and (in Howard's revised edition, after the publication of *Anticipations*) H. G. Wells [22]. Howard is also appreciative of the works of William Morris and Peter Kropotkin (both of whom he met in London in the 1880s and 1890s). Morris's utopian romance, *News from Nowhere* (serialized in 1890 and published as a book in 1891) offered an evocative picture of the population of London and other big cities freely migrating to new villages and small towns in a reconstructed society that had rid itself of the afflictions that troubled the minds of radical thinkers at that time. It is difficult, too, to miss the obvious connections and similarities with the decentralist ideas of Peter Kropotkin, who, like Howard, saw electricity and modern technology as key elements in his social model of 'fields, factories and workshops' [23].

It has also been noted that, in the formative period before the publication of *To-morrow*, Howard takes more than a passing interest in spiritualism. Although he had himself been a lay, nonconformist preacher, it is argued that his attachment to spiritualism served to strengthen his own drift towards an unshakeable belief in cooperative values. In place of more traditional forms of Christianity, 'came an abiding conviction that love was the embodiment of the 'Supreme Power' and inevitably led man to new forms of co-operation and progress.' [24]

Howard, then, drew on a rich mix of ideas, but this alone is not enough to explain his subsequent influence. After all, the nineteenth century was strewn with a legacy of failed utopian plans, each in their own way drawing on the strengths of each other, and each launched with no less optimism than that of Howard's scheme [25]. One essential feature, however, which distinguishes the garden city idea from many other visions in the same 'genre' is its practicability – 'I have taken a leaf out of the books of each type of reformer and bound them together by a thread of practicability' [26] – combined with its political acceptability. It was, above all, a reformist plan, 'a peaceful path to real reform', rather than a blueprint for revolution. As Howard himself was at pains to emphasize, it could enjoy a broad measure of support.

In political terms, the path that Howard sought was that which followed a line between total individualism and total collectivism, 'an even course between the Scylla of anarchy and the Charybidis of despotism.' [27] It was a radical scheme (not least of all because of its communal ownership), which, if carried through to its logical end, would have implications for the organization of society as a whole. And yet Howard was at pains to avoid any sense of coercion, stressing that his scheme should not be regarded as a straitjacket into which all had to fit. He was undoubtedly right when he observed that past utopian schemes had often failed because they had asked too much of human nature [28]. His own approach was to seek to create a climate in which social experiment could flourish, but not to impose a single way of doing things. In the agricultural belt, for instance, he could imagine that the farms would be managed by a mixture of capitalist, cooperative and small individual methods, as best befits the size of the holding and the preferences of the farmer. 'Here, as in every feature of the experiment, it will be seen that it is not the area of rights which is contracted, but the area of choice which is enlarged.' [29]

In a similar way, Howard addressed the overall balance that should be struck between municipal and private enterprise. He contrasted the views of the socialist and the individualist, each of which favoured one form of enterprise rather than the other, and concluded that 'probably the true answer is to be found at neither extreme, is only to be gained by experiment, and will differ in different communities, and at different periods.' [30] His own preference was to see an extension of municipal activity, but this would best come about gradually through the example of merit and should, in any case, never claim a 'rigid monopoly' [31]. Elsewhere, Howard described this approach as one of Social Individualism, where the association of individuals for the common good would come about as a natural rather than as an imposed and artificial way of doing things [32].

Eschewing extremes, Howard appealed to capitalists and working class alike for their support. With his 'gift of sweet reasonableness', Howard looked for that area of common ground that so often lies at the heart of reformist campaigns [33]. Once the logic of the garden city idea was widely known, he thought it inevitable that vested interests and resistance would fall away in the face of overwhelming popular demands. The immediate need, though, was to make a start with an experimental scheme, and for that to happen existing sources of power and influence had to be tapped.

Reassurance was all-important at this stage, and Howard was adept in addressing his audience: '. . . my proposal appeals not only to individuals but to co-operators, manufacturers, philanthropic societies, and others experienced in organisation, and with organisations under their control, to come and place themselves under conditions involving no new restraints but rather securing wider freedom.' [34]

While a middle course is a gathering ground for support, there will always be some for whom this kind of approach does not go far enough. For some, the idea of a garden city was too radical to contemplate, another fanciful scheme that threatened to turn the known world upside down [35]. At the same time, for others it failed to address the immediate problems of the day, escaping to green fields rather than marshalling the forces of labour in a frontal assault on the bastions of capitalism [36].

But in its moderation more could be attracted to the idea than alienated. In theory at least, capitalists could find common ground with trade unionists and cooperators, and Liberal politicians, especially, were able to lend the scheme their support [37]. Culturally, too, it fitted comfortably into a deep-flowing, Romantic tradition of *rus in urbe* that was at once (with examples like Bedford Park and Bournville) both radical and respectable [38]. Howard's biographer, Robert Beevers, locates his views within an English tradition of dissent and radical ideas that stem back to the seventeenth century. Yet Beevers also shows how Howard consciously moderated his presentation to maximize its appeal, even to the point of working through several drafts for a title until he finally alighted on 'garden city', with its 'beguilingly soft English attraction about it.' [39]

The garden city, then, for all its radical pretensions was presented in a spirit of consensus, and the importance attached to consensus was to characterize the early years of the pressure group. That these events took place when they did was of no less significance. There is undoubtedly a sense in which the time was right for a proposal of this sort.

'A PEACEFUL PATH TO REAL REFORM'

In these days of strong party feeling and of keenly contested social and religious issues, it might perhaps be thought difficult to find a single question having a vital bearing upon national life and well-being on which all persons, no matter of what political party, or of what shade of sociological opinion, would be found to be fully and entirely agreed . . . There is, however, a question in regard to which one can scarcely find any difference of opinion. It is wellnigh universally agreed by men of all parties, not only in England, but all over Europe and America and our colonies, that it is deeply to be deplored that the people should continue to stream into the already over-crowded cities, and should thus further deplete the country districts. (From Ebenezer Howard's introduction to *To-morrow: A Peaceful Path to Real Reform*, 1898).

There is a critical sense in which the seed of the idea of garden cities was sown on fertile ground. In the late-Victorian period (and, subsequently, during the Edwardian years), deplorable conditions in the countryside as well as in the cities, and the urgent need for improvement, had become (as Howard was to claim in the introduction to his book) an issue impinging on the consciousness of widely-differing groups. The ground was enriched by an unusual mix of compassion and blatant self-interest, combining to produce conditions conducive to the growth of the garden city idea. The GCA, as a pressure group, sought to define and redefine the common ground – a general concern about the urban problem – rather than taking a more selective approach that might have alienated one group at the expense of another. No opportunity was lost to remind people of the great domestic problem of their time, and of a solution that could appeal to all.

In the last quarter of the nineteenth century the ground had already been prepared. Practical reformers in the field of housing, philanthropic schemes for model settlements, and utopian idealism, all served to turn over the barren soil of *laisser faire*. Across a wide political spectrum, attention was turned to the problems unearthed by a generation of intrepid social explorers. Andrew Mearns, General Booth, Charles Booth and Seebohm Rowntree were amongst those who ventured into a world of poverty and destitution that was to raise uncomfortable questions for the rest of society. In their various investigations, the overwhelming conclusion was that, for all the strides that had been taken in technology and industry, and in imperial expansion, the conditions of large numbers of the work-force of the nation were deplorable. What is more, the 'facts about sweating, overcrowding, unemployment and casual employment, endemic diseases and drink were filtering into the drawing-rooms of the West End.' [40]

Thus, for instance, the publication in 1883 of the findings of Mearns (in the form of a penny pamphlet, 'The Bitter Cry of Outcast London: An Enquiry into the Condition of the Abject Poor', reproduced in the *Pall Mall Gazette*) 'caused an immediate sensation' [41]. A moral as well as a material problem, the wretched conditions of the poor called for immediate action, and if the mission halls that took root in the slum districts towards the turn of the century were not a direct outcome of this particular exhortation, they were at least representa-tive of the general approach [42]. Following a similar route, the founder of the Salvation Army, General Booth also crossed into 'Darkest England' and returned with harrowing tales of a forgotten race – a 'population sodden with drink, steeped in vice, eaten up by every social and physical malady . . .' [43] His namesake, Charles Booth, uncovered the existence of comparable conditions, but did so through extensive and systematic surveys that could not be easily ignored [44].

What these and other studies revealed was the extent of misery that existed in the capital city. Perhaps even more unsettling, though, were the statistics gathered in York by Seebohm Rowntree, and published in 1901 as a book, *Poverty: A Study of Town Life* [45]. It was one thing to discover poverty in the metropolis, but even more revealing to find that a similar proportion of the population existed under conditions of poverty in a town that was relatively free of large industry. Rowntree, driven by the belief that there was 'an over-powering amount of work to be done' [46], was understandably sympathetic to the garden city movement. In December 1901 he attended a meeting of the Association to tell his audience of his findings in York, and to urge 'the very great necessity of taking some action to try and improve the conditions under which people were living at the present time.' He said he was glad to give a hearty welcome to Howard's scheme, and spoke from experience of the advantages which resulted from moving factories into the country [47]. Over the years, in his relentless campaign for better housing, Rowntree was to remain an important friend of the Association – even to the point (as his biographer notes) of being 'somewhat uncritical' of the idea of garden cities [48].

With the problem unearthed, what, though, was to be done about it? Certainly, Howard's idea of establishing new colonies in the countryside was not in itself new (as Howard himself acknowledged). William Morris and John Ruskin, for instance, had already aroused the socialist imagination with a romantic vision of new settlements founded on lost values of harmony and community [49]. As early as 1874, Morris was contemplating a world where 'people lived in little communities among gardens and green fields, so that you could be in the country in five minutes' walk . . .' [50]

And, similarly, attached to the formal text of the Association's Annual Report in 1903 was an extract from Ruskin's *Lectures on Art* (entitled with liberal editorial licence, 'Ruskin on the Need for Garden Cities'):

It is not possible to have any right morality, happiness, or art, in any country where the cities are clotted and coagulated together; spots of a dreadful mildew spreading by patches and blotches over the country they consume. You must have lovely cities, crystallised not coagulated in form; limited in size, and not casting out the scum and scurf of them into an encircling eruption of shame, but girded each with its sacred pomoerium, and with garlands of gardens, tall blossoming trees, and softly-guided streams [51].

In the latter years of the nineteenth century, there was no shortage of popular writings contrasting conditions as they were with how they might be. Inspired more by Morris (who had adapted the ideas of Marx to English culture and tradition) than by Ruskin, the socialist writer, Thomas Blatchford (under the pseudonym of Nunquam), attracted more than a million readers with the publication of his book, *Merrie England*, in 1893 [52]. That present conditions were abysmal he regarded as incontrovertible:

Look through any great industrial town, in the colliery, the iron, the silk, the cotton, or the woollen industries, and you will find hard work, unhealthy work, vile air, overcrowding, disease, ugliness, drunkenness, and a high death-rate. These are *facts* [53].

Workers bought the book, not simply to read about the misery that they knew firsthand, but because there was also a message of hope. 'My ideal is that each individual should seek his advantage in co-operation with his fellows . . .' Given this cooperation 'this country would, in return, for very little toil, yield abundance for all.' [54]

But this period was marked by political action as well as the mere presentation of ideas, a period when 'British politics had become distinguished for their ferocity and confusion. . . .' [55] Against a background of periodic recessions, the labour movement was asserting itself as a collective force, demonstrating its 'new unionism' on the streets of London in the 1889 Dock Strike; while socialism was emerging along both revolutionary and Parliamentary lines – the former evidenced by the formation of the Social Democratic Federation in 1881, and the latter by the Fabian Society (dating from 1884) and the Independent Labour Party of 1893. For these movements, the way ahead lay in the advance of the unions and the appropriation of the power of the State by one means or another. In the early days of the garden city movement, there was little in Howard's ideas to interest the soldiers of revolution.

Nearer to the heart of Howard's approach, however, were the radicals – 'their faces which have no elegance and little humour but much hope and integrity' [56] – forming organizations that campaigned for every type of social improvement. J. Bruce Wallace, one of the founder members of the Association, had, in 1893, formed his own Brotherhood Church, and its branches became something of a magnet for these various radical causes:

> Every kind of 'crank' came and aired his views on the open platform, which was provided every Sunday afternoon. Atheists, Spiritualists, Individualists, Communists, Anarchists, ordinary politicians, Vegetarians, Anti-Vivisectionists and Anti-Vaccinationists – in fact, every kind of 'anti' had a welcome and a hearing and had to stand a lively criticism in the discussion which followed' [57].

London was a hotbed for all these activities [58], and it was to the capital that Howard came on his return from a stay in America in 1876. His work as a shorthand writer and stenographer, coupled with his growing interest in social problems, brought him into contact with this ferment of ideas, though his own preferences steered him more towards radical circles as opposed to outright socialism. Here he found people who 'devoutly believed in progress . . . rejecting what were to be the two great engines of social change, government intervention and the labour movement.' [59] Two organizations which particularly attracted Howard's attention were the Land Nationalisation Society and the Nationalisation of Labour Society, the former dating from 1888 (superseding the earlier Land Nationalisation League) and the latter from 1890. Both organizations were to offer a network of ideas and contacts, with the Land Nationalisation Society being instrumental not only in supporting the launch of the Garden City Association but also, in the following year, the National Housing Reform Council [60].

Howard's interest in the LNS stemmed, no doubt, from its commitment to the ideas of Henry George, but there was also a growing bond between Howard and the founder of the LNS, A. R. Wallace, who was himself a longstanding advocate of new communities. This mutual interest is affirmed by Stanley Buder, who notes that Howard was 'sympathetic to the Wallace organisation's view on land policies and on occasion was employed by them to take notes of meetings. In turn the Land Nationalisation Society provided most early supporters of the Garden City.' [61]

Of the NLS, established to promote the ideas of Edward Bellamy in England, Howard was himself one of the twenty founder members [62]. In the three years the organization lasted, a magazine (*Nationalisation News*) was circulated, yellow vans toured the country to spread the message, and, significantly, plans were laid for a new community, the Home Integral Cooperative Colony. Not only were the plans for the community unsuccessful, but the early ending of the society as a whole revealed problems that Howard himself was to face within a few years. There were problems to do with funds and general organization, and also a failure to attract support from working-class movements. In a similar tone to that which was later used to pour scorn on the Association's plans, Sidney Webb dismissed attempts to create new communities as utopian. The cooperative commonwealth would not be created overnight, but through 'such pettifogging work as slowly and with infinite difficulty building up a Municipal Works Department under the London County Council . . .' [63]

Undeterred by the failure of such groups in the 1890s, and fired more by the need to address the problems publicized by the social explorers and others – problems which showed no sign of going away without a new approach – Howard persisted with his own ideas. In the cauldron of debate and latent violence at the time, the subtitle of his book, 'A Peaceful Path to Real Reform' was used advisedly. In its context, it was both reassuring and challenging.

NOTES

Formation of the Garden City Association

1. GCA Minutes of Proceedings, 10th June 1899. The names and addresses of the thirteen who attended the first meeting (held at 70 Finsbury Pavement) were:

Alfred Bishop	'Barnwood', Turnbridge Wells.
George Crosoer	39, Icleford Road, Hitchin.
Joseph Johnson	80, Rectory Road, N.
George King	166, Evening Road, Upper Clapton, N.E.
Ebenezer Howard	50, Durley Road, Stamford Hill.
Joseph Hyder	432, Strand, W.C.
Herbert Mansford	53, Aldergate Street, E.C.
Alexander W. Payne	70, Finsbury Pavement, E.C.

W. Charter Piggott   40, Oliphant St, Queens Park, W.
W. Sheowring   24, Bethune Road, Stoke Newington.
A. H. Singleton   6, Drapers' Gardens, E.C.
Francis W. Steere   7, Archibald Road, Tufnell Park.
J. Bruce Wallace   59, St John's Park, N.

2. Buder (1969), p. 394. Fishman (1977), p. 56, demonstrates the continuing influence of the Land Nationalisation Society in the early years of the GCA: 'At first, the Garden City Association seemed little more than an adjunct of the LNS. A corner in the LNS office was designated as the headquarters of the Garden City Association, and a majority of its members were prominent in the older body.'
3. Armytage (1961), chapter 7, traces the overlapping interests of Wallace with the garden city enthusiasts.
4. *Ibid.*
5. Howard (1902), pp. 164–165. The first Chairman, T. H. W. Idris, was a London County Council Liberal Member, as well as being the owner of a company manufacturing mineral waters.
6. GCA Tract No. 1, 'The Garden City Project', September 1899.
7. The second tract is mentioned in Tract No. 1, *op. cit.*, but it has not been possible to trace a copy.
8. Constitution and Rules of the GCA.
9. *Ibid.*
10. Howard (1902), p. 165.
11. The development of Howard's ideas before the publication of *To-morrow* is best described in Buder (1969) and Fishman (1977). They show how, during the 1880s, Howard imbibed the ideas of London radicals as well as being attracted to spiritualism. In 1893 Howard proposed the formation of a 'Co-operative Commonwealth' (comparable to his subsequent proposal for garden cities), and was involved in an unsuccessful attempt to create such a scheme on a site in Essex. It was after this experience that he set about writing his book, seeing this as a more effective way to publicise his ideas.

The Idea of the Garden City

12. Howard (1898), p. 7.
13. See, for instance, Culpin (1913), Purdom (1949), Osborn (1946a), Eden (1947), Creese (1966), and Fishman (1977).
14. These details are derived directly from Howard (1898 and 1902). Howard made a number of revisions to the 1898 edition, including the omission of a chapter in the first book, 'Administration – A Bird's Eye View' and the development of his ideas on the extension of municipal activity. The 1902 edition contains a Postscript, with helpful information on the first years of the GCA.
15. This was the title of chapter 11, Howard (1898). An effective exploration of the origins of Howard's ideas remains Eden (1947).
16. Howard (1898, chapter 11) referred specifically to Wakefield's advice on the establishment of imperial colonies (as published in a book in

1849, *Art of Colonisation*), recommending a balanced social mix of population as well as a balance between town and country. Marshall, in contrast, was a contemporary of Howard, and was looking for ways to relocate people and industry from London. Elsewhere, Howard (*GCTP*, Vol. XVI, No. 5, May–June, 1926, p. 133) claims that his work as a shorthand stenographer had enabled him in the 1880s, not only to listen to politicians and others, but also to put his own ideas to the likes of Marshall. He recalls that after the Association was formed, Marshall invited Howard to his home in Cambridge, and took a keen interest in the work of the Association.

17. The question of land values and land ownership was central to Howard's scheme, and he pays particular attention to the ideas of Thomas Spence a century previously. What appeals particularly to Howard is the concept of the community as a whole enjoying the benefits of the rents which everyone pays to the parish. Spencer revives the idea of common land ownership (without involving the population in a full socialization of goods), but, in Howard's opinion, he puts too much faith in the State as the corporate landlord (1898, chapter 11).

18. Of the various proposals contained in James Silk Buckingham's utopian settlement, Victoria, (*National Evils and Practical Remedies*, 1849), that which appeals to Howard (1898, chapter 11) is the concept of a medium-sized town surrounded by an agricultural estate – an illustration of the balance that Howard sought between town and country.

19. Howard's recollections, in *GCTP*, Vol. XVI, No. 5, May–June 1926, pp. 132–134. In this, Howard claims credit for persuading a publisher to produce an English version of the book.

20. Quoted in Buder (1969), p. 391.

21. Howard acknowledged his debt to George in a footnote at the end of his chapter, 'The Path Followed Up' (Howard, 1946, p. 136).

22. For a fuller discussion of these diverse connections see, especially, Eden (1947), Petersen (1968) and Fishman (1977).

23. Howard was full of admiration for Kropotkin. In his draft autobiography he wrote that Kropotkin was 'the greatest democrat ever born to wealth and power' (Howard Papers, Folio 10, quoted in Fishman, 1977, p. 37).

24. Buder (1969), p. 391.

25. See, for instance, Armytage (1961) and Hardy (1979).

26. Howard (1898), p. 119.

27. *Ibid*, extract from *Daily Chronicle* article on this theme, quoted at the start of chapter 9.

28. Fishman (1977), pp. 35–36, refers to Howard's interest in Topolobampo, a utopian colony in Mexico where over-centralized leadership contributed to the colony's decline.

29. Howard (1898), p. 18.

30. *Ibid*, p. 64.

31. *Ibid*, p. 65.

32. This concept precedes a fuller development of his thoughts on

municipal activity (as expressed in *To-morrow*), and is explained in a short essay (undated) in the Howard Papers, Folio 20.
33. Lewis Mumford, in his introduction to Howard (1946), p. 37.
34. Howard (1902), p. 116.
35. A sense of the scepticism (if not of fear) that greeted Howard's proposal can be seen in various reports included in Howard's scrapbook of press cuttings (Osborn Papers). For example, 'Many of Mr Howard's suggestions concerning social cities and the future of London are as impracticable as those of the late Mr Bellamy . . .' (*Daily Mail*, 14 October 1898); '. . . the reformer may mend a bit here and there, but he cannot rub the figures from the slate and begin anew.' (*Pall Mall Gazette*, 29 October 1898).
36. In *Fabian News* (December 1898), for instance, the scheme is dismissed: 'We have got to make the best of our existing cities, and proposals for building new ones are about as useful as would be arrangements for protection against visits from Mr Wells's Martians.' Quoted in F. J. Osborn's Preface to Howard (1946).
37. Howard's notion of Social Individualism blended most easily with Liberal philosophy, although there were components within his scheme which appealed to Conservatives (the philanthropic side of the scheme) and Labour politicians (who could see the attraction of common land ownership). It is not until 1918, however, that the Labour Party, as such, lent its official support to the garden city movement.
38. This tendency was strengthened when Raymond Unwin and Barry Parker were commissioned to design Letchworth, and succeeded in transforming Howard's two dimensional scheme into the picturesque architecture and landscaping of the first garden city.
39. Beevers (1988), p. 54. Earlier titles for Howard's scheme included 'The Master Key' and 'Unionville', the latter likened by Beevers to a raw railroad town on the American prairie.

'A Peaceful Path to Real Reform'

40. Macfadyen (1970), p. 35.
41. Keating (1976), p. 91.
42. Possibly the best known of these outposts in the slums, Toynbee Hall (opened in 1885), is directly attributable to a response to Mearns's pamphlet, in the form of the Reverend Samuel Barnett urging members of Oxford University to lend assistance in the battle against poverty.
43. Booth (1890), pp. 14–15. Within a year of publication, 200,000 copies were sold, Seebohm Rowntree being amongst those who were influenced.
44. The first volume of Charles Booth's extensive survey of poverty in East London, published in 1889 (with the complete works appearing in 1902), was of fundamental influence as a source of information for reformers.

45. For an account of the context, as well as the content, of this work, see Briggs (1961).
46. Rowntree, quoted in Briggs (1961), p. 15.
47. Rowntree, speaking at a public meeting of the GCA, held at the Westminster Palace Hotel, 10th December 1901.
48. Briggs (1961), p. 73.
49. Reference has already been made to Morris's *News from Nowhere* (1890), in which a picture is drawn of London and other big cities losing population in favour of new and revived country settlements. Ruskin not only wrote in a similar vein, but, in his enthusiasm for recovering the order of a lost age, had even created a society, The Guild of St. George, to put his ideas into practice. See Hardy (1979), pp. 78–81.
50. A letter from William Morris, quoted in Morton (1978), p. 203.
51. From Ruskin's *Lectures on Art*, Part IV, p. 143, in the GCA Annual Report for the year ending 31st October 1903.
52. *Merrie England* was first published in the form of articles in the *Clarion*, in 1892–1893. The book by Blatchford (1893), originally sold for one penny.
53. Blatchford (1893), p. 9.
54. *Ibid*, pp. 2–3.
55. Bowman (1962), p. 96.
56. Fishman (1977), p. 30, referring to photographs in radical pamphlets.
57. Nellie Shaw, describing Sunday afternoons at the Croydon Brotherhood Church, in Hardy (1979), p. 177.
58. This theme is partially pursued by Hulse (1970).
59. Fishman (1977), p. 31.
60. *The Housing Reformer*, Vol. 1, No. 1, p. 1: 'During 1898, 1899 and the early months of 1900, special Housing and Land Reform Conferences were arranged by the Land Nationalisation Society . . . and early in 1900 the National Housing Reform Council was established.' To set the Land Nationalisation Society in the context of rural issues, see, for instance, Douglas (1976). Armytage (1961) offers some interesting connections with the new community movement.
61. Buder (1969), p. 392.
62. For a detailed account of the NLS, see Marshall (1962).
63. Sidney Webb, quoted in Marshall (1962), p. 106.

3

CHOOSING THE GROUND
1899–1914

It is no coincidence that the first fifteen years of the GCA, from the time of its formation in 1899 through to the outbreak of the First World War in 1914, were a period of active social and political reform. Those very conditions which favoured the formation and development of the Association were no less conducive to social progress on a variety of fronts, not only in Britain but also in other countries which had reached a comparable stage of industrial and political development. Indeed, the international parallels and connections in the campaign for garden cities is a distinguishing feature of this period.

As well as noting this wider context in which the Association emerged, a notable characteristic of its early development is the way in which its original aims were broadened. From a significant, but restricted, set of aims to do with the establishment of garden cities, the Association was soon to be drawn into a wider arena of town planning and general housing reform. A change of name in 1909 to the Garden Cities and Town Planning Association reflected this broadening interest. In certain respects the Association became not a specialized arm of a wider movement, but a focal point for gathering forces pursuing environmental improvements through the introduction of an effective town planning system. Some of the Association's members were to see this new role (drawing it away from its original preoccupation with garden cities) as a mixed blessing, attracting publicity and support but damaging the long-term interests of the movement.

Additionally, these first fifteen years offer a fascinating insight into the working of a pressure group. How did the Association set about its business? What was it about this particular group which enabled it not merely to survive this period, but to mark it as simply the first stage in a life which may well span at least the whole of the twentieth century?

In terms of what was done, it was not simply a question of surviving its first difficult years, but also of achieving some of its original aims. By 1914 the garden city pioneers could look back on the solid achievement of the establishment of the first garden city, and on an increasingly popular acceptance of views which were once widely seen to be, at the very least, impractical. At the end of the Edwardian era, the idea of leaving urban growth and the lives of urban dwellers solely to the dictates of market forces had finally been laid to rest. Marking a new approach, the first footings of town planning, as a statutory and professional activity, were already in place. An agenda for town planning had been set, and the GCTPA had cast for itself an important role in the impending programme.

GARDEN CITIES AND TOWN PLANNING

How was it that the young organization was able to see one of its prime aims, the creation of a garden city, fulfilled within a few years of its own inception as a pressure group? Then, with Letchworth under way, what was the Association's role in a growing campaign for town planning legislation? And where did a bulging portfolio of interests leave the garden city in the Association's list of priorities? Was it still the basic creed of the Association?

Edwardian Reformism

The social conditions of the British people in the early years of the twentieth century cannot be contemplated without deep anxiety. (Winston Churchill, President of the Board of Trade, 1909, in Bruce, 1966, p. 146)

Reference has already been made in the previous chapter to the groundswell of reformist activity in the 1880s and 1890s, carrying issues like poverty, housing and public health from a Victorian backwater into the political mainstream. The turn of the century saw this groundswell continue on its course, gathering momentum through the inflow of new currents of social information and political awareness. Now, though, instead of being held back, floodgates were judiciously opened – enough to draw off the main flow, without allowing all to be swept away. Thus, from 1906 to 1914, successive Liberal Administrations acknowledged the growing pressures, with a reformist programme that eroded familiar landmarks while leaving the basic contours of the country unchanged [1].

For the Association, events of this magnitude were of central importance to its own campaign. The organization benefited from the fact that issues of concern to its own members were, at the same time, attracting national attention. Building on the tradition of late-Victorian studies, for instance, the Edwardian years saw a succession of large-scale inquiries, with statistics amassed on related topics of poverty, housing and unemployment. As one contemporary observer noted – recalling 'the interest excited by Seebohm Rowntree's study of industrial conditions in York, by Chiozza Money's *Riches and Poverty*, by Charles Masterman's *The Condition of England* and by the Anti-Sweating Exhibition of 1906' – such challenges to complacency, 'following on the grim revelations of Charles Booth, reminded us that we were only just beginning to build Jerusalem in England's green and pleasant land.' [2]

If observers knew that this 'green and pleasant land' was not yet to be found in the towns, they also knew that it could not be found in the country. Thus, no less in the public consciousness was the plight of the countryside, with years of agricultural depression forcing labourers to leave the land and with farmland in an increasing state of neglect and decline. Since the 1870s, successive reports and campaigners had pointed to the threat that this situation posed for the nation, swelling the number of unemployed and adding to existing housing problems in the towns, and at the same time draining the nation of its home-grown food supply and of the rich traditions of country life. A Royal Commission in 1881, for instance, had revealed that 700,000 farm labourers and their families had left the land in the previous nine years, and to this were added the Census findings of a 10 per cent fall in the number of farmers over a decade. Nor, indeed, was the plight of the land to be confined to labourers and tenant farmers, as indicated by Lloyd George's later reference to a 'great slump in Dukes' [3].

The 'Land Question' remained high on the political agenda from the 1870s through to 1914, reflecting not just a concern for the immediate problems that had arisen, but also a deeper assault on the landowning class [4]. For the Liberals, champions of Free Trade and of those solid non-conformist citizens of the industrial towns whose fortunes were tied to the growth of manufacturing, the large land-owners – relics of an old order – were both an easy and an obvious target. The power base of the landlords was already diminishing, and it has since been questioned whether the Liberal strategy was simply one of diverting attention from the source of the real class enemy, namely, that of industrial capital [5]. Whatever the motives, however, the fact is that the garden city movement gained from the interest that was focused on the land as an arena for political action. Howard's garden city solution was as much addressed to the problems of the country as of the town, and proponents of his scheme were able to draw on an influential well of sympathy and support in this respect.

The prospect of bringing people back to the land, perhaps even of recovering a 'lost order', was composed of powerful images – powerful enough to cut through a broad swathe of public opinion.

Particular credit for making connections between the garden city movement and the issue of rural regeneration must be attributed to Thomas Adams. Acting as the first full-time official of the Association, Adams (who himself came from a farming background), with the support of another doughty campaigner for rural improvement, the author and Norfolk landowner, H. Rider Haggard, later organized a conference and wrote a book based on the proceedings, *Garden City and Agriculture: How to solve the problem of rural depopulation* [6]. Adams was under no illusions that garden cities alone would solve all of the problems of the countryside, and his book explored a range of agrarian reforms. Like many who campaigned for such reforms, he subscribed to a vision where 'a new race of sturdy English yeomen will grow up to form the bulwarks of our Empire.' [7]

This vision of a new race was itself part of an ideology of national efficiency that gained a strong hold on the Edwardian imagination [8]. One issue that aroused particular concern was that of physical degeneracy – brought to light at the turn of the century by the evidence of frail bodies lining up in the recruiting halls for the South African War. An Inter-Departmental Committee on Physical Degeneration, formed to look into the matter, published its findings in 1904 [9]. It could not find irrefutable evidence of any general physical deterioration, but it did show clear causal links between overcrowding and pollution in the cities and a poor state of health. In any case, by the time the Committee reported, the die had already been cast, and reformers were able to exploit popular fears and hopes of building a stronger race. The eugenics movement (with academic bodies like The Eugenic Education Society and London University's National Eugenic Laboratory to sustain it, and journals like *The Race-Builder*, devoted to the cause of improving the national stock) reached out into all aspects of reformist activity [10]. As such, the garden city movement was an obvious enough source of interest, and *The Race-Builder* had no hesitation in commending it to its readers, seeing garden cities as a means of 'purifying men's blood by bringing them back into invigorating touch with the soil and quickening their minds by social contact in a friendly atmosphere. These are not trifling considerations in the building of a race.' [11]

The cause of racial improvement and national efficiency became a strong platform on which to mount reforming campaigns, something of which the GCA was keenly aware. Throughout the period before the First World War, the case for garden cities was linked to the fulfilment of wider patriotic aims. Industrialists and politicians, who might otherwise have paid little attention to yet another philanthropic cause, themselves pursued the arguments with vigour. Thus, reflecting these interests, Ralph Neville (as Chairman of the Association) returned frequently to the links he saw between urban and rural improvement on the one hand, and military and economic strength on the other. At his first public address to the Association he rallied the members with a warning:

> A physical degeneration was proceeding, and proceeding in some places at a very rapid rate. Nothing could prevent the ultimate destruction and decadence of the race if they did not see that the mass of the people led lives which were inconsistent with sound physical development . . . Looking at it as a question of national rivalry, there were reasons for saying that unless they discovered some means of mitigating the evil, of restoring healthy conditions of life, they were inevitably doomed to failure in the fierce rivalry which they had to undergo [12].

When referring to the question of rivalry, Neville and others were in no doubt that it was Germany that Britain had most to fear. It was a constant source of irritation and concern that of all countries Germany appeared to be the most advanced in terms of the way its towns were planned. With his particular knowledge of that country, the planning pioneer, Thomas Coglan Horsfall, frequently told GCA supporters of Germany's superiority in this respect, and of the benefits that accrued through a healthy labour force [13]. In January 1905, for instance, he addressed the Sixth Annual Meeting of the Association, deploring 'the environment of our less fortunate classes', and contrasting the haphazard way we allowed our towns to grow compared with how it was done in Germany, 'where you cannot examine a German town without seeing that it gains immensely from having its growth guided by a carefully-prepared plan.' [14] Henry Vivian (a Liberal MP, and another leading member of the Association) was less circumspect, warning that unless we (the nation) began to improve the state of our towns, 'we may as well hand over our trade, our colonies, our whole influence in the world, to Germany without undergoing all the trouble of a struggle in which we condemn ourselves beforehand to certain failure.' [15]

A separate strand to that of eugenics and the whole national efficiency movement, but related in its causal links between environmental and social improvement, is that of civics – 'a school attempting to reassert the importance of environmental factors in human evolution and to refute any sociology or biology which set heredity and environment in opposition to each other.' [16] Although based on the ideas of Le Play, the promotion of the movement in Britain and its contribution to the emergence of town planning is closely associated with the name of Patrick Geddes. Of particular interest to the garden city movement, with its joint concern in town and country, was his advocacy of regional surveys as an essential step towards social improvement [17].

The early records of the Association show the garden city movement within this nexus of intellectual and moral concern, with the various threads of civics, eugenics, land reform and housing improvement entwined around a common cause. Although (as a later section, on the first garden city, will show) the Association was able to make progress on specific fronts, it was not until after 1906, with the election of a Liberal Administration with an overall majority, that a national reform programme was initiated. On the election of the Liberals to office, Beatrice Webb was undoubtedly not alone in viewing the prospects with caution: 'We do not deceive ourselves by the notion that this wave of Liberalism is wholly progressive in character . . .' [18] But the fact is that reform is as much a product of fear and self-interest as it is of compassion and progressive ideals, and the warnings of physical degeneracy and a failure to compete with the emergent industrial nations, coupled with the arrival in the House of the first sizeable minority of Labour MPs, were in themselves a spur to do something. Whatever the motives, the outcome in the years through to 1914 was the enactment of a reform programme that later writers commonly acknowledge as having laid the foundations for the modern Welfare State [19]. The 'new Liberalism' differed from the old in its formal abandonment of *laisser faire* as the essential doctrine, and, while retaining a belief in individualism, admitted a larger role for the State. Thus, for all her reservations, Webb was right in noting that 'all the active factors are collectivist.' [20]

Poverty, education, health, housing and planning were all to be tackled as the Edwardian era drew to a close. But the problems ran deep, and on the eve of the First World War the sense of urgency amongst reformers was undiminished. For the Garden City Association, while a start had been made, the problems it was addressing had barely been touched. In November 1913, one of the Association's leading campaginers, Charles Reade, argued that 'the blot on English civilisation' was still ignored. Each week, he showed, more people died of tuberculosis than had perished in the *Titanic*, and yet still the tragic conditions in which disease flourished were allowed to persist. On all grounds the costs to the nation were enormous: 'The prodigious waste of public and municipal resources, the fabulous loss of industrial and social efficiency, the drain upon the national vitality . . .' [21] The arguments were comprehensive and irrefutable, and although those who accepted the need for reform were not necessarily drawn to the conclusion that garden cities were the answer, the campaigners for new settlements nevertheless found themselves amidst convergent currents of public concern. Their early progress and influence in the years before 1914 is very much a reflection of this wider context of reform.

Ideas and Action

> To promote discussion of the project as suggested by Mr Ebenezer Howard in his book *To-morrow*.
> To take the initial steps towards the formation in Great Britain, either by public Company or otherwise, of Garden Cities, wherein shall be found the maximum attainable of comfort and convenience to the inhabitants, who shall themselves become in a corporate capacity the owners of the site subject to the fullest recognition of individual as well as mutual and public interests. (Constitution of the Association, 1899)

The original aims of the Garden City Association were, quite simply, to pursue the ideals and objectives as laid out in Ebenezer Howard's book on garden cities. In the Association's original constitution this amounted to both a propagandist role for the Association, and also a practical role to initiate the first garden city. If all this was clear enough, however, it was not to remain so in the future. Reflecting the Association's wider involvement in town planning, the aims of the organization were regularly revised and reviewed – a process that was not without attendant controversy and confusion. A brief review of the changes offers an introduction to the issues that mark the Association's early history, and shows how difficult it was to choose the ground on which to sustain a campaign [22].

In July 1903, shortly after land was secured at Letchworth for the first garden city, a special general meeting was called to broaden the original aims of the Association [23]. While the proposition in Howard's book remained paramount, the interests of the GCA were redefined as the general promotion of the relief of overcrowded areas and the achievement of a wider distribution of the population. Garden cities were seen as the best way to secure this, but secondary aims were to be through encouraging manufacturers to remove their works from congested areas to the country; by cooperating with or advising firms, public bodies, and other associations to secure better housing accommodation for workers near to their place of employment; by taking steps to promote effective legislation with this end in view; by generally advocating the ordered design and development of towns; and by promoting the practice of well-designed houses with gardens [24].

This redefinition of aims is significant. Internally, within the organization, it reflected a feeling that, with plans to build the first garden city now underway, the role of the GCA might usefully become more wide-ranging. It was felt that the GCA should leave the development company to the practicalities of building the first garden city, while it, in turn, concentrated on persuading others of the wisdom of this kind of reform. 'The Association is entirely educational, the Company entirely practical.' [25]

It seems that Thomas Adams (who at the time occupied a dual role for the Company and the Association) was instrumental in clarifying the path the Association should take. In his dual role he found himself in a difficult position, and was sensitive to criticism and confusion amongst members as to what the Association should be doing now that the building of a garden city was under way. A memorandum was written by Herbert Warren, Chairman of the Association's Executive, warning that, with the establishment of the Company, the Association might well languish as its main *raison d'être* had been achieved. Perhaps it would be better, he suggested, to concentrate the energies of the Association into the Letchworth experiment. The Association might become the Agents of the Company, doing things on the estate which the Company wished to be done but which it could not do itself. The publication of a magazine for the new residents was suggested as one activity [26].

Adams disagreed strongly that the Association should be relegated to an agency role, but he acknowledged that the current situation was untenable. Looking back to the original aims, Adams felt that an unusual feature of the Association was that it was formed without any definite principles. Its brief was simply to discuss Howard's book and to take initial steps to put the ideas contained in that book into practice. The whole edifice of the Association, then, rested on what was contained in Howard's book. But, as Adams pointed out, when the scheme was put to the test the original proposition was quite radically modified. Letchworth was not going to be the literal embodiment of Howard's book. So where did that leave the Association? Did it any longer have a right to collect and use members' subscriptions for activities which had, in the course of practice, changed? The way forward, Adams recommended to his Executive, was to redefine the objects of the Association so that it could take a broader and longer-term view than a preoccupation with the first practical experiment would allow. 'The function of the Garden City Association is surely the higher one of the teaching of sound principles in regard to a particular aspect of social reform, and not in acting as an advertising agent of the Company.' [27]

Externally, the accepted redefinition of the Association's aims meant that already, by 1903, a pressure group was in existence with a national brief to promote the idea of a more dispersed (and, by implication, less congested) pattern of settlement and industry. Its brief was not simply to spread the original gospel, but to arouse public opinion and to begin to lobby for effective legislation to ensure that improvements would not be restricted to scattered, local initiatives. Although the Association remained firmly committed to voluntary effort, and although at this stage an interest in intervention is confined to the prospect of enabling legislation, the attention of the State was already being sought. The cause of garden cities had been placed on a public agenda.

In the event, just as the achievement of Letchworth led to a reappraisal of the original aims, so, too, did the passing of the 1909 Housing and Town Planning Act have its own effect on the Association. In formal terms, the most direct result of the 1909 Act was a constitutional change, including a change in the title of the organization, now to be known as the Garden Cities and Town Planning Association. The change was significant in two respects. It was accompanied by a redefinition of aims, and it offered a fresh opportunity to rally support. Thus, in the words of an editorial:

> . . . this is not merely a change of title. It means the enlargement of the whole of the Association's activities. It will necessitate the enlisting of new sympathisers; and it will assuredly mean a widening of our opportunities for working for the well-being of the people . . . Every political body, every religious order, every type of thought is able to take part in our movement, and to every reader of these words is addressed the urgent request, 'Come and help!' [28]

The redefinition of aims is especially significant, even though the constitutional changes were really little more than a recognition of what the Association was already doing. The fact is that over the years the Association had drifted markedly away from its original preoccupation with the formation of garden cities. The new aims indicated not just a change in the breadth of the Association's work, but also a shift in priorities. The first aim was now 'To promote Town Planning' – a change that reflected the Association's own perception that it had become 'the principal organisation concerned with the promotion of town planning' [29], and that it intended to remain in that position. Clearly, in advance of the formation of the Town Planning Institute, there was a gap to be filled, and it was explained that 'the Association was approached by influential persons with the suggestion that such an enlargement of its activities would not only be beneficial to the Association, but would be very valuable to the community.' [30]

While few would have wished to dispute the first aim of promoting town planning (if only because in such a generalized form it could embrace a variety of more specific objectives and favoured schemes), a second aim – which linked garden cities with other forms of settlement – laid the foundations for considerable debate in the future about the priorities and scope of the Association. For now there was formal recognition that garden cities were not the only kind of development that deserved the Association's support, the aim being 'To advise on, draw up schemes for, and promote Garden Cities, Garden Suburbs and Garden Villages.' This really was a rewriting of the gospel, and the Association was quick to assure its members that:

> The original aims of the Association in the establishment of separate garden cities will still be the great aim. We are not content, and never shall be content, with Letchworth as the only example of the complete application of Mr Ebenezer Howard's ideas, but . . . in the meantime we cannot be idle. The ameliorative work of the Garden Suburb idea must be attended to, and the efforts of all enthusiasts for the Garden Suburb idea must have their focusing point. This, too, will be the Association's work [31].

Reflecting, and perhaps anticipating, the sensitivity that could be aroused by effectively downgrading the original aim of the Association, Sir Ralph Neville, in his Presidential address following the 1909 Act felt compelled to nail his colours to the garden city mast. He showed his concern at the proliferation of garden suburbs and garden villages, which would only add to the problems of large cities. And as for the 1909 Act, that, he contended, would only give licence to forms of development which purported to do more than they possibly could. Members were reminded that these lesser schemes were but palliatives of the evils which the Association sought to eradicate, and that 'The real remedy lies in the completion of Letchworth and the multiplication of similar enterprises.' [32] As Neville undoubtedly sensed, this was an issue that would be raised again in the future.

Constitutionally, then, the Association was set on what was intended to be a broader and firmer footing. The changes were presented less as a departure from the original gospel, and more as a rationalization of where the Association had reached and an opportunity to reaffirm the faith. Members were encouraged to look forward to a new era in the Association's activities:

> New committees will be appointed; fresh enthusiasm is being brought to bear; new counsellors, expert upon their subjects, are coming to our aid; and there is every reason to believe that our new departure will not only strengthen the approval of our present

members, but will gain us hundreds of fresh adherents . . . We have unique opportunities [33].

The First Garden City

No more in sunless cities, grim and grey,
Thro' brick-built conduits shall the nation pour
Her dwindling life in torment . . .
For you in league with sunshine and sweet air,
With comfortable grass and healing flowers,
Have sworn to bring man back his natural good,
Have planned a Garden City, fresh and fair,
When Work and Thought and Rest may ply their powers,
And joy go hand in hand with Brotherhood.
('The Garden City', Rev. Canon Rawnsley, *GC*,
Vol. I, No. 2, February 1905, p. 9)

As indicated in the previous section, in its pioneer days the idea of forming garden cities was the life-blood of the early GCA. Its members were drawn to the Association in the fervent belief that the new organization would achieve more than words. Within months of its formation, committees were actively considering the problems with which the first garden city would have to deal – land tenure, housing, labour, engineering, architecture, education, liquor traffic, and manufactures – while a sites committee set about inspecting possible estates [34]. As a result, in May 1900, the Association resolved to form a limited company, Garden City Limited, with a share capital of £50,000, to pioneer the way.

The initiative, however, proved to be premature. The Association's own small membership was unequal to the financial demands called for, and external investors saw little in the project to attract them. It was a case of going back to the drawing board, with a view to increasing the number of members and putting the Association on a sounder footing.

By the beginning of 1901 the membership had been increased to 350, and the internal organization was improved. A new Chairman, Ralph Neville, KC, was elected, and 'though our financial position hardly justified such a step, we took an office of our own, and engaged a paid secretary, who agreed to devote his whole time to the work.' [35] The new appointment was Thomas Adams, who, as well as writing out 'receipts for half-crown subscriptions and a few guineas' [36], greatly increased the effectiveness of the Association's propaganda. It was Adams who initiated two important conferences, at the model settlements of Bournville and Port Sunlight, confident in the belief that the exemplary environments would inspire others to create something similar. Or, as Howard said at Bournville, 'A Garden Village has been built; A Garden City is but a step beyond.' [37]

Although Neville brought to the Association influence and sound leadership [38], there is a sense in which the value of his involvement was questionable. A more critical view is that Howard in his innocence was rather taken over by Neville and his fellow businessmen, to the extent that idealism gave way to hard business sense [39]. The kind of money that was needed to build a new city drew Howard away from any immediate hope of financing the venture primarily from within the ranks of fellow radicals, excited by the prospect of a 'co-operative commonwealth', and, increasingly, into the world of Edwardian company boardrooms and the panelled lounges of gentlemen's clubs [40]. To the extent that this was so, the whole rationale for the scheme was inverted. 'For Howard, the Garden City was an environment in which capitalism could be peacefully superseded. Most of his supporters, however, looked to the Garden City as the place where capitalism could be most easily preserved.' [41]

It was against this background of a new leadership that conferences were held at Bournville and Port Sunlight, and, following the latter in July 1902, the First Garden City Pioneer Company was registered with a capital of £20,000 [42]. The prospectus explained that the company had been formed with the object of taking initial steps towards the creation of a larger company to put into effect Howard's scheme (although it was also pointed out that the company could not be bound literally by the details of the scheme). Capital was needed to finance the investigation of suitable sites, the preparation of plans, the calculation of rents, and for negotiations with manufacturers and others who might be attracted to the new settlement. Ralph Neville took on the Chairmanship and, as well as Ebenezer Howard, the other Directors were Edward Cadbury (chocolate manufacturer), T. H. W. Idris (mineral water manufacturer), Howard Pearsall (civil engineer), Franklin Thomasson (cotton spinner), Thomas Purvis Ritzema (newspaper proprietor) and Aneurin Williams (ironmaster). This time, compared with the previous attempt to float a company, the whole of the £20,000 was subscribed before December 1902. George Cadbury, Alfred Harmsworth, W. H. Lever and J. B. Thomasson each bought shares worth £1,000, and Harmsworth also offered the company free advertising space in the *Daily Mail* [43].

Apart from the practical outcome of the Company's formation, it is interesting to see that philanthropy on a business footing could appeal to a very wide set of interests. Different groups were attracted to the idea of garden cities for different reasons, and it is the strength of a pressure group to be able to weave a coherent pattern from diverse threads. Thus, news of the Company's formation was widely reported in August 1902, and the press was generally enthusiastic [44]. Religious interests found much in the scheme to applaud. The *Methodist Times* was 'convinced that in this direction lies the best hope of solving the pressing problem of overcrowding and of realising the old cry of "Back to the Land". We heartily commend this courageous experiment to the attention of our readers . . .' [45] The *Jewish Chronicle* started from a different basis, but reached a similar conclusion. 'The Jewish community has very pressing interests in the break up of the great city aggregations and their dispersion into the country . . . Our community will, therefore, view with a little more than mere platonic sympathy the remarkable programme of the GCA.' [46]

In turn, specialist groups warmed to the proposal. The *Temperance Record* believed that there could be no doubt that 'the effect to bring sweetness and light into the lives of the workers is sound business. We wish the workers would come half way to meet the GCA and give some indication that they desire something more than beer and skittles and the perusal of the half-penny rags that publish the racing odds and betting news.' [47] Readers of *The Vegetarian* were similarly urged to support the scheme. 'Undoubtedly there is room for a great object lesson of this kind, and those who have faith in the practicability of the proposal, and have sympathy with the ideals of the promoters, should, if they have the means, give the scheme their support.' [48]

As the *Municipal Journal* pointed out, 'The Garden City Co. appeals to all, irrespective of political, social or economic views.' [49] The claim may not have been entirely true, but sufficiently so to explain the successful start which the Company enjoyed. Two permanent officers were appointed, an accountant, Harold Craske – impeccable with his 'waxed moustache, top-hat, and frock-coat' and treating 'the whole affair as rather amusing' – and a junior clerk, C. B. Purdom, whose first reaction was that 'this was not what I had expected, and some resolution was required to keep me there.' [50] As the search for a site got underway, Purdom complained that there was no real organization of the work. The Company shared the GCA's office, but there was 'nothing short of chaos, and the office floor was covered with maps and offers of sites, extending from fifty acres to large estates, sent from all over the country.' [51]

The search was on for a greenfield site of 6,000 acres, and only at the eleventh hour was Letchworth chosen in favour of an estate at Chartley, near Stafford. What attracted the Directors to Hertfordshire was its proximity to London, and the fact that the land (a product of years of agricultural depression) was practically deserted. It was smaller than hoped for (under 4,000 acres), and an aggregate of fifteen separate parcels, but in other respects it seemed ideal.

The Hon. Mr. Justice Neville, whose portrait occupies the central space, has been compelled, by reason of his appointment to be one of his Majesty's Judges, to retire from the Chairmanship of the Board of Directors of First Garden City Limited. He still retains his interest in the scheme and will continue to act as Chairman of the Council of the Garden City Association.

Board of Directors on First Garden City Ltd (formed 1903). Ralph Neville, Chairman, is in the centre.

Contracts were signed in the Spring of 1903 at what proved to be the competitive price of about £40 per acre. Later that year, in September, First Garden City Ltd. was registered with an authorized capital of £300,000, and the first prospectus was issued, inviting subscriptions for £80,000 share capital. The Pioneer Company was duly wound up [52].

Within four years of its own inception, then, the Association could look forward to a new phase in its development. The Association and First Garden City Ltd. had to sort out their respective roles, but if that could be done the future looked bright for both. Letchworth would mean not simply the fulfilment of a primary objective of the parent organization, but the publicity surrounding the experiment could be used to further the cause of garden cities throughout the nation. Just as the model villages of Bournville and Port Sunlight had, by their own examples, helped to make the case for Letchworth, so, in turn, the new settlement might encourage others to do the same. Progress by example was a well-established technique amongst reformers, and the Association was by now adept in using the press and other means to tell the world of its bold experiment.

Orchestrated visits to Letchworth became a regular diet for the press, even before the first bricks were laid. For instance, in October

OPENING DAY AT LETCHWORTH. LEAVING LETCHWORTH HALL HOTEL.

The first garden city was publicized in various ways, starting with the Opening Day in 1903.

1903, to mark the acquisition of the estate, some two hundred press representatives were taken on a tour of the site, followed by a separate visit by more than a thousand members and supporters of the movement. It rained throughout the press visit, and some reports on the prospect of building the New Jerusalem in the sodden fields of Hertfordshire were less then enthusiastic. Overall, though, the GCA was satisfied with the response:

> The widespread and generally favourable notices of the enterprise that subsequently appeared in these journals have greatly increased our already heavy obligations to the Press . . . and there is no doubt that all present on both days of the Inspection received a new and stronger impression of the reality and practical nature of the scheme [53].

In addition to the annual reports of the Association (circulated to a far wider network than the Company alone could reach), there were

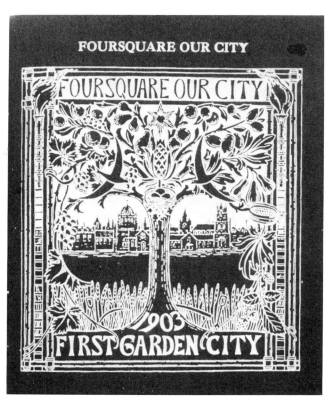

A representation of Letchworth on a banner by Edmund Hunter (c. 1909).

regular news items on the garden city in the Association's journal. Progress at Letchworth was carefully monitored, and the good news was passed on to an international readership. Visits to Letchworth and summer gatherings of GCA members and supporters were organized as an exercise in public relations. In the summer of 1905 alone, it was reported that some 60,000 visitors came to see for themselves early progress with the new city [54].

For his part in raising sights above the day-to-day details of site development, and, instead, projecting the kind of image that would benefit the wider movement, a key role has been attributed to the

Illustration reflecting the Bohemian character of Letchworth. (From *The City*, 1909)

Poster extolling the attraction of Letchworth as a place to live.

Company's Secretary, Thomas Adams [55]. As well as promoting the welfare of the Company, Adams realized the need to broaden the base of the movement's support. A wide variety of groups was hosted at Letchworth, including adult education bodies, cyclists, women Liberals, vegetarians, the Christian Social Union, and MPs from all parties. 'By these means, Adams spread the word of Garden City and helped to integrate it into the mainstream of social reform.' [56]

Radicals were attracted to Letchworth, to settle there amongst like-minded idealists as well as simply to visit – 'for here a town was to be built that would, they thought, change the face of England.' [57] There had been many false dawns amongst the community experiments of the nineteenth century, but this time the illusory shoreline of utopia seemed within sight. Tolstoyans, Ruskinian socialists, and members of the Independent Labour Party were amongst those who made their home at Letchworth [58]. To outsiders, they seemed an odd set, 'a typical Garden citizen clad in knickerbockers and, of course, sandals, a vegetarian and member of the Theosophical Society who kept two tortoises which he polishes regularly with best Lucca oil. Over his mantlepiece was a large photo of Madame Blatavsky and on his library shelves were *Isis Unveiled* and the works of William Morris, H. G. Wells and Tolstoy.' [59]

But, for all the radical hopes attached to it, the new settlement took its place as a reformist experiment rather than as a wedge to undermine the capitalist system. An article in *The Race-Builder* was probably right in locating the first garden city as an evolutionary experiment. 'The revolutionist may regard it as a last ditch for the hard-pressed forces of capitalism, but the evolutionists should surely see in it an effort to find a way out of the competitive chaos towards a well-ordered society. If the scheme retains some old evils, it introduces new qualifying virtues . . .' [60]

In Letchworth's pioneering days, much publicity was given by the Association to the progressive forms of new housing, to novel industrial ventures (like Garden City Press, a cooperative set up by Aneurin Williams), to the variety of schooling within the small town (its population barely exceeding 10,000 until after 1914), to the rich opportunities for community life (including convivial evenings spent at the 'non-alcoholic' Skittles Inn), and to the healthy environment [61]. In one sense, then, Letchworth was the Association's beacon to signal the movement's early progress. But there was also a sense in which it threatened to leave the parent body in the shade. For one thing, the formation of the Company and the interest that the young settlement attracted was, at least in part, at the expense of the Association [62]. It consumed some of the organizational energies of the Association (Adams, for instance, for a while tried to divide his time between the two bodies), and financial support which would otherwise have gone to the Association was diverted to the Company. These, however, proved to be relatively short-term problems.

More enduring in its effects on the future development of the Association was the important fact that, in putting Howard's ideas

An example of early housing development at Letchworth.

into practice, the original principles were diluted in the process. The new town was by no means a replica of Howard's blueprint. Acknowledging the significance of this, Adams identified key areas of comparison between the garden city project as outlined in *To-morrow*, and what was happening on the ground at Letchworth [63]. He pointed to differences in methods of raising capital, administration, ownership of the sites and public services, land tenure, the size of the estate, the proportion reserved for agriculture, restrictions on growth, layout, and the system of distribution. What Adams regarded as 'fundamental principles' had been lost to what appears as a mixture of pragmatism and an ideological preference for a more commercial approach than Howard originally envisaged. The GCA could either come to terms with these changes, or reject Letchworth as an errant offspring. It chose the former course, the logical consequence of which was that its future was bound up with the broadest of garden city principles, rather than with the literal interpretation of a particular proposal. The importance of Letchworth in the history of the Association is that this is where the choice, however unwittingly, was made.

Lobbying for Town Planning

> There is no doubt that the ready acceptance given to the main principles of town planning by all parties and in all quarters is largely due to the work of the Association in educating the country to the possibilities which lie behind the adoption of a scientific system of planning and building . . . On the introduction of the Bill, one newspaper remarked: 'Actually, of course, the authorship of the Bill belongs to Ebenezer Howard.' (GCA Tenth Annual Report, presented to the Annual Meeting, 27 January 1908).

Clearly, as the above quote indicates (referring to the Bill to introduce town planning legislation) the Association believed not only that it had a wider role to play, but also that it was a leading actor in the unfolding drama of events. With the passing of the first town planning legislation in 1909, it is understandable, up to a point, that the Association should claim some credit for the enactment [64]. The Association could, after all, point to the example of Letchworth as a living embodiment of town planning principles. That was undoubtedly a powerful propagandist tool, and the publicity attached to Letchworth belied the relatively slow progress on the ground [65]. And, as well as generally promoting the cause of garden cities, the Association had been active in the specific task of lobbying for a town planning Act.

Initially, the Association put its trust in voluntary effort, rather than State intervention, to build garden cities. Collective ownership would follow, rather than precede, the establishment of a new settlement. Indeed, it was even surmised that perhaps there was already too much in the way of laws and regulations instead of too little; and Letchworth was held up, less as an argument for legislation, and more as an object lesson of what could be done without government involvement. What was needed, argued the purists within the garden city movement, was more of the law of natural liberty [66].

Yet, at about this time, there were already signs that the climate of opinion was changing. The ideological heartland of the Association in the Edwardian era remained in the area of 'associated individualism' [67]. From 1906, however (with the new Liberal Administration and, especially, after 1908, when Asquith becomes Prime Minister) the basic belief in self-reliance within the Association was challenged by a more directive approach. Moreover, the belief of members was also shaken by the evidence that most new housing developments in this period were taking place in a form that bore little or no resemblance to their own high ideals. This dual challenge, ideological and empirical, caused many within the Association to question its purist roots. Could it any longer afford to ignore the potential of the State to support its own aims? As will be seen in the following section, not all were convinced that a reappraisal of this sort was in order, but a majority within the Association believed that this was the right course. What was needed, now, argued the protagonists for change, was legislation that would *compel* developers to lay out new developments along garden city lines. If whole new settlements could not be built, then at least some of the better principles of design and layout (evidenced at Letchworth, but also in a modified form at Hampstead Garden Suburb) should be safeguarded [68].

In its new, more committed role as a champion of legislation, the Association sought to ensure that its own particular view of what was needed would gain wider acceptance. Two conferences were organized to pave the way for impending legislation. The first of these, in March 1906, attracted 150 representatives from local authorities as well as Members of Parliament [69]. More important, though, was the second conference, Town Planning in Theory and Practice, in October 1907, held when legislation was already being drafted. An air of immediacy surrounded this, and every local authority was urged to prepare itself for the coming legislation [70].

To promote its own view, the Association took the opportunity to circulate a memorandum to all of the 1907 conference participants, setting out its priorities. Three reforms were proposed, which the Association regarded as essential for 'securing for the future not only more wholesome and more suitably arranged dwellings for families of the poorer classes, but also whole separate towns of reasonable size and desirable amenity, adding health and pleasure to the mere convenience and subsistence of town life.' [71] The first change that was proposed for inclusion in the new legislation was for General Development Schemes, where local authorities (in conjunction with a central authority, such as the Local Government Board) would authorize the form of town extensions and the planning of new towns. A second proposal was to give local authorities powers to acquire land for the creation of new towns, with compulsory purchase procedures to be strengthened. Finally, the Association called for government loans for public and other bodies to assist in the building of garden cities or garden suburbs.

In 1907 and 1908 the propagandist work of the Association increased. On a day-to-day basis, it was reported that 'a large part of the endeavours of the Association have been concentrated on the question of Town-planning' [72], with pamphlets produced and lectures arranged in all parts of the country. The various sub-committees of the Association – the Legal and Parliamentary Committee, the Prospecting and Development Committee, and the Architectural and Building Committee – were all hard at work in preparing material designed to influence the shape of the legislation. Members of Parliament were briefed, and in June 1907 the Association could report that its aims had been advanced by the unopposed adoption of a motion in favour of town planning powers being granted to local authorities [73]. Satisfaction was drawn from the fact that, in moving the proposal in the House, Mr Whitwell Wilson referred explicitly to the garden city style of development as a model to be emulated in new suburban extensions. He also pointed to the healthier conditions of the garden city environment, citing the evidence of lower mortality rates, to support his general case for legislation [74].

It was an active period of lobbying, but the work did not stop when the Housing, Town Planning, etc. Act was finally passed in 1909. Later in that same year, the Association organized another conference, The Practical Application of Town Planning Powers, designed this time to ensure that the new powers available to local authorities were wisely and effectively used.

In his subsequent report of the conference, the Secretary of the Association, Ewart Culpin, took the opportunity to thump the table for his organization, arguing that it was the obvious leader of the town planning movement. He offered a variety of reasons to support his claim:

(1) It is entirely non-partisan and non-sectarian.
(2) It is the oldest organisation working for the better housing of the people combined with good Town Planning.

(3) It is the only organisation which maintains a central London office and staff for the purpose of dealing with inquiries and giving advice on both Town Planning and housing matters.

(4) The first Garden City at Letchworth, the Hampstead Garden Suburb, and the numerous schemes on Garden City lines throughout the country, have resulted from its work.

(5) It is the only organisation equipped for the providing of free lectures all over the country, and several thousand lectures and meetings have already been held.

(6) Through its agency similar organisations have been formed in several Continental countries and in America.

(7) Its organisation includes committees of experts dealing with prospecting and planning, legal and Parliamentary, housing and public health, architecture and building, etc.

(8) Free literature is distributed in large quantities, and the Association issues the only periodical dealing with the subject of Town Planning, under the title of *Garden Cities and Town Planning* [75].

For an organization which prided itself on its impartiality, this kind of undisguised propaganda on its own behalf, in a report of a conference to promote general aims, must have struck a discordant note for a number of its readers. The Association was undoubtedly a significant agent in the whole business of getting town planning onto the statute books, but its role has been greatly exaggerated by its advocates. Extravagant claims of primacy can be qualified in three ways.

For a start, behind the public rhetoric of acclaim, the 1909 Act fell some way short of what the Association had actually been seeking. The signs of this were already apparent when the Bill was introduced in 1908. A caustic editorial in the journal referred to the Bill as a 'suburb planning and not a town planning Bill, (that) would give no facilities for new town creation.' The editor also bemoaned the fact that the President of the Local Government Board, Mr Burns, in his Second Reading speech, 'made no mention whatever of Letchworth' although he alluded to lesser schemes [76]. Undaunted, the Association proposed a number of amendments, and there was sufficient support in Parliament to ensure that they were tabled [77]. The end result, though, was still to be an Act that was designed to cope with suburbs rather than new towns, and not very effectively at that. It can hardly be said, then, that the first town planning legislation expressed the fulfilment of the main aims of an organization dedicated to the promotion of new self-standing settlements, even though some common ground could be found in the pursuit of better environmental standards.

A second reason why the claims of the Association need to be qualified is that, as the attendence record of their various conferences illustrates, it was just one amongst a number of influential pressure groups and progressive local authorities that were all campaigning for town planning measures [78]. The demand for town planning was, in fact, coming from a wide range of groups, and 'in part from those who would be responsible for the execution of town planning if it were introduced.' [79] As a propagandist body, the National Housing Reform Council was especially effective, and it was that body (at a joint meeting with the Workmen's National Housing Council at Leeds in 1904) that passed the first recorded resolution explicitly in favour of town planning in Britain. At the same time, professional opinion was expressed through organizations such as the Royal Institute of British Architects, the Surveyors' Institution, and the Association of Municipal and County Engineers. Additionally, of the more progressive local authorities in the town planning campaign, Birmingham City Council's Housing Committee passed a resolution in favour of town planning and municipal land purchases in 1906 [80]. The Association was prominent in the general campaign, but it did not have the monopoly that it sometimes inferred in the partisan pages of the journal.

Finally, the most important reservation about the role of the Association has less to do with the details of their campaign and their relative influence compared with other lobbies, and more to do with their structural position as a pressure group. This is itself a major debate that will be explored as a separate issue [81]. It is enough, though, simply to note at this point that, while it is perfectly under-standable for a pressure group to over-estimate its own influence when it appears that its aims are being realized, the view from within the frenetic world of meetings, lectures, lobbies and publication deadlines will inevitably be a partial one. In focusing on a specific Act of Parliament, and assessing its own part in it, there are wider issues that can be missed. Whatever altruistic motives were offered for the first town planning legislation, the fact remains that other compelling motives were also in the legislators' minds. These, it has already been argued, had more to do with the changing political profile at home (with the emergence of the Labour Party and the rise of the trade union movement, both of which put new pressures on established interests to make some social concessions, if only to stave off more radical demands), with a wider assault on traditional landed interests, and with the industrial and military threat from overseas (both of which added weight to the case for providing the conditions for a healthy working and fighting force). In this context, pressure groups can be seen as caught up in an overwhelming tide of change, in which their own part can easily be exaggerated. Such groups are not, in themselves, responsible for the source or the turn of a tide, but they might be right if they claim, at least, a localized influence.

In the case of the Association, while it would be hard to sustain the extravagant claim that the passing of the 1909 Act was the direct result of their own campaign, it would, however, be legitimate to look for more subtle links. Letchworth had undoubtedly made its mark, and the kind of planning that went onto the statute books might have been different had all the pressure come, instead, from the large metropolitan authorities. If the 1909 Act favoured the development of suburbs rather than garden cities, that was still a gain of sorts for the garden city campaigners, compared with what might have been. It was not wholly what the Association wanted, nor was it what they claimed was their main contribution. But the fact remains that a vision of low-density, cottage style development (which its critics have persistently referred to as anti-urban) [82] has proved, nevertheless, to be a significant legacy to the type of town planning that has evolved in the twentieth century.

Garden Cities and Garden Suburbs

> More and more the Garden City Association became a lobbying group for planning in general, with Garden Cities but one arrow in its quiver. Indeed, for a while it was not only neglected by the Association, but also in danger of being forgotten. (Buder, 1969, p. 396).

When Ewart Culpin (as the Secretary of the Association) reviewed the situation in 1913, in his book *The Garden City Movement Up-to-date*, he noted how the breadth of the Association's interests had increased over the years. As a general environmental pressure group it had engaged in a wide range of issues, and the growth of the movement in 1913 alone was regarded as 'phenomenal':

> The activity in every branch is remarkable, despite adverse conditions in regard to the building trade and an increasing tightness of money. Large additions have been made to the number of new schemes now afoot . . . The educative work which has been done by the Garden Cities and Town Planning Association has spread far beyond what was at first thought to be its borders. Lectures are being given everywhere; literature is being supplied by thousands of copies; the monthly magazine, *Garden Cities and Town Planning*, is acquiring a firmer hold and has obtained a wider circulation, being recognised as the chief educative factor in civic improvement in this country . . . (and) there is not a portion of the

civilised world to which the Garden City message is not now being sent regularly [83].

Culpin could report that developments planned on garden city lines (with profit restrictions as well as a garden city type of layout) were being built in all parts of the country, and that these alone would grow to accommodate some 300,000 people. What was more, the Association was being looked to, increasingly, by landowners seeking advice on how to plan new housing on garden suburb, if not garden city, principles. In the minds of some of the leaders of the movement, the promotion of garden cities and garden suburbs had, in fact, become almost one and the same thing [84]. At a dinner in honour of Howard in 1912, well-planned garden suburbs were not only acknowledged in their own right, but were also commended as a worthy source of support amongst garden city campaigners. Presiding over

Map showing 'developments on garden city lines'. (From Culpin's *Garden City Movement Up-to-date*, 1913)

the event, Earl Grey hoped that everyone would play their part 'in spreading the gospel of the Garden City, Garden City Suburb movement.' He went on to urge the ladies in the gathering, especially, to see garden suburbs for themselves. 'It is so easy to go down to Hampstead Garden Suburb in a taxi . . . and I will venture to make this prophecy, that if they once go there . . . then they will realise that there is a charm, a happiness, a peace and content in living in these Garden Cities and Suburbs which is absent from the greater part of the urban centres in other parts of the Kingdom.' [85]

As well as supporting the garden suburb movement (a strategy that was later to be questioned as a serious breach of faith, with the role of Culpin himself particularly suspect) [86] the Association also adopted a campaigning role in a number of development issues. For instance, at the new naval base at Rosyth in Scotland the Association pressed for appropriate housing, and the officers in London worked closely with their counterparts in the Scottish Branch [87]. But Culpin lamented that an 'opportunity of providing a world example is, alas! being lost through the Admiralty's attitude in regard to the proposal

6.—HER MAJESTY QUEEN MARY, LORD EMMOTT AND DAME HENRIETTA BARNETT viewing the east end of the Suburb and the flats built for Officers' families from the Institute.

Visitors of all levels in society were encouraged to see Hampstead Garden Suburb as a model of good housing.

to create a model town.' [88] There was a similar story in London, where the Association negotiated with the Port of London Authority, with a view to securing model 'workman's housing' to the north of the docks. But, in this case, 'the extraordinary improvidence of the Port of London Authority as to its responsibilities for the people who will have to live in the neighbourhood of the new Docks is not encouraging for those who look in high quarters for help in these matters.' [89] The Association also became involved in a long campaign, opposing plans for the Northern Railway Junction, the issue being that it was considered that the proposed new line would do serious damage to the natural beauty of a stretch of countryside on the north-west outskirts of London [90].

Elsewhere, attention was drawn to less conspicuous, everyday activities which kept the officers busy. They travelled to all parts of the country on a variety of assignments – helping in the preservation of a group of trees in Devon, suggesting the best way to lay out some land donated for use as a public park, attending meetings in connection with proposals for a garden village for the Kent coalfields, organizing conferences, and joining in deputations to the Prime Minister to continue to press for more effective town planning.

However, for all the diversification in activities, the garden city remained the essential creed of the Association. Some ten years on, Letchworth (despite its slow growth, with a population of only 7,500 in 1912) was consistently projected as the shining star in the firmament of new developments. The Association's journal, for instance, carried regular full-page advertisements, with headings such as 'What no other town can offer you' and 'The success of Letchworth'. Foreign visitors with an interest in housing improvements made pilgrimages to the small Hertfordshire town – 'the mecca of the housing reformer and the town planner throughout the world' – paying due tribute to Ebenezer Howard, and invariably enjoying displays of Old English dancing and tea supplied by the Letchworth Residents' Union [91].

Yet, strangely perhaps, the pride and enthusiasm in the first garden city did not, before 1914, lead to the building of a second one. From time to time, though, members were reminded that this was what they should be doing. A bold initiative in 1910 to commemorate the death of the late king with a new garden city, to be called King Edward's Town, came to nothing. The Association was advised that the new king wished to see local memorials rather than a national gesture of this sort. Although that particular proposal was rejected, Howard persisted with the idea that the time was right for a second garden city, whatever it was called [92].

Howard stated his case. The prime propagandist tool would be to demonstrate to the public the claimed success of Letchworth. This kind of argument was familiar, but an important new departure was to raise the idea that the new garden city could well be a State-aided enterprise. It was a qualified form of intervention, with the State providing the freehold of the estate and perhaps some capital towards its development, and with private capital and local initiative doing the rest. But the very idea of moving away from a total dependence on private and voluntary effort is significant, and reflects both the experience of trying to raise the kind of capital involved without some form of support, and, no doubt, a new political environment where State intervention was gradually being seen to be more acceptable.

Probably, Howard (who, himself, was by no means an advocate of unqualified State intervention) was ahead of the field in anticipating a version of State-sponsored new towns. When the issue was discussed at a meeting of the Council, Howard asked the members to concentrate on the principle of whether or not to initiate a new garden city, rather than to get sidetracked on the question of State aid, which he now played down as being 'the smallest part of the scheme.' [93] Opening the discussion, Neville reinforced his already well-known views that the whole success of garden cities 'depended upon being able to prove that this was a business conception. If it was merely philanthropy, there was little or nothing in it. . . .' [94] In turn, the Liberal MP, Aneurin Williams (speaking as the Chairman of First Garden City Ltd.) agreed that a new initiative was called for, but thought that Howard should first write another propagandist book, this time called *Garden Cities in Being* [95]. Like Neville, Williams did not look to the State, but thought that a business trust could be created on the basis of the anticipated financial success of the company that had built Letchworth.

If there were disagreements as to method, though, the essential belief in the idea of the garden city within the Association remained firm – at least for the time being [96]. When the architect, A. Trystan Edwards, openly criticized the garden city movement in the pages of the new journal, *Town Planning Review*, ranks were tightly closed [97]. It was a weighty attack, arguing in some detail that garden cities led to a kind of development that was an affront to beauty, convenience and economy. Far from combining the best of town and country, the garden city was an unsatisfactory hybrid. If the real cities were properly arranged and improved, then no-one, contended Edwards, would choose to live in what he saw as fictions of rusticity. The ideals behind the movement expressed 'a tiredness of the spirit and lack of historic sense.' [98] It may be contended, he concluded, that 'the garden city movement had served its purpose. It was from the beginning a sectarian movement . . .' [99]

The editor of *Town Planning Review* reported that this attack on the garden city movement (embodying, as it did, a polarization between urbanist and anti-urbanist approaches to planning) had evoked considerable discussion.

The Association, through an article by Charles Reade, offered its own response under the heading 'A Defence of the Garden City Movement'. It was a systematic response, reiterating the main arguments in favour of garden cities. What is significant about this debate (and about that of whether the State should be a part of the process) is that, in retrospect, the issues that were raised then were to become the subject of a more spirited debate in the years ahead. Certainly, there is no evidence to suggest that the course of the Association was diverted at this stage. Nor, indeed, that the Association was anything other than active and optimistic, up to the outbreak of the First World War, when 'prospects were probably brighter than at any previous time in the history of the Association.' [100]

ORGANIZING FOR PRESSURE

Having surveyed the general progress of the Association before 1914, and the issues that it confronted, how did it manage its business? How was it actually organized, and what was the situation regarding membership and finance? What methods did the new pressure group employ to promote the idea of the garden city? What importance was attached to gaining the support of influential figures, and to what extent was the original radicalism of the garden city idea compromised in the process? How were the special interests of women, and the particular claims of the regions reconciled with the general objectives of the Association? And, at a time when the cause of environmental reform was attracting the interest of other groups, was there any attempt to work together to achieve common ends? Finally, how active was the Association in seeking to spread its central ideas abroad? Together, the answers to these questions offer an interesting profile of an early twentieth-century pressure group.

Internal Organization

> The offices were at the top of an old building adjoining Lincoln's Inn, and were sub-rented from Arthur Blott, well known as an anarchist solicitor, a friend of Howard's, but who had nothing to do with this project. The rooms were poor and dilapidated, and I found myself sitting in a partitioned-off part of Blott's own office, without daylight or heating. (Purdom, 1951, p. 37, describing his appointment as a junior clerk at the GCA in 1902)

Although common amongst pressure groups, it is sometimes unexpected to find an organization with a national (or even an international) reputation tucked away in modest and overcrowded premises, overworked and understaffed. Yet visitors to the GCA (and subsequently the GCTPA) in the years before 1914 would have found just this type of situation – modest office accommodation on the edge of the City, leased when possible at favourable rates from a landlord with sympathies for the cause. Several moves were made in this period, as leases ran out or at times when more spacious accommodation was needed. The Association started life in shared office space at 432 West Strand, lent by the supportive Land Nationalisation Society. A move from this represented an improvement in one sense, but poor C. B. Purdom blamed his ceaseless working in an office 'that was a sort of Black Hole' as the source of later health problems [101]. But at least he did not have to endure those particular premises, at 77 Chancery Lane, for too long. Within a couple of years the organization had moved on to 345 Birkbeck Bank Chambers, followed some three years later by a move to larger offices in the same building. There was one further change before 1914, to another nearby Holborn address, 3 Gray's Inn Place [102].

Undoubtedly frequent moves were disruptive, but the efficiency of the organization was to depend much more on the abilities of its few staff. In particular, much depended on the effectiveness and on the pioneering role of its main paid official, the Secretary, Thomas Adams [103].

The advertised post in 1901 called for someone with a sympathetic acquaintance with Howard's book. Adams is reputed to have read the book for the first time on the train from Edinburgh to his London interview, and to have been seduced more by the underlying philosophy of associated individualism than by the idea of garden cities as such [104]. Notwithstanding any initial doubts on the part of Adams, he was offered and took up the post immediately. His duties, he soon found, were 'ill-defined and the organisation was somewhat casual.' [105] In contrast, his own qualities were the very opposite, and his contribution in the formative years, when the Association could well have slipped into obscurity as just another quaint indulgence of a visionary, was undoubtedly crucial.

With Howard's ideas and Neville's influence, Adams made up the third side of a triangle which, as a result, held together. Adams's own particular contribution was as a very good organizer. He was quietly efficient, building a sound base, but with sufficient vision to launch initiatives (notably the Bournville and Port Sunlight conferences) that attracted national interest [106]. 'His great gifts of charm, persuasion, patience, practicality, dynamism, shrewdness and lucidity were allied to substantial talents for organization, administration and publicity and were harnessed most effectively in his work for the emerging profession of planning.' [107] C. B. Purdom, who worked with Adams, and who complained so bitterly about the state of the office and even about another of his colleagues, the GCA's accountant, Harold Craske (whose mind, Purdom discovered to his concern, was 'quite blank' on the subject of garden cities), confirms the view that Adams was doing a very effective job: '. . . robust and energetic . . . he worked whole-heartedly, believing utterly in Howard's ideas.' [108]

With the start of Letchworth, Adams left to devote most of his energies to the new enterprise, with a new Secretary, George J. H. Northcroft, taking over at the Association. After a two year period, however, Adams returned to his old job. Northcroft, a journalist by trade, proved to be a poor organizer and he resigned in August 1905. Adams returned to find the office in total disarray; new subscriptions had almost dried up and old ones had not been renewed, the branches were complaining of neglect and little had been done to organize lectures [109]. A special committee was set up to look for ways of improving the organization. It was asked to consider how the scope of the Association could be widened, and whether this could be promoted by forming local councils in the large centres throughout the country [110].

The problem proved to be not simply a problem of office efficiency, but also one of the Association's role now that the first garden city was under way. As Adams had earlier observed, 'considering that many people consider that our "raison d'être" had ceased . . . we can understand why many subscriptions are not renewed.' [111] An important part of revitalizing the Association, then, was to redefine its role so that it could be seen as more than the mere agent of the First Garden City Company. The future of the Association lay in a complementary but quite separate role, dedicated to spreading the idea of garden cities as a wider movement. Within nine months of resuming his post, Adams was credited with restoring the financial situation and organization, 'and it is safe to say that the credit of the Association never stood higher in general estimation than it does today.' [112] With the fortunes of the Association thus revived, Adams resigned in 1906 in favour of a new appointment, Ewart G. Culpin. The new Secretary proved to be a good choice, working consistently for the cause in Britain and overseas [113]. In the years through to 1914, the Association experienced the odd financial crisis that is the lot of every pressure group, but in other respects the machinery that had been established by Adams functioned reasonably well [114].

Whether or not the Association was working as efficiently as possible is another matter. The constitution and rules of the Association were revised from time to time, though the dual structure of a Council and an Executive (with sub-committees known as Sections) was retained. It was the plethora of sub-committees that attracted the interest of critics. Particularly in its early days, the Association established committees for a variety of purposes, some of them surviving only for short periods and apparently achieving very little. At various times there were committees to liaise with the Co-operative Societies, to monitor Liquor Traffic, to organize foreign tours, to handle the Association's publications, to organize lectures, and to campaign for smallholdings and agricultural land reform [115]. It was a wide spread of activities for a small organization, and there may have been substance in the view of the Fabians (admittedly already looking for reasons to discredit such a voluntaristic approach) who attributed some of their doubts to such a fragmented organiz-ation: 'We fear it is somewhat futile to wish success to a project so impractical. No less than twelve sub-committees have been appointed to carry on the work.' [116] Although the central aim of the Association remained clear, there were undoubtedly times when the small organization seemed to be in danger of over-extending itself.

Membership and Finance

I think people imagine that in some mysterious way the Garden Cities (sic) Association is making a profit out of the various schemes on Garden City lines that have come into existence, and do not realise that we are purely a propagandist body and gain nothing by the spread of our ideas except the satisfaction of spreading them. (Sir Ralph Neville, speaking at the Fourteenth Annual Meeting of the Association, 5th February 1913)

The issue of membership and finance is one that is endemic to the activities of any pressure group. How important is it in political terms to demonstrate a large and, preferably, growing membership? Is it, perhaps more important to secure a sound financial base to enable the various activities of the group to be promoted, regardless of whether this revenue stems from a large membership or from a few wealthy sponsors? Especially in the early years of the Association, questions such as these were, at least implicitly, on the business agenda. No doubt this was in part because a new pressure group will inevitably be sensitive to demonstrate to the rest of the world that it should be taken seriously, and citing evidence of growing membership would be one way to do this. It is also a case that a new group experiences (perhaps more than a mature organization) an obvious tension between the vitality of its ideas and ambitious goals, and the task of spending time in building the financial base that will enable its goals to be achieved.

Early reports of the Association reveal this initial gap between small beginnings and lofty aspirations. At the same time, these reports also indicate a sense of optimism and material progress. By the end of the first full year of the Association, in August 1900, the membership stood at 325. Annual subscriptions were set at a minimum of one shilling per member – 'the democratic shilling, so that none should be shut out' [117] – and the total income in the first year was £176.7s.6d (against total expenditure of £84.15s.6d). The one shilling subscribers were full members, but higher subscriptions were always invited. For 2s.6d, membership carried with it the attraction of receiving any literature produced by the Association (an offer that preceded the publication of a regular journal). Life membership could be bought through donations of five guineas and upwards. Subscriptions apart, the Council could also create Corresponding and Honorary members, the latter in recognition of some service to the Association or to humanity [118].

In subsequent years the Association could point to an increase in both membership numbers and income [119]. The 1900 figure of 325 members rose to 530 in the following year, and (undoubtedly stimulated by the success and publicity surrounding the Bournville and Port Sunlight conferences, and the interest in Letchworth) on to 1800 and 2500 in 1902 and 1903, respectively.

Similarly, the total income of £176 at the end of 1900 had risen to £202 by 1901. After that, a change in the presentation of the accounts makes comparisons difficult, though a total income figure of £915 over a fourteen month period through to October 1902 indicates substantial growth (linked to the big increase in membership). In the following year, (relating to a twelve month period) the income total, however, drops to £797.

Contemporary comments on these early trends offer a mixture of optimism tinged with disappointment that the movement had not attracted more of a mass following. Thus, at the end of 1901 the Annual Report concluded that the growth in income

> does not satisfy us that the claims of the Association for public support are adequately recognised. For a time education had been necessary, and propaganda work had to be carried on with the object of creating public interest in our objects. But . . . it seems to us that we ought soon to get past the stage of education and embark upon the first practical experiment. To carry out that purpose we wish to make an urgent appeal for further support . . . [120]

There was also an interesting comment on the significance of the membership figures. While an increase in the first years was obviously welcomed in itself, the modest scale of this increase called for some explanation. The general feeling was that these numbers in no way reflected the real strength of the movement's ideas, but perhaps mere numbers were not really what counted. The fact was, asserted the Association, that 'the greater part of those who have recently become identified with the movement are men and women of considerable influence, many of whom occupy positions of eminence in the country.' [121] Was influence, then, going to count for more than numbers in the subsequent growth of the Association? The fact is that while an increase in numbers might have some immediate propaganda value, in reality 'these figures meant little. Lecturers signed up people from the audience for a donation of one shilling per annum, and this usually ended the new member's participation.' [122]

In contrast with the debate about membership numbers, the need to secure a firm financial base was beyond contention. Throughout the period to 1914 the state of the Association's finances remained prominent in the minds of the organizers. The accounts for the financial year ending 31st August 1901 illustrate the kind of balancing act that was involved. Set against a balance carried forward of £109, augmented by income during the year amounting to £202, the expenditure was itemized. Rent for the Association's new offices at 77, Chancery Lane amounted to £15 for a full year, while the appointment of a Secretary half way through the year, together with clerical assistance, yielded costs of £49. Then there was expenditure incurred for printing and publication (£52), postage (£28), stationery (£6), meeting costs (£5), preparations to date for the Bournville Conference (£5), advertising (£3), office fittings (£4), and sundries (£4). At the end of all this a balance of £142 could be carried forward to the following year. Although the Association remained solvent and was able to sustain a range of activities, it was not in all years that even a modest surplus of this sort could be recorded [123].

From 1904 the publication of the Association's own journal offered a new opportunity not only to spread the idea of the garden city, but also to launch a series of appeals and campaigns to increase the organization's revenue. Membership subscriptions remained the financial lifeblood of the Association, and the pages of the journal periodically listed the names of subscribers and, pointedly, the amount of their contributions. Any donations of particular generosity were warmly acknowledged in the journal, no doubt in part *pour encourager les autres*. Under the heading 'A Generous Offer', news was given of Mr Harold Moore's offer of £25 per year for three years, provided nine other members would do the same by the end of that month. The money was to be used to obtain information on the building of country cottages and to advance the cause of adequate rural housing. In the event of the fund not being achieved (and there is no further evidence that it was), Mr Moore called for all members to follow his own example by doubling their annual subscriptions.

There is no evidence of this happening either [124]. Exemplifying a less personal approach to fund-raising, the Association in 1907 launched a special appeal for £500. The money was needed, quite simply, 'to place the Association on a firm financial basis.' [125] In spite of all the publicity surrounding Letchworth, the Association was concerned that its own role and slender financial resources were misunderstood in the minds of the public, who had been led to believe that the Association had some share in the capital subscribed to First Garden City Ltd. Appeals of this sort were at pains to show that this was not the case, and that any funds gained would be used purely for its promotional activities. Later that year, and linked to the fund-raising objective, the Association called for members to help in recruiting 1000 new members. 'The labours of the Association were never more highly appreciated than they are today, but unfortunately it is not always realised that we have no settled income, and are dependent upon voluntary contributions.' [126]

In spite of modest progress from time to time, the 'firm financial basis' that was constantly sought proved to be an elusive goal. Thus, at the end of 1907 the Chairman could look back on a year when the financial position was 'in a more satisfactory condition than at any period in the history of the Association.' [127] Yet in the following year regret was noted that 'the financial position of the Association has not been maintained.' [128] The sudden change of fortune had been brought about, it was claimed, by a substantial loss on the publication of the journal as a result of the default and mismanagement of an agent who was handling the advertising; by a fall in donations; and, in particular, by 'a great falling off in the amount received from women members, who are interested in the suffrage question, and devoting all efforts to that end.' [129]

As this last example of the suffrage movement illustrates, and as subsequent experience endorsed, the Association, like other pressure groups, was operating in a competitive situation amongst a wide range of worthy causes. In 1912, for instance, a new appeal was launched, this time for £1000. By the end of that year, extra subscriptions combined with special donations had brought in £350, still well short of the target. Part of the problem, it was surmised, was that the public had been seduced by more dramatic appeals (notably, the fund-raising that followed the sinking of the Titanic), and distracted by other issues affecting the world at that time (the Dock Strike, the Balkan War, and 'other lamentable occurrences') [130].

In calling for more funds, a sense of frustration is evident in what was perennially seen as a gap between the enormity of the task and the extent of public support to achieve it. Equally, there was a sense of optimism and faith that the gates to the New Jerusalem were at least within sight:

Only the lack of a few hundred pounds a year now stands in the way of completing its programme of lecturers, organisers, and travelling exhibitions, and again we appeal to all those interested in the highest welfare of the land, the truest advancement of the people, to come and help in the work which we conceive to be nothing less than a peaceful revolution from what is seriously and even fundamentally wrong with Housing and Planning in our cities [131].

Arguably, more than a few hundred pounds was needed to set this 'peaceful revolution' on its way, but hope was not dimmed until the outbreak of the First World War 'brought an entire change in our prospects . . .' [132]

Patterns of Propaganda

The tendency of public thought on the question (of housing reform) is now almost entirely in accord with the objects of the Garden City Association, which a few years ago had practically no following. It is hoped that members of the Association and supporters of the Garden City Company will begin to realise how great an educational force their movement has been, and how necessary it is to actively maintain the propaganda in order to take full advantage of the work that has already been done. (*GC*, Vol. I, No. 5, November 1905, p. 70)

From its inception, the Garden City Association, and its successor the Garden Cities and Town Planning Association, was in the business of communicating an idea and of urging others to put this idea into practice. The Association was never itself directly involved with building and development. It remained throughout, in its own terms, a propagandist body.

In some respects the task of the Association was easier in the years before Letchworth, in that the object of propaganda was more sharply focused. Once the building of the first garden city had been secured, the Association was forced to adapt to somewhat more diffuse educational aims. But in spite of a broadening role, the methods employed in the period through to 1914 were fairly consistent. There were some methods that it favoured, and other means of propaganda which seem hardly to have been tried.

The Association sought consistently to attract the interest of the press, and offered newsworthy items on its main activities – through publicizing conferences, exhibitions and tours, through its own publications and a regular journal, and through public meetings and lectures up and down the country [133]. There is evidence, too, of 'quiet influence' to persuade politicians and potential sponsors of the worth of their cause, but (although it attracted the support of MPs) there was not an organized political lobby of the sort that was pursued, say, by the National Housing Reform Council [134]. Nor was there a hint of seeking the favours of any one political party rather than another. 'The Garden City Association has no political opinions' [135] was the misleading, but obviously well-intentioned, rationale for its bipartisan approach [136].

Obviously, the starting point in terms of propaganda was the publication of *To-morrow*, with its subsequent reviews and public lectures. It is debatable, though, whether the momentum could have been sustained without the campaigning flair of Thomas Adams. His decision to base the Association's conference at Bournville rested on a belief that public attention could be drawn to the success of the existing model village, and that the lessons of this for future experiments would become apparent [137].

Delegates to the two-day conference, in September 1901, came from local authorities, religious denominations, trade unions, cooperative societies, and friendly societies, though manufacturers were poorly represented. Howard and Unwin were amongst those who gave papers, and George Bernard Shaw (who, as a Fabian, had his doubts about the voluntary approach, yet retained a keen interest in the movement and warm admiration for Howard) rose from the audience to warn the gathering not to trust municipal authorities as they were currently constituted. As intended, the gathering attracted plenty of publicity, and the gains to the Association were various. One outcome was that 'some of the critics of the garden city idea have, by their visit to Bournville, been converted into enthusiasts.' [138] The Association could also point to the recruitment of nearly one hundred new members and a substantial increase in income. And, in his subsequent annual report, the Chairman acknowledged the interest shown by the press, and how the 'favourable and extensive notice given in the columns of the public journals after the Bournville Conference has been consistently maintained ever since.' [139]

In terms of the publicity it brought, an even more successful conference was held in the following year at Port Sunlight. Attracting more than a thousand delegates, the chairman this time hailed it as the 'most remarkable gathering yet held under the auspices of the Association.' [140] Within the space of ten months, two conferences had been held which had subsequently been interpreted as 'decisive steps in the propaganda which led to the creation of Letchworth.' [141] Conferences thereafter became an important part of the Association's repertoire.

From time to time, conferences were held on specific themes. Three of the more important examples in this period before 1914 were those in connection with the 1909 planning legislation [142]. The first two of these conferences, in March 1906 and October 1907, were described as the first town planning conferences of their kind. The latter was an especially prestigious event, held in the Guildhall, that was designed to reinforce and to articulate the growing campaign for town planning. This conference was followed by a comparable gathering (also in London's Guildhall), immediately after the 1909 Act was passed, to discuss the practical applications of town planning powers. These were by no means isolated events, but it is significant that the Association was seen to be taking a leading role in pressing for reforms which, in fact, went beyond its own more specific brief.

In addition to conferences, the Association looked for opportunities to hold or contribute to exhibitions where its cause could be furthered. In 1908, for instance, different themes were explored at three separate exhibitions [143]. In conjunction with First Garden City Ltd., a display was mounted at the Franco-British Exhibition apparently earning for the Association not only considerable interest but also winning the Diploma of Honour (the highest award at the event). Then, at the Scottish Exhibition a model of Letchworth was the special feature, presented with a view to stimulating others to initiate a similar garden city experiment in Scotland. Finally, the Association also had an exhibit at the Municipal Exhibition in London.

As well as organizing major events, the Association was also responsible for a steady output of literature in pursuit of its ideals. Apart from *To-morrow*, other pioneers in the movement wrote their own contributions, in the form of both leaflets and books [144]. Thomas Adams, for instance, voiced his concern about rural depopulation in a publication in 1905, *Garden City and Agriculture: How to solve the problem of rural depopulation*. In turn, two of the town planning conferences were subsequently reported in separate publications, one in the name of the Association and the other edited by Ewart Culpin. There was also a number of books, advocating the case for garden cities, such as G. Montagu Harris's *The Garden City Movement* and A. R. Sennett's *Garden Cities in Theory and Practice*. And, in 1912, Ewart Culpin prepared a set of fifty photographic postcards to illustrate garden city development (for sale at a cost of 5s. 6d.), though his more important contribution was the publication in the following year, *The Garden City Movement Up-to-Date*. As a regular source of ideas and news, however, it was the Association's own journal that was particularly important.

Although it passed through the hands of successive editors, and was changed in format and frequency, *The Garden City* (from 1904 to 1908) and subsequently *Garden Cities and Town Planning* offered the most consistent source of information on the early progress of the Association. Its columns included news of the Association itself, briefings on the garden city movement generally (in Britain and abroad), and material to help and inspire campaigners in the field. It must be assumed that most of the copies were for the Association's own members, although at one stage a reference to sales through W. H. Smith indicates a concern to reach a more general readership [145].

Probably the most characteristic source of propaganda in this early period was not that of conferences, exhibitions or publications, but the use of public meetings and lectures on a whole variety of garden city topics:

The work of educating public opinion by means of lectures and meetings has always been a special feature of our Association, and the hundreds of lectures and meetings which have been arranged by us in the past few years must have had a most valuable influence upon public opinion throughout the country. There is hardly a

'The Choice' (reproduced from *The Housing Reformer*) in *GCTP*, March 1912, with the caption: 'There is little doubt about the miner's choice; the difficulty is in the realisation of his hopes.'

town of any importance in the country to which our missionaries have not gone expounding the principles of Garden Cities and town planning, and still much more must be done on the same lines [146].

There is something very distinctive about this particular way of spreading the message. It lends itself to an evangelistic style of seeking converts (the Apostles of Better Environment is how the Association's lecturers were described in *The Garden City*) [147]; it has a distinctly Edwardian feel about it, an image of reforming zeal, the quest for improvement, and an austere world of draughty halls; and it raises questions about the efficacy of a campaign which puts so much energy into a method that can have only a piecemeal impact. It rests on a basic belief that rationality will win the day, and, in the interests of independence and the purity of its own ideals, turns its back on mass political movements. Whatever reservations one might have, though, the evidence of commitment to the cause is compelling. A small band of campaigners worked tirelessly, year after year, touring the country with their message.

Between August and December 1902, for instance, there were no fewer than 106 lecture engagements in all parts of the country. The GCA published a lecture circular with details of these events, and an appeal to 'Educational, Social, Political, Co-operative, Municipal, Religious and Temperance Societies and Institutions', inviting requests for further lectures on the subject of garden cities as a solution of the housing problem. A large collection of lantern slides had already been collected, including colour slides of Bournville, Port Sunlight and other garden villages, and applicants were asked if they wanted an illustrated lecture [148].

In the following winter, 1903–4, the number of lectures was far greater, and all manner of organizations were addressed. Literary societies, working men's institutes, the William Morris Labour Church, vegetarian societies, art and camera clubs, the Beautiful Oldham Society, the C.H.A. Rambling Club, 'Back to the Land' branches, and a whole variety of church and political clubs hosted one of the garden city missionaries [149]. Ebenezer Howard's own name was prominent on the lecture list, and all the signs are that he maintained this record throughout the decade. His youthful days attending chapel, when he was told by his minister that he should become a preacher, followed by some later experience in the pulpit, may have offered a valuable apprenticeship for this evangelizing role [150].

When the Liberal Administration announced its intention to implement town planning legislation, the Association was quick to mount a new programme of lectures to explain the principles of reform, with Howard heavily involved in another winter tour. Thus, in three months at the end of 1908 Howard gave thirty-eight lectures on this subject, fourteen of the lectures 'being in Lancashire, where the lack of town planning is especially noticeable.' [151] In that same programme, the Secretary of the Association, Ewart Culpin, was also very active, with some thirty lectures to his name.

Interestingly, a less publicized and very different pattern of lectures and meetings took place in comfortable drawing rooms and private gardens. Normally, these were hosted by ladies in fashionable parts of London and the home counties, with an apparent aim of securing for housing reform and garden cities a place on the unwritten list of 'good causes'. During the summer, 'members in London and the neighbourhood' were urged 'to place their gardens at the disposal of the Association for the purpose of garden parties.' [152]

Perhaps, though, some of the initial missionary zeal waned a little over time, for in 1912 there was a call for new 'active missionaries in garden city work'. It was said that 'Mr Culpin was the only lecturer on behalf of the movement, though there were other gentlemen who lectured from time to time.' [153] Admittedly, overseas lecturing was now attracting some of the best lecturers of the Association, but the fact remains that, first with the building of Letchworth and later with the passing of town planning legislation, some of the sting might have been taken out of the original message. In any case, after more than a decade of campaigning, it might reasonably have been argued that the idea of the garden city, novel in its day, was now quite widely understood. It had, as Howard and others frequently pointed out, become an accepted part of the English language, and that in itself was a product of the earlier campaign.

The 'Great and the Good'

The scene at the (Bournville) conference was richly symbolic of the future direction of the movement. The 'little men' to whom Howard had originally addressed the Garden City were nowhere to be found. At his side were millionaires, and in front of him were government officials. Neither group wanted to hear of the co-operative commonwealth or radical social change. They looked to the Garden City as a plausible and thrifty means to relieve urban overcrowding. Already the Garden City design was being separated from its original purpose; the broad Radical coalition that Howard had envisioned was narrowed and refocused to an elite of notables and bureaucrats. The Garden City was succeeding not as a social movement but as a planning movement. (Fishman, 1977, pp. 61–62)

Ebenezer Howard, born in 1850, grew up in a respectable, mid-Victorian setting, his father in trade and his mother a farmer's daughter. A variety of clerical posts, several years spent in the Mid-West of the United States, an inventive mind which led him from a mastery of shorthand to the invention of a shorthand machine, some experience as a preacher and more than a passing interest in spiritualism provided the background to Howard's social and political circle of the 1890s [154]. In promoting his idea of garden cities, Howard's natural constituency was the world of public meetings and the many radical, religious and political journals where inquisitive minds reflected on the ill ways of society and eagerly turned over new ideas that offered a route to salvation. Vegetarianism, theosophism, spiritualism, anarchism, socialism and associated individualism were amongst these various sources of interest and inspiration at the turn of the century.

It was in this context that the idea of garden cities enjoyed a wide appeal; an idea with a radical ring about it, yet an idea which was not as threatening to established interests as some of the more strident calls for fundamental change that were also in the air at that time. It is not, however, the strength of ideas alone that assures a pressure group of influence, let alone success, so much as its ability to communicate those ideas and to know how best to translate them into action. Thus, the first year or so of the Association's existence suggested that the campaign might well fail – a cause that would be earnestly discussed by well-meaning intellectuals and moralists, but which was destined to founder in the face of financial and organizational limitations.

Then, in 1901, 'a change suddenly came over the Association.' [155] Almost by chance, the Association veered away from its honest, but possibly ineffectual, background of people of good intent, and towards a more effective (though also less radical) circle of influence; 'away from the crowded parlours of English radicalism into the more affluent drawing rooms of English liberalism.' [156] A key figure in this change of direction proved to be Ralph Neville. It is Howard who is most closely associated with the origins and early years of the Association, yet in some ways it is the lesser-known Neville who had most influence on the type of pressure group it became [157].

Ralph Neville was a London lawyer (later a judge) with strongly-held views about human progress. Society, he contended, is subject to natural laws which we ignore to our cost. If our lives are not in harmony with the natural order of things, then degeneracy is the only outcome. And that (or physical deterioration at least) was what had happened in industrial England. The way out, however, was not to attempt the impossible task of reversing the process of capitalism, but rather to seek to improve the conditions in which so many people lived. Of Howard's ideas for garden cities, Neville wrote: 'Without pledging myself to every detail – for we still await lessons of experience – it may confidently be asserted that the idea is based upon sound economic principle.' [158] Howard immediately persuaded Neville not only to join the Association but also to become its Chairman [159].

For the Association, the elevation of Neville to the Chairmanship (and subsequently to the Presidency, until his death at the end of 1918) had its costs as well as its benefits. Under his leadership, it was not the radicalism of Howard's ideas which was to be more actively promoted, so much as the conciliatory and more moderate, reformist features. Neville had already shown interest in the idea of co-partnership, in which workers would be encouraged to hold shares in their own place of employment, and he had been actively involved in the Labour Association for Promoting Co-operative Production Based on Co-partnership of the Workers [160]. The idea of the Garden City, in which the workers would share in the profits of the community, was consistent with his general beliefs. In the circle in which he mixed – the Liberal politicians, lawyers and businessmen of the day – Neville was able to offer a sense of assurance that outsiders like Howard were denied. So much so, in fact, that through his direct influence he attracted to the GCA more than half of his associates on the board of his Co-partnership Association [161].

However, for more radical factions, already sceptical about another scheme to build the New Jerusalem on the foundations of capitalism, the course of the pressure group, directed through the corridors of power, seemed to be moving away from their own priorities. Although individual members held more than a passing interest, the bulk of the trade union movement, the Fabians and the emergent Labour Party had little to do with the Association in its formative years.

Illustrative of this tendency, the Workmen's Housing Council (founded in 1898 'to induce Municipal Authorities to provide cheap and good houses for the people') was sceptical about the way the Association was moving. Its Secretary, Fred Knee, reluctantly attended the Port Sunlight conference, returning with strong criticism over what he saw as the unwarranted influence of industrialists with a vested interest, at the expense of democratic local authorities. Garden cities, he thought, would simply play into the hands of these industrialists: 'What little cohesiveness workmen have obtained by closer association would easily be dispelled, which, of course, would be and is excellent for the manufacturer!' Knee concluded that 'we had better put up with our slums, else we enter a worse servitude than now.' [162] The inherent contradiction which this view illustrates (between ends which are promoted as being essentially universal, and means which can be, to an extent, elitist) is a theme that will be pursued subsequently.

For garden city enthusiasts at the time, however, the enrolment of Neville and fellow Liberals was undoubtedly seen as a gain. Howard, himself, was euphoric: 'Now our movement will go ahead, for we shall secure a truly doughty and courageous Chairman.' [163] Successive notes in the Association's journal at this time endorsed this view, and show the extent to which the leadership of the Association was very much in the hands of Neville. 'It is a great advantage to the Association to have at the head of its affairs a man of Mr Neville's influence and ripe wisdom. By his suggestion as to our work and attendance at our meetings he places us under a large and growing obligation.' [164]

Within the Association, Neville was supported by a long list of Vice Presidents, selected for the additional influence they could offer. There were, for instance, no fewer than ninety-six Vice Presidents in 1902, a total that had increased to 138 by 1906. In recording the new Vice Presidents elected during 1903, Neville explained how the list 'indicates most significantly the appeal which the work of the Association makes to many persons of distinction who differ widely upon a variety of subjects. It is our boast that the Garden City Association is non-political and non-sectarian in the widest sense; and this fact is well illustrated by the names of . . . the Right Hon. the Earl Grey, the Lady Florence Dixie, the Lord Bishop of Ripon, the Rev. C. H. Kelly, Mr G. F. Watts R.A., Major General Owen-Jones C. B., Mr H.Rider Haggard, and Mr Malcolm Morris F.R.C.S.' [165]

The Association also enjoyed the support of a number of philanthropic industrialists, reassured of the legitimacy of the organization by the presence of Neville, and attracted by the practical goals of Letchworth [166]. Looking back, in 1911, a two-part feature in the Association's journal acknowledged the respective roles of George Cadbury, W. H. Lever and Joseph Rowntree as the core pioneers of the movement [167]. Each had demonstrated his own model experiment, and had, in turn, given his support in one way or another to the Association's aims. Moreover, other members of both the Cadbury and Rowntree families were to take an active interest in the promotion of garden cities. In addition to the chocolate and soap dynasties, the journal might also have acknowledged the generous support of the newspaper family headed by Alfred Harmsworth. He, in turn, encouraged his brother, Cecil, to work for the movement [168]. As well as industrialists the Association could also list, in 1906, thirty-seven Members of Parliament who were members of the Garden City Association or shareholders in First Garden City Limited.

It would be wrong, however, to suggest that the Association was totally appropriated by industrial and political interests. Complementing this source of influence, the idea of garden cities consistently attracted leading professionals and campaigners in their own fields of housing and town planning. Apart from its own officers, the Association gained enormously from the contribution of Raymond Unwin, not to mention Barry Parker, Henry Vivian, J. S. Nettlefold, G. L. Pepler, Henry Aldridge, T. C. Horsfall and Professor Adshead, all of whom either served on the Council or were directly involved in some other way in the work of the Association. Patrick Geddes was also associated with the movement – including a brief period on the Council, and an honorary position as Vice President – but his main energies at this time were devoted to the promotion of Civics and the Sociological Society [169].

Unwin's role deserves special mention [170]. For the Association it was significant in two respects. On the one hand, Unwin contributed directly to the garden city movement in both a practical and a theoretical sense, each underpinned by firmly held socialist beliefs. In practical terms, Unwin, with Parker, translated the idea of the garden city into the organic reality of Letchworth, expressing his understanding of community and his essentially humanist values. In the same period, before 1914, his wide-ranging professional activities as an architect were matched by his propagandist work as a writer and educator. His advice was freely given to the Association, and one of his influential publications, *Nothing Gained by Over-crowding*, was published by the GCTPA in 1912. On the other hand, as well as his direct contribution, Unwin was an important link for the Association between the various contacts in a growing network of professional town planning. He was no less active, for instance, in the work of the National Housing Reform Council, with Hampstead Garden Suburb and its connections to the wider garden suburb movement, with co-partnership housing schemes, the RIBA and, towards the end of this period, with the newly-formed TPI. During the First World War and after he assumes important governmental roles, and remains committed to the work of the Association through to his death in 1940 [171]. Described as 'the father of modern town planning' [172], Unwin was a valuable person to have around as the Association sought professional as well as political respectability.

Other notable Edwardians were mentioned from time to time for their interest in the Association. H. G. Wells (at one time a Vice President) attended the odd meeting or wrote the occasional commentary, but had more time for Fabianism and the socialist movement. Another Fabian, George Bernard Shaw, felt less constrained by his collectivist beliefs and showed more than a passing interest in the garden city idea. 'We middle-class people, having always had physical comfort and good order, do not realise the disaster to character in being without . . .', he argued, in defending the theme of his play *Major Barbara* to Beatrice Webb. But Webb could not forgive 'the anti-climax of evangelising the Garden City!' [173] Then there was G. K. Chesterton, intrigued by the spirit of revolt and undoubtedly attracted by the decentralist aims of the movement. Addressing the Association at its Sixth Annual Meeting in 1905, he told its members that a great many people detested the very idea of the garden city, and the utopians who tried to bring it into practice, but that, far from being dismayed, they should rejoice. 'Because until you are thoroughly detested you may be perfectly certain that no very serious advance has been made.' [174]

Drawing together the many contacts, the one single event which best illustrates the web of influence woven around the Association is the dinner that was held at the Holborn Restaurant on the 19th March 1912 for Ebenezer Howard, in recognition of 'his work for humanity'. Organized by the Association, it was a gala event, attended by some 400 guests at a cost of six shillings each. Half as many again were expected, had it not been for the effects of the Coal Strike (as Edward Cadbury, for instance, explained in a letter saying that it would be impossible for him to travel from Bournville on the day, 'in view of the disorganised Railway service') [175].

The notable attendance list was seen by the Association as 'a splendid testimony to the catholicity of the Garden City idea' [176], and, affirming its place in the centre of the town planning stage, a message from Professor Adshead and the Liverpool University School of Town Planning congratulated Howard as the 'originator of the modern system of town planning.' [177] The journal reported that not only was there:

a strong representation – as might be expected – of the Garden Cities and Town Planning Association and of Letchworth itself, but practically every housing association in the country united to do Mr Howard honour. Over a score of public organisations and propagandist bodies were represented . . . Church and Parliament, Bench and Bar, Art and Literature, combined with the idealist and the practical business man to show their admiration of the man who more than anyone else in this generation has been responsible for changing the methods of estate development throughout the world, and who had given a new meaning to the desire for a fuller life. The tributes received from foreign countries and from leaders of English thought were especially striking . . . [178]

Neville proposed the toast of the evening, and Howard responded, saying again that 'if Sir Ralph Neville had not joined the movement at the time he did the project might still have been in the clouds.' [179] Further speeches were made by Earl Grey, who reminded the gathering that their task was 'to create a public opinion which would be strong enough to spread the movement' [180]; Aneurin Williams, who spoke of the practical success of Letchworth; Henrietta Barnett, making links betgween garden suburbs and garden cities; Captain Swinton, speaking not only as Chairman of the London County Council, but also as someone who was shortly to depart to plan the new Imperial City of Delhi, fired by the example of Howard; Henry Vivian, presiding over a table of forty representatives of the Co-partnership Tenants movement; Cecil Harmsworth, who took the opportunity as Chairman of the Council, to call for a yearly income for the Association of at least £1000; and, finally, Lord Robert Cecil who, in proposing the toast to the Chairman, set the seal on an unprecedented evening. It is unlikely if there has been, before or since, a comparable event where so many leading figures in the world of planning and housing were so closely connected within an enlightened fringe of the Establishment.

The Women's League

> Woman's influence is too often ignored. When Garden City is built, as it shortly will be, woman's share in the work will be found to have been a large one. Women are among our most active missionaries. (Howard, 1902, Postscript)

The role of women in the early garden city movement is ambiguous. It reflects a mixture of a Victorian 'lady bountiful' approach, where the gentle hand of woman is offered to lead the slum-dweller to a better land, and the promise of a more radical approach, where the traditional role of women itself is challenged [181].

In formal terms, women were not strongly represented in the Association's positions of office. In 1901, for instance, there were just three women on a Council of twenty-one – Mrs Ashton Jonson, Miss Jessie Currie, and Mrs E. Howard. At no time before 1914 did a woman hold one of the executive posts [182]. At the same time, in 1903 a Women's League was formed, open to all members of the Association at no extra subscription cost. The aim of the League was to promote the aims of the Association as a whole, 'more especially with regard to the claims of the home from the standpoint of wives and mothers.' [183] There were plans for advisory committees on a county basis, which would, in turn, report to a central council in London. Members of the League were urged by the first Secretary, Viscountess Helmsley, to do what they could as individuals to further the cause [184]. She suggested ways in which this could be done: by talking to friends and persuading them to join; by sending the League's leaflet to women elsewhere; by trying to arrange meetings and lectures; by encouraging people to buy shares in First Garden

City Ltd.; and by speaking about the movement at mothers' meetings, girls' clubs, and other local gatherings.

Viscountess Helmsley believed that 'if the women clearly understood the benefits of living in an atmosphere such as Garden City will afford, they would demand a change from the slums, and would influence their mankind and children to go and live where homes – real homes, not barracks – can be procured for less rent in a wholesome area, thus helping the children to grow up stronger and healthier in mind and body. The healthfulness of our youth is a most important national question . . .' [185] In spite of the strength of her case (linking it, as she did, to national concern about physical degeneracy), the League itself had a chequered history. Perhaps because at that time energies were consumed by the Letchworth experiment, or because it was thought that the wider cause of the women's suffrage movement came first, the fact remains that the initial plans and ambitions came to little.

Two years later, in 1907, an attempt was made to revive the League [186]. Again, it was Lady (formerly Viscountess) Helmsley who took the initiative. She called a meeting of the original League members, held at her Chelsea home. This proved to be the start of a modest revival, and in the following year Lady Helmsley reported on a successful meeting at her home, when it was decided to raise money to finance the building of two cottages at Letchworth [187]. Some drawing-room meetings were arranged, together with a sale of work. There is little evidence after this, however, of the League playing an important role in the Association.

In contrast to this approach, a more radical view was aired. The doughty communitarian and campaigner for land nationalization, Evacustes A. Phipson [188], wrote to the editor of *The Garden City*, with an article which asked the question 'Why not associated homes?' [189] The place of women was not his sole concern, although that was an important part of his scheme. What he had in mind (and which he thought a garden city experiment would be in an ideal position to promote) was for clusters of up to ten homes that would enjoy their own privacy for some functions, but which would be connected to a communal kitchen, dining-room, nursery, laundry and bathroom. For the 'poor harassed wives' the labour and worry would 'be easily reduced by at least one half'. And 'instead of one woman having to light and stoke fires, sweep and scrub floors, dust furniture, clean up dishes, cook up to three or four meals a day, mind babies, black boots, wash and mend clothes, go shopping, and perform all the other multifarious functions which are considered a wife's duty, the various co-operators could either take turns to do such work, whether singly, or in pairs or threes, as was found necessary . . .' It was radical in the sense that it challenged the concept of the single family household, and yet conservative in the sense that it retained a traditional division of labour. Women may well be working together, under more amenable conditions, but it was still envisaged that they would continue to do the tasks that had come to be expected of them.

Significantly, Howard, too, had himself long nursed the idea of experimenting with new forms of social organization based on cooperative principles [190]. There is a hint of this in *To-morrow*, when Howard refers in passing to some of the housing having common gardens and cooperative kitchens [191], and in 1906 he takes this idea a stage further [192]. The time had come, asserted Howard, when cooperative principles could be tried 'as one of the central ideas of domestic life.' He described a scheme that he had devised in conjunction with the architect, H. Clapham Lander, for twenty-four homes around a square, linked by a cloister, ('after the fashion of a college quad'), and sharing kitchen and dining room facilities. It was clearly intended for middle-class residents, less concerned with the emancipation of women from traditional tasks and more with reducing dependence on tiresome servants.

For all the limitations of this original scheme, Howard remained convinced of the possibilities and potential of the concept. He became directly involved in two modest experiments at Letchworth, and some years later wrote from his home in one of them, 'Homesgarth', to reaffirm his belief in the practicability, as well as simply the ideal, of what he called 'a new way of house-keeping' [193]. He acknowledged that for many people the very idea of sharing some facilities was beyond comprehension [194], but he also reminded his readers that far-sighted individuals like H. G. Wells foresaw cooperative dwellings as soon becoming the norm rather than the exception. The fact was, contended Howard, that in his experience the idea actually worked in practice. He pointed to the balance that could be struck between community and privacy and, again, to this kind of scheme as a way of easing the domestic 'tiresome servant' problem.

It was this last point that caught the eye of Bernard Shaw's sister, Lucy Carr Shaw, living at the time in a fashionable part of London. She immediately wrote to Howard, asking for more information and explaining how the new way of housekeeping would so adequately meet her own needs:

I am a much harassed person, in delicate health, nearly worried to death by the curse of house-keeping and the intolerable incompetency (sic) of servants, who seem to treat one worse and worse the more one tries to consider their comfort. One of your £64 houses presents itself to me as a paradise after the turmoil of private house-keeping. Are there any more co-operative establishments likely to be built nearer London, as Letchworth is rather too far away for an inveterate theatre-goer [195]?

Howard's radical instinct, however, also led him to show how this type of scheme could be accessible to people on low incomes as well as the 'moderate means' which characterized the Letchworth experiment. In another article, 'A new outlet for women's energy' [196], Howard illustrated a potential project where a four-acre plot is divided into two equal parts, one for houses built around three sides of a square, and the rest of the land for allotments. What was novel about the proposal was the inclusion of a kitchen where all the cooking was undertaken for the tenants, a communal wash-house, and a creche with 'a kind motherly body in charge'. He foresaw that many women who would otherwise be unable to leave the home might choose to work in the local factories. It was a proposal which Howard believed had 'wrapped up within it the germ of what will help greatly towards a new and brighter, a juster and a happier social order – an order, too, in which women will play a far larger part than she plays today . . .' [197]

Regional Connections

> The Council hope that the formation of Local Centres will be a help rather than a hindrance to the Association financially, and while carrying out the local organisation in an efficient manner care should be taken not to burden the Central Body with expenses beyond the amount of the local subscriptions. It should be the object of all local centres to advance the principles of the Garden City Association loyally, and to secure the adhesion of all who sympathise with its aims. (Recommendations by the Council with reference to the constitution of Local Centres, GCA, June 1902)

For an Association whose very lifeblood was the idea of dispersal, it is understandable that its protagonists travelled to the provinces whenever they could, lecturing to interested organizations and seeking to encourage others to promote garden city schemes in their own locality. Although the Association has always remained a London-based organization itself, regional connections have played their own part in the spread of the garden city movement. Big cities throughout the country were obvious sources of interest for an Association which sought a process of urban decentralization.

Reviewing progress over a fourteen-month period through to October 1902, it was noted that the Association had forty local correspondents in the provincial towns, with two 'exceptionally strong' branches formed in Manchester and Liverpool with a combined membership of 300 [198]. Some evidence of progress in the Manchester branch remains in a minute book for the period 1902 to 1908 [199]. It appears that interest in garden cities had for some time been restricted to scattered individuals, and that an early attempt to formalize this interest had failed. The turning point was when Ebenezer Howard visited Manchester in November 1901, and lectured to the Manchester Ruskin Society. On the very next day, a group of enthusiasts who had attended the lecture met with Howard at the Grand Hotel, with a view to proceeding with the idea of a local association. Included in the small gathering was Archdeacon Wilson and a man who was to play an important part in furthering the cause of housing reform, Thomas Coglan Horsfall [200]. It was a promising start with plans laid for a public meeting, but then 'matters did not develop just as was expected. They seemed to drift somewhat aimlessly . . .' [201], and it took a visit from Thomas Adams in March 1902 to galvanize the group again.

Following the Adams visit, an Executive was formed (with Barry Parker and Raymond Unwin amongst its members), and arrangements were made not simply to spread the idea of the garden city to the Manchester public, but also to see whether a practical scheme could be started in the region. Letters were sent to local sympathizers, public meetings were planned, and a lecture programme sought to carry the idea to a variety of local associations. The winter of 1902–3 saw members of the Executive out and about in the region, lecturing to the Moss Side Unitarian Debating Society, Sale Social Guild, Leigh Literary Society, Failsworth Co-operative Society, and the Hooley Bridge Liberal Club, to name but a few. It was also proposed to add the subject of garden cities to the syllabus for lectures to the educational sections of working men's clubs.

Distinctive though it was, with its specific interest in garden cities, the new organization was undoubtedly enriched by the fact that it existed within an environment where housing reform movements were already active. Michael Harrison has ably demonstrated not simply the strength of the housing and town planning movement in Manchester before 1914, but also the inter-connections between reforming bodies [202]. This latter point is amply illustrated by the arrival of the Garden City Association, where its leading lights were also active in parallel organizations. Horsfall, for instance, was a link with the National Housing Reform Council, as well as being an active local campaigner. Another activist in the Association, and one who also enjoyed a national reputation, was T. C. Marr. A one-time assistant to Patrick Geddes (helping to run the Outlook Tower in Edinburgh), Marr proved to be an indefatigable reformer in Manchester before 1914. Known locally as 'Citizen Marr', for his work in the Citizens Association for the Improvement of the Unwholesome Dwellings and Surroundings of the People (an organization in which Horsfall was also active), he was a key figure in the Manchester University Settlement, chairman of two co-partnership tenant societies, and a city councillor from 1905.

As well as benefiting from overlapping memberships, the Manchester Centre of the Garden City Association (as it was originally called) sought formal and informal contact with other organizations. An early affiliation, for instance, was that in April 1902 to the National Housing Reform Council. And, as part of its internal programme, members were invited to take part in a picnic outing to Port Sunlight, there no doubt to gain inspiration but also to meet fellow garden city campaigners from Liverpool.

Free offices were obtained for the organization in November 1902 at 55 Market Street, and regular committee meetings were held to discuss how best to spend their limited funds on local propaganda. The question of a practical scheme also arose, and a proposal was put to consider the formation of a Company or Trust with the object of establishing 'garden villages similar to Bournville' [203]. It was decided, however, that the Branch (as it was then called) should not become directly involved, although its members might wish to do so as individuals. Four years later, when presented with an opportunity to promote a scheme at Alkrington, the Branch found that they could not agree to pursue the proposal, leaving it to others to see it to fruition [204]. It was, then, as a propagandist rather than as a practical body that the local organization is best known.

Elsewhere in the country, the record of GCA branches is mixed. In the Annual Report at the end of 1907, the welcome news was that the Association's branches were active, with three involved in practical schemes. At the same time there were also disappointments to record. It seems that, as well as Manchester, there had also been hopes with other development proposals 'which have been submitted to the Association and upon which much time has been spent. In each instance, however, after the bestowal of much patient endeavour, and in many cases much laborious work, upon the schemes, it was not found possible to secure their completion.' [205]

From time to time, the Association's journal recorded the formation of new branches. In 1908, for instance, progress was reported at Bristol, new branches were formed at Edinburgh and Glasgow, and 'a promising organisation has come into being in East London, under the title of the East London Garden Suburbs and Town Planning Association. The definite object of this branch is to arouse public opinion in this part of London . . . and if possible to provide an object lesson.' [206]

At the Association's Annual Meeting in February 1912, Professor

Stanley Jevons made a strong plea for more regional involvement, and, specifically, for the siting of a National Congress on Garden Cities and Town Planning to be held in Cardiff. In his address, he connected the 'bitter strikes', for which South Wales was renowned, with the idea of the garden city, on the basis that, in his opinion, a good deal of the industrial unrest at the time was due to the very bad housing conditions prevailing [207]. Largely as a result of the Jevons initiative, a South Wales Garden Cities and Town Planning Association was duly formed and formally affiliated.

Certainly, by 1914, local organizations had helped to carry the ideas of the garden city movement into the regions [208]. The Association remained very much a London-based national body, but its propagandist role was undoubtedly assisted by local initiatives of this sort.

An Alliance of Interests

The Garden City Association, under whose auspices an important Conference was held at the Guildhall, London, yesterday, affords a very striking example of what can be accomplished in the direction of solving the most difficult problems when they are earnestly attacked by a body of thoughtful, practical and enthusiastic men. It is only a very short time since the Association came into existence, but it has speedily grown into a robust, vigorous organisation, which has not only been instrumental in the formulation of several interesting schemes in various parts of the country, but is exercising the minds of thoughtful men of all classes, and representing a variety of shades of political opinion by means of systematic propaganda work . . . (*Birmingham Mail*, 26th October 1907)

It is, perhaps, a hallmark of an effective pressure group that it should not simply pursue its own distinctive aims in isolation, but that it should also seek areas of overlap and common affinity, combining with other groups in a broader alliance of interests. Illustrative of this wider network, when the Garden City Association organized its conference in the London Guildhall in October 1907, the participants included a wide range of propagandist and professional bodies sharing a common interest in the general cause of town planning [209].

Particularly before 1914, co-partnership housing was an important ally for the garden city movement [210]. Co-partnership carried with it the idea that housing was about more than individual dwellings, and that tenants could enjoy a share in the quality and value of their general surroundings. Raymond Unwin offered a link between the two movements, combining his commitment to garden cities with an

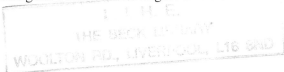

active involvement in co-partnership schemes. What appealed to him about the latter was that:

> . . . instead of the buildings being mere endless rows, or the repetition of isolated houses having no connection one with the other, they will naturally gather themselves into groups, and the groups again clustered around the greens will form larger units, and the interest and beauty of grouping will at once arise. The principle of sharing, therefore, not only causes each individual house to become more attractive, but gives to the whole area covered that coherence which, springing from the common life of the community, expresses itself in the harmony and beauty of the whole . . . [211]

Apart from his contribution to these principles, where 'architecture was the expression of community values' [212], at Letchworth and Hampstead Garden Suburb, Unwin advised co-partnership tenants' associations at Ealing, Leicester and Sevenoaks.

It was, in fact, at Ealing in 1901 that the first co-partnership scheme was launched, and by 1910 there were twelve co-partnership societies around the country. They could boast 'living accommodation at least as good, in the way of air space, as any others within the neighbourhood, but also (they) give the tenants the privilege of using clubrooms, tennis courts, bowling greens, play spaces for the children, and fields for athletics.' [213] Local societies were registered, in turn, with an umbrella organization, Co-partnership Tenants Ltd. (which helped to raise capital for local schemes), and with a parallel propagandist organization, Co-partnership Tenants Housing Council.

Henry Vivian (who was also a Liberal MP) was Chairman of the latter, and advanced the cause of co-partnership and garden city principles with equal fervour. The two movements could be seen as complementary, and there is no evidence of the kind of friction which sometimes mars the joint work of pressure groups in related areas. Indeed, Vivian was acknowledged as one of the pioneers of the garden city movement [214], and he, in turn, said that those connected with co-partnership were particularly indebted to Ebenezer Howard for his idea. Speaking at the dinner in 1912 in honour of Howard, Vivian said that all those at the co-partnership table were only too pleased if they had been able to make their contribution towards the realization of the garden city ideal [215]. By 1913, Vivian had become a member of the Council of the GCTPA, and the interests of co-partnership became increasingly merged with those of the Association [216].

Howard's own enthusiasm for co-partnership can be traced to a long-standing commitment to cooperative principles, dating back for some years before the publication of *To-morrow* in 1898 [217]. The modest success for the Association that resulted from collaboration with the co-partnership movement may have helped to compensate for what must be seen as the relative failure to involve the broader cooperative movement to the extent that was originally hoped for. Howard was not the first to see the enormous potential of the cooperative movement to raise capital and to seek better living and working conditions for their members [218]. Undaunted, though, by previous failures to establish cooperative communities on the scale that always seemed possible, Howard persevered with the idea, especially in the early years of the Association. Thus, in December 1901, it was reported that cooperators were prominent among the Association's membership, that a special committee would be set up to deal with Co-operative Societies, and that there were plans for joint conferences with Co-operative Societies to be held in the coming year:

> We do not under-estimate the importance of securing the help of Co-operative Societies to carry out the Garden City project, and we are sure the members of that great movement recognise how necessary it is for industry to secure a share of the unearned increment from the land, in order that Co-operative principles may be more effective in securing the true welfare of the people and the proper reward of labour [219].

An important personal link between the two movements was another Liberal MP, Aneurin Williams (one of the Directors of the First Garden City Company. As President of the Labour Association (a body with which the GCA also had links, in the form, for instance, of joint meetings and exhibitions), he consistently spoke in favour of a much greater contribution that could be made by the cooperative movement. At a joint conference in November 1901, between the Coventry branch of the Cooperative Union and the GCA, Williams argued that the development of a garden city could be very largely carried out by Cooperative Societies [220]. Although there is evidence of further collaboration between the GCA and the Co-operative Union (with the Garden City case put at every annual Cooperative Congress between 1900 and 1909) [221], and of active support by individual cooperators for the first garden city, the kind of partnership that might have arisen failed to materialize [222].

A less ambitious, but in its way perhaps a more effective alliance in the cause of environmental improvements, was that with the National Housing Reform Council (founded in 1900, and from 1909 renamed the National Housing and Town Planning Council) [223]. In one important respect, the interests of the two organizations were divergent, with the NHRC focusing on the need for better housing within cities, including well-planned town extensions, and not necessarily on new communities. Their prime objective was to enhance the powers of local authorities, and to ensure that existing housing powers were used more effectively. At the same time, the Council's founder, Henry R. Aldridge, was also at pains to point out what the two organizations had in common:

The Garden City Association and the National Housing Reform Council are working for objects and ideals closely allied.

Both organisations have as a cardinal point in their programmes the betterment of the home conditions of the workers. It is true that in one way the aims of the Garden City Association are wider and more complete. You desire not only to secure better homes for the people, but better and healthier conditions of labour as well. You desire to decentralise industry by taking the factory from the dark, back lanes of a squalid and ill-planned town, and to rebuild it on modern scientific lines in the country, where proper provision can be made for the health of the workers.

We, on our part, are striving to persuade Local Authorities to completely reform the methods of developing new housing areas . . . We are demanding that Town and District Councils should realise and fulfil their responsibilities. We are urging them to copy the example of the great German cities and secure that every new housing area shall be planned to secure wide streets, gardens, and public playgrounds – in fact, shall largely conform to the ideal of the Garden City Association [224].

Aldridge (who, like some of the founders of the GCA, had previous connections with the Land Nationalisation Society) could point to the fact that some of the Council's most influential members were also active supporters of the GCA. Amongst these were Seebohm Rowntree, George Cadbury, Raymond Unwin and Aneurin Williams. As a propagandist organization, as with the GCA, conferences and lecture tours constituted an important part of the work of the Council, and it was not uncommon to find the representatives of one organization at an event convened by the other. Probably the Council was the more effective of the two in terms of its procedures for lobbying politicians – its aims more closely directed to practicable legislative changes, and enjoying strong municipal support – but there is no evidence of rivalry between the two and every sign that progress achieved by one organization benefited the other no less. An overlapping membership helped to ensure that common aims were kept in view [225].

Taking a broader view of the reformist network, Gaskell has

identified four organizations that were central to the emergence of town planning in the years before 1914 [226]. In addition to the GCTPA and the NHTPC, there was the Royal Institute of British Architects and the Civics Committee of the Sociological Society (very largely the work of Patrick Geddes) [227]. Compared with the NHTPC, there is no evidence that links between the GCTPA and these other two bodies were especially strong, though, equally, there is no evidence of antagonism. Where links were made these were important, and as Gaskell concludes: 'It was the inter-relationship and fusion of all these movements, and the ideas and ideals underpinning them, that forged the town planning movement in the first decade of the twentieth century.' [228]

With the establishment of the Town Planning Institute in 1913, however, the role of the GCPTA in contributing to a broad alliance of town planning interests changed. The case for advancing the cause of planning still had to be made, but the new Institute became an obvious focus for this general work, leaving the various special interest groups to concentrate on their own specific priorities. What is significant, though, is that the garden city viewpoint was effectively projected within the offices of the new Institute, less now through the well-tried propaganda methods of the Association's early years, and more by means of the quiet influence of planners who had grown up as professionals within the garden city movement. At the Institute's Council meeting on the 12th December 1913, the first elections resulted in notable successes for garden city proponents. Thomas Adams was elected President, and Raymond Unwin one of the two Vice Presidents. Another GCTPA activist, William Davidge, had been on the Provisional Committee (which paved the way for the formation of the Council), and Barry Parker's name was on the first list of members [229].

Such were the linkages that by 1940 no less than twelve of the twenty-six annual Presidents of the Institute were also at one time Council or Executive members of the Association [230]. It would be erroneous to suggest that these and other joint members used their positions to advance the special cause of garden cities to the exclusion of the wider interests of the Institute. Apart from anything else, garden cities were by no means the sole route by which they as individuals necessarily thought that town planning could be advanced. At the same time, as a source of influence, it was undoubtedly the case that the garden city viewpoint could be more effectively promoted in what were formative years in the evolution of the town planning profession. In pressure group terms, the GCPTA could now enjoy something of an 'insider' role, exerting influence in a new planning Establishment of professionals and bureaucrats.

By 1914, then, there was still as much work as ever to be done, but the first phase – to communicate the idea of the garden city – was over. The idea was now well known, not least amongst those in the forefront of town planning and housing reform.

International Networks

The extent to which this idea has spread outside the limits of our own country is certainly astonishing, and I think since we last met we have had enquiries from Russia, Poland and Spain – countries which, in our ignorance, we looked upon as somewhat behindhand in social matters – and we find now that they are coming to the front of the Garden City Movement. Indeed I sometimes fear that if we are not careful we shall be outstripped by our Continental neighbours, because they have taken up the idea with such fervour and with such persistence that I think we shall have to look to our laurels. Glad as I am to see the idea spreading and the efforts made to carry it out in other countries, I must say that with me the Empire stands first, and I should be sorry to find in this respect the Empire lagging behind. It would be rather a sad thing if England, after having saved others, herself should be a castaway. (Sir Ralph Neville, Chairman of the GCPTA, addressing the Association's Fourteenth Annual Meeting, 5th February, 1913)

An evangelistic zeal to spread the message, national pride and a spirit of competition, a genuine desire to learn from other countries, and perhaps the kind of kudos that comes from a world-wide reputation, together stimulated an international role for the Association from the outset. This diffusion of the idea of garden cities exemplifies what has been referred to elsewhere as the export of planning [231]. The early twentieth century is a significant period, in the sense that the emergence of theory, ideology, legislation and professionalism in Britain is also characterized by the 'export' of these ideas to other parts of the world. The process is intimately related to that of reinforcing imperial values and interests, and of maintaining a healthy and productive labour force at home. Garden city enthusiasts were always delighted to see the adoption of their ideas abroad, but less so if Britain showed signs of falling behind. Thus, the MP, Sir Walter Foster, expressed a typical mixture of pride and concern:

So far as this feeling abroad is concerned, the other day when I was on the other side of the Atlantic, I was quite haunted by the Garden City. They were talking about it in New York: I heard it mentioned in several cities I visited; and at St. Louis I found the exhibit there had a remarkable effect in awakening public interest and public sympathy. Throughout the States there is a very strong desire to seize hold of the idea and develop it for the public good; a condition of things very likely to be a serious rival to you in your progress, for they have a way in that young country of doing things on a large scale, and doing them rapidly [232].

Howard's original book itself attracted a wide interest that was not confined to Britain, but it was the formation of the GCA which provided an obvious focus for enquiries from abroad. Letters requesting information, visitors who came to see progress at Letchworth and other model schemes firsthand, conferences organized by the Association, and overseas lecture tours became an important part of the pressure group's programme.

In July 1904 the first International Garden City Congress was held in London. It showed that at that time the main centres of interest overseas were in Germany and France (each with their own Garden City Associations) and the United States, but letters were also received from Budapest, Stockholm and Brussels. Other correspondence already on the Association's files included letters from Japan, Australia and Switzerland.

The Garden City regularly carried news of foreign contacts, including a section, *Continental Notes*. It showed, for instance, that the embryo interest of correspondents in Brussels had developed by 1905 into a Belgian Garden City Association, distinguished by a commercial rather than a propagandist bias [233]. In the following year, a Garden Cities Association was formed in the United States (although it appears to have survived for no more than a year), and, elsewhere, there is evidence that the garden city idea had also been adopted in Japan [234]. But undoubtedly one of the most influential sources of contact was that with Germany [235].

As a result of the 1904 International Congress in London, a representative of the Association (Montagu Harris, then a member of the Council) accompanied Bernhart Kampffmeyer, the Secretary of the newly-formed German Garden City Association, to a Housing Congress in Frankfurt. From the German side, the presence of a representative from Britain was seen as significant, helping to convince sceptics that the garden city movement was practical and worthwhile. 'Mr Harris's speech has given a new authority to our statements which have formerly been regarded as somewhat fantastic. People now consider the Garden City movement as something real and important.' [236]

Some, however, viewed the enthusiastic interest from Germany and the United States, especially, with caution. It was noted that the countries showing the greatest interest were also Britain's keenest industrial competitors. Attributing to garden cities a direct relation-

GCTPA members in the woods at Stuttgart, on one of the member visits to Germany before 1914.

ship with national vitality, the Chairman of the Association warned that 'we must see to it in this country, where the pressure is greatest, we are not outstripped by others in the practical application of our own remedy.' [237]

In spite of reservations, on the basis of international competition, over the years overseas links were strengthened, and a continuing exchange of ideas and visits became an important aspect of the Association's own development. Germany continued to hold a particular fascination, with British observers no less guilty of trying to extract the secret of German industrial supremacy, in a way that they feared was happening in reverse. The efficacy of Prussian town plans and building codes was frequently cited, especially in the lobbying and debates preceding the first town planning legislation in this country. Garden city enthusiasts were keen to see for themselves just how the German system operated, and regular visits were made [238].

In turn, German garden city propagandists clearly believed that they had much to learn by coming to this country, and tours were arranged and hosted by the Association. One of several such tours took place in July 1911, when a party of about sixty members of the German Garden City Association arrived in England to visit housing experiments. They were led by Adolf Otto, the new Secretary of the German Garden City Association, and by his GCTPA counterpart, Ewart Culpin. The party consisted mainly of officers from Municipal

Corporations, together with some private architects. Their itinerary and the people they met in each place was very much a 'Cook's tour' of who and what were worth seeing [239].

Predictably, the first stop was at Letchworth, where the party was received by directors of First Garden City Ltd., and by the Residents Union. After that there was a visit to the Exhibition of Cottages at Romford, *en route* to Hampstead Garden Suburb, where Raymond Unwin explained the thinking behind the estate. Another day was spent looking at the work of the London County Council, before the party left for Birmingham. Councillor Nettlefold addressed the party on the principles of town planning, and George Cadbury welcomed them to Bournville. In turn, Liverpool's councillors hosted a day in their city, prior to a visit to meet Sir William Lever at Port Sunlight. There it was said that Lever's reception was heartiness itself, and his explanation of the prosperity-sharing system at Port Sunlight attracted particular interest amongst the German visitors. The party then crossed the Pennines to visit New Earswick as the guests, this time, of the Rowntree family. Displays of Morris Dancing and swimming exhibitions by children of these healthy new environments undoubtedly struck a familiar note for the 'race-builders' in the party [240]. The only inkling of nagging doubts about it all came in an address from Ralph Neville, who looked forward to the time when the only rivalry between the two nations would be that of social endeavour, and as such reminded everyone that rivalry was indeed very much on their joint agenda.

Visits to and from the Continent became relatively frequent, although, in spite of close personal and institutional links, the original garden city idea was variously interpreted along the way. One reason for this was that 'several countries each had a home-grown garden city advocate, who would – and sometimes did – claim that he thought of the idea independently.' [241] Compared to excursions to and from the Continent when the Secretary of the Association, Ewart Culpin, set sail to America in 1913 it was seen as a major event. A lecture tour was arranged in response to requests from a variety of North American organizations, and in giving it its official blessing the GCTPA was hoping that Culpin's tour would help to lay the foundations for a similar Association in America. While the outcome did not quite take this form, a number of branches of the GCTPA were formed and the word was spread to many towns and cities receptive to ideas for more rational lines of development.

Ewart Culpin travelled some 30,000 miles, and on his return the Association's Council entertained him at the Holborn Restaurant (a popular meeting place for the Association), and heard his account of the visit. Reports in the journal claimed that the outstanding feature of the tour had been the remarkable and enthusiastic reception of the

BACK FROM THE UNITED STATES AND CANADA
AFTER A HIGHLY SUCCESSFUL TOUR

Mr Ewart G. Culpin, Secretary of the Garden Cities
and Town Planning Association, and Editor of this
Magazine.

Ewart Culpin, one of the two most widely travelled exponents of the
garden city idea.

message of the Garden City. The Association received numerous
enquiries from American and Canadian organizations seeking more
information and advice. There were also letters of praise, like that
from Regina, Saskatchewan, which thanked Mr Culpin for contributing to a climate of urban reform, and saying that after the meeting a

Charles Reade, the second of the most widely travelled exponents of the garden city idea.

City Planning Association had been formed [242]. Successful though it was, a brief visit could hope to do little more than to sow some seeds, and it was to be a former Secretary of the Association, Thomas Adams, who would make the greater impact in taking the idea of town planning to North America [243].

Of all the overseas contacts, though, the transmission of the Association's aims to what were referred to in journal reports as the 'Dominion beyond the Seas' encouraged something akin to missionary zeal. There was none of the ambivalence about assisting Britain's 'rivals' when it came to dealing with colonial territories. In 1912 it was reported that this sphere of activity was growing rapidly, 'and during the year constant negotiations have been going on with a view of getting into touch with various associations in the Colonies, having for their aims the improvement of the conditions of life.' [244] A Colonial Committee was set up to promote the good work, and plans were laid to despatch pamphlets and lantern slides, and from time to time the Association's own representatives, to the far-flung outposts of the Empire. In this latter context, for instance, William Davidge undertook a tour of Australasia, and returned in 1914 with the news that 'Throughout the whole tour the utmost enthusiasm was experienced, and the reports and statements received indicated that a good deal of permanent good work had been done.' [245]

The Australian connection is effectively explored by Robert Freestone [246]. He indicates that the year 1914 saw the clearest expression of a concerted British planning 'export' campaign, with the presence of Sir William Lever in Sydney, sessions on town planning at the Australian meetings of the British Association for the Advancement of Science, and another GCTPA lecture tour organized (conducted this time by Charles Reade as well as Davidge). The ideas enjoyed a good reception, but Freestone concludes that garden city advocates at that time 'represented less of a "movement" than an informal coalition . . .' [247].

Taken together, the success of the Association's propaganda, and the timeliness of the message, led to a constant flow of letters seeking advice and telling of progress in all parts of the world. Continental Europe (together with Russia), North America, South Africa and even the Belgian Congo were mentioned in a report in 1912 on this aspect of the Association's work [248]. In the following year, no fewer than 21,799 postal packets were sent out to all parts of the world, 'each of which contained some matter explanatory of the aims of the Association.' [249]

A logical sequel to this expanding network was the formation of the International Garden Cities and Town Planning Association in 1913 [250]. This, very much the brainchild of Ewart Culpin, was urged as a means of supporting the growing volume of overseas activity, particularly those initiatives that were otherwise isolated. Representatives from Germany, France, Norway, Poland, the United States and Japan were present at the launch of the International Association, but the dominance of the British movement is evidenced by the fact that Culpin became the first Honorary Secretary, G. Montagu Harris the Chairman, and Howard the President. What is more, the officers used were those of the GCTPA in London.

In the following year, representatives from the original member states and from other countries (including Austria, Canada, Italy, Russia and Spain) attended the First Congress of the International Association in London, and went on a tour around England to see examples of what it was they wanted to promote [251]. In practical terms, it transpired that although the new Association was by no means inactive, there were clearly limits as to what could be done to further its common cause until after the First World War. The very formation of such an organization was, however, in itself a sign of the progress of the garden city movement.

NOTES

Edwardian Reformism

1. For instance, Freeden (1978) explains the 'New Liberalism' as a reformist rather than a revolutionary creed. Likewise, see Morris's explanation of Edwardian radicalism (1974).
2. G. P. Gooch, quoted in Briggs (1961), p. 59. Gooch was a Liberal MP, an active member of the Association, and (from 1910 to 1913) Chairman of the Executive.
3. Lloyd George, quoted in Douglas (1976), p. 41.
4. See, for instance, Douglas (1976) and McDougall (1979).
5. A summary of this debate is included in Reade (1987), pp. 36–41.
6. Adams (1905).
7. *Ibid*, p. 37.
8. A comprehensive account of national efficiency in the period before 1914 is provided by Searle (1971).
9. Report of the Inter-Departmental Committe on Physical Deterioration (1904).
10. For general works on eugenics in this period, see Young (1980) and Jones (1986); for its particular relationship to town planning and sociology, see Halliday (1968) and Garside (1988).
11. *The Race-Builder*, May 1986, reprinted in *GC* Vol. I, No. 7, August 1906, p. 159.
12. Neville, speaking at the Association's Conference at Bournville, reported in *The Times*, 21st September 1901, p. 2.
13. A fuller account of the importance of Germany as a model, and the views of T. C. Horsfall, is provided later in this chapter. See also Horsfall (1904) and Sutcliffe (1984).
14. T. C. Horsfall, in *GC*, Vol. I, No. 2, February 1905, p. 3.
15. Henry Vivian, quoted in Ashworth (1954), p. 169.
16. Halliday (1968), p. 380.
17. *Ibid*. See also Meller (1990).
18. Beatrice Webb, in N. and J. MacKenzie (eds) (1984), p. 25.

19. On the 1906–1914 reforms and the New Liberalism, see, for instance, Bruce (1966), Morris (1974), Freeden (1978) and Fraser (1984).
20. Beatrice Webb, in MacKenzie and MacKenzie (1984), p. 25.
21. *GCTP*, Vol. III, No. 11, November 1913, pp. 268–269.

Ideas and Action

22. The aims of the Association were changed seven times in the period 1899–1946.
23. The resolution of the special general meeting at Essex Hall on 9th July 1903 is copied in Culpin (1913), pp. 14–15.
24. Culpin (1913), p. 15, regards this as 'the first pronouncement of any society or body in England in favour of municipal Town-planning, although that name does not appear yet in the rules.'
25. *GC*, Vol. I, No. 1, p. 6, October 1904.
26. Appendix to the Adams Memorandum: Memorandum by the Secretary as to the 'raison d'être' of the Association, its relationship to the Garden City Company and other matters which require consideration. Undated but probably 1903.
27. *Ibid.*
28. Editorial, *GCTP* NS, Vol. IV, No. 34, August 1909, p. 215.
29. *Ibid.*
30. *Ibid.*
31. *Ibid*, p. 216.
32. Annual Meeting of the GCTPA, April 1910.
33. Editorial, *GCTP* NS, Vol. IV, No. 34, August 1909, p. 216.

The First Garden City

34. See Macfadyen (1970), p. 40.
35. Howard (1902), p. 166.
36. Simpson (1985), p. 11.
37. Howard, in Simpson (1985), p. 13.
38. Neville's source of interest in the garden city idea and his contribution to the Association is explained more fully later in this chapter (2.4).
39. Fishman (1977), p. 58.
40. Although caution is urged in drawing conclusions from the evidence, it is interesting to trace the overlapping memberships of London Clubs amongst leading members of the Association before 1914:

	Athenaeum	Reform	National Liberal
R. Neville	X		
Lord Salisbury	X		
T. W. Idris			X
S. Rowntree		X	
C. Harmsworth		X	
A. Williams		X	X
E. Howard			X

Source: *Who Was Who*.

41. Fishman (1977), p. 65.
42. A copy of the prospectus of the Garden City Pioneer Company, and other details about the company, are held in the Garden City Museum. Macfadyen (1970), pp. 41–43, also provides a useful account of the formation of the company.
43. Neville's part in recruiting such influential support is consistently acknowledged within the Association. As financial sponsors, the recruitment of George Cadbury and W. H. Lever was particularly important, although, in the long term, the support of the Harmsworth family may have been of greater effect. A broader context for the support of 'enlightened entrepreneurs' is provided in Bradley (1987).
44. An extensive collection of press cuttings on this and other stages in the history of the first garden city is held at the Garden City Museum.
45. *Methodist Times*, 9th August 1902.
46. *Jewish Chronicle*, 9th August 1902.
47. *Temperance Record*, 7th August 1902.
48. *The Vegetarian*, 22nd August 1902.
49. *Municipal Journal*, 8th August 1902.
50. Purdom (1951), p. 37.
51. *Ibid*, p. 39.
52. Letchworth is an important milestone in modern planning history, with a variety of helpful accounts of the town's development – for instance, Purdom (1913), Culpin (1914), Creese (1966), Macfadyen (1970), and Miller (1989).
53. Fifth Annual Report of the GCA, for the year ending 31st October 1903.
54. *GC*, Vol. I, No. 5, November 1905, p. 69.
55. See, for instance, Purdom (1951) – who worked with Adams at Letchworth – and Simpson (1985).
56. Simpson (1985), p. 22.
57. Purdom (1951), p. 41.
58. See Armytage (1961), chapter 7: From Rurisville to Garden City, 1898–1918, pp. 370–384.
59. From a diary of Letchworth events, in Armytage (1961), p. 374.
60. Article from *The Race-Builder*, May 1906, copied in *GC*, Vol. I, No. 7, August 1906, p. 159.
61. Extensive sources on the early development of Letchworth are available in the Garden City Museum. A sensitive summary of developments in this period is provided by Marsh (1982), chapter 14.
62. It will be seen that the second garden city, Welwyn, had a more direct effect on the Association in terms of diverting energies and skills from the parent body.
63. Garden City Association: Memorandum by the Secretary as to the 'raison d'être' of the Association, its relationship to the Garden City Company, and other matters which require consideration. Undated, but probably 1903.

Lobbying for Town Planning

64. For an account of the processes leading to the Housing and Town Planning, etc. Act, 1909, see Minett (1974) and Cherry (1974a). In neither of these accounts does the Association get the credit it claimed for itself. There were clearly other groups arguing the case, and Bournville, Port Sunlight and Hampstead Garden Suburb offered more convincing examples of town planning than the infant garden city.

65. Development of the garden city got off to a slow start. By the end of 1905 (more than two years after its purchase) the original population of 450 had increased to 1,000; and then to 4,500 to 1907. More important than its actual growth was the publicity attracted to specific projects, such as Miss Annie Lawrence's open-air school, the Cheap Cottages Exhibition, and the location of industrial firms like W. H. Smith's bookbinding works and the new plant for Idris drinks.

    In propagandist terms, Letchworth was also used to demonstrate that garden cities offered a healthier environment than traditional towns; the death rate in Letchworth, for instance, was 4.8 per 1,000 in 1909, as compared with 20.3 per 1,000 in Middlesbrough (given, however, that the statistical basis for this kind of comparison is questionable).

66. Editorial, *GC*, Vol. I, No. 6, July 1906, p. 127.

67. Simpson (1985) shows that Thomas Adams is attracted to Howard's original scheme by the idea of 'associated individualism'. In turn, a two-page essay by Howard explains the concept as 'a state of society in which manufacturing, trade, industry, professional life, are carried on by individuals or groups of individuals who are as far as possible free from the need of governmental or other external control or regulation . . .' (Howard Papers, Folio 20).

68. This growing call for legislation is evidenced in the pages of the journal, following the establishment of Letchworth. Thus, in November 1905, for instance, Thomas Adams wrote that Letchworth marked just 'the first stage of a new era of housing reform and industrial betterment . . . Progressive municipalities in all the most advanced nations of the world now consider the planning of new suburbs as an essential part of their work. Soon the object lesson of Letchworth will show how new towns can be established on agricultural land, isolated from existing populous areas, and how the increased value of the land created by the people can be secured for the public benefit. All this will soon have its effect on the legislation of the country.' (*GC*, Vol. I, No. 5, November 1905, p. 70).

69. This conference was reported in the pages of the journal, including the Report on the Annual Meeting for 1906. (*GC* NS, Vol. I, No. 3, April 1906, p. 68).

70. Proceedings of the conference were published by the GCA in 1908, under the title of the conference, *Town Planning: In Theory and Practice*.

71. The memorandum was copied as an appendix of the GCA conference proceedings (1908), *op.cit.*

72. *GCA* (1908), *op.cit.*, p. 66.
73. *GC* (NS), Vol. II, No. 17, June 1907, p. 362.
74. *Ibid*, p. 354.
75. Culpin (1910), pp. 2–3. In a paper to the Fourth International Planning History Conference, Bournville, 1989, Anthony Sutcliffe provides additional evidence of the Association's 'bullishness'. He refers to a letter from Culpin (December 1909), urging the NHTPC to withdraw from town planning work, thus allowing the GCTPA to operate as the sole promotional body in this field. See Sutcliffe (1989).
76. *GCTP* (NS), Vol. III, No. 19, August 1908, pp. 89–92.
77. In particular, the Association could call on the support of thirty-seven MPs who were members of the Garden City Association, or shareholders in First Garden City Ltd.
78. The range of groups involved is considered more fully later in this chapter.
79. Ashworth (1954), p. 180.
80. Ashworth (1954) and Cherry (1974*b*) offer helpful accounts of this emergent planning lobby.
81. This is a theme that is explored consistently throughout the thesis, but particular reference can be made to the Association's comparable claims for the establishment of the 'Barlow Committee' in 1937 and the 1946 New Towns Act.
82. The Association's campaign in this period, as a 'bridge' between nineteenth-century anti-urbanist thought and twentieth-century planning, is discussed in Petersen (1968).

Garden Cities and Garden Suburbs

83. Culpin (1913), p. 9.
84. As Swenarton (1981) and Gaskell (1987) show, the 'garden city movement' had become the term to describe a wide range of development, most of it being of a garden suburb type. 'The garden city movement was not, as the term might seem to imply, a homogeneous group with a single ideology, but was rather a heterogeneous collection of different groups and interests, linked only by a common commitment to bringing about a transformation in what was referred to as "the housing and surroundings of the people".' (Swenarton, p. 5).
85. Earl Grey, in 'Proceedings at a Complimentary Dinner, to Mr Ebenezer Howard, Garden Cities and Town Planning Association, 19th March 1912' (Osborn Papers).
86. Many years later, in 1974, Frederic Osborn wrote in a confidential note that he was not alone in thinking that it was largely Culpin's 'fault that the Association had allowed the essential G.C. idea to be submerged in the fashion for open housing estates and garden suburbs.' (Notes to David Hall, March 1974, Osborn Papers).
87. The branch system of the Association is explained later in this chapter.

88. Culpin, *op.cit.*, p. 10.
89. *Ibid*, p. 11.
90. Information on this and the other campaigns in this period have been gleaned from the GCTPA General Minute Book, and from successive Annual Reports before 1914, as well as news items in the journal.
91. The quote of Letchworth as a mecca, and related details, is extracted from a lengthy report of a visit by representatives of the German Garden City Association, *GCTP* (NS), Vol. II, No. 9, September 1912, pp. 195–203.
92. Howard's ideas were included in a report (entitled 'A National Garden City Trust') at the quarterly meeting of the Council of the GCTPA, 25th October 1911, in *GCTP* (NS), Vol. I, No. 10, November–December 1911, pp. 226–229.
93. *Ibid*, p. 227.
94. *Ibid*, p. 228.
95. *Ibid*, p. 229.
96. It will be shown in the following chapter that a schism – based on whether or not the Association should devote itself solely to the idea of the garden city – opened towards the end of the First World War. There was consistency, though, in advocating garden cities as open, low-density developments, in opposition to the kind of model proposed by Trystan Edwards and, later, by Thomas Sharp.
97. Articles were published between July 1913 and February 1914 in the *TPR* on the pros and cons of the garden city movement; A. T. Edwards, 'A Criticism of the Garden City Movement', Vol. 4, No. 2, pp. 150–157; Charles C. Reade, 'A Defence of the Garden City Movement', Vol. 4, No. 3, pp. 245–251; an editorial comment, 'A Controversy', Vol. 4, No. 4, p. 275; A. T. Edwards, 'A Further Criticism of the Garden City Movement', Vol. 4, No. 4, pp. 312–318.
98. Edwards, *op.cit.*, p. 157.
99. Edwards, *op.cit.*, p. 317.
100. GCTPA Executive Committee, 16th September 1914: General Minute Book 1913–1916.

Internal Organization

101. Purdom (1951), p. 38.
102. The Association then remained at 3 Gray's Inn Place until 1935.
103. Information on Adams and his role in the Association is provided in Simpson (1985).
104. Simpson (1985), p. 9.
105. *Ibid*, p. 11.
106. In Howard's book of Press Cuttings (Osborn Papers), it is apparent that the two conferences at Bournville and Port Sunlight put the Association 'on the map' as a viable organization with a wide source of appeal.
107. Simpson (1985), p. 192.
108. Purdom (1951), pp. 37–38.

109. Simpson (1985), p. 36.
110. *GC*, Vol. I, No. 5, November 1905, p. 79.
111. Adams Memorandum, c. 1903, discussed in the earlier section on the aims of the Association.
112. *GC*, (NS) Vol. I, No. 7, August 1906, p. 154.
113. Culpin remained in this post until he left the Association in 1921. His role would repay a separate study, particularly because of the international connections he developed. In spite of his obvious contribution, however, Osborn later (1974) refused to include Culpin in a list of 'Key Figures in the garden city movement' because of Culpin's catholic interpretation of the basic concept.
114. In the period before 1914, apart from the Annual Reports, the journal carried more details about the internal workings of the Association than it did subsequently.
115. When it was constituted in 1899, there were twelve sections – Finance; Literature, Lectures and Public Meetings; Land Tenure; Manufactures and Trade; Co-operative Societies; Labour; Housing; Liquor Traffic; Education; Art; Domestic Economy; and Health.
116. *Fabian News*, October 1899, quoted in Buder (1969), p. 394.

Membership and Finance

117. Howard (1902), p. 165.
118. Subscription details are included in the Annual Reports and in various leaflets, all at the Garden City Museum.
119. Membership figures were normally recorded in the Annual Reports in the early years; where this has not been done an estimate has been based on the entry for subscriptions and donations in the financial accounts.
120. GCA Annual Report, for the year ending 31st August 1901.
121. *Ibid.*
122. Buder (1969), p. 395.
123. Howard (1902), p. 165, complained that the Association suffered from the fact that 'some who could afford much more (than the minimum subscription) were content to subscribe that sum.'
124. *GC*, Vol. I, No. 2, February 1905, p. 5.
125. *GC* (NS), Vol. II, No. 13, February 1907, p. 272.
126. *GC* (NS), Vol. II, No. 17, June 1907, p. 353.
127. GCA Annual Report for 1907.
128. GCA Annual Report for 1908.
129. *Ibid.*
130. GCA Annual Report for 1912.
131. *Ibid.*
132. GCTPA Executive Committee, 16th September 1914, General Minute Book 1913–1916.

Patterns of Propaganda

133. As Howard's own book of Press Cuttings shows, the Association attracted a wide range of interest in the press at particular times in its early development. As well as national and local newspapers, its progress was reported in publications as diverse as *Journal of Gas Lighting*, *The Field*, *The Spectator*, *Co-operative News*, *Pall Mall Gazette* and *Building Societies*.

134. The National Housing Reform Council, from the date of its own formation in 1900, had a more direct interest in general housing legislation, and the extension of local authority powers.

135. *GC* (NS), Vol. I, No. 1, February 1906, p. 21.

136. Although the Association tried to attract politicians from all parties, in the early period its greatest appeal was to Liberals. Of the thirty-seven MPs in 1906 who were members of the Association or shareholders in First Garden City Ltd., no less than thirty-three were Liberals. The remaining four were Conservatives, with no representation at all for the Labour Party.

137. This important event is well-recorded in Simpson (1985) and in press cuttings in the Garden City Museum and in the Osborn Papers.

138. *Councillor and Guardian*, 28th September 1901.

139. GCA Annual Report, for the fourteen months ending 31st October 1902.

140. *Ibid*.

141. Purdom (1951), p. 25.

142. Full details of these three conferences have already been given. The point here is that, as well as being a source of lobbying influence, they were also of wider propagandist value in terms of promoting the work of the Association.

143. GCA Annual Report for 1908.

144. These are detailed in the Bibliography, with titles shown here to indicate the scope of interest.

145. A minute of the Executive Committee on the 22nd January 1913 reports that W. H. Smith was taking 1300 copies of the Association's journal each month.

146. Editorial, *GCTP* (NS), Vol. IV, No. 34, August 1909, p. 216.

147. *GC*, Vol. I, No. 3, April 1905, p. 48.

148. GCA Lecture Circular, 1902–1903.

149. Lecture details are obtained from successive copies of the journal in this period.

150. See Macfadyen (1970), chapter 1.

151. GCA Annual Report for 1908.

152. *GC* (NS), Vol. II, No. 17, June 1907, p. 353.

153. GCTPA Annual Report for 1911.

The 'Great and the Good'

154. Howard's role in the Association is reviewed in the following chapter.
155. Howard (1902), p. 166.
156. Fishman (1977), p. 58.
157. In addition to Macfadyen's own account of Neville (1970), there is Neville's own collection of writings (n.d.)
158. From an article by Neville in 1901, quoted in Macfadyen (1970), p. 48.
159. In Macfadyen (1970), p. 48, Howard recalls how he enlisted the support of Neville: 'In 1901, I had already seen much of Mr Neville, for I had taken shorthand notes of his speeches and his examination of witnesses at the High Court, and had become impressed with his great ability and his rare fairness. So, when in March of that year I found that he had been endorsing the proposals of the Garden City Association in *Labour Co-partnership* . . . I at once called at his chambers in Old Square. He received me most cordially, and at once agreed to join the Association.'
160. See Fishman (1977), p. 58.
161. *Ibid*, p. 59.
162. *The Housing Journal* No. 25, August 1902, pp. 2–3.
163. Howard, quoted in Macfadyen (1970), p. 48.
164. *GC*, Vol. I, No. 3, April 1905, p. 39.
165. GCA Annual Report for 1903.
166. Purdom (1951), p. 38, emphasizes the practicality of the garden city as a source of attraction. It was consistent with the 'philanthropy + 5%' approach of late Victorian 'enlightened entrepreneurs'.
167. *GCTP* (NS), Vol. I, Nos. 1 and 2, February and March 1911, pp. 10–11 and 34–35.
168. Particularly after 1914, Cecil Harmsworth becomes an important figure in the Association.
169. See, for instance, Halliday (1968) and Meller (1990) on the role of Geddes in the town planning movement.
170. Apart from frequent references in the journal, Unwin's role is discussed in Sutcliffe (1981a) and Jackson (1985).
171. A review of Unwin's work for the Association is provided in a report of a dinner in his honour (when he was awarded the Howard Memorial Medal) in November 1938. See *TCP*, Vol. VII, No. 26, January–March 1939, pp. 41–47.
172. Hawtree, in Sutcliffe (1981a), p. 84.
173. From Beatrice Webb's diary entries, 29th November and 2nd December 1905, in Mackenzie and Mackenzie (1984), pp. 12–16.
174. Report of the Sixth Annual Meeting of the GCA, in *GC*, Vol. I, No. 2, February 1905, pp. 4–5.
175. Letters and other details of the event, including the full attendance list, are included in the Howard Papers, Folio 24.
176. *GCTP*, Vol. II, No. 4, April 1912, p. 69.
177. *Ibid*, p. 73.
178. *Ibid*, p. 69.

179. *Ibid*, p. 74.
180. *Ibid*, p. 75.

The Women's League

181. This dichotomy between charitable and radical approaches is explored in the work of recent feminist writers. I am indebted to Beverley Taylor (London Borough of Ealing) and Clara Greed (Bristol Polytechnic) for correspondence on this issue, and for other comments on this section. Greed notes, for instance, that in Edwardian times to call an active women reformer 'just a sewers and drains feminist' was even more insulting than the dismissive 'just a lady bountiful'.

182. This is a poor record, but both Taylor and Greed (*ibid*) point to a consistently low level of representation in the environmental professions – particularly where they become increasingly concerned with legislation and statutory duties, as opposed to welfare reform.

183. *GC* Vol. I, No. 2, February 1905, p. 12.

184. Viscountess Muriel Helmsley was herself a local Conservative politician in Islington, and amongst her varied activities she was Chairman of the National Society of Day Nurseries, and Honorary Secretary of the Women's Institute Training College Branch for Nursing.

185. *GC*, Vol. I, No. 2, February 1905, p. 12.

186. *GC* (NS), Vol. II, No. 17, June 1907, p. 354.

187. *GC* (NS), Vol. III, No. 25, February 1908, p. 11.

188. Phipson's persistent quest for a communitarian utopia is referred to in Armytage (1961) pp. 314, 316 and 373. His interest in Letchworth illustrates the hopes that were attached to the new garden city by many, like him, who had failed to found their own settlement.

189. *GC*, Vol. I, No. 4, July 1905, p. 64.

190. Clara Greed (*op.cit.*, Note 181) suggests that many of Howard's ideas in this field were not original, but were, in fact, derived from the work of earlier women town planners and architects. For example, a model of a new community based on groups of 44 row houses with cooperative housekeeping facilities was exhibited by Mary Coleman Stuckert of Chicago at the Columbian Exposition in the 'Women's Building' section in 1893. Earlier she had developed a scheme for a city block based on cooperative living in Denver between 1878 and 1893, which incorporated kitchens, a laundry and kindergarten. See also Hayden (1981) and the comprehensive analysis of 'cooperative living' in Pearson (1988).

191. Howard (1898), p. 15.

192. Reference is made in *GC* to a leaflet produced by Howard in 1906, *Domestic industry as it might be*, but this source cannot be traced. However, in *GC* (NS), Vol. I, No. 8, August 1906, p. 170, an article by Howard that was published in *The Daily Mail* is reproduced under the heading, 'Co-operative Housekeeping'.

193. 'A new way of house-keeping', *The Daily Mail*, 27th March 1913. There is also a useful chapter on this theme in Purdom (1913), pp. 98–103.
194. Howard's article of the 27th March, 1913 (*op.cit.*) was, in fact, a riposte to an article a few days earlier (19th March), also in *The Daily Mail*, headed 'Our Co-operative Housekeeping'. In this, the author (signed D.L.) recounts what he refers to as an amusing story of a family experiment in which two families share a spacious house and experiment with joint housekeeping.

  The author (the husband and father in one of the families) attributes the source of the idea to the two women, who sought to simplify and economize on their household responsibilities. Although the women were intent on making the experiment work, they were to disagree to the point of an *impasse* on how to treat their measle-ridden children. The men were disparaging, treating the failure of the experiment as inevitable, and dismissing it all as ' a feminine notion (with) an oddly feminine ending'.
195. Letter from Lucy Carr Shaw to Howard, 3rd April 1913, in the Howard Papers, Folio 25.
196. *GCTP* (NS), Vol. III, No. 6, June 1913, pp. 152–159.
197. *Ibid*, p. 157.

Regional Connections

198. GCA Annual Report, for the fourteen months ending 31st October 1902.
199. Minutes of the Manchester Branch of the GCA, 1902–1908. The book is included in the TCPA archives.
200. See Reynolds (1952).
201. Minutes of the Manchester Branch, *op.cit.*, 1st April 1902.
202. Harrison (1981).
203. Minutes of the Manchester Branch, *op.cit.*, 30th November 1902.
204. Gaskell (1981), p. 42.
205. *GCTP* (NS), Vol. III, No. 26, March 1908, p. 23.
206. *GCTP* (NS), Vol. IV, No. 32, January–February 1909, p. 174.
207. *GCTP* (NS), Vol. II, No. 3, March 1912, p. 55.
208. To the extent that the Association's name and interests were at stake, it is understandable that, constitutionally, the position and status of branches became more formalized than in the early days when they were simply encouraged. In Ewart Culpin's review of the garden city movement in 1913, it is shown (p. 74) that the formation of branches had to be authorized by the Executive Committee. In exchange for a 20 per cent levy of branch subscriptions, the local organization received copies of the journal and other literature, the advice of the secretariat and the services of lecturers on the basis of expenses, and representation on the Council. The Association accepted no financial liability for its branches, and required all branches to recognize the journal as its official organ and outlet for local information.

An Alliance of Interests

209. The report of this conference has already been referred to in the context of lobbying for the 1909 Act. For a published report of the proceedings, see GCA (1908).

    At the Guildhall were representatives of First Garden City Limited, Hampstead Garden Suburb Trust, Association of Municipal Corporations, Co-partnership Tenants Limited, the Royal Institute of British Architects, Society of Architects, Institute of Sanitary Engineers, Metropolitan Public Gardens Association, Mansion House Council on the Dwellings of the Poor, National Housing Reform Council, Incorporated Institute of Hygiene, Surveyors Institute, Land Nationalisation Society, Institute of Builders, League of Physical Educators and the Sociological Society. This was a unique gathering, but, to differing degrees, these were also the organizations with which the Association had contact on a more regular basis. Two of these groups, in particular, feature in the activities of the Association before 1914, the Co-Partnership Tenants Ltd. and the National Housing Reform Council.

210. See, for instance, Gaskell (1981), pp. 29–30.
211. Unwin, probably 1910, quoted in Hawtree (1981), p. 87.
212. *Ibid*.
213. *GCTP* (NS), Vol. IV, No. 36, February 1910, p. 272.
214. *GCTP* (NS), Vol. I, No. 2, March 1911, p. 34.
215. *GCTP* (NS), Vol. II, No. 4, April 1912, p. 76.
216. See Cherry (1974*b*), p. 43.
217. See, for instance, Buder (1969).
218. See Hardy (1979), chapter 2, for a record of various cooperative community experiments in the nineteenth century.
219. GCA Annual Report, for the year ending 31st August 1901.
220. *Municipal Reformer*, December 1901.
221. Fishman (1977), p. 65.
222. It is interesting to note that the National Housing Reform Council, in its first ten years (1900–1910) was also disappointed that the cooperative movement as a body had not responded as positively as had been hoped for to the cause of housing reform. See NHTPC (1910), p. 3.
223. The records of the NHTPC are available at the Council's offices. Minute books are incomplete for this early period, but two useful papers are the NHTPC's *1900–1910: A record of 10 years' work for housing and town planning reform*, undated but probably 1910, and Baker (1970).
224. *GC*, Vol. I, No. 2, February 1905, p. 11.
225. The NHTPC's membership list in 1910, for instance, includes the names of Ebenezer Howard, Thomas Adams, W. R. Davidge, G. L. Pepler and T. C. Horsfall.
226. Gaskell (1981), pp. 17–19.
227. On the role of the Sociological Society, see, especially, Halliday (1968). See also Meller (1990).

228. Gaskell (1981), p. 19.
229. Cherry (1974*b*), pp. 57–60.
230. Cherry (1974*b*), Appendix 1, lists the Presidents of the Institute.

International Networks

231. This is the thesis of King (1980), seeing planning as an aspect of a wider process of imperial expansion and control.
232. Sir Walter Foster, MP, addressing the Sixth Annual Meeting of the GCA, 17th January 1905.
233. *GC*, Vol. I, No. 2, February 1905, p. 12.
234. Dr S. J. Watanabe explains (in an abstract for his paper, 'The Japanese Garden City versus the Land Question', for the Fourth International Planning History Conference, Bournville, 1989) that it was Sennet's book (1905) rather than Howard's that was translated by the Japanese Home Ministry. Following that, in 1908, one of the Ministry's staff visited Howard in Letchworth.
235. A valuable account of the international aspects of the garden city movement, in particular the links with Germany, is provided in Sutcliffe (1984), pp. 37–42.
236. *GC*, Vol. I, No. 2, February 1905, p. 12.
237. Ralph Neville, in *GC*, Vol. I, No. 2, February 1905, p. 12.
238. Of particular influence in reformist circles was T. C. Horsfall, whose book (1904) and firsthand experience of the German system was frequently cited. As well as his own writings, see Reynolds (1952).
239. A copy of the programme and itinerary is contained in the *Garden City Museum*.
240. In an interesting report of a conference, Miller (1986) refers to a paper by Wolfgang Voigt which links pre-1914 eugenics with a Nazi attachment to *volkisch* architecture in the 1930s.
241. Hall (1988), p. 112.
242. *GCTP* (NS), Vol. III, No. 4, April 1913, p. 94.
243. See Simpson (1985).
244. *GCTP* (NS), Vol. II, No. 3, March 1912, p. 60.
245. GCTPA General Minute Book, 22nd October 1914.
246. See Freestone (1986).
247. Freestone (1986), p. 68.
248. *GCTP* (NS), Vol. II, No. 3, March 1912, p. 56.
249. GCTPA Annual Report for 1913.
250. Batchelor (1969), p. 199, acknowledges the importance of the IGCTPA, but also draws attention to other international networks which contributed to the spread of garden city ideas – notably, the conference organized by the RIBA in London in 1910, the Vienna International Congress of Architects in 1908, the two Universal City Building Exhibitions in Berlin and Dusseldorf in 1910, and the German Werkbund of 1914.
251. The First Annual Report of the International Association (published in 1915) provides a comprehensive review and information on contacts and representation.

4

THE LONG CAMPAIGN
1914–1939

The fortunes of the GCTPA between 1914 and 1939 closely reflect the wider changes experienced in Britain in this period. The Great War itself imposed a double stamp on the work of the Association, constraining what it (like other organizations) could hope to do in wartime, but also opening the way for a national reconstruction debate with housing high on the political agenda. With the ending of the war, and the promise of unprecedented State intervention, it proved to be an active phase for the Association – cajoling Government and seeking to enlighten public opinion, as well as seeing the building of a second garden city. It also proved to be a short-lived phase and, when the Government's reconstruction plans were withdrawn, the Association entered a long period of relative quietude, lasting through to the second half of the 1930s. It was not so much that the Association was inactive as that it was ineffective, powerless to do very much in the face of a persistent governmental reluctance to plan (in the widest sense) more than it had to, and in the face of a relentless tide of suburban housing development as opposed to garden cities. In the few years before the outbreak of the Second World War, however, the Association's campaign gained from a wider interest in economic and physical planning, and, once again, the level of political involvement to secure its aims increased. It was a long campaign, with relatively little to show for it, but, arguably, by 1939 the Association was well-placed to play an important part in the new debate about planning and reconstruction that lay ahead.

In terms of the workings of a pressure group this long campaign lends support to opposing arguments. On the one hand, the general pattern of activity and effectiveness – with its peaks and troughs – supports the view that the fortunes of pressure groups can best be explained in terms of wider changes within society. Thus, the Association fared better in those years when governments, through force of economic and political circumstances, were already disposed to reform. Yet, on the other hand, the evidence of this period is that one cannot ignore the role of individuals within the organization, contributing, in different degrees, to its effectiveness. The work of the Association was affected, for instance, by the withdrawal of key figures in the early 1920s, who chose to devote their energies to the building of the second garden city, and, conversely, by the influx of new skills in the late 1930s. This balance of forces – those of structure, and those of agency – offer an important context for examining the work of the Association over a twenty-five year period.

CAMPAIGNING IN THE GREAT WAR

In the cauldron of the 1914–1918 War, idealism, far from being diminished, was if anything enriched. While the nation's thoughts were turned to the horrors of the trenches so, too, in a spirit of defiance, people resolved to 'keep the home fires burning' and, in turn, to plan ahead for their returning heroes. Reflecting the nation's mood, the GCTPA continued to champion the cause of garden cities, first, in the way they had always done and, then, as a contribution to the reconstruction debate. And, at the same time, the spectacle of international conflict only served to strengthen the case for an international garden city movement to build again when the war ended. The Association's own history in these turbulent years reflects something of the old world as well as of the new.

Business as Usual

The pessimists who thought that the outbreak of war would mean general financial and commercial ruin, and particularly the annihilation of propagandist societies, have been proved altogether wrong as far as the experience of the Garden Cities and Town Planning Association is concerned. (*GCTP* NS, Vol. 4, No. 11, November 1914)

In spite of gloomy forebodings that the outbreak of war would inevitably lead to a suspension of the activities of the Association [1], the evidence is that there was a sustained attempt throughout the war years to continue business as usual. Thus, in November 1914, the Association could report an actual increase in activities, with several special meetings to deal with pressing issues, and the maintenance of the prewar level of funding. Although the number of subscriptions had fallen, this loss of income was balanced by more generous donations received during the year [2]. Nor was this viability simply a feature of the early months of the four-year war. The Association took pride in the continuing circulation of its journal, stressing its value 'in view of the position which has to be faced after the war.' [3] In 1915 attendance levels at meetings were reported as being above average [4], while in the Annual Report for 1917 the record is one of 'continuous expansion such as to give satisfaction in every branch of the Association's undertakings.' [5]

What is also evident, though, is that, in keeping its doors open, the Association was only doing what was commonplace. The First World War was fought on foreign soil and, for all the heavy sacrifices that had to be made, many aspects of life at home could go on much as usual. Encouraged by trading interests, and then reinforced by politicians, the phrase 'Business as Usual' reflected a popular mood of the moment. Harrods was among the first to demonstrate (through an advertising campaign proclaiming that the store's policy for the war would be one of business as usual) that what was good for shopkeepers would also be good for the rest of the nation [6].

In this context, the Association continued to campaign on a variety of familiar fronts. Developments in the first garden city were regularly reported in the journal under the heading 'Progress at Letchworth' [7], the Association being determined to keep the experiment in the public eye as a model for the future. To this end, it was always important to protect the integrity of the garden city concept. In part, this was a question of taking every opportunity to define and redefine its meaning and, in particular, to distinguish it from other settlements which had appropriated the name of 'garden city'. A central aim of the Association remained 'to dissipate the confusion prevailing in the popular mind as to the real meaning of First Garden City and to make it known that only under such conditions as are found at Letchworth

Table 1. GCTPA volume of correspondence, 1914 and 1917.

Type of correspondence	Britain		Colonial		American		Foreign	
	1914	1917	1914	1917	1914	1917	1914	1917
General Information	2805	2421	126	82	225	188	97	66
Specific Advice	206	359	3	4	17	15	1	2
Literature	403	268	32	16	41	63	11	18
Magazine	426	133	50	2	25	9	12	2
Lantern Slides	113	51	8	4	19	2	12	4
Conducted Visits	403	–	15	–	56	2	179	–
Lectures	285	122	–	–	31	5	12	–
Exhibitions	108	–	1	–	38	–	35	–
Australasian Tour	173	–	143	–	1	–	–	–
Belgium	–	52	–	–	–	–	–	6
Public Utility Societies	–	227	–	–	–	–	–	–
Totals	4922	3633	378	108	453	284	359	98

can Mr Howard's famous design be carried out in its beneficent entirety.' [8] In part, too the defence of the concept included the rebuttal of popular misrepresentations of Letchworth that appeared from time to time in the press. Understandably, for instance, the Association was quick to respond to an article in the *Daily Sketch* purporting to explain the steady increase in the size of Letchworth as being due to 'the influx of the hatless and long-haired, silly intellectual and intellectually silly males and females.' The number of residents who lived the ordinary life of honest British people was infinitesimal, claimed the article, with sub-headings of 'Honest People Rare' and 'Some Astonishing Conditions at Letchworth Garden City' to press home the point. The Association feared that years of patient propaganda were put at risk by the writings of an 'unmuzzled lunatic' of this sort [9].

Although the rate of new building in the country slumped in the war years, as a propagandist body the Association remained busy in offering guidance to others and disseminating ideas. Some indication of the activities of the office is provided by the volume of correspondence that was handled. The table opposite compares the total entries for 1914 and 1917, showing a decrease as the war progresses but still a high level of activity [10].

To undertake this continuing stream of routine tasks, as well as to respond to the particular challenges imposed by the war, the Association could not afford to neglect the efficiency of its own workings as a pressure group. As a 'good housekeeping' measure the status of the Association was changed in 1915 through its registration under the Companies Acts (1908 to 1913) to that of a company not trading for profits. Although it continued to be known by its old name for everyday business, it was now officially registered as 'The British Garden Cities and Town Planning Association (Incorporated)'. Members were assured that this would strengthen the financial position of the Association, while in no way impeding its work along traditional lines [11]. Technical changes apart, the Chairman of the Association (from 1911 to 1919), Cecil Harmsworth [12], was of the same view as his predecessor, Ralph Neville, in seeking to strengthen the role of the pressure group through attracting people of influence. There is a sense in which his task was easier than that of Neville, in that, some ten years on, some of the Association's existing members were themselves now finding their way into positions of influence within a newly-forming planning and housing 'Establishment'. Thomas Adams had been the first to gain a position of this sort, with his appointment as Town Planning Advisor to the Local Government Board in 1909, and from there going from strength to strength, including his appointment to the first Presidency of the Town Planning Institute. The Association's 1914 Annual Report could also record the appointment of Raymond Unwin (who was already the Vice President of the Town Planning Institute, and who in 1915 assumed the Presidency following the resignation of Thomas Adams) as Chief Town Planning Inspector to the Local Government Board, and G. L. Pepler as Town Planning Inspector. Another member, S. D. Adshead, became the first Professor of Town Planning at the University of London (a post which had been consistently urged by the Association to support the progress that had been made on the legislative front). Most prestigious, though, was the promotion in 1915 of Cecil Harmsworth to the Government post of Under Secretary of State for Home Affairs. While there is no conclusive evidence that this, or other such appointments to posts of influence, materially strengthened the position of the Association, it certainly can have done no harm. Each of the above members carried a mixed portfolio, and was not a supporter of garden cities to the exclusion of all else. But none of them was averse to the cause and, compared with the early years when the movement was striving for credibility, these were at least signs of a growing maturity. It was never expected that the campaign for garden cities would be a mass movement (although it was always hoped that the idea of garden cities would enjoy a popular following), so that 'quiet influence' in the corridors of power was consistently (from the time of Neville's involvement) seen as an appropriate way forward for the Association.

If this was progress, however, it was not yet enough for Harmsworth. What the Association wants, claimed the Chairman in 1918, is 'new blood, new and active recruits . . . I should like to see brought into this Association a larger number of influential men and women belonging to the different classes of political thought . . . I am thinking of them as public people, people of influence, people who can make our propaganda effective.' [13] Being an astute politician, Harmsworth realized that it was important to see beyond the narrow circle of Liberal politicians and businessmen that had sustained the Association to date, and to tap the growing strength of the Labour Party. 'I was saying only the other day to Mr Howard that I thought it would be an invaluable thing if we could enlist the active sympathy of this great new Labour Party which is forming itself in our midst . . . men full of public spirit who, if they but knew and understood the objects that we have in view, would be, I am sure, among our best and most powerful friends.' [14]

In attending to the routine business of the Association, then, progress was maintained on a variety of fronts. It would be misleading, though, to see it all as business as usual. Occasional reports in the journal told of members who were on active service overseas, sometimes with tragic consequences. A poignant reminder of the realities of the period came in a letter from a mother to the Association, in memory of her soldier son listed among the missing: 'His heart was so much in your work that we would like to continue his subscription in his own name as some memory of him.' [15] But the outcome was not always one of sadness, and one member had special reason to rejoice in his long commitment to the garden city movement. Imprisoned as a suspected spy in Germany, he recalled later that his release was due to the fact that the officer in charge had once visited Hampstead Garden Suburb with a party of German visitors [16].

Reconstruction

> . . . a maximum effort must therefore be put into building which in the circumstances . . . private enterprise cannot be expected to supply. Communal action will be required . . . It is the duty of the State, in the emergency which will arise at the end of the War, to make adequate provision to supply the deficiency of houses of a decent standard. (Record of first meeting of Second Reconstruction Committee, 19th April 1917, in Johnson, 1968, p. 59)

If 'business as usual' was the keynote for the Association in the first phase of the war, there is no doubt that the theme of reconstruction dominated thinking thereafter. In both phases the interests and priorities of the Association were closely reflecting national trends.

Thus, from 1916 thoughts of Britain after the war assume a greater importance on the national agenda. It was in March of that year that the Prime Minister, Mr Asquith, established a committee (soon to be known as the Reconstruction Committee) to look ahead to what needed to be done when the war ended [17]. Although this reconstruction debate was officially located in Whitehall, it is significant to note that 'Government and Parliament did not work alone.' [18] Various groups (including the GCTPA) were to be actively involved in what was seen as a period of opportunity when reformist ideas, previously considered too radical or impractical, could attract serious attention in official circles. It seemed that the winds of change were at last beginning to blow. If the old order did not exactly topple, the heavy demands of wartime had at least served to show that the whole system of society rested less securely on the twin pillars of capitalism and imperialism than had once been thought.

The public debate on how Britain might emerge after the war impinged on the development of the GCTPA in two ways. At one level, the debate brought to the fore discussion on the role of the State, advocating a more interventionist stance than had been the rule previously. And, at a more detailed level, prominence was given in ideas about reconstruction to both housing policy and land settlement, issues that were central to the Association's own interests.

In one respect, in that it signalled a fundamental shift in the whole basis for public policy and welfare reforms, the more general debate about the role of the State was to have the greater effect. Although the reconstruction strategy was, in fact, to achieve less than it promised, its very occurrence reflected (even temporarily) political concern and a new sense of social vision. As a measure of the importance attached to it, by July 1917 the whole business of reconstruction had been passed on to a new Government Ministry (headed by Christopher Addison), with a wider brief than the initial committee. Politicians were concerned not simply about the practical problems that would accompany demobilization, but also about ways of sustaining morale as the war dragged on. With one eye on the growing power of the Labour Party, as an expression of working-class interests, politicians looked uneasily at events then unfolding in Russia. Continuing industrial unrest in 1917 added to these fears, and there was open talk of the threat of Bolshevism [19].

Whatever the motives (and these were by no means confined to cynicism and fear) [20], the rhetoric and message of hope that emerged was compelling. Strengthened by its inevitably interventionist role in the war, the State could now be portrayed as a source of salvation in peace. Under the leadership of the State, the nation was encourged to raise its sights, forgetting for a moment the immediacy of conflict and looking ahead rather than back. The War Cabinet itself offered reconstruction as 'not so much a question of rebuilding society as it was before the war, but of moulding a better world out of the social and economic conditions which have come into being during the war.' [21] A reformist role for the State was, of course, not new in itself [22], but previously it had been applied almost as an 'apologia' when all else failed. It is arguable that in the First World War the reconstruction debate contributed to a new climate of opinion where, in the future, intervention 'looked less and less like contestable belief, and became increasingly the broad starting point for argument, rather than its disputed conclusion.' [23] It will certainly be seen that the GCTPA looks more to the State as an agent of change in the years after 1918 than it did previously.

A more specific outcome of the reconstruction debate, and of direct interest to the work of the Association, was the importance attached to housing policy and land settlement. When it was formed, in March 1916, the Reconstruction Committee had its sights on 'the problems that will arise on the conclusion of Peace' [24], rather than on broader welfare plans. By the end of that year, however, the scope of the committee had been transformed to include a range of welfare issues, of which housing was the most important – 'no mere item but a program conceived on a scale without precedent.' [25]

Having put housing on the national agenda it was left to a new

Reconstruction Committee (reconstituted in March 1917 by the new Prime Minister, Lloyd George, and with a more radical membership) to map out the details of a policy. A specialist Housing Panel was established with Lord Salisbury (President of the GCTPA) as Chairman, and another GCTPA activist, Seebohm Rowntree, as a member. Although the Panel set its sights high, there was already something of a consensus that a serious shortage of housing existed and, significantly, that solutions could no longer be left to the private sector. The housing shortage arose because an existing backlog of housing need had been exacerbated by the near cessation of general housebuilding during the war. Moreover, it was predicted that the costs of skilled labour, building materials and capital would be high when the war ended, and that cheap housing could not be provided without some form of State assistance [26]. It was also predicted that house costs would fall within a few years of the end of the war, and that the prospect of falling house prices would discourage the private sector in the initial period when construction would be most urgently needed. If there was, at least, a broad agreement on goals, differences arose when it came to quantifying the extent of the housing shortage, and in resolving just how State assistance should be organized. Both of these dilemmas were addressed in a report by Rowntree to the Reconstruction Committee's Housing Panel [27].

For one thing, Rowntree dismissed the Local Government Board's figure of 120,000 as a gross underestimate of the housing shortage, replacing it instead with a minimum of 300,000 (a total that Lord Salisbury quickly endorsed and which was then widely accepted as a measure of what was needed). The knottier problem was that of whether the State should take on the job itself, or whether the programme should be channelled wholly through the local authorities. Rowntree's preference was for a mixed solution, in which the State underwrote the building costs and the value of the housing, and controlled the overall programme, while the local authorities assumed ownership and management responsibilities for the new houses. The Local Government Board was urged to begin work immediately by locating where housing was most urgently needed, and ensuring that land was made available to enable a rapid start when the time came.

But a fundamental difference emerged between the Local Government Board, which wanted more responsibility to rest with the local authorities, with less compulsion by the State, and the Housing Panel (from July 1917 installed within the new Ministry of Reconstruction), which was now proposing housing commissioners and default powers for the State if local authorities did not meet their goals. The Minister of Reconstruction, Christopher Addison, himself took a close interest in this issue, coming to the firm conclusion that the balance of power had to swing more towards the State and away from the local authorities. Quite simply, Addison contended, the local authorities were not equal to the task in hand. They were claiming responsibility for building 300,000 new houses, and yet they had never before erected more than 4,000 houses in a year [28]. By early 1918 Addison was raising the stakes, calling for a building programme of half a million houses to be started immediately the war ended. But, for the time being at least, the Local Government Board with the support of the Treasury was once again drawing back the balance of power in favour of the local authorities. In March 1918 the Cabinet approved the plan emanating from the Board, which (compared with the Housing Panel's proposals) loosened the hold of the State and which, its critics claimed, 'now ruined the plans for cottage-building on an extensive scale.' [29]

Housing and reconstruction was a vital debate, addressing radical issues that had previously only been the subject of public meetings and articles in reformist publications, but which were now discussed at Cabinet level. This shift, from outside to within the doors of Government, is significant. But where in all this did the GCTPA feature? Had it, at least indirectly, laid the ground for the high level consideration that, from 1916, took place? Did it remain an outsider in these discussions, or was it able in any way to influence events in this decisive period of policy formation? Reconstruction was certainly high on the agenda of the Association's business, and can best be considered in terms of three related but distinct strands of the same issue – that of how best to provide the new housing which would be built after the war. The three strands of policy are those of land settlement, housing policy in general, and the Association's particular proposal for new towns.

(a)   Land Settlement

One aspect of rehousing which attracted the interest of the Association was that of a land settlement programme for returning soldiers and sailors. The proposal itself was presented in 1916 in the form of a report by a Departmental Committee of the Board of Agriculture, the 'Report of the Departmental Committee on Land Settlement for Discharged Sailors and Soldiers' [30]. The kernel of the scheme was for the Government to establish three experimental colonies, each for about 100 families, to enable a select group of men and women to start a new life on the land. The scheme was limited in its extent, but the President of the Board of Agriculture hoped that, if successful, the example might be replicated on a larger scale. His own aspiration was that 'many of those men (from the Navy and Army) would live to own a part of the land which they had saved.' [31]

What the Board had in mind hardly amounted to garden cities, but they were new settlements of sorts and the whole scheme offered a contribution to the old problem of rural regeneration. These were both issues that were close to the heart of the GCTPA and, understandably, the Association responded enthusiastically to the principles embodied in the proposal. In its own report, the Association likened the proposed colonies to garden villages, which it claimed to have 'anticipated almost entirely in one way or another.' [32] With its own experience in these matters the Association hoped that it would be asked to contribute to the implementation of the plan. At least, in a practical way, it saw itself able to assist with propaganda, 'by the exhibition of lantern slides showing the conditions of country life as compared with the crowded town, and depicting scenes in some of the Garden Villages already started' to 'bring home the actual material advantages which would result from settlement in one of these colonies.' [33] A special architectural committee of the Association (with Barry Parker as an active member) even went so far as to produce its own representation of how the colonies might best be arranged to maximize the social amenities of village life. It suggested that most of the plots should be grouped in a ring around a central complex of social and agricultural buildings.

The South Wales branch of the GCTPA went further than its parent body, supporting the scheme in principle but also calling for a practical experiment to be located in the Principality. In a pamphlet entitled 'A State Farm Colony for Wales', six reasons were offered to support the claim. The branch pointed to the fact that Welshmen fighting in the war should have the chance to return to their own land; that rural decline had long been a more serious problem in Wales than in England; that a great demand already existed for smallholdings; that there was plenty of experience of small mixed farms; that ready markets would ensure the new farms of good prices for their output; and that there was an appropriate infrastructure in the form of educational and economic facilities [34].

For all this initial enthusiasm, however, doubts about the limited scale of the scheme soon turned to open criticism. It is probable that the Association had hoped that the Government might have been encouraged to authorize an expanded version, but that did not happen. The proposals in the Departmental Report were accepted as they were, and the verdict was that an opportunity had been lost. 'The proposals, so far as they have at present seen light, do not appear to be very heroic . . .' [35] In stirring terms, Ewart Culpin wrote on behalf of the Association to *The Times*, calling on Members of Parliament to insist on a scheme 'which shall not only be worthy of a great and grateful country, but shall also be worthy of the brave men in whose interest it is framed.' [36]

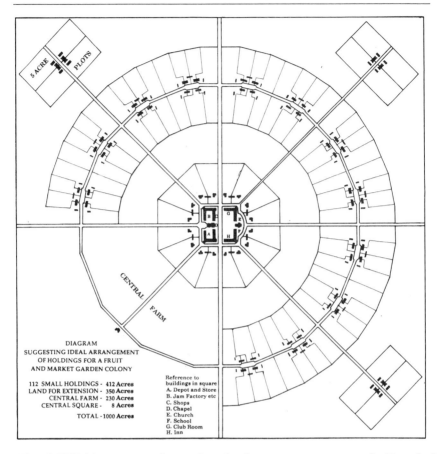

DIAGRAM
SUGGESTING IDEAL ARRANGEMENT
OF HOLDINGS FOR A FRUIT
AND MARKET GARDEN COLONY

112 SMALL HOLDINGS -	**412 Acres**
LAND FOR EXTENSION -	**350 Acres**
CENTRAL FARM -	**230 Acres**
CENTRAL SQUARE -	**8 Acres**
TOTAL -	**1000 Acres**

Reference to buildings in square
A. Depot and Store
B. Jam Factory etc
C. Shops
D. Chapel
E. Church
F. School
G. Club Room
H. Inn

The GCTPA's concept of agricultural colonies, in response to the Board of Agriculture's wartime report on the subject.

To pursue not just this specific case but also the wider cause of rural reconstruction, the Association took the lead in setting up in May 1916 an informal Round-Table Conference (which evolved, in turn, into a more formal network known as the Rural Organisation Council). The members of the initial body were drawn from existing organizations with an interest in rural development, as well as supportive Members from both Houses of Parliament [37]. Resolutions were passed, calling for a bolder approach to rural problems, and the Association itself recorded 'its deep regret that such a fine opportunity for the social reconstruction of rural England by State action was thus missed.' [38]

(b) Housing Policy
On the broad issues of housing policy after the war, the Association

made only a limited contribution. Its special brief was to build on the experience of Letchworth and to promote new settlements. But the broader issues were not unrelated, and from time to time particular representations were made.

That housing was a priority in any plans for reconstruction was never in doubt, and members were frequently reminded that the war had simply added to the urgency of the housing problems of the nation that had been the spur to all the Association had done to date. In an article in the *GCTP*, 'Housing after the War', support was given to the views of Seebohm Rowntree, who was publicly arguing that a massive housebuilding programme would be a way of combating unemployment as well as the housing shortage. The article also endorsed the view that the task could not be left to the private sector, and that public authorities should already be preparing the ground [39].

One type of public authority that was especially favoured by the Association was that of the Public Utility Society. Registered under the Industrial and Provident Societies Acts, they were limited by their rules to a 5 per cent maximum annual interest or dividend. The 1909 Act had made it easier for them to obtain cheap loans, and, since then, Public Utility Societies had sponsored a number of garden suburb schemes. Seeing in these societies a potential means of launching new garden cities, the Association was prominent in seeking for them a more important role in postwar housing. Thus, in a deputation in 1916 to the President of the Local Government Board, attended by a wide range of housing organizations, it was Ewart Culpin who was asked to present the case for Public Utility Societies. Culpin pointed to the fact that there were then some seventy such societies in existence, and that they could play an important role alongside local authorities in the years ahead. But first, he contended, various changes in the law were needed to make them more effective [40]. The Association was also instrumental in calling a National Conference of Public Utility Societies (held at the offices of the Association in October 1916), which then discussed an 'After-the-War Policy'. There is no evidence, however, that in Government circles Public Utility Societies were considered at that time as a serious option, compared with the local authorities or more direct control of public housing [41].

As well as general lobbying a tangible source of achievement claimed by the Association was that of the quality and form of emergency housing built by the Government during the war for munitions workers. The Association's Chairman reported that the advice of the organization had been sought on a number of occasions, and that 'it was a tribute to the principles which they had advocated that practically all the permanent housing work done in war-time had been more or less upon the lines they had laid down.' [42] For several years before the war the Association had lobbied the Admiralty for a high standard of housing at the new dockyards at Rosyth, but the types of scheme that attracted particular praise were the estates of Well Hall and Gretna. Although of contrasting styles (the Well Hall houses being more picturesque and ornamental, as opposed to a simpler, plainer style at Gretna), the two estates were interpreted as a sign of official endorsement of garden suburb (if not garden city) housing [43]. As such, they represented an important link between the Association's prewar campaign and the advent of State housing on a large scale when the war ended.

In addition to its role in advising on detailed schemes, the Association was also called on from time to time to comment on more general policy issues. Although there is no evidence of a major impact on the course of policy in this period, it is significant, at least, that the Association was acknowledged as one of the country's leading housing campaigners and that its views were sought on a number of occasions by the reconstruction committees [44]. For example, the Secretary of the first Reconstruction Committee, doubtful about the advice submitted by the Local Government Board, invited a number of housing reform organizations (including the GCTPA) to give their assessment of the housing problem. By the time of the Housing Panel and the second Reconstruction Committee, one view was that 'the voice of unofficial campaigners had now become a voice *within* the circles of government.' [45] And when Addison was facing difficulties in the Cabinet with the resistance of the Local Government Board to any diminution of the powers of local authorities, he could at least count on the support of organizations such as the GCTPA that were campaigning for the more forceful approach that he represented [46]. Although there is little in the way of any tangible evidence of influencing events, to the extent that the Association was now readily consulted on housing issues, there were signs, at least, of a new phase in its activities – within as well as without the corridors of power.

(c)   New Towns

Of all the issues, however, the one in which the Association could offer the sharpest contribution to the reconstruction debate was that of including in the postwar plans provision for the building of new settlements along the lines of the first garden city. Strangely, though, it was this issue that led to one of the stormiest periods in the Association's history, dividing its members in the process. The source of contention was whether or not the Association should concentrate all its energies on propaganda for new garden cities after the war, as opposed to a more broad-based campaign along the lines it was currently pursuing.

Largely at the instigation of C. B. Purdom (who, in 1917, published a pamphlet arguing for new housing to be built on garden city principles) [47], a breakaway group was formed to rekindle the flame of garden city idealism. Frustrated by what he saw as the GCTPA's 'failing as custodian of the garden city idea' [48], and by his own inability to persuade leading figures at Letchworth to spread the fruits of the first experiment after the war, Purdom joined with Howard and W. G. Taylor (a director of the publishers, Dent and Sons) to form the National Garden Cities Committee. Their common goal was to see the creation of Government-sponsored new towns [49]. Others who were attracted to the idea and who joined the group included F. J. Osborn, Professor Abercrombie and G. D. H. Cole. Of these, it was Osborn whom Purdom persuaded to write a book to publicize their cause. The outcome was a small book, *New Towns after the War*, published in 1918 under the author's pseudonym of 'New Townsmen' [50].

As a source of propaganda, Osborn's book amounted to a reaffirmation and updating of Howard's original garden city tract. Twenty years on, and with the experience of Letchworth to call on, the

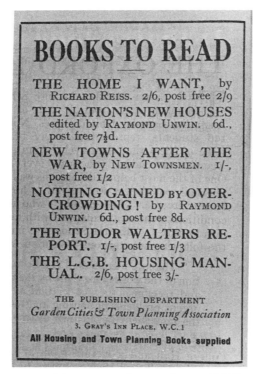

BOOKS TO READ

THE HOME I WANT, by RICHARD REISS. 2/6, post free 2/9

THE NATION'S NEW HOUSES edited by RAYMOND UNWIN. 6d., post free 7½d.

NEW TOWNS AFTER THE WAR, by NEW TOWNSMEN. 1/-, post free 1/2

NOTHING GAINED BY OVER-CROWDING! by RAYMOND UNWIN. 6d., post free 8d.

THE TUDOR WALTERS RE-PORT. 1/-, post free 1/3

THE L.G.B. HOUSING MAN-UAL. 2/6, post free 3/-

THE PUBLISHING DEPARTMENT
Garden Cities & Town Planning Association
3, GRAY'S INN PLACE, W.C.1
All Housing and Town Planning Books supplied

Wartime planning publications advertised in *GCTP*, including *New Towns after the War*.

updating introduced some new features. Significantly, in 1918, the need for new housing was not in public contention, and Osborn could start from the premise that a national plan was called for. His estimate was that as many as a million houses would have to be built in the first five years of peacetime, and that this formidable target could best be achieved through the construction of 100 new towns. With considerable foresight he argued that this massive construction programme should be seen as part of a wider restructuring of British capital, renewing the country's industrial plant as well as its housing.

What distinguished it most from Howard's original arguments was the unequivocal role that was to be attributed to the State. There were different ways of organizing this in detail, but there could be no question of an enterprise on this scale without the State assuming a basic responsibility: 'Such a programme appears heroic' conceded Osborn, 'but that is no point against it if it is also practicable.' [51] And of that the New Townsmen entertained no doubts.

The ideas in the book were well enough received in some quarters [52]. And they were entirely consistent with the essential creed of the GCTPA, advocating just the kind of new settlement that the Association had promoted since its own formation. But the manner in which these ideas were now promoted, through a splinter group beyond the control of the parent body, and the challenge it posed to the other activities of the Association, was too much for the main body of the organization to accommodate. Strenuous efforts were then made to bring the radicals into line [53].

The issue was openly discussed at the Annual Meeting of the Association in March 1918, and a conciliatory resolution was passed which called for special propaganda being started throughout the country to ensure that garden city principles were incorporated in reconstruction plans. In moving the resolution Mr Montagu Harris (a member of the Council) was careful to affirm that the Association had been right to adopt a wide brief, rather than to confine itself solely to new towns propaganda. However, he recognized that the time was now right for a major campaign on the latter theme, and that it might be necessary to establish a special committee *within* the Association to do it. The Association's Executive was less circumspect as to what needed to be done, requesting that 'the members of this Executive who are also members of the National Garden Cities Committee be asked either to see their way to merge their Committee's work in the proper Garden City work of this long-established and recognised national Association of those interested in Garden Cities and bring their personnel into that work, *or* if they desire to be at liberty to work as a separate society to take immediate steps to drop the words "National Garden Cities" from their name.' [54] The option of a merger was subsequently agreed, with Purdom acting jointly as the new Propaganda Committee Secretary and the Association's Assistant Secretary at an annual salary of £300 [55]. Although the whole episode did not show the Association in a particularly positive light, at least it had emerged intact and ready to play a part in the years of reconstruction ahead.

Related to the work of the Association, but not seen as a direct challenge to policy in the way of the National Garden Cities Committee, was another group, the New Town Council [56]. Largely a Quaker organization, the immediate aim in this case was not a frontal assault on national policy, but, instead, to build a small new town as an example of what might be done: 'a social experiment in the provision of a fit environment for the minds and bodies of men and women to enter the joy of active service together for the glory of God.' [57] A Trust was formed to investigate sites, based in one of the rooms in the Association's own offices. In the event, though, the Trust soon abandoned its own plans, being drawn instead to Howard's postwar scheme of building a second garden city at Welwyn, with some of its members subsequently going to live and work there [58].

Internationalism

> With so many doors of activity closed to it, the work of the International Garden Cities and Town Planning Association might well have been suspended during the progress of a war which had involved nearly the whole of the countries actively engaged in garden city propaganda . . . Despite everything, it was seen that the activities of the Association are, perhaps, as great as ever, and that in some directions they have considerably enlarged. (*GCTP* NS, Vol. VI, No. 7, October 1916, p. 117)

Launched in the year before the outbreak of a world war, the International Garden Cities and Town Planning Association might well have been wound up, at least for the duration of the conflict. Business as usual was one thing on the home front, but quite another when it came to building confidence and contacts between warring nations. At the very heart of the new organization were the close ties which had been fostered between Britain and Germany, and it is these which were now the most seriously challenged. Only days before war was declared, arrangements had been put in hand to hold the Second International Conference in Dusseldorf in 1915, and members of the GCTPA found 'the thought of the conflict of arms between the two nations almost unbelievable.' [59] In spite of everything, members were urged to remember how much the town planning world had to thank the German nation for [60].

But the old order had already changed, and continuing links along the lines proposed when the international organization was formed to disseminate the garden city idea, were no longer possible. Despite C. B. Purdom's dismissive view that during the war there was nothing for this body to do [61], the record shows that the organization engaged actively in both routine tasks to keep itself in business and also in a specific campaign that attracted widespread interest and support. The Secretary, Ewart Culpin, proved to be a key figure in both sets of activity.

At the routine level, the viability of the International Association was assisted by the fact that all correspondence was handled in the GCTPA's office, and by Culpin's own 'initiative, energy, and unceasing and devoted service.' [62] The funds of the IGCTPA were, in fact, pitifully low in these years of currency controls [63], and it could not have survived as an autonomous organization. Even so, although some lines of communication were now blocked other contacts thrived. Up until the Bolshevik Revolution in 1917, the International Association was in touch with garden city enthusiasts in Russia and could report on plans there for the creation of a garden city on similar lines to Letchworth [64]. There were notes to the effect that the garden city flame was at least still flickering in other countries in mainland Europe, including Spain and France. Understandably, though, the most optimistic reports came from those parts of the world furthest from the field of conflict. Links with the United States were strengthened, with an actual increase in the volume of correspondence between the two countries and visits made by garden city advocates in both directions. In 1917 there were hopes that the American Government would adopt garden city principles for its own wartime housing schemes for munitions workers [65].

The most regular reports, though, were from Australia, where one of the more prominent garden city 'missionaries', Charles Reade, had arranged a tour of the continent in 1914–1915 to spread the gospel. Accompanied for part of this time by W. C. Davidge, the intrepid pair travelled extensively from government offices to local meeting halls throughout the country, exhorting their audiences to adopt garden city principles for their new settlements. Armed with 'a set of lantern slides which is not approached elsewhere' [66], the two fulfilled twenty-six engagements in September 1914 alone [67]. In the Melbourne area, for instance, their audiences varied from the Royal Victoria Institute of Architects to the Melbourne Socialists at the Bijou Theatre, and from the Geelong Mechanics' Institute to an organization of Liberal workers. Both lecturers reported an enthusiastic response, and for some time after the tour both the GCA and IGCTPA in London received letters of enquiry and congratulations. Charles Reade remained in South Australia at the end of the tour to advise on town planning in the State, and the International Association took some credit not simply for that source of influence but also for the formation of Town Planning Associations and local civic groups that were seen as an outcome of the lectures [68].

Of all the issues, however, the one that came closest to the heart of the new Association and which did most to unite its far-flung members was that of the proposed reconstruction of Belgium. Nothing symbolized more the need for international action than the cause of that ravaged country, in the very crucible of war. Apart from civilian losses and the problem of refugees, the German invasion resulted in substantial destruction of the nation's heritage. As well as historic centrepieces like the University of Louvain, and the Cloth Hall at Ypres, 'scores of beautiful public buildings have been outraged, and it is safe to say that well over ten thousand houses have been totally or partially destroyed. Besides these, farms and factories, hospitals and schools, churches and stations have been rendered impossible of renovation.' [69] The question was one of what could be done in the midst of war to plan for the rebuilding of Belgium in peacetime.

Under the guidance of Ewart Culpin, the International Association took the lead in setting up appropriate administrative arrangements to tackle the problem. Initially, it was thought that a division of tasks could be organized, with the International Association concentrating on the propaganda side and the Town Planning Institute dealing with the technical issues.

This division was soon seen to be needlessly cumbersome and, instead, a single body, 'The Belgium Town Planning Committee', was formed in 1915. Raymond Unwin was elected Chairman, and Ewart Culpin added the Secretaryship to his existing secretarial posts. For the rest, the committee was composed of representatives of Belgian and other housing and town planning organizations [70].

The new committee had as its central aim the task of providing 'facilities to enable Belgian architects, engineers, surveyors, lawyers, and other professional men to study the problems involved in replanning and rebuilding the towns, villages, and means of communication in Belgium, and in particular to prepare draft enactments and preliminary schemes for rebuilding.' [71] To achieve this, the committee did three things. It initiated the formation of study groups for nominees of the Belgian Government and expatriate professionals; it mounted a Town Planning Exhibition to illustrate the conditions and needs of Belgium; and it organized a series of lectures and conferences in London and provincial centres. A base for the committee's activities was provided in the new building of the School of Architecture and Town Planning at University College, London.

Culpin himself became passionately involved in promoting the cause. Although he acknowledged that some of the towns would have

THE REMAKING OF BELGIUM

This is a reproduction of the striking poster which **Mr. Frank Brangwyn,
A.R.A.**, designed for the **Belgium Town Planning Committee**. Specially
printed signed copies of the original may be obtained at one guinea each,
or in black and white 5s. each.

(Reproduced in GCTP NS, Vol. V, No. 5, 1915, p. 95).

to be reconstructed on their former lines, he also saw attractive opportunities for the application of garden city principles. One of the more emotive proposals was for plans to include an international garden city, 'where all the forces of civilisation shall unite in producing a perfect city of health, a city residential, commercial, industrial, and agricultural, responding to all the several and varying needs of humanity, preserving the facilities of the city, and above all, serving as a monument and a testimony from humanity the world over to the valour and the honour of Belgium today.' [72]

The practical difficulties of the committee were immense, but at least proposals such as that for an international city could offer hope and inspiration at a time when this was in short supply. More than that, the Belgian campaign also had the effect of helping to keep open lines of communication between members of the International Association in the darkest hours of the war.

A GLIMPSE OF UTOPIA

While the guns still fired across the mudfields of northern France, a vision formed of a green and pleasant land – a land fit for returning heroes. With all its hitherto little-used capacity to intervene in order to do good, the State now cast itself as the instrument of change. A brave new world beckoned, with jobs and decent housing for all.

The GCTPA had not previously seen the State as the architect of utopia. But now the promises looked sound enough, and the Association was hardly going to stand by at this crucial juncture of history. It would be a disaster if the building blocks of utopia were wrongly assembled, and the Association's mission in the immediate postwar years was to ensure that their own longstanding ideals were not ignored. Led by events, the thrust of the Association's work in this period was to seek to influence the shape of housing policy and, within that, to lay the foundations for a nation of garden cities. The glimpse of utopia was alluring, and in the aftermath of war the deepest emotions of idealism were aroused.

War and Peace

We cannot return to the old conditions . . . Timidity is fatal to great action, and these are the days when great action is required. (Lloyd George, as reported in *The Times*, 18th November 1918, in Hurwitz, 1949, p. 291)

For the GCTPA, having clung to a raft of its own making in the stormy waters of the war (ensuring the survival not only of the domestic organization, but also, more remarkably, of the international association too), it might well have seemed that the shores of the millennium were now in sight. That, at least, was how the nation in general was encouraged to see things, putting behind it the grief of 800,000 dead and dismissing thoughts of Bolshevism as the way forward. Inevitably, the Association, with its reformist outlook, was carried along on this tide of euphoria, enjoying the exultation of the immediate postwar year, before, like the rest of the nation, confronting the cruel realization that the tide had already started to turn and that the promised land was fast slipping out of sight.

During the war, not one but contrasting visions formed of what Britain could be like when peace returned. For some, it was a question of turning back the clock to restore the world of 1914 [73]. For others, expressed by but not confined to the recommendations of the Ministry of Reconstruction (and representing a vision with which the GCTPA could most closely identify), there would be social reforms the likes of which had not been seen before. Housing, education, social insurance, and the prospect of the public control of the mines and railways were all on the agenda [74]. In contrast, the Bolshevik Revolution in Russia in 1917 inspired new political factions in Britain and other European countries to reject any idea of further bargaining with a corrupt capitalist system [75].

This relationship between the war and thoughts of change is seen by some historians as a predictable enough outcome. Wars disrupt, if not destroy, existing processes of government and social activity, and in the vacuum that is created the possibility of new patterns can be entertained. In his analysis of the whole reconstruction debate at the time of the First World War, Paul Johnson discusses this relationship in terms of 'Mars and the Millennium'. [76] He shows how reconstructionists believed that the war served the goals of reform in two ways – in an objective sense, through the sheer momentum of trends that it generated, and, subjectively, by the creation of a new mentality and a new purpose. The language itself frequently expressed the millennial hopes of those who took this view: 'Since August, 1914, England has broken with her past and entered an entirely new epoch. Today can never be as yesterday.' [77] Samuel Hurwitz (writing before Johnson) takes a comparable view, arguing that the level of hopes that were aroused was almost in a direct ratio to the level of suffering endured. On this basis, the sheer horrors of war ensured a high degree of millennial expectation [78].

Politicians were quick to exploit this underlying current of need and hope for a brave new world, in whatever form this might take. The guns stopped firing on the eleventh hour of the eleventh day of 1918, and Lloyd George, the Prime Minister of the Coalition Government which had brought victory, called a General Election for the 14th December. The people were offered another coalition (consisting of Lloyd George's Liberals, and Conservatives under Bonar Law), with Asquith's Independent Liberals and the Labour Party as the main alternatives. Electioneering was focused around the twin issues of punishing the Germans and securing an honourable peace, and of achieving at home (in Lloyd George's terms) a 'land fit for returning heroes' – this latter goal being dependent on the State playing a bigger part than it had done before the war. Thus, when Lloyd George was returned with an overwhelming majority, his new Government could confidently call for resolute action:

> We must stop at no sacrifice of interest or prejudice to stamp out unmerited poverty, to diminish unemployment and mitigate its sufferings, to provide decent homes, to improve the nation's health, and to raise the standard of well-being throughout the community [79].

The GCTPA was not alone in anticipating that the prospects for achieving at least a measure of social reform were better than they had been before. Severe industrial action in 1919, coupled with an even more threatening situation posed by the demobilization of a disaffected fighting force, served to enhance the case for reform. And, indeed, some concessions were made in the first year of the new Government. Of particular interest to the Association was the State's enlarged role in housing, and the formation of a Ministry of Health (one of the recommendations of the Reconstruction Ministry) with responsibilities in public and environmental health that went well beyond the old 'poor law' approach. More generally, the climate of opinion and acknowledgement of social problems on which the Association had for long campaigned seemed to offer an encouraging basis for progress. In material terms, an industrial boom as the economy changed into its peacetime gear added to the sense of a potential for improvement.

And yet, even before 1919 drew to an end, hopes were already beginning to dim. Beatrice Webb had sensed from the outset that it might turn out this way, viewing the postwar euphoria with a healthy cynicism:

> The two great parties are gathering up their forces, coalescing on the boom of victory and the fear of revolution – the two most potent emotions of today . . . All that can be said is that the governing class is willing to promise anything that is unanimously demanded by the labour movement rather than endanger their hold on the seat of power. Whether after they have won the election they will be equally complacent is not so certain . . . [80]

Some, like T. E. Lawrence, laid the blame for lost hopes on personalities; for all the rhetoric of radical change, the Coalition Government was composed of 'yesterday's men', who had taken from the people 'our victory and remade it in the likeness of the former world they knew.' [81] J. M. Keynes saw it more in terms of exhaustion: 'we have been moved already beyond endurance and need rest.' [82] Nor did Lloyd George escape criticism, closeting himself with his closest advisers in what was popularly termed the 'garden suburb', [83] and becoming a scapegoat for broken promises. A more probable explanation, however, is that the commitment to reform lost momentum when the threats and fears that drove the Government to do something themselves lost their force. Organized labour had underplayed its own strengths, and the demobilized forces returned to their jobs in the booming factories rather than to the barricades. 'By the end of the year, though there had been several more strikes, some of them of a very serious character, the cutting edge of revolution and of reconstruction alike had been blunted.' [84] The millennium, a land fit for returning heroes, was (like all millennia) an ideological creation that, as it transpired, could be dissolved just as easily as it had been created.

During 1920 the engine of reform still has some power within it, but by the end of that year the postwar economic boom is over, and Britain entered the first of the interwar recessions, in this case lasting in its severest form until the end of 1922. With two million unemployed the strength of organized labour was reduced, and newspaper campaigns were mounted to urge the Coalition to stop wasting public funds on activities, such as housing, that the private sector could do better. 'Anti-waste' and 'end squandermania' became popular catch phrases that served to buttress the ideological backlash against further reform [85]. In late 1922, on a slogan of 'Tranquillity', a Conservative Administration (under, first, Bonar Law, and then Stanley Baldwin) was returned to power for the first time since 1905, and the fate of reconstruction was finally sealed. Some hope amongst reformers was later revived in 1924 when, following a General Election, Labour assumed power, for the first time, as a Minority Government. Although its brief period of office was not without some achievement (not least of all in the field of housing), its potential for change was hamstrung by the restraining influence of its Liberal allies. By the end of 1924 the first Labour Government was out of office [86].

For the GCTPA, the aftermath of war, from 1918 through to the early 1920s, was (reflecting the changing fortunes of the country as a whole) a turbulent period. The years 1919 and 1920 were particularly busy, with the activities of the pressure group enhanced by a keen public interest in housing reform. Politicians and newspapers constantly debated issues that had previously attracted far less attention, and the Association had little trouble in packing meeting halls and collecting donations. When the tide turned, however, the Association returned to a more quiescent role, patiently campaigning for the time when new opportunities would arise. If there is a general lesson from all this it is that a pressure group, while not entirely at the mercy of wider social forces, is nevertheless very closely dependent on what is happening in politics, in the economy, and in public opinion. When the tide of change is running in its favour, it is itself at its strongest; when the tide changes it can, at best, stay afloat, reserving its strength for better times.

Paradise Postponed: Homes Unfit for Heroes

The old year ended with something like a dirge over the still-born body of the new world. The land fit for heroes had become an uneasy memory . . . The economic difficulties that are crowding upon us are in danger of making people lose their wits. The clamour of the newspapers in the name of economy is having a powerful effect upon the unthinking . . . (Editorial, *GCTP*, Vol. XI, No. 1, January 1921, p. 1)

Under extreme duress, towards the end of and immediately after the war, the Coalition Governments led by Lloyd George conceded the promise of rich social rewards to the nation in exchange for political stability. The brightest jewel in the crown of reforms was that of housing. In an enduring phrase (that long outlived the content of what was promised) Lloyd George pledged to the electorate in 1918 that he would secure 'habitations that are fit for the heroes who have won the war.' [87]

'Homes fit for heroes' became a popular catch phrase, embodying not simply the quantitative goals of housing policy but also the question of quality. Numbers were important, with an immediate target of 500,000 new houses over a three-year period, but so, too, was the standard of what was to be built. Published in the same week as the Armistice, when Government fears about social order (in the face of returning troops and the prospect of unemployment as the munitions factories closed down) were at their most acute, the Tudor Walters Report offered a blueprint for higher standards of design and comfort as a further source of State largesse [88]. When, subsequently, general housing legislation was framed, the whole question of raising standards was considered to be at least as important as the question of numbers. Moreover, the way in which this was to be done was strongly influenced by the report's recommendations which, in turn, bear the strong imprint of the only architect on the committee, Raymond Unwin [89]. For Unwin, with his previous record of designing in the 'garden city' style (characteristically, cottages, grouped sympathetically at modest densities, and in settings that respected the natural features of the landscape) the report offered an exceptional opportunity to promote these ideas. And, indeed, these recommendations proved to be extremely influential in setting the pattern for municipal housebuilding, especially, in the interwar years.

To give effect to these and other ideas about State subsidized housing that had been discussed towards the end of the war, Christopher Addison was moved from Reconstruction to the Local Government Board (and then, on its dissolution in July 1919, to the Ministry of Health). Under his guidance, a new Housing and Town Planning Act was framed and steered easily through a Parliament eager for support in what amounted to a campaign to win the confidence of the working class [90]. Under the Act, subsidies were introduced which offered the potential for half a million houses to be built and let at low rents, without financially committing the local authorities (through which the scheme was operated) to more than the proceeds of a penny rate. Every local authority was required to make a survey within three months of housing needs within their area, and then (with the approval of the Ministry of Health) to prepare plans to meet these needs. Launched amidst acclaim, just two years after the Act came onto the statute books, in July 1921, the programme was officially disbanded. A legacy was bequeathed in the form of some houses (about 170,000) which were, at least, of a higher standard than had been commonplace before [91], and although the idea of subsidized housing was to be shelved for the next two years it proved to be a resilient concept. Thus, in 1923 and 1924, two subsequent housing Acts reintroduced State subsidies – the first of these Acts promoted by Neville Chamberlain in a Conservative Administration, and designed primarily to stimulate the private sector, and the second, the work of Joseph Wheatley in the short-lived Labour Administration, putting the emphasis on direct subsidies to assist local authorities. Neither of these measures could be compared with the radical promises of 1918 and 1919, but the latter Act at least provided a sound basis for the extension of public housing provision. Together, the 1923 and 1924 Acts led to the building of some 580,000 houses (characteristically with gardens) until subsidies were abolished in 1933 [92].

This whole episode of hopes raised and confounded has been carefully documented by a number of writers [93], and while drawing on this work it is not the intention here to repeat it. Instead, what matters in this context is how this transformation of housing policy (where, for all the disappointments, the State emerged as a key agent in housing provision) can be related to the work and aspirations of the GCPTA. Did the Association influence in any way the new policies, and, in turn, did these events affect what the Association did?

Undoubtedly, this was a challenging episode in the life of the Association. On the one hand, it (along with other housing reformers) had for years been calling for a vast programme of new housebuilding. Now that this appeared to be within reach, the Association could hardly flinch from the challenge of trying to ensure that what was built accorded with its own ideals. Yet there was a fine balance to be struck between responding positively to an initiative that was welcome in principle, and at the same time trying to safeguard its own position. In wider terms, it was a question of whether the Association (or for that matter any individual pressure group) would prove to be strong enough to channel the powerful tide of events or simply be swept along by it.

At least, at the start of 1919, there was no doubt as to the enormity of the challenge, and the Association defined its own position. 'With the coming of peace the Garden City movement has the greatest opportunity that has yet appeared of influencing housing and industrial developments in this country in accordance with the principles that it has maintained for so many years.' [94] The Association cast itself a dual role – to promote garden city principles, and to mount its own campaign in all parts of the country to ensure that its principles were widely known and applied. In February 1919 a Memorandum was submitted to the President of the Local Government Board, calling for the adoption of the garden city principle as a national policy. This, it was argued, would not only provide a sound basis for the new housing but would also offer a way of tackling related problems of industrial and agricultural reconstruction [95].

Against a background of growing industrial and political unrest in the country at large, the Association pressed for urgent action rather than mere words. For all the signs of activity in the Local Government Board, the fact was that 'time is passing, the men are being demobilized, and the country is not "fit for heroes to live in", because there are no houses for them . . . unless a start is made upon the houses without delay, we shall be faced with a state of affairs that none of us dare to contemplate.' [96] At that time, in early 1919, the Government needed no urging, and Cabinet discussions of the Housing Bill were framed in the context of doing something that would offer the people of the country 'a sense of confidence' in the State [97].

The Bill, then, was concocted in a setting of desperation and hope, and when it appeared, in March 1919, it was sufficiently potent to appeal to the exacting demands of housing reformers. Thus, the Association welcomed the Bill (subsequently enacted as the Housing and Town Planning Act in July 1919) as a 'revolutionary measure', heralding it as the beginning of a new system of housing. The provision of housing could no longer be regarded as incidental to the sanitary duties of local authorities, but now as a distinct branch of local government activity. Its warm reception was confined to the housing clauses of the Bill, rather than the town planning sections (which were regarded as 'altogether inadequate'). And the Association warned that its own task to educate public opinion was more urgent than ever if high standards of building were to be achieved [98].

By the end of the year, however, the honeymoon period was over,

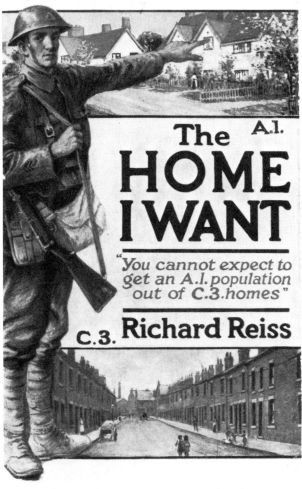

Richard Reiss (author of this postwar housing book) was an influential figure in the housing and garden city campaign. (By courtesy of the Bodleian Library)

and the Association was already fearing that the best-laid plans of Addison would come to naught. There were less than 10,000 new houses in the pipeline, as opposed to the promised 100,000 by that time. 'If speed in building were the very essence of the Government's scheme, it is certain that the scheme had failed.' [99] People simply did not understand why houses were not being built, claimed the Association, before offering its own explanations. In common with other critics, the Association pointed to the failure of Government to control the building industry, and of the inexperience and inability of some local authorities to handle the programme. The real weakness of the scheme was that it left the distribution of houses to local considerations, rather than to considerations of national interests. Even the inclusion of a supplementary clause which provided for the acquisition of land for garden cities failed to placate the Association [100]. When the scheme was finally abandoned, in July 1921, the Association could have taken little joy in concluding that 'we always believed it to be impossible. We never saw anything commendable in a scheme that meant the violent stimulation of municipal building apart from town planning control. And we believed that a satisfactory housing scheme required a permanent basis.' [101]

In terms of the workings of the pressure group, what is interesting in relation to all this is the way the Association mounted its own campaign to seek to influence events in this period. Under the banner of a National Housing Campaign, the Association started work in 1918 'to develop an enlightened public opinion throughout the country for dealing with housing on an adequate scale and on sound principles.' [102] In the same month, July, as the 1919 Act was passed, details were reported of the campaign to date. Compared with prewar campaigns, the scale and professionalism of the new operation was unprecedented. It was estimated that the full cost of the campaign would be £10,000, mainly to enable the employment of full-time local organizers. Members were exhorted to send donations to make it all possible, the Association's expenditure being contrasted with an estimated £300,000,000 to be spent by the Government. £10,000 was a small outlay, it was argued, if it led to the larger sum being wisely spent.

If the nature of the exercise was new for the organization, the sheer energy and missionary zeal that it attracted was familiar enough. From all parts of the country, local organizers reported enthusiastically on what they were doing [103]. P. R. Marrison, the organizer for the Western Counties, based in Bristol, told of lantern lectures to the boys of Clifton College and to the girls of Clifton High School; and of a gathering of 1000 people at the Bristol Hippodrome to see the Association's films on housing schemes, featuring scenes of Letchworth (to which the audience responded with applause and cries of 'why can't we have the same?'). From Birmingham, J. C. Haig reported on meetings he had addressed at the Cathedral Rectory, the Women's Labour Party Rooms, and a lunchtime gathering of 400 to 500 men at the General Electric Works. It was certainly not just a question of preaching to the converted. In the North East, F. D. Stuart explained that his group had concentrated on educational work in the areas of local authorities that had the worst record for housing improvements. Likewise, in the Eastern Counties, the Association's missionaries ventured to the outlying rural districts, spurring reformers with tales of three families living in a tiny cottage, and of one man who told a gathering that when it rained he slept with an umbrella over him. It was not just private landlords who were to blame. In the Home Counties the Association came across the case of a local authority that had resorted to roofing over some cattle sheds and then letting them at 2s 6d per week. The local organizer concluded (in terms that were apt for the whole campaign) that it could all too readily be seen that the work they were carrying out was essential.

Popular interest and support for the Association's National Housing Campaign coincided with the high political profile attached to housing policy at the time of the Addison Act. When the Government perceived that the urgency for radical reform had receded, and, in the face of economic recession between 1921 and 1923, housing policy slipped slowly down the political agenda, there was little that the Association or, for that matter, any other pressure group could do to recover the situation. It had been the threat of revolution that had forced the State to make bold concessions, not the force of rational argument.

Ever optimistic, though, even before the Addison Act had been buried the Association was trying to lay the basis for a new policy. Articles appeared in the journal in 1921 [104] analysing what had gone wrong and suggesting what needed to be done. But the political tide had turned, and it was to be another two years before a new initiative came, this time in the form of a Housing Act primarily to stimulate the private sector. It was not what the Association wanted, but it could not be readily dismissed. On the whole, the Association concluded, 'it represents a perfectly honest attempt by a Conservative Government to do what can be done to alleviate the housing situation without departing from Conservative principles.' [105] Wheatley's Act in the following year was more to the Association's liking, but even this had been weakened by concessions forced on the minority Labour Government. The Association was prepared to see both Acts used to the full, though both fell short of their own ideals. The garden suburbs that resulted around towns and cities throughout the country were welcome in themselves (the design of which reflected the very considerable influence of Raymond Unwin and other garden city architects), but they represented only part of what the Association wanted.

Garden Cities and Satellite Towns

The superstition that the Garden City is an enthusiast's dream takes an unconscionable time in dying. In the backwoods of social thought still survive many persons who have never visited a garden city, but nevertheless 'can easily imagine what it is like'; they picture a pinchbeck paradise inhabited by a peculiar people, part high-brow and part bumpkin, who tend sartorially to djibbahs and sandals, intellectually to all that is fantastic, and practically to fads. Very slowly dawns on these sociological backwoodsmen the truth that garden city dwellers are much as other men, though more fortunate in, because more consciously the masters of, their environment, and that the garden city is a break with the past because those who have learned most from the present are determined to plan and build for a better future. (*GCTP*, Vol. XIII, No. 1, January 1923, p. 1)

Intertwined with the postwar housing campaign, the Association sought to ensure that new houses were discussed within a wider context of garden cities and town planning. Government ministers and officials were approached directly, but also (as the above editorial indicates) the Association believed that there was still a wider role to be performed in informing public opinion. Overall, though, the general thrust of the Association's work in this period was that it was a time of opportunity, and that official endorsement for the idea of planned towns was within reach.

Garden cities, it was argued, made good sense for a nation about to embark on a housebuilding programme of the scale projected. Part of the Association's campaign was simply to reaffirm that. In 1920 the organization celebrated its twenty-first anniversary, and took the opportunity to assert that the original ideals which had brought it into being in the first place were as fresh and applicable as ever. At the same time, a redefinition of aims was prepared, reflecting (in the context of the then housing programme) an appreciation of the need to deal with the problems of existing towns as well as turning to green fields. The new policy of the Association contained five aims:

1. The establishment of garden cities on suitably chosen areas with a view to the relief of congestion and overcrowding in existing towns and the development of the resources of the country.
2. The development of existing small towns on the garden city principle where they are suitably placed for such extension.

3. The application of the garden city principle to existing large
   towns with the object of preventing their extension, except by
   the establishment of satellite garden cities separated from the
   main town by an adequate rural belt.
4. The improvement of village life and the development of agriculture by securing the better planning of villages and the close
   co-ordination of village and town life.
5. The good administration of the Housing and Town Planning
   Acts [106].

The Association promoted its cause by restating the general advantages of garden cities, and by demonstrating why they were particularly appropriate at that time. In general terms, an important
argument advanced was that garden cities were based on sound
economic principles. Proponents pointed to the crucial factor of
agricultural land values as the initial cost of development; to the
efficiency of a compact and well-designed town for industrial production (arguing that there would be very few industries requiring towns
of more than 50,000 people, shipbuilding being one example); to the
economy attached to a purpose-built transport system; and to the
easy access for supplies of fresh food. In contrast, large cities, made
even larger through accretions of garden suburbs, were expensive
and inefficient to operate. Beyond that, there were the obvious social
and environmental advantages of a planned community, and a vague
supposition that citizenship would thrive in a garden city with finite
limits [107].

Acknowledging the propagandist role of the Association in this
sphere, Professor Adshead (who certainly did not agree with all that
the Association wanted) [108], in his Presidential address to the Town
Planning Institute said that he was glad that he was not alone in
wanting to see entirely new towns in some cases, and that he was sure
that 'we shall all be interested in the work of the Garden Cities
Association (*sic*) in this direction.' [109]

As well as the general arguments, the Association was also quick to
adapt these to the specific conditions of postwar Britain. Apart from
the solution they offered in distributing the Addison houses, it was
claimed that they would also remove some of the sources of industrial
unrest. Sometimes, with a naivety that only true believers show,
particular news items were adapted to make the point. There was, for
instance, the case of a strike of 3,000 workers at the Lancing works of
the London, Brighton and South Coast Railway Company. A dispute
about travelling time, along with a similar case involving engineering
workers at Barrow, was heralded as evidence that people would not
for much longer put up with the 'discomfort, inconvenience, expense
and waste of time and energy' experienced in long journeys to work,

and that these disputes 'bring the end of suburban development within sight . . .' [110] More dramatically, a future editor of the Association's journal contemplated garden cities not as a bulwark to radical social change but as an appropriate social unit in the reconstructed society. After the revolution, he assured his readers, 'we should be ready with our garden cities, built to function and demonstrating their attractive qualities and usefulness . . . They will be cities of refuge from social chaos.' [111]

At a more pragmatic level, the Association concentrated on the immediate tasks of negotiating with successive governments to secure official support for the cause of garden cities. In this respect, the 1919 Act was itself a disappointment. It concentrated on the business of a subsidized housing programme, and although it was jointly titled Housing and Town Planning it introduced only minimal changes to the latter. Planning schemes became less cumbersome to get approved than they had been under the 1909 Act and it became obligatory for the larger authorities to prepare schemes [112], but, compared with the challenge of radical social change that was in the air at the time, the new measures were something of a lost opportunity. This was certainly the view of the Association which, apart from deploring the fact that the Government had failed to address the issue of garden cities, took a broader view of the perceived folly of building houses without a plan. Surely, it concluded, we 'simply cannot afford a huge scheme of house-building that does not proceed hand in hand with town-planning.' [113]

Small consolation came to the Association at the end of 1919, in the form of a clause in the Housing (Additional Powers) Act, to the effect that powers were now available for the public acquisition of land for garden cities. Simply enabling the acquisition of land was not enough, however, contended the Association, and the Ministry of Health itself should be empowered to take a more positive role in initiating schemes. What was more, in referring to garden suburbs and garden villages, as well as garden cities, the new legislation would simply add to the existing confusion in the public mind as to what a garden city really was [114]. To clarify things, the Association felt moved to provide its own definition, describing a garden city as

a town planned for healthy living and organised for industry, of a size that makes possible a full measure of social life, but not larger; surrounded by a rural belt; the whole of the land being in public ownership [115].

The term, 'garden city' had been in use for long enough, but, increasingly, another term, 'satellite town', came into popular usage. It had the comparable meaning of a planned settlement, but also related to the idea of a constellation, with satellites within the sphere of a central 'planet' (the planets being the major conurbations). Frederic Osborn considers that the first use of the term satellite town was in 1919, referring to the idea of a detached town, dependent on local industry and girdled by a country belt, but having economic linkages (in that case) with London [116]. In 1920, Lt. Col. F. E. Fremantle (a Member of Parliament, who became Chairman of the Council of the Association from 1921) asked the Minister of Health whether he had any plans for new satellite towns for London, and whether additional legislation would be required to do this. The Association followed the discussion keenly, disagreeing with the Minister's reply that in his opinion fresh legislation was not needed [117]. Undeterred by the Minister's rebuttal, Fremantle used the opportunity of a Government amendment to its Housing Act to propose the insertion of a clause to enable the Public Works Loan Commissioners to lend money to approved garden city companies with a limited dividend. In spite of the argument that it was 'the only specific piece of garden city legislation that Parliament has ever been asked to consider, and it could not fail to have practical results' [118], it failed to reach the statute books.

Within a few months, however, in March 1921, a new Housing Bill (the previous one having foundered) included from the outset a garden cities clause along the lines of Fremantle's earlier proposal. Although Public Utility Societies enjoyed existing powers to build houses, this clause enabled them to extend their activities into garden cities. The significance of the measure was that the 'State is now enabled for the first time to provide finance for the development of garden cities . . . It is at once taken out of the sphere of private experiment and put upon a different plane.' [119]

Understandably, the Association was quick to claim some credit for this, urging its members to write in support to their MPs, and pointing out that the proposal was for loans rather than subsidies, so that it would not add in any way to either taxes or rates. Indeed, at a time when housing policy was entering the doldrums, and economy was everywhere being sought, the garden city clause was acclaimed as a sound contribution to a national campaign of 'anti-waste' [120].

The 1921 Act was regarded as a step forward (if only in winning support from MPs of all parties), but in itself the Association rightly predicted that it would not lead to the kind of programme that was needed. For that, nothing short of direct State intervention was called for, and to that end a Memorandum was drafted by the Council of the Association, reaffirming the case for garden cities (the case now being strengthened by the contributions that new garden cities could make to the growing problem of unemployment) and appending a proposed Garden Cities General Powers Bill. In this, the Ministry of Health would have crucial powers in enabling garden city developers to acquire the land compulsorily if necessary, and at agricultural land values [121]. It was a statement of intent rather than a serious political manoeuvre, but it reflected how far the Association had come in terms of seeing the future of new town development as a function of State rather than private enterprise.

The 1921 Memorandum also reflected a conscious shift in the Association's policy, away from its 1918–1919 position of devoting most of its efforts to the Addison housing initiative (in the hope that garden cities would somehow follow). From the early 1920s the thrust of the Association's argument is reversed, with the promotion of garden cities and satellite towns as the spearhead of its approach. Thus, in the Annual Report for 1920, it is already noted that 'the housing propaganda undertaken by the Association has gradually been replaced by work of a more solid educational character in which definite emphasis has been laid upon town planning and the garden city principle.' [122] The Association was returning to its roots.

It was at this stage that in propaganda terms the Association received what proved to be an important boost to its campaign. In 1919, Neville Chamberlain, newly elected to Parliament, was appointed by Addison to chair a committee (known originally as the Slum Areas Committee, and then, more generally, as the Unhealthy Areas Committee) to look into the whole problem of slum clearance and rebuilding. Its Interim Report in 1920 (confirmed in the Final Report in the following year) included the significant recommendation that 'the development of self-contained garden cities, either round an existing nucleus or on new sites, should be encouraged and hastened by State assistance in the early stages.' [123]

Although it was not immediately acted upon it embodied the principle of planned dispersal that was to become a crucial feature of future planning strategies. In personal terms, the importance of Neville Chamberlain's attachment to this approach, given his influential role in the years ahead, has also been stressed [124]. The Committee's recommendation for garden cities was seen as a clear endorsement for the Association's policy. There were, indeed, two members of the Association on Chamberlain's Committee, namely, R. L. Reiss and G. L. Pepler, and the former at least (as Chairman of the Executive at the time), would have been active in promoting the case for garden cities from his position 'within' government. At the same time, it has to be acknowledged that Chamberlain was already an experienced reformer (at the municipal level), and 'had no need simply to be the mouthpiece of a propagandist body.' [125]

In propagandist terms, the findings of the Unhealthy Areas Committee were significant. But, as well as operating at a national level, the Association also had some success in lobbying local authorities.

At this level, their strongest influence appears to have been in London, where Herbert Morrison especialy (as Secretary to the London Labour Party, and a former resident of Letchworth) espoused the cause with enthusiasm. Even before the end of the war the Association had submitted a Memorandum to the London local authorities, sowing the seeds of the garden city idea in the great reconstruction programme that was predicted [126]. Then, as part of the *Daily Mail* Ideal Home Exhibition in February 1920, the Associ-

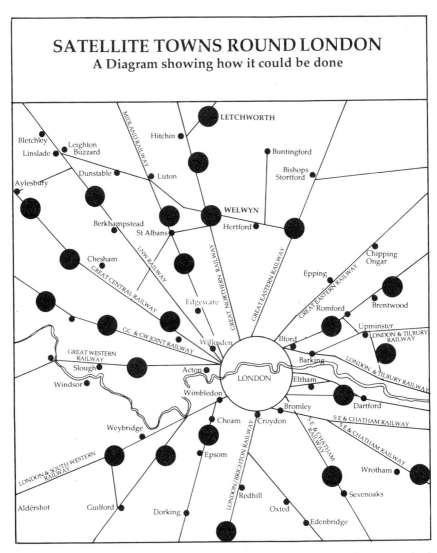

GCTPA proposal (prepared by C. B. Purdom and shown at the 1920 Ideal Home Exhibition) for satellite towns around London.

ation mounted a conference on Satellite Towns for Greater London. Purdom put the Association's case, explaining that it was because of its belief that 'housing is a much larger question than the sizes of rooms or heights of ceilings, or even the supply of building trade labour or material' that satellite towns were proposed [127].

A proposal was made for a system of twenty-three satellite towns around London (a forerunner of the Greater London Plan of 1944).

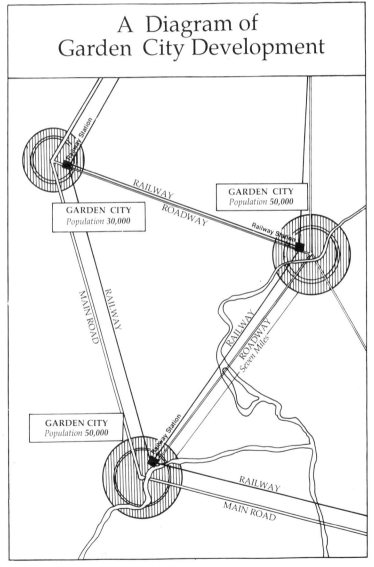

A second diagram displayed at the 1920 Ideal Home Exhibition.

Morrison responded eloquently to the proposal, asking his colleagues to 'conceive London as the sun with a whole series of planetary towns scattered round it at suitable points in the Home Counties', and urging them 'not to treat this garden city proposal as if it were a hazy idea on the summit of the Welsh mountains.' [128] But if for Purdom and Morrison the idea was already clear enough, for others it was to be another twenty years or more before the haze cleared sufficiently for general progress to be made.

The Second Garden City

Did you ever hear of Ebenezer Howard
And the little bit of land he found . . .
The owner said he'd never sell it
For less than a hundred million pound;
But Ebenezer told him that the whole estate he'd sold him,
And the green grass grew all around.
(From Frederic Osborn's 'The Green Belt Song', in
Osborn, 1959, p. 99)

The above verse, written by Frederic Osborn for the children of Welwyn Garden City, conveys a sense of the impishness that surrounded the formation of the new town. The year 1919 was a fearful one, with industrial unrest and talk of revolution, but there was Howard pacing the fields of Hertfordshire as if these were still the golden days of an Edwardian summer. The world had changed since the pioneers had broken the soil at Letchworth, and while the GCTPA retained the aim of more garden cities at the top of its agenda it no longer seemed appropriate to rely on individualistic acts to achieve it. But Howard, the gentle idealist, loyal to the cause but somehow oblivious to the dictates of history, simply went off and did it his way. The formation of Welwyn was, in itself, a remarkable achievement, and, in retrospect, may have been the most effective way of demonstrating the value of new towns to the nation. At the time, though, it seemed to run counter to the drift of the Association's own priorities, drawing away some of its key campaigners in the process.

Howard's apparent waywardness stemmed from a healthy enough disbelief in the immediate likelihood of a government programme of building garden cities: '. . . if you wait for the Government to do it you will be as old as Methuselah before they start.' [129] But if Howard was impatient it was not simply with the laggardliness of governments. His action during the war in banding together with Purdom, Osborn and Taylor to form the National Garden Cities Committee reflected some impatience, too, with the inability of the

GCTPA to move beyond Letchworth. But even his collaborators in the breakaway group had not realized that Howard was about to take matters into his own hands. Purdom and Osborn recall that towards the end of 1918 the two of them were led by Howard around a stretch of farmland that all had observed many times before from the train to King's Cross.

Howard's companions agreed that it was a possible site to bear in mind, 'but we did not contemplate proposing a specific scheme for a town on it.' [130] And, certainly, the Association was not involved at this stage. At the end of 1918 it was more concerned with the promise of radical housing legislation on a national scale.

Entirely on his own initiative, in April 1919, Howard made a direct approach to the owner of some of the land, Lord Salisbury (who was also, significantly, President of the GCTPA) to see if he would be willing to sell part of his estate to support a scheme for a second garden city. Extracts from the ensuing correspondence are worth quoting, if only to illustrate at first the naive but disarming honesty of the approach, and then (as at Letchworth) the importance attached to gaining the support of a respectable group of gentlemen with sound business connections to underwrite the scheme [131].

30th April 1919

My Lord,

As I intimated to your Lordship in my very short interview I have a matter of very great national importance to lay before you . . . The site that I had in mind when writing this letter lies on both sides of the Great Northern Railway a little to the North of Hatfield Station . . .

I remember with how much real feeling you spoke (at a meeting of the Royal Sanitary Institute) of the call there is on every one of us to serve our country in this difficult and critical juncture, and am persuaded that if you were once convinced that by selling such portion of this site as may belong to you and as may be necessary for the purpose at a fair price you would greatly aid in the solution of many difficult problems . . .

I remember, too, a remark you made about the great value of private enterprise, and that in this connection you referred with much appreciation to the Garden City movement in its relation to Housing. In that remark I was one of the few present who agreed with you. For I believe most fervently that private enterprise when it is pervaded by public spirit can accomplish really marvellous things – by putting into operation spiritual forces which have not yet reached far enough down among the constituent elements of

Society to permit of things being done by the State which in a democratic country implies that the Nation is ready for them . . .

Surely, if financial steps towards the carrying out of such an enterprise are taken by private individuals who can act much more quickly than could the slow-moving machinery of the Government, then it will be possible to unite all classes together in the realisation of a great and beneficial aim. Afterwards what has been wisely begun may be carried out more completely by other forms of administrative machinery and a great and wide-spread National movement will follow in due course . . .

1st May 1919

Dear Mr. Ebenezer Howard

. . . I had not any inkling that there was any such suggestion on foot and I need not tell you that it is a matter of such great importance to me that this reply must be of a purely preliminary character.

I need not go into the general question. You know that I am very much interested in the Garden City method of development to which I have publicly testified on many occasions but its application to particular sites requires of course very careful investigation in detail . . . I have as you will imagine considered the residential development of my Hertfordshire Estate to some extent but the idea which has been in my mind is the development to the South of Hatfield rather than to the North . . . if you thought it worthwhile let me know whether there is any reason why the land to the North of Hatfield is preferable to the land to the South.

4th May 1919

Dear Lord Salisbury

. . . I think there are strong and sufficient reasons for greatly preferring, for the purpose I have in mind, the land to the North . . . I will, in another letter if it will interest you, suggest what appear to me to be some of the chief lessons to be learned from Letchworth and show why much more rapid and much finer results should issue out of that experience and from the greater inherent advantages of the site, as well as from recent changes which have arisen in public opinion and practice.

23rd May 1919

Dear Mr. Howard

I need not tell you that I have not allowed your suggestion to me to be absent from my thoughts for a single day . . . I am afraid however that I cannot give you a favourable reply . . . I do not say that under no circumstances would I favourably entertain a proposal to sell land to the North of Hatfield on a large scale for the purpose of the erection of a Garden City but it would be useless to consider the matter further until I had become convinced that I was acting in harmony with the wishes of the great body of those upon whose enterprise and business capacity the success hitherto of the movement has depended. I know of course of your wish and you are indeed a very notable example amongst the pioneers of the movement but in a matter of business even so distinguished a representative of garden city progress would not be sufficient. I do not think it would be reasonable (to proceed) . . . unless a firm proposal by those who have control of the business part of the Garden City movement were put forward.

Coincidentally, at the same time as the above correspondence, Howard received details of the proposed sale at the end of May of Lord Desborough's adjoining Panshanger Estate which, in fact, included the greater part of the land in which Howard was interested [132]. Once again (as at Letchworth) Howard turned to wealthy industrial philanthropists for most of the £5,000 deposit that he needed for the auction on the 30th May [133]. An area of nearly 1700 acres was bought, the nucleus of the garden city, but Salisbury had to be approached again to secure some of his estate as well. The terms of any fresh negotiations had been laid out in Salisbury's letter of the 23rd May, and (in spite of another false start occasioned by Howard's indiscretion) [134] a credible group was soon assembled – as a pioneer company, Second Garden City Ltd. At the head of the list was J. R. Farquharson (an industrialist with his own firm, and also a director of Letchworth Cottages and Buildings Ltd. and of the Howard Cottage Society Ltd.) [135], Lt. Col. F. E. Fremantle (a member of the London County Council, and consulting Medical Officer of Health for Hertfordshire), Walter Layton (the distinguished economist, later Lord Layton), Capt. R. L. Reiss (Chairman of the GCTPA Executive Committee, and a member of the Government Advisory Housing Committee), H. Bolton Smart (a Director of First Garden City Ltd.), C. B. Purdom (who was by then Secretary of the GCTPA), and Howard. It was intimated that others would be invited to join the first Board of Directors of the new Garden City Company.

The line-up seemed to satisfy Salisbury this time, and, in October 1919, 700 acres from Salisbury's estate were added to the initial purchase of 1700 acres, together with an extra 250 acres bought from Lord Desborough after the auction [136].

Meanwhile, the hunt was on to augment the initial seven members of the Company with others of money and influence. Osborn recalls that he and Howard approached J. Ramsay Macdonald, and 'treated the future Prime Minister to a frugal lunch at an ABC teashop in Holborn' [137], but he declined to join the board as he thought he might attract too much controversy. He suggested another leading Labour MP, J. R. Clynes, who was keen to accept, except that his trade union would have none of it, contending that its members had no part to play as directors of capitalist enterprises. The aristocracy, however, had no such qualms, and Lord Lytton (the second Earl) willingly joined, only to leave for India within a few months (though, on returning, he became President of the GCTPA from 1929 to 1947). Others enlisted at this time were Samuel Smethurst (described as a successful builder in the North of England), and Sir John Mann (a leading Scottish accountant). The main coup, though, was to attract Sir Theodore G. Chambers, KBE, a surveyor by background, with experience in estate administration, a director of companies in Africa and Asia, and Controller of the National Savings Committee during the war. 'An undoubted Tory in every fibre of his being' [138], he became Chairman of the Company in November 1919, championing the cause as 'a patriotic enterprise of the first order' [139], and, not least of all, using his personal influence with the Chairman of the Midland Bank to secure an immediate overdraft for the Company of £100,000. Thus was the second garden city born, a product of energy, idealism and influence [140].

These events left the GCTPA in something of an ambiguous position. On the one hand, although some of its leading members were responsible for the venture, the Association had not itself campagined directly for Welwyn. Indeed, one view is that it was at that time 'dead against any more garden cities being started by private enterprise.' [141] On the other hand, the exercise was entirely consistent with its general aims, and as a propagandist body there was undoubtedly political capital to be gained through publicizing the experiment. Establishing a second garden city was not what it had chosen to do at that particular time, nor in that way, but now that it had happened there was valuable work to be done.

For the Association, the main opportunity was to promote Welwyn as a demonstration project for a Government and local authorities in the process of finding ways to implement the 1919 Act. In this way, underlying tensions between Howard's private initiative approach and the Association's new found trust in the State were eased. The

Welwyn pioneers themselves saw it this way, declaring that the object of the company was to build Welwyn 'as an illustration of the right way to provide for the expansion of the industries and population of a great city . . . It is urgently necessary that a convincing demonstration of the garden city principle of town development shall be given in time to influence the national housing programme.' [142] In its own reports, the Association endorsed this view, giving no indication of a basic policy rift. Welwyn was presented, not just as a general model for the 1919 Act to follow, but, particularly, as a direct contribution to the campaign for satellite towns around London. While it was likened to Letchworth, it was also pointed out that Welwyn had been located to encourage firms needing to be near London to move there. It was the first of the proposed satellites, and it was hoped that 'the establishment of the new garden city will lead the way to a series of such towns in the Home Counties.' [143]

As a demonstration project, Welwyn was firmly rooted in garden city principles. What was proposed was a self-contained town with a population of 40,000 to 50,000 living close to their work and to social, recreational and civic needs. Firms were encouraged to move to Welwyn with the promise of 'healthy and well-equipped factories . . . grouped in scientific relation to transport facilities.' [144] The freehold was to be retained in the company's ownership in trust for the future community, and an agricultural belt would be permanently reserved around the town. In its crucial elements it was comparable to Letchworth, but Welwyn could build on the experience of the first garden city and, significantly, it could take advantage of the new housing legislation to provide accommodation. Howard (for all his distrust of the State) was glad to note that Addison 'has written expressing great interest in our scheme and a desire to assist it, and there is every reason to suppose that the local authorities, with the support of the Ministry of Health, will provide houses for the workers as soon as they are satisfied that industries are coming to the new town.' [145] The first houses were, in fact, built at the end of the 1920s, and by 1945 the population had reached a figure of 18,000.

Like Letchworth, Welwyn attracted plenty of publicity, and as a result of one scheme (that of building a model village as part of the *Daily Mail* Ideal Home Exhibition) it was known for some years as the '*Daily Mail* town' [146]. Welwyn put the whole garden city movement under the spotlight once again, and the Association was in no doubt that the success of the new project was essential to its own success on a wider front. Indeed (perhaps influenced by diminishing hopes in the Addison Act, and coming round to Howard's view that the State was not going to launch a major garden city initiative) the Association underwent an extraordinary transformation in claiming credit for the whole experiment.

Although it had been Howard, acting independently (though with the help of others, notably Osborn and Purdom), who had been responsible for the formation of the Second Garden City Company, in 1920 the Association claimed that it had itself 'promoted this comapny'. More accurately, in the same statement, the Association took credit for having given 'help to the scheme in its initial stages.' [147] But a year later, in 1921, the rewriting of history had been completed, and the Annual Report records that the 'initiative of Welwyn Garden City was directly due to the work of the Association . . .' [148]

In a way, of course, the Association's interpretation of events is not as misleading as it seems. Led by Howard, the initial promoters of the scheme were all themselves leading members of the Association, the difference being that they were acting independently and along lines of their own choosing. The Association was undoubtedly

Above and opposite: Posters extolling the virtues of the second garden city. (By courtesy of the Central Library, Welwyn).

weakened by this diversion of energy when so much else was going on nationally, and while Welwyn was indeed to serve its purpose as a demonstration of garden cities, it remains questionable whether the timing was as helpful as it might have been. While the likes of Purdom and Osborn battled with the sticky ground and even stickier finances at Welwyn, the Association failed to make much of an impression in the national housing campaign between 1919 and 1921, and then rather seems to slip into a somnolent phase in the middle 1920s. There was plenty happening at Welwyn in the 1920s, but, perhaps not without coincidence, far less in the Association's offices at Gray's Inn.

COMING OF AGE

In 1920 the Association had been in existence for twenty-one years. As a sign of its growing maturity, it was consulted by various bodies (including Government) as a leading housing and town planning reform group. Some of its own pioneers had secured for themselves a place in the new planning 'Establishment' of professional and government officials. It had two garden cities to its name, and the concept embodied in Howard's original book continued to attract international interest. Yet, in other respects, the Association carried on much as before, bereft of funds, appealing for more members, writing letters to the 'great and the good', and tirelessly touring the country to win the hearts and minds of the British public.

Organization and Finance

The Garden Cities and Town Planning Association will celebrate its twenty-first anniversary this year. It is desired to make the event an occasion for increasing the membership to 5,000. With the programme that the Association has, affecting as it does all classes of people throughout the whole country, it should not be difficult to reach that result . . . (In a note headed 'The Five Thousand', *GCTP*, Vol. X, No. 1, January 1920, p. 2.)

The Association's coming of age in 1920 was an obvious occasion for taking stock and urging its members to greater things. The occasion, not without some cause for celebration, was marked by an anniversary dinner at the Criterion Restaurant in London. One hundred and thirty members and guests attended (including representatives of the Ministry of Health and old allies in the campaign for better housing, like the National Housing and Town Planning Council and the Royal Institute of British Architects), and speeches were made acknowledging the building of two garden cities to date and the need and promise of more [149].

The truth was that, behind the glitter of ceremonial dinners and the esteem of deputations to government ministries, the Association remained a small and impecunious body. It enjoyed a shortlived surge of support immediately after the war, at the height of the National Housing Campaign, but in the early 1920s the level of support fell back again. It was one thing to mark its twenty-first anniversary with an appeal for 5000 members, but even in its best years the highest number reached fell far short of that, albeit 'representing all classes of society.' [150] The evidence suggests that subscriptions were gratefully handed to the Association's organizers in meeting halls when radical housing reform was on the agenda, only to lapse with disappointed hopes in the following years. Thus, in the early 1920s, membership totals stabilized at around 500 [151].

Regular appeals were made (in the Annual Reports and in special notes in the journal), urging existing members to bring in at least one new member, but without any great success. The problem was not simply a lack of numbers for its own sake as a source of political influence (though that was important enough), so much as a source of funding. Faced with annual deficits, subscriptions were raised in 1920 from the figure of 7s. 6d. that members had been paying since the war to a new total of 10s. 6d., and then in the following year it was doubled to 21s.

Even this was regarded as a minimum, and there was a constant effort to supplement the basic subscription income with donations and legacies. £860 was raised in this way in 1918, and (with the help of the Joseph Rowntree Trust) £2600 in 1919, at the height of the Association's National Housing Campaign. But in 1920 a special appeal for donations to prevent a deficit at the end of the year yielded only £75 [152]. 'The Association's work means social economics', claimed the Treasurer, but the financial situation remained parlous [53]. As the nation's housing policy entered the doldrums and Welwyn attracted less national publicity the situation became worse. In 1923 a deficit of about £287 was recorded, and it was all too easy to blame the general public for not coming forward 'for the furtherance of the most constructive social policy of the day.' [154]

The declining fortunes of the Association in the early 1920s were reflected in staff cuts. In its heyday in 1919 and 1920, as well as temporary local organizers for the National Housing Campaign, there was a paid Secretary and an Assistant Secretary supported by a small team comprising Mr H. Chapman (who was responsible for the library, exhibition and tours), Mr A. T. Pike (who organized the lectures and conferences) and Miss Browning (who managed the new Women's Section, formed in 1920). Progressively, for reasons of economy, the team was reduced. Miss Browning's position in charge of the Women's Section appears only to have been temporary, and Mr Pike moved into the vacant post of Assistant Secretary, taking with him his previous job of organizing lectures and conferences. Reflecting the gravity of the situation the Annual Report for 1922 opens with the statement that 'the past year has of necessity been one of consolidation rather than of extension of work. The staff of the Association has been reduced more stringently than the volume of work performed has justified.' [155]

There were also important changes of personnel. At a time of internal difficulties, the Association could not have been helped by successive changes in the post of Secretary. Ewart Culpin left in 1918 'to pursue his commercial and professional interests in connection with industrial housing.' [156] He had been in the post since Thomas Adams left in 1906, and had been instrumental in guiding the

Association along the broad path of 'garden city housing' as opposed simply to garden cities. This was not to everyone's liking, not least of all his successor, C. B. Purdom, who recalls that he took over when the Association 'had been practically moribund for a long time', and that with his own coming it 'was thus galvanised into new life.' [157]

Culpin had, in fact, been a very active Secretary (not least of all on the international front), and Purdom's disparaging comment could only have been referring to the fact that, in his opinion, the Association had been led up a blind alley. A broad-based housing reform movement was based on well-meant but misplaced logic. He was himself in no doubt that the Association stood for garden cities, and that everything should be directed to that central purpose. To that end, it was Purdom who claimed to have recruited R. L. Reiss to the Chairmanship of the Executive Committee. Reiss had previously worked at the Ministry of Reconstruction, and it was largely through him (as a close friend of Seebohm Rowntree) that funds from the Joseph Rowntree Trust had been allocated to the Association for their National Housing Campaign [158]. He was not at that stage totally committed to garden cities as the only way forward, but Purdom saw strengths in Reiss and so set about converting him. 'I succeeded', concluded Purdom [159], and to the extent that both men threw their energies into Welwyn perhaps it was a justified claim. Purdom resigned his post in 1921, to be succeeded by W. Mc G. Eagar, who had been working for the previous two years as an inspector at the London Housing Board of the Ministry of Health. He, in turn, left after three years, 'which is perhaps a respectable period for anyone so full of energy and ability' [160], and A. T. Pike (who had started with the Association as a Regional Organizer in the National Housing Campaign) was promoted from his job as lecture and conference organizer to become the new Secretary (a post he retained until 1936).

In other ways, too, it was an unsettled period. One of the costs of coming of age was that some of the early firebrands had run out of steam, and, more poignantly, obituaries had become a regular news item in the journal [161]. Howard now spent most of his time at Letchworth (his home) and Welwyn, Thomas Adams was building on his reputation in North America, and Raymond Unwin was tackling housing and town planning on a broader front than the single cause of garden cities. Although he had not been active in the Association for several years, the death of Ralph Neville in 1918 also marked the end of the beginning in the organization's history. Howard penned a suitable appreciation for the journal, recalling Neville's pioneering work, and describing him as 'an evolutionist in the best sense of the word.' [162] Neville's contribution in setting the Association on a sound footing and in helping to launch Letchworth was rightly acknowledged, but perhaps no less significant was the style of patronage and influence that he imposed on the Association. This was something that was to mark its approach long after he had himself departed, and which cannot fail to have had a subtle but lasting effect on both the policies and politics of the Association in the years ahead [163].

There is also a sense in which the character of the organization was reflected, if not reinforced, in a decision about its accommodation. Throughout this period it remained in genteel surroundings at 3 Gray's Inn Place (premises that had originally been made available through the Association's strong legal contacts), and the view onto 'the lawn, the plane trees and broad undeviating walks of Gray's Inn

The Association's genteel surroundings in Gray's Inn Place were contrasted with the poor conditions that many for whom it campaigned endured.

Gardens' was greatly appreciated by the staff [164]. The quality of environment was not, however, taken for granted. 'Our staff is small; our work is generally heavy. But we owe too much to the peace and beauty of our immediate surroundings to ignore the effects of uproar and squalor on the life and work of others whose homes and workplaces give on to mean and crowded streets.' [165] Perhaps, though, the genteel surroundings were overvalued, for, in September 1924, when the lease was due for renewal, the Association rejected an opportunity to move to another part of London where it could share accommodation with 'certain societies which exist for policies sympathetic to our aims, and are staffed by officials whose companionship would be delightful.' [166] Although the other societies are not specified it is interesting to speculate that an alternative decision about accommodation, placing it alongside other groups, might well have influenced the course of development of the Association. Speculation aside, the Association stayed where it was, paid a higher rent, and was forced once again to appeal to its members for donations and new subscriptions.

There is another sense, too, in which the Association appears to have added to its own difficulties. For a small organization, with its staff constantly under pressure, it maintained what can only be seen as a cumbersome committee structure. At the peak of the elaborate hierarchy were the nominal posts of President and a panoply of Vice Presidents. Below that was the Council, for which fresh elections were held each year, and which in the early 1920s had in the region of fifty members (with others joining through cooptions). In turn, this was supported by an Executive Committee of some fourteen members, and a varying pattern of sub-committees. In relation to what was achieved (remembering that the one tangible achievement in this period, namely, the formation of Welwyn, was largely the result of efforts undertaken outside the main organization) it must remain questionable, however, as to whether this was necessarily the best way to proceed. If the Association was seeking to infiltrate the corridors of power, one is left with the view that a great deal of effort was expended without really getting beyond the antechambers.

If, however, one is critical of the overall structure, there is no doubt that the officers worked tirelessly for their cause, nor that some of the sectional work of the Association is particularly worthy of note. Two examples are those to do with the Women's Section and the work of the branches. Of the former, the Women's Section was formed in 1920, as a direct outcome of a conference of women's organizations initiated by the Association in February 1920, as part of the *Daily Mail* Ideal Home Exhibition. The conference was clearly designed to demonstrate the importance of a woman's perspective in the great housing debate. There were five sessions during the day, on 'The Planning of the Home', 'Labour Saving Kitchens', 'Central Hot Water Systems and Central Heating', 'Communal Arrangements' and 'The Need for Women on Housing Committees' [167]. Some 600 women attended, and at a subsequent conference at the Association's offices in May 1920 a Women's Section was formed [168].

The objective of the new group was reported as being to provide information on women's work on housing committees, and to enable the Association to act as a central bureau of information on housing and town planning for women's organizations throughout the country. It was chaired by Lady Emmott, and the following societies affiliated – Association of Women's Home Property Managers, Federation of Women's Village Councils, London Society for Women's Service, Women's Political and Industrial League, Women's Local Government Society, National Baby Week Council, Queen Victoria's Institute for Nurses, Rural Housing Association, Fabian Society Women's Group, and the Women's Imperial Health Association [169].

The Women's Section lost no time in gaining the support of Lady Astor, MP, and, on a practical front, in preparing comments on house designs published by the Ministry of Health in 1920. A questionnaire was circulated to obtain information about the best kind of labour-saving devices for new houses. Assistance was given to a scheme of the Women's Village Councils for the improvement of sanitary conditions in rural areas. And a report was prepared and publicized to promote the role of women as property managers [170]. A further progress report in 1923 shows that the work of the Women's Section was by then concentrating on internal house design and new gadgets on the market – an American gas cooker and electrical fittings attracting special attention [171]. Important though this was, there is no evidence of what might have been a more radical role in shaping housing policy, and in March 1924 it was reported that 'the necessity of a separate section comprised of women's organisations no longer exists.' [172]

In terms of regional activity, this does not appear to have been as vigorous as it was in the period before 1914. However, there is some evidence of active branches, particularly in Manchester (where there had for long been a strong base) and Bristol. As with the Women's Section the most active period coincides with that of the greatest national interest in housing issues, after which the level of activity wanes. Thus, in November 1920 the Annual Meeting of the North-western Branch at Manchester could look back on a busy year, with over a hundred public lectures, weekend conferences on town planning and housing, and a Regional Town Planning (*sic*) conference addressed by Professor Abercrombie and Ebenezer Howard amongst others. Discussions were opened with Manchester Corporation, proposing that the Wythenshawe estate be developed as a satellite town rather than as a suburb [173].

Similarly, in Bristol, 1919 was an active time, with a branch formed in May and a full programme of meetings and conferences to discuss the 1919 housing legislation. Breaking with a tradition of male-dominated branch committees, the Bristol Chairman (*sic*) was Miss Hilda Cashmere, with Mrs R. Burman and Mrs G. A. Falk as Hon. Secretaries. All three were, in turn, members of the Bristol Women's Advisory Housing Committee, and it is significant that women's organizations feature in the branch's lecture programme [174]. There is evidence that the branch continued in business after 1920 (in 1922, for instance, lobbying candidates in local elections), but it is unlikely that its meetings continued to attract the same level of interest that was reported when the branch was formed. If there is a broader lesson to draw from this it is that pressure groups ride high on the crest of a wave, but making waves in the first place is a different matter. The Association and its sectional interests were undoubtedly buoyed up by the great wave of housing reform in 1919 and 1920, but suffered badly when the wave broke in the early 1920s. Although there was important work to be done, it was to be some years before the Association rode high again.

Politics and Propaganda

The Garden Cities and Town Planning Association has been given by Sir Oswald Stoll the free use of the Alhambra Theatre . . . to give an exhibition of cinema films of Letchworth, Hampstead, Well Hall, Gretna, Port Sunlight and Bournville . . . In view of the great interest of the Royal Family in the problem of Housing, I have been requested through your Lordship to invite the King, the Queen and the Prince of Wales, as well as other members of the Royal Family, to be present. Naturally, if they are able to do this, they will be aiding us in a very marked degree in the carrying on of our work. (Letter dated 5th May 1919, from Howard to The Rt. Hon. the Lord Stamfordham, Buckingham Palace, Howard Papers, Folio 25)

Although the King and Queen did not attend the above event, the Prince of Wales did. From the inception of the Association (or, at least, from the time of Neville's involvement), importance had been attached to gaining the seal of Establishment approval for its work. The panoply of one hundred or more Vice Presidents, a cross section of the 'great and the good', was one way in which this was achieved.

But to extend the influence of the Association, Howard, above all, was tireless in writing letters to the powerful in the land, inviting their support through attendance at a dinner, through a note of support that could then be cited, and through donations to a worthy cause.

In 1921, for instance, Howard wrote personal letters in search of funds for the Welwyn venture, and, again, in 1923 when 'the Garden City Association (*sic*) is in very low water.' [175] On neither occasion does the success rate appear to have been very high. Sometimes, replies were simply polite but evasive. J. J. Astor sidestepped the request by wishing Howard well in his forthcoming 'mission to the Riviera.' [176]

Edward Cadbury wrote from Bournville, simply affirming that he was already a subscriber to the Association [177]. On other occasions Howard's letters touched a raw nerve, revealing the impecunity of the correspondent, like Wedgwood Benn, who wished Howard well but lamented 'I am not in touch with anyone of means, that is my difficulty.' [178] George Bernard Shaw was characteristically more forthright: 'Nothing doing, alas! Do you expect me to build Garden Cities on £4.10.0 a year? Let this illiterate country perish: it does not deserve your efforts.' [179] There was always the chance, too, that asking a favour would elicit a reciprocal request. H. G. Wells penned a footnote to Howard, urging 'I wish you would join the Fabian Society.' [180] It was, as Wells surely knew, a forlorn hope, with Howard by then in his seventies more entrenched than ever in his view that putting one's trust in the State was not the best way forward.

If winning friends in high places was one strategy, it was, at the same time, always seen to be important to tread carefully on the tightrope of impartiality. This had been an axiom of Howard's book, namely, that the idea of the garden city could appeal to a spectrum of political persuasions, and the Association had consistently sought to distance itself from any one sphere of influence. In an article in 1920 it was claimed that the Association had, in fact, been successful in this respect:

> avoiding attachment to any one of the great political parties which contend for power in the State. It would have been fatal to the success of the movement, as it is, obviously to so many others, if in the minds of the public it had been hitched to a party star – even of the greatest magnitude. No such star is safe enough in its course, or sure enough of its destiny, to pilot the movement to the haven we wish it to reach [181].

Compared with the pre-1914 period, however, the rise of the Labour Party as a new force in British politics posed the Association with something of a dilemma. On the one hand, the Association could not forget 'the chill effect of Fabian logic on successive waves of idealists', and the fact that the 'Socialists have left community schemes alone for decades in order to concentrate upon the effort to conquer governmental institutions . . .' [182] Yet, on the other hand, it was the Labour Party, at the local level (through politicians like Herbert Morrison) as well as at the national level, that was most receptive to the ideas that the Association was promoting. The Association, then, was drawn towards the party that stood for State intervention, but at the same time it was at pains to demonstrate that its attachments remained broad-based. Thus, in explaining the rationale for Welwyn, Purdom was keen to encourage his socialist audience that the scheme 'should go far enough to satisfy the modern socialist', while at the same time assuring more timorous souls that 'there is nothing revolutionary, nothing subversive of society, in the principle upon which the garden city is based.' [183] Some years later, in 1924, in a submission to the then Labour Minister of Health, the Association was keen to point to the strength of Labour support (citing the Chairman of the Executive, R. L. Reiss, and two members of the Council, W. Graham, MP and G. D. H. Cole, as Party members), and recalling the Party Conference resolution in January 1918 which had endorsed a garden city policy. But it was also careful (no doubt with an eye on the precarious state of the Minority Government in 1924) to demonstrate that it enjoyed support from other parties too. The President, Cecil Harmsworth, was an eminent Liberal politician, and the late Aneurin Williams (who was at one time Chairman of First Garden City Ltd) had also been a Liberal MP. As for the Conservatives, the Chairman of the GCTPA Council, Col. F. E. Fremantle, was a Tory MP, and the Association also cited the supportive work of Neville Chamberlain (in his role as Chairman of the Unhealthy Areas Committee) to argue the case for their bipartisanship [184].

Eschewing party patronage, then, the Association promoted itself as 'an educational body, doing work that had produced great results in the past and will produce great results in the future.' [185] Most of this work was based on well-tried propaganda techniques, but the Association was also proud to offer for hire its own 'cinematograph films', featuring scenes of 'garden city housing' (as opposed to just garden cities). A more traditional resource was its classified collection of lantern slides, of which 'no less than ten sets are always out, and others are available to illustrate any aspect of housing, town planning, and the garden city.' [186] The Association also offered access to its Library, with 'probably the most useful collection of its kind available in the country.' [187] The student of housing and town planning should not take a narrow view, urged the Association, and to enable the broadest of studies its collection was organized into the categories of: Garden Cities, Town Planning, Housing, Transport and Traffic, Health and Sanitation, Parks, Rural, Legal, Textbooks, Periodicals, and General Social. A reputation was also gained for what was termed its Information Bureau, an enquiry service based on the Association's growing expertise in the housing and planning field.

With the ending of war, the journal appeared monthly on a regular basis again, progressively adopting a more reflective approach, with articles on town planning experience in history and overseas, rather than more of a news bulletin style that marked its early editions. It still carried some business news as well, however, and the editorials pursued a campaigning role, determined in their aims but moderate in tone. A comparison was made with the more strident editorials of *The Municipal Journal*, where headings such as 'A Useless Ministry', 'The Absurd Ministry', and 'The Moribund Ministry' were a product, it was surmised, of the fact that it was by then into its thirtieth volume [188]. The editors of *GCTP* chose not to do things this way, reflecting the Association's long-term interest in spreading the gospel without giving offence [189].

If it was the journal which most consistently presented the public face of the Association, there were other ways, too, in which it sought to tell the world about garden cities. Material had been prepared for exhibitions in the prewar period and while this practice continued in a similar way, a new opportunity arose through Associated Newspapers' invitation for the Association to present its wares at successive *Daily Mail* Ideal Home Exhibitions. Starting from 1920, garden city propaganda enjoyed an annual exposure to national publicity. At the first of these events, the Association was granted the use of the Conference Room at the London Olympia, and three conferences were arranged during the duration of the main exhibition. Two years later, in 1922, a far more ambitious programme included daily conferences for most of March, with topics ranging from 'Labour saving fittings for the small house' to 'Open spaces for city dwellers' [190].

Probably, though, the most characteristic propaganda technique was still that of public lectures. At the time of the National Housing Campaign, extra lectures were recruited through special training schools. In April and May 1919, for instance, prospective lecturers attended schools (each lasting for several days) at Newcastle, Oxford, Cardiff and Exeter, to be briefed by the likes of R. L. Reiss, Raymond Unwin and C. B. Purdom on the needs and nuances of housing policy [191]. The demand for lectures at that time was at its peak, with more than 500 engagements in 300 towns during 1919. By the early 1920s, when public interest had subsided, the number of lectures settled down to an annual total of about 100. Reflecting the

Association's critical view of successive governments in treating housing policy almost in isolation from broader issues, a theme of their work in this period was that of educational work in town planning. Programmes of lectures were arranged through the London County Council and the Workers' Educational Association, amongst others, and the Association explained why it was particularly well-suited to raise public awareness of town planning principles: 'That educational work can better be done by a voluntary organisation than a State department. It can be done more efficiently, more economically, and with greater freedom by such a body.' [192] Reinforcing its concern for getting across the message of planning, the Association later produced a leaflet, 'Town-Planning: what it is and why it is needed' (opening with the timely claim that town planning is a means of saving, not spending, money) [193].

The Association's lecturers trod a well-worn path around the meeting halls speaking to political organizations, women's groups, and evening institutes. Courses were offered at different times at the London School of Economics, and at University of London Summer Schools. But those that were most highly valued were the lectures to Rotary Clubs. 'The Executive Committee considers that it is of supreme importance that the business community should understand the industrial and economic importance of town-planning, and the Rotary Club audiences, consisting as they do of representative business men, give a great opportunity for effective educational work.' [194] The sound business bases of town and regional planning was to be an important argument promoted by the Association in the years ahead, particularly when the Government came to consider new towns as part of official policy.

Overseas Relations

Great as was the need of a vast extension of garden city enterprise before the war, that need had now become intensified. Vast fields of destruction were calling loudly for reparation, and the vital necessities of life, of which there was such a terrible shortage throughout Europe, demanded the widest acceptance of garden city principles . . . the International Association would be found an ally of tremendous power and value to the League of Nations. (Report of the Presidential Address by Ebenezer Howard to the Conference of the IGCTPA, February 1920)

Appropriately, the first international gathering after the war to invoke the role of garden city planning in Europe's reconstruction was held in Belgium [195]. The conference in September 1919 was arranged jointly by the Belgian hosts, L'Union des Villes et Communes Belges and the IGCTPA. A delegation of twenty-five members from England was amongst those who toured the battlefields of western Flanders, and who saw amidst the devastation the true need for reconstruction. Howard made 'a short but inspiring speech' [196], committing himself to the cause of an International Garden City in Belgium as a living memorial to all that had been lost in the war. With plans for the League of Nations close to fruition, it was a time when talk of international collaboration was warmly received.

In the following year, the postwar revival of the International Association was marked by its own conference, attended by some 150 delegates from around the world. The conference was accommodated at London's Olympia, as part of the *Daily Mail* Ideal Home Exhibition [197]. Papers were presented on a range of topics, but the event which was to test the loyalties of the organization was a letter from the Austro-German Garden City Association asking for affiliation, and another from the officials of the original German Association calling for the restoration of old relations. Howard hoped that recent wounds could be healed, but French and Belgian delegates asked for a little more time, at least to allow for some progress with rebuilding. A decision was deferred for the time being, but in a spirit which encouraged the view that the International Association was giving a lead, not simply in the advancement of town planning, but also in international relations [198]. Within a few months, in June 1920, the two General Secretaries of the International Association (Culpin and Purdom) travelled to Cologne to meet with officials of the German Garden City Association to pave the way for an early return of the organization that had been a source of strength in the movement before the war [199].

In other respects, too, it seemed as if the intention was to turn the clock back. The International Association was still administered from the offices of the GCTPA, and the officers elected in 1920 were all from Britain. Howard continued in the post of President, with G. Montagu Harris as Chairman, Raymond Unwin as Treasurer, and Ewart Culpin and C. B. Purdom sharing the secretarial post. It was an arrangement that had served well enough in launching the movement in the first place, and in getting it restarted after the war, but by the early 1920s strains were beginning to show. Purdom recalls that the British executive 'wanted to keep the international as a mere extension of its activities (at home), to be conducted for its advantage, which did not fit in with my ideas or with those of some of the more prominent continental members, who felt there was a place for a genuine international housing and town-planning body.' [200] As a result, the hold of the British organization was gradually loosened. In 1922 the International Association acquired its own office (still at 3,

Gray's Inn Place, but now separated from the GCTPA), and a full-time Organizing Secretary was appointed (described 'as the least internationally minded of men') [201]. The name of the organization was amended to that of The International Garden Cities and Town Planning Federation. In the following year, Montagu Harris was replaced as Chairman by a Frenchman, Henri Sellier, though most of the original British contingent continued to serve in an honorary capacity. In 1929 another link with the past was severed when the organization changed its name again to that of the International Federation for Housing and Town Planning.

During the 1930s it seems to have suffered from the turbulence of European politics, and by 1936 Purdom (who had remained until then in the honorary capacity) concluded that 'the federation passed back into a nominal phase of existence, the Germans secured control, removed the central office to Brussels, but allowed the British to hold presidential and other positions . . .' [202]

Although, compared with the early days when Culpin ran the two organizations almost single-handed from the same office, the GCTPA no longer retained this degree of control, internationalism was to remain a distinctive feature of the British Association. Culpin, Howard and others had performed a valuable role in strengthening the international basis of the movement, but it was right and proper that the new organization should, in its own time, seek autonomy. The GCTPA continued, however, throughout the 1920s and 1930s with an active overseas programme, sending speakers to international conferences, hosting foreign visitors on traditional pilgrimages to Letchworth and Welwyn, and arranging overseas tours for their own members [203]. The organizational framework had changed, but the pioneering spirit and missionary zeal of those early years had certainly not been extinguished.

TOWN AND COUNTRY

An important context for the work of the Association in the interwar period is the great 'explosion' of urban development and activities, in the form of suburban extensions and the recreational use of the countryside. Described in the Association's own terms as the 'movement outwards', the question then was to ask what could be done about it. The Association had two answers. One was to pose the garden city as an alternative to the suburbs; the other was to lend support to a growing realization that settlement planning could best operate within a regional context.

'The Movement Outwards'

> Nina looked down and saw inclined at an odd angle an horizon of
> straggling red suburb, arterial roads dotted with little cars, factor-
> ies, some of them working, others empty and decaying, a disused
> canal, some distant hills sown with bungalows, wireless masts, and
> overhead power cables. 'I think I am going to be sick,' said Nina.
> (From Evelyn Waugh's *Vile Bodies*, quoted in Williams-Ellis,
> 1938, pp. xiv–xv)

The fictional Nina's revulsion for the sheer ugliness of English
townscape expressed sentiments that were real enough. In a period
when traditional values were under attack along a wider front – when
international economic and political crises threatened to sweep away
the very foundations of democratic society – the defenders of the old
order rallied at home behind a banner of preservation. What had
been the point of staving off a foreign foe, only to succumb to new
forces within: 'It may be well to preserve England, but better to have
an England worth preserving.' [204] The towns and cities, already
bad enough in themselves (and long the object of campaigns for
housing reform) were now bursting their boundaries, creating hybrid
suburbs and threatening the beauty and economy of the countryside.
Monitoring these changes with dismay, the GCTPA noted in 1928
that this 'Movement Outwards' was one of the most remarkable
trends of the day matched only by the 'Movement Southwards' [205].

Events through to 1939 proved the Association right. The 'movement outwards' was to have an inescapable impact – on the ground (in
terms of the physical extension of cities), in the lives of the new
suburbanites, and in its effects on public opinion and on the work of
organizations like the GCTPA. It occurred in all parts of the country,
though nowhere did it attract more attention than in the case of
London [206]. Between 1919 and 1939 the population of Greater
London increased from six million to eight million, but in the same
period the built-up area grew by a factor of five. This growth followed
the lines of the London Underground and electric railways, with the
gaps between stations and between the radial routes soon filled in
with the help of a network of buses. Characteristically, what emerged
was a broad ring of suburban housing, built at a density of not more
than twelve houses per acre. Beyond this suburban ring, and in other
parts of the country, a less even spread of development occurred.
New houses were scattered along country roads (creating the reviled
'ribbon' development), or as random 'blots' on the landscape. The
relentless energy behind this outward movement, and its tentacular
form, encouraged descriptions in organic terms (as if it all had a life of

its own) and expressions of fear as to where it would all end. Typically, C. E. M. Joad voiced a popular nightmare:

> Every year the pink tentacles spread further and further into the heart of the green, while round every corner there perks up the inflamed little villa of angry red. In fifty years time, if present tendencies continue, there will be neither town nor country but a single dispersed suburb sprawling untidily from London to the coast [207].

There was, however, nothing mystical about the power behind this outward movement. Both the State (through its own direct housebuilding activities, coupled with a reluctance to impose more stringent controls on general development), and the private sector (inducing as well as responding to popular demands) were directly responsible [208]. For the State, with the authority of the Addison and Wheatley Acts, this kind of out-of-town building was a new venture, but one which it soon set about with relish. With a well-worn copy of Tudor Walters by the drawing-board, and a mounting casebook to testify to the popularity of garden suburbs, the municipal architects redrew the map of working-class housing. Vast estates of houses with gardens – like Becontree to the east of London (a single estate with a population exceeding 100,000 in 1932), Kirkby near Liverpool, and Longbridge on the outskirts of Birmingham – were the building blocks in a new State edifice. Some 800,000 houses were built in this way, before new priorities took effect in 1934 in favour of slum clearance and inner urban redevelopment [209].

By comparison, though, the more active role in terms of suburban housebuilding was that of the private sector. This was especially so after 1934, when the State withdrew from fresh developments in the suburbs, leaving private builders free to continue (at an even faster rate than previously) the job of creating the world of 'Dunroamin' – the world of the 'suburban semi', 'unsung and unpraised, but by no means unloved.' [210] Aided and abetted by the building societies (in turn, assisted by cheap interest rates), private builders were responsible for some 2.9 million houses between the wars. The peak of this activity occurred between 1935 and 1939, with an average annual output of 265,000 houses [211]. Taken together, the public and private sectors built nearly four million new houses in the interwar period, of which more than 90 per cent were in the suburbs [212]. This alone represented a transformation in the housing stock of the country, and a victory of sorts for the garden suburb lobby.

Socially, there was much about the new housing to commend it. Something like a quarter of the population was relocated in low-density and low-rise housing, with a garden of their own. The new occupants enjoyed the luxury of built-in baths, and kitchens with gadgets that operated at the flick of a switch. They bought all kinds of items for the home from the Woolworths along the shopping arcades, and paid a weekly visit to the local Odeon. The popularity of the *Daily Mail* Ideal Home Exhibitions illustrated the newfound interest in the home, and the rise in personal consumption habits that went with it. At the end of this period, Mass Observation endorsed what all but the experts already knew, namely, that there was a high degree of satisfaction with the new housing, and that a majority defined the 'ideal home' as a small house in a garden [213]. By 1939 few things could illustrate better than the suburban lifestyle how far some of the more fortunate members of society, at least, had come since 1914. And yet there were also few things which attracted more opprobrium. In some quarters (not least of all, in the Association) the suburban dream was nothing short of a nightmare.

The suburbs were to be loved or hated (usually depending on whether the commentators lived in a 'semi' or not), and few expressed the ambivalence of views as well as J. B. Priestley, on his journey through England in 1933 [214]. For Priestley, the suburbs belonged to Modern England, a world of 'arterial and by-pass roads, of filling stations and factories that look like exhibition buildings, of giant cinemas and dance-halls and cafes, bungalows with tiny garages, cocktail bars, Woolworths, motor-coaches, wireless, hiking, factory girls looking like actresses, greyhound racing and dirt tracks, swimming pools, and everything given away for cigarette coupons.' [215] What was to be admired was the sense of opportunity it offered an England without privilege, where democracy might have some meaning. But Priestley also voiced wider doubts, that somehow it was all 'a bit too cheap . . . lacking in character, in zest, gusto, flavour, bite, drive, originality . . .' [216] It was his doubts that struck the more familiar chord amongst the intelligentsia.

The arguments against suburbanization were well rehearsed. The quality and design of the housing came in for a lot of criticism; as did the siting of estates without a proper regard for the services required for the new population. An especially strong source of concern was the voracious appetite of suburban housing for land, consuming acres of cherished countryside and threatening popular beauty spots. Additionally, the Association, in the forefront of anti-metropolitanism, argued against the future extension of the conurbations, taking them 'up to the limit of human tolerance of strap-hanging.' [217] To add insult to injury, the Association discovered on numerous occasions that unscrupulous developers, while eschewing garden city principles, were widely marketing their developments 'on garden city lines' [218]. Above all, the whole suburban process seemed to the Association to amount to a wasted opportunity

– an unprecedented flow of housing investment that could, instead, have been used to create genuine garden cities. In this respect, garden suburbs, for all the improvements in housing standards that they brought, ranked as a very poor second.

The Association was certainly not alone in its battle against the suburbs. Of all the sources of opposition, that which aroused the strongest public opinion had to do with the desecration of the countryside. Arising from this, the Association, which had previously found most of its allies amongst the housing reformers, now gained from a new alliance of preservationists. It was to prove a partial alliance (with the Association's development interests not necessarily at one with the diehard preservationists), but there was enough in common within the new lobby to make it an effective force. Writing in 1928, Abercrombie (who was a founder member of the Council for the Preservation of Rural England, and who, like Adams and Unwin, combined an active membership of the Association with a similar involvement in other bodies in the environmental movement) identified the various partners in the alliance – pressure groups, professional institutes, local authorities, landowners, countryside users, the National Trust, and the 'real country people'. For all their differences, he explained, 'when we sit round a table there is unanimity that the country should be preserved and decently developed.' [219] The Association itself affiliated to the CPRE.

Ten years later, in 1938, after a decade of largely uncontrolled development, this consensus of resistance had widened to embrace a view that voluntary action and weak legislation was no longer enough [220]. If town and country were to be kept apart, then the State had to exert greater powers than it had done to date. By then, in a wider campaign for planning, the Association was able to marshal the support of the preservationist lobby.

Before this later period, however, in the 1920s and for at least the first half of the 1930s, the Association battled against suburban and ill-sited countryside development on two fronts. It championed the cause of garden cities in a straight contest against suburban extensions. Additionally, acknowledging the inter-related problems of town and country, it welcomed and encouraged the growth of intra-regional planning. As a result of this double-fronted campaign, there is some evidence that the Association was winning more hearts and minds, but no evidence throughout the entire interwar period that the great tide of development was in any way checked. Little wonder that an editorial in the journal in December 1939 was to conclude, despairingly, that the interwar campaign had been lost. 'We did our best, with our little stirrup pump, to project a spray of commonsense into the heart of this red-hot madness. We failed.' [221]

An Antidote to Sprawl

> . . . if this movement were really to take on the proportions that were necessary to make a substantial contribution towards our social problem, it seemed to him that we should have to enlist the aid of the machinery of organisation of Government either locally or nationally or, perhaps, both. In his opinion the time was not ripe for an advance of that kind just yet. He did not think the financial position of the country would allow it. He was not at all sure that public opinion had advanced sufficiently to give the necessary support and drive to a proposal of that kind; but he thought it might come in the future. (Report of a speech on garden cities by Neville Chamberlain, 4th February 1927, in *GCTP*, Vol. XVII, No. 3, March 1927, pp. 61–63)

In its interwar campaign, Neville Chamberlain was a good friend of the garden city movement. It was his Unhealthy Areas Committee that had, as early as 1920, recommended garden cities as an answer to the slums [222]. In turn, the Association was careful to foster this friendship, inviting him to address gatherings such as the one cited above (a dinner at Letchworth in honour of Ebenezer Howard's knighthood), and frequently quoting his influential endorsement of their work. But Chamberlain, genuinely attracted to the idea of the garden city as he appears to be, was also a politician who, with great skill, knew how to hedge his bets. His reading of the situation in the mid-1920s was that a continued support for subsidized housing (to which he had contributed his own legislation in 1923, apart from fulfilling the aims of the more important Wheatley Act of 1924) was probably as far as he could then carry his Conservative colleagues and a wider public. At that time, he could do no more than offer the prospect of a brighter future, and himself seek opportunities to advance the case for garden cities in the years ahead. He was also shown to be correct in his observation (as quoted above) that future initiatives would have to come from the State rather than from the private sector.

Although by 1939 not a single garden city had been added to the two pioneer settlements, it nevertheless proved to be a formative period during which the general philosophy of the Association became, if not the conventional wisdom, then at least an important strand in official thinking on what could be done about metropolitan sprawl. The problem for any pressure group with a long campaign is that moods can change from a heady optimism when a report or a speech is made in its favour, to prolonged pessimism when the effort of campaigning goes unrewarded. Osborn struck a realistic note in an article in 1926, warning against complacency, but also reaffirming the essential faith. The movement had to accept the fact, he argued, that it had failed to impress its ideas upon the nation at the point of historic time (after 1918) when its ideas were most necessary and might most easily have been put into effect. Referring to Letchworth and Welwyn, he condemned the movement for 'petting our two ewe lambs with almost indecent fondness, but we show no realisation that they are already threatened with old-maidish sterility.' [223] He urged again (as he had done after the war) a more aggressive stance, refusing to compromise with garden suburb schemes, and reminding the organization that it had a specific propagandist job to do. The pity, perhaps, for the Association was that Osborn himself continued to be preoccupied with Welwyn, and it was to be more than a decade before he personally devoted himself to the policy he was then advocating. The Association was left for the time being to continue in its own way.

In the long campaign of the interwar years, winning the hearts and minds of a wider public meant not simply arguing the case for garden cities but also rebutting false claims, alternative strategies, and outright criticism. In spite of Osborn's admonishment, the Association remained ambiguous about the merits or otherwise of garden suburbs. These were not what it wanted, but houses in gardens went at least some way towards its own ideals. What was intolerable, though, was the misappropriation of the term 'garden city' by speculative (and even municipal) developers, who either misunderstood the full meaning of the term or wilfully used it to convey an image which was clearly beginning to enjoy a market value. In the face of the great wave of suburban development in this period, the Association adopted what was perhaps too self-righteous a role, recording in its journal the latest examples of misnomers. Thus, in one editorial, news was given of a 'garden city' at Holly Lodge, within five minutes of Kentish Town; of the 'New Garden City', proposed for Morden in Surrey, with the opening of the area by the City and South London Railway; of talk of another Surrey development, Merton Garden City; and even of a proposal to turn the land occupied by the Wembley Exhibition into a garden city [224]. At Peacehaven, as far from the ideals of the garden city architects as any, the developer, Charles Neville, proudly proclaimed the arrival of the first 'Garden City by the Sea' [225].

As well as the misuse of the term, the Association was also forced to defend the concept in the face of intellectual criticism and practical alternatives to the garden city approach. Reflecting the extent to which garden city ideas had achieved a hold on the town planning and architectural professions, the Association was not often put into this position. Certainly, compared with the Continent, an urbanist movement had, as yet, nothing like the same influence on events [226]. But higher density (if not high rise) housing advocates were beginning to articulate alternative ideas, and to question the basis of the garden city movement in the process. Of these, the most outspoken was Thomas Sharp, whose views first came to the attention of the Association on the publication, in 1932, of his book *Town and Countryside*. Sharp (who even at this stage was not averse to the idea of satellite cities, so long as they were high density) was uncompromising in his attack on what he saw as the undisciplined, low density development for which he thought the garden city movement stood. Far from uniting the best of town and country, he accused Howard and his disciples of contributing to the destruction of two separate entities. 'Howard's new hope, new life, new civilisation, Town-County, is a hermaphrodite; sterile, imbecile, a monster; abhorrent and loathsome to the Nature which he worships.' [227]

Familiar enough with passive indifference to its work, but unused to a diatribe of this sort, the Association responded indignantly. Sharp was, at best, misguided, was the thrust of the response. 'He ignores the harrassing difficulties, forgets the world war, never mentions finance, and goes all over the world with his muck-rake to collect mistakes which other people have made and to label them "garden cities".' [228] Perceptively, though, it was acknowledged that, in essence, Sharp's book was about one issue – that of open or closed development for town structure – and that was how others came to see it too. Five years after its publication, architects were invited to conclude that *Town and Countryside* marked the end of an epoch, 'the first epoch in English official planning in which one school could dominate practice without effective interference. Mr Sharp was not the first to argue that all was not well, nor even the first to propound an ideal halfway between the garden city of Howard and the Ville Radieuse of Le Corbusier, but his arguments were so downright and closely reasoned that they immediately attracted attention . . .' [229] By the end of the 1930s, as a result of increased interest in alternatives to garden city and garden suburb ideas, the Association was drawn more into debate as opposed merely to promoting its own cause in preference to the *status quo*. When Osborn became Honorary Secretary of the Association in 1936, he was keen to demonstrate that the Association was opposed not simply to the old, Victorian housing, nor even just to the new suburbs, but also to what he perceived as the growing menace of high flats and tenements. Signalling the start of a campaign that was to become intense in the postwar years, he succeeded in 1937 in adding a statement of opposition to this kind of development as an aspect of the Association's policy [230].

If the modernists were at least kept at bay for the time being, the fact remains that the garden city movement itself failed to achieve even a third garden city. It could score propagandist points, but somehow never managed to win a game. On more than one occasion, though, there were high hopes of progress. For instance, in 1925 there was talk of the next garden city (following in the Letchworth-Welwyn lineage) being built on a site near Glasgow. A prospectus was produced, and the intention was to form a public utility company to carry out the work. Goodwill messages were received from the Prime Minister, the Minister of Health, and the Secretary for Scotland, but it appears that it was a failure to raise sufficient capital which prevented development [231].

In contrast, the example of Wythenshawe, first hailed as a garden city for Manchester, was based on sounder foundations. Instead of an embryo company, on this occasion the proposal stemmed directly from a recommendation of Manchester City Council's Housing Committee. It was, from the outset, an ambitious scheme, with plans to acquire no less than 5000 acres and to resettle up to 100,000 people, and the Association watched the plans unfold with keen interest. Abercrombie was commissioned to assess the feasibility of the scheme, and Barry Parker was subsequently appointed as the architect. Even though the logistics of municipal city building on this scale (beyond their own boundary) proved to be daunting, the portents, in terms of a progressive ideal, were encouraging. A self-contained garden city proved to be impossible, but the Association (although rather dismissively referring to it as a 'semi-garden city') [232] acknowledged that it did, at least, in part fulfil its own ideals [233]. Reflecting on its progress in the 1930s, the former Chairman of the Manchester Housing Committee, Sir Ernest Simon, thought (in spite of the Association's reservations) that the scheme offered lessons for the garden city movement. It showed, in his opinion, the potential of municipalities, with their capital to acquire land and build houses and factories, in preference to private companies or the Government (which would not itself undertake the local development). 'That is the importance of the Wythenshawe experiment. If the garden city movement is to extend it must be sponsored by our great cities.' [234]

Less practical than Wythenshawe but indicative of a wider support for new settlements was the Hundred New Towns scheme. First brought to the attention of the public in the unusual form of a procession of ex-servicemen marching through the slums of London on Armistice Day, 1933, the scheme was further publicized in a letter to *The Times* in February 1934, and in two booklets [235]. A Hundred New Towns Association was duly formed, and was active throughout the rest of the 1930s and during the Second World War. It was the letter to *The Times* that attracted the attention of the GCTPA, and, in principle, the Association (although it did not like the idea of basing the location of the new towns on existing county boundaries) extended to the scheme 'a cordial reception'. [236] Hopes were expressed that the scheme might be brought closer within the ambit of the Association, but the new organization (underpinned with strong religious principles) followed an independent line. Moreover, when the Hundred New Towns Association enlisted the support of the architect, A. Trystan Edwards, any lingering possibility of closer collaboration must then have disappeared. Trystan Edwards had some years earlier voiced his doubts about garden city principles [237], and in his own publication showing how a hundred new towns could be built he made it clear that they 'would not be, or become, Garden Cities in "open development" . . .' [238] His own preference was for 'very compact' towns.

Interesting though these other schemes were in themselves, for the most part the Association pursued its own line, lobbying politicians and, increasingly, seeking the direct support of the State (ideally, as an initiator, rather than simply as an enabler of new garden cities). Certainly, one gets the sense that the time for individual experiments had passed, and that what was needed was a concerted effort:

> If once the State would recognise the complex of evils which afflicts people through urban congestion and would guide the younger and adventurous inhabitants and mobile industries *outwards*, not in ribbons but to new towns and old, a process of decentralisation would begin which would decant, aerate, and finally empty the slums [239].

To give effect to its continuing concern, the Association in 1929 and 1930 issued two policy memoranda. The first (presented in October 1929 in a submission to the then Labour Minister of Health, Arthur Greenwood) called for the establishment of a special body 'with the definite duty of fostering development of Garden Cities, located in accordance with regional plans.' [240] This new body would have powers to acquire land, to raise capital for a basic infrastructure, and to lease areas to public utility companies or local authorities to develop. The Minister warned that he would not be prepared to support a proposal which threatened to interfere so much with the rights and powers of local authorities. As a result, the Association drafted a new statement, this time naming the 'special body' as a Development Board or Commission and stressing that local authorities would be strongly represented on such a Board [241]. Particularly with the subsequent departure of Greenwood and his Labour colleagues from high office, the prospect of an interventionist measure of this sort once again receded. The idea, however, of a public corporation with a responsibility for development, and of a regional system of garden cities, had again been planted in the minds of national and local politicians, and, as events were to show, was yet to have its day.

For the time being, although there was to be no immediate breakthrough, there were at least some crumbs of comfort for the Association. In July 1931, Arthur Greenwood (heeding the advice of the Chelmsford Committee) [242] established a new committee, under the Chairmanship of Lord Marley, to review the experience of garden cities to date. More specifically, the Marley Committee was asked to consider 'the steps, if any, which should be taken by the Government or local authorities to extend the practice of such garden cities and villages and satellite towns.' [243] The Committee was asked to pay particular attention to the question of industrial growth, to financial and administrative arrangements, and to the possible application of planning of this kind to the extension of existing towns. Amongst the fifteen members was Sir Theodore Chambers (Chairman of the Welwyn development, and a vigorous proponent of garden cities) and the ubiquitous Raymond Unwin [244].

Politically, the potential of this initiative was blunted before it started, and then overtaken by events. Internal Departmental papers [245] show that while Greenwood was prepared to give the Committee a positive brief – accepting at the outset the basic idea that more garden cities would be a good thing, and looking more for detailed advice on implementation – representations from Philip Snowden at the Treasury led to something more neutral. Clearly concerned that Greenwood might be opening the gates for a flood of public expenditure, Snowden also objected to an original membership list for the Committee, 'too heavily weighted with people who quite clearly have preconceived ideas on the subject' [246], and insisting that the 'garden city people' be limited to two. Lord Marley was not the first choice Chairman, and the GCTPA Council member, T. Alwyn Lloyd, was left out in favour of Alderman Rose Davies (who, apart from not being a member of the Association, was considered to be more suitable on account of being a woman, coming from Wales, and – although a direct connection was not made with her new task – of having experience of Mental Deficiency Colonies) [247]. Attempts to get a representative from Letchworth included on the Committee were rejected out of hand [248].

If these were ill enough omens, external events conspired to dim the prospects of the Committee still further. Before it could even meet, the Government of the day had fallen and, in the depths of economic depression, a Conservative Government was returned to power in October 1931. The Association, ever optimistic, hoped that 'when the clouds of the crisis have rolled by – or displayed their golden lining – the labours of the Committee will begin.' [249] It might have been unrealistically hopeful to take this view, but the

Association thought at least that the process of taking evidence would offer an important opportunity to 'bring our movement into the very heart of current political thought, to which it rightly belongs.' [250] But in spite of the Association's optimism, it remained an inauspicious start. Even the Chairman had been left without guidance when the new Government took office, and, in desperation, he took the unusual step of complaining in a letter to *The Times* in December 1931 that his Committee had been prevented from meeting and 'now appears to have faded away.' [251] However, an embargo on its work was lifted within a few months, and June 1932 saw the first of twenty meetings, together with visits by the whole Committee to Letchworth, Welwyn and Wythenshawe, and a trip to Russia by Lord Marley (now enthused by the whole idea of garden cities) to see some of the new satellite towns in that country.

For its own evidence to the Committee, the Association prepared a full and detailed submission that offers a comprehensive review of its policy on garden cities to date, and its wishes for the future [252]. Along the lines of its previous policy memoranda in 1929 and 1930, the Association's main recommendation was for a central body to be set up, with the definite duty of fostering development of garden cities and satellite towns.

For all the Committee's industry, it was not until 1935 that its findings were finally published. The Association found itself 'cordially in agreement with the substance of the Report.' [253] In a wide-ranging set of recommendations, endorsing garden cities as a key element in town, regional and national planning, a proposal was made for a new Planning Board (appointed by the Minister of Health) to provide a basis for land development and redevelopment throughout the country. The Board would not itself undertake development, but would pass on this responsibility to the local authorities. In the opinion of the Committee, there were already sufficient garden city powers under the Planning Acts to enable a start to be made. More than one national newspaper announced the publication of the Report with headlines of 'Garden Cities all over the country', but the Association, while welcoming such enthusiasm, was less sanguine about the possibility [254].

The Association had, no doubt, learnt through the hard experience of dealing with a Conservative Government since 1931 that there was a world of difference between ideas on paper and a will to commit them to practice. It had, for instance, already suffered disappointments in the passing of the 1932 Town and Country Planning Act [255]. In its response to the Marley Report the Association was also no doubt aware, not only of the obvious ideological resistance to more interventionist policies amongst Conservative politicians, but of the even more deep-rooted resistance amongst senior civil servants in the Ministry of Health. Separate memoranda advised the Minister that the recommendations were 'rather a demonstration than anything else', and that 'it is difficult to suggest that the presentation of this report serves any useful purpose whatsoever.' [256] A handwritten note added a final note of damnation: 'My own view . . . is that the experience obtained is not such as to support the conclusion that there is much advantage in trying to found new communities in virgin areas . . . Things do not happen in that way . . .' [257]

At root, the real source of disaffection had less to do with garden cities as such, and more with the very idea of planning. 'The Committee . . . moved by Sir Raymond Unwin, have gone off into a highly ridiculous notion of a National Planning Board . . . The pity of it is that in these days one most readily obtains credit for statesmanship in many quarters by the mere suggestion of a Board as the cure for all evils and this Report may give us trouble.' [258] To minimize any trouble, the Minister was advised to publish the Report without comment and with no steps to secure press coverage.

In such an unpromising political and economic climate, the Association could do little more for most of the 1930s than to try, at least, to keep its ideas in the public mind. It could retain a propagandist role, even if the prospect of achieving very much was limited. In its favour it could draw on a growing sense of concern about urban sprawl and ribbon development, and right through to 1939 pamphlets were produced to carry the message to a wider audience than politicians and government committees. In a series of sixpenny pamphlets for instance, Rose Simpson (as General Secretary of the English Women's Co-operative Guild) wrote on the practicability of garden cities, and Norman Macfadyen presented a case on the health aspects [259]. But at the outbreak of the Second World War, there was still only Letchworth and Welwyn, cast in the image for which the Association campaigned. Largely through the efforts of the Association the garden city idea had become well known, but, compared with the endless acres of suburban development built during this period, in material terms the interwar campaign can hardly be judged to have been an unqualified success.

The Emergence of Regional Planning

. . . the idea of national and regional surveys as preliminary to the solution of the housing problem has taken a certain hold in official circles; what is now needed is its extension as a popular idea, including not only housing but problems of industry, transport and population. ('A National Housing Policy', *GCTP*, Vol. XI, No. 5, May 1921, p. 107)

During this period the promotion of garden cities and the emergence of regional planning were closely related. Intra-regional planning emerged largely as an instrument of housing policy [260]. It was, in fact, the Minister of Health who, in February 1920, set up a body known as the South Wales Regional Survey Committee to provide a basis for allocating State expenditure for new housing in the South Wales coalfield. The establishment of the Committee was in itself a recognition that housing could not reasonably be left to individual local authorities, some of which in that region could offer only small pockets of land in steeply-sided valleys. The Committee examined industrial trends as well as housing needs and concluded that new housing should be located to the south of the valleys on the agricultural plain. Of particular interest to the GCTPA was the proposal that some of this housing should be concentrated in two new dormitory towns. To implement the proposals, four Joint Town Planning Committees were recommended, and a Regional Town Planning Board with the task of preparing an overall development plan [261].

For the GCTPA, campaigning for the rational distribution of new housing, the South Wales example added weight to the Association's call for a coordinated national approach, with plans to be prepared on a regional basis. Prejudging the outcome of such a process, it was confidently predicted that 'this will probably mean the prevention of the continued growth of the largest towns, reasonable proposals for the increase of many smaller towns, and finally, the creation of new towns planned on garden city principles on sites selected for their natural suitability and because of their relation to other portions of the region.' [262] Howard's original scheme (as published in 1898) was itself a blueprint for intra-regional planning, with an overall plan for town and country, and it was fundamental to the Association's belief in garden cities that urban growth should no longer be left to localized initiatives; on that basis, the best to be hoped for might only be garden suburbs, with large cities simply becoming larger. Thus, the Association welcomed signs of growing acceptance and support for a regional approach.

For a start, it could be claimed that 'almost every Government Department has, for its own purposes, divided England into large areas' [263], though in most cases these divisions followed existing local government boundaries that were not necessarily appropriate for the particular task in hand. There were, however, three novel schemes between 1919 and 1921 that attracted the Association's interest. One was an idea conceived within the Ministry of Health, suggesting the subdivision of the country into fifteen natural 'regions' (based largely on the lines of watersheds) and fifty-nine 'sub-regions' [264]. The other two schemes lacked official standing, but took a broader view of the country's administrative arrangements, and contributed to a growing regional debate in the interwar period. The first of these, that of C. B. Fawcett, was published in 1919 as a book with the title of *Provinces of England*. Advocating a subdivision of the country into twelve provinces, boundaries were carefully drawn on the basis of geographical criteria, and a provincial capital was selected in each case [265]. The other scheme was the work of G. D. H. Cole, *The Future of Local Government*, and in this nine provinces were proposed as a basis for a new system of local government. The determining factor in identifying these provinces was the location of suitable cities to serve as regional centres [266].

In addition to engaging in debate at a national level, the Association also became directly involved in promoting more locally-based regional solutions, in the first place for the conurbations of London and Manchester. From as early as October 1918, the Association was calling for a Greater London Town Planning Commission 'to exercise control with regard to housing, industrial and residential development and all means of suburban communication, over the whole region which is in direct and continuous economic dependence upon London.' [267] In the same submission, the Association (anticipating by some twenty-six years the Greater London Plan of 1944) made a specific proposal for garden cities to be located between twelve and forty miles from the centre of London, as a way of relieving pressure on the 'insanitary districts'. A Greater London campaign was to be pursued consistently throughout the interwar years. The Association, for instance, took a close interest in the Royal Commission on London Government (which started work in December 1921), urging that the metropolis be conceived as three spheres – London, Greater London and Greatest London. 'In a word', concluded the Association, 'we should be thinking of the Metropolitan Province or Region of London . . .' [268] Although the danger of drawing away too many jobs from the capital was noted by critics even at that stage, the case for planned decentralization was considered by the Association, at least, to be overwhelming [269].

Manchester was also seen to be in need of urgent regional attention. At a conference organized by the Association in May 1920 a proposal (made by Professor Abercrombie, then at the University of Liverpool) for a regional town planning commission for South Lancashire was adopted as a basis for lobbying the Ministry of Health. The South Wales initiative was cited as a suitable model, worth emulating not only in South Lancashire but in other parts of the country too, and the Ministry was congratulated for its policy of encouraging regional studies into 'the relations between housing, industry, communications and recreation in the urban areas of this country.' [270] Whether or not a direct outcome of the conference, the Association could at least take satisfaction in seeing the formation of the Manchester and District Town Planning Advisory Committee.

Joint advisory committees of this sort (empowered in the 1919 Act) became a familiar and important feature of town and regional planning in the 1920s. If they fell short of the Association's own hopes for regional planning – 'joint town-planning is not necessarily regional planning' [271] – they nevertheless represented an improvement of sorts on a system based solely on the work of individual authorities. The number of joint committees increased steadily, from seventeen in 1923 to fifty-seven by the end of 1928, by which time more than one-fifth of the country was covered and the Association felt able to claim that it was its own educational work that had contributed to this [272]. Plans produced for these committees were regularly monitored, and the Association took particular interest in those (such as that for East Kent) which proposed garden cities as part of a regional development strategy [273]. As if to explain the connection, the Association was also keen to point out that some of its own members were proving to be prominent in the ranks of this new breed of regional planners [274].

In its propaganda, regional planning was promoted by the Association as a consensual issue that cut across political boundaries. After the turbulence of the war and immediate postwar years, with strikes and talk of revolution, the Association looked ahead, seeing no reason why 'this refashioning of the physical side of our life should not become of intense interest, and . . . the people may learn to turn aside from vague and romantic cries to those questions which, after all, will concern our economic, hygienic and social life much more closely than former generations believed.' [275] In the mid-1920s, regional planning was urged as an issue 'as yet untarnished by party strife.' [276] Moreover, it was now being promoted as an approach that could offer far more than the solution of housing problems alone. 'The talk about coal and power, roads and transport, railway reform and house construction should all lead on to serious thoughts on regional planning . . .' [277] Indeed, it was argued from time to time, that regional planning should itself ideally be located within a planning hierarchy, midway between a national and a local tier: '. . . just as town-planning called for regional-planning, so regional-planning seems the necessity of national-planning as a logical outcome of its labours.' [278]

The logic of the Association's case is difficult to dispute, but there is also a sense in which its regional campaign was remarkably unfocused. Its initial coherence, where it was argued that regional planning should be seen as part and parcel of a massive programme of housebuilding after 1918, was somehow overtaken by events. Joint committees evolved in an *ad hoc* way, and the Association's tacit support for these gave way in time to a more critical stance. As well as the fact that the committees initially lacked executive powers, R. L. Reiss drew attention in 1927 to some of the shortcomings in the plans so far produced [279]. He questioned whether the methods and principles adopted had been satisfactory, and whether the plans had succeeded in doing any more than confronting immediate problems as opposed to taking a more synoptic view. Reiss, as Chairman of the Association's Executive Committee, looked outwards to the flimsy apparatus of regional planning for his reasons to explain limited progress to date. Several years later, and with the benefit of his ongoing experience of examining the regional problems of London, Raymond Unwin wondered if the Association's own campaign might also have been lacking. It seemed, suggested Unwin, as if the Association was in danger of keeping its head in the clouds, and losing sight of what was actually happening on the ground. During the 1920s the population of Greater London had grown by a million people, and yet the only new garden city was that of Welwyn:

> As a movement it behoves us to consider how it is that we have worked for thirty years, and have only succeeded in that period in accommodating about 24,000 persons in the two garden cities of Letchworth and Welwyn; whereas during the last ten years that number of available persons have settled in the greater London area every twelve weeks . . . Is it not possible that our movement has exhibited, beyond the date when it was necessary, too much desire to keep the garden city movement a purist movement free from the contamination of town expansion, with the result that we have somewhat lost the influence which we should be exerting in this matter? [280]

If anyone was in a position to question the role of the Association at this time it was Unwin. Not only had he, himself, a long involvement with the Association, remaining loyal to the idea of the garden city (although, significantly, not to the exclusion of all else), but he had from early 1929 assumed a new role as Technical Adviser to the Greater London Regional Planning Committee. Although this, like other joint committees, was purely advisory, its work (mainly attributable to Unwin) proved to be something of a landmark in the emergence of regional planning. Its brief was to examine an area within a radius of some twenty-five miles from the centre of London, and the Committee was composed of representatives of all the local authorities covered by the survey. From at least the end of the war, there had been an active lobby calling for a comprehensive approach to deal with the development of Greater London [281]. The GCTPA had been active in this lobby, and was understandably pleased when at last something seemed to be happening: 'It has been a great year for us in that we have witnessed the acceptance by the Government of the idea which we have put forward for many years, the idea of planning, on a large scale, for the future development of Greater London.' [282] In fact, while the Association contributed to the formation of this new body, its own role does not appear to have been instrumental. Instead, on this occasion, it was the TPI which initiated a petition to the Prime Minister in January 1926, calling for a regional policy for London and the Home Counties [283].

The GCTPA was a signatory, but so too (as well as the TPI) was the London Society, the Royal Institute of British Architects, the Commons and Footpaths Preservation Society, the Institute of Mechanical and Civil Engineers, the National Playing Fields Association, the National Housing and Town Planning Council, the Roads Improvement Association and the Metropolitan Public Gardens Association. The call for regional planning was broadly based, and it was fortunate that the deputation was invited to meet the Minister of Health, Neville Chamberlain – a senior politician already informed and sympathetic to the idea.

Chamberlain's response was to set up the Greater London Regional Planning Committee, with a modest budget of £300 per annum, which at least enabled the appointment of Raymond Unwin from the start of 1929. It is not insignificant, too, that the part-time Secretary of the Committee was another garden city pioneer, G. Montagu Harris (previously the first Chairman of the International Garden Cities and Town Planning Association). As an official in the Ministry of Health, there is evidence that he (along with others) was in a position to advise Chamberlain on this issue [284].

The Committee produced its First Report at the end of 1929, two Interim Reports (one on decentralization, and one on open spaces) at the beginning of 1931, and a Second Report in 1933 [285]. The reports were not weighty, but between them they offered a coherent statement on what intra-regional planning could achieve. From the perspective of the GCTPA, it was also a powerful endorsement of the whole garden city idea. Amongst the recommendations was the idea of regional open spaces and a 'green girdle' around London (a precursor of the subsequent Green Belt). The pattern of outward growth could be articulated within successive rings, starting with planned suburbs on the outskirts of London ('as self-contained as practicable'), and beyond these development would be directed to self-contained satellite towns up to twelve miles from the centre of the city, with 'still more complete industrial garden cities' in a ring between twelve and twenty-five miles from Charing Cross [286]. To create these new settlements, it was suggested that the Government should play a leading role by providing grants or guarantees.

But neither Government nor local authorities responded to the proposals. With dwindling financial support for the Committee, Unwin personally subsidized the publication of the second and final report in 1933. The recommendations lay dormant, but, with hindsight, one can see how, at least, they represented another link in the chain of regional thinking that was slowly becoming clearer. It was proving to be a long and frustrating campaign for the GCTPA (and Unwin was probably right in implying that the Association might have been more effective in that period) but at least the garden city enthusiasts could take satisfaction from the fact that their original gospel was still offering a topical message. Indeed, in the face of a relentless outward spread of development from all the major cities, the need for a regional solution seemed stronger than ever.

The early 1930s was not a time of bold action, and a similar pattern of hope giving way to frustration can be seen in another regional planning initiative in these years. Responding to the growing number of planning reports produced by joint local authority committees, in January 1931 the Labour Minister of Health set up a Departmental Committee (under the Chairmanship of Lord Chelmsford) to consider what needed to be done to implement some of the proposals [287]. The Committee was particularly asked to look at those proposals that could lead to schemes of work to relieve unemployment. By then, there were some sixty Joint Advisory and twenty Joint Executive Committees in England and Wales, involving some 880 local authorities [288], and their reports were already of keen interest to the Association. Indeed, in a survey of recommendations at about that time the Association discovered that no less than fifteen of the reports contained proposals for new settlements. It was consequently argued that 'few adequate regional plans can be made without the establishment of new communities planned according to the garden city principle.' [289]

The Chelmsford Committee included amongst its fourteen members four prominent members of the Association, R. L. Reiss, Raymond Unwin, T. Alwyn Lloyd and W. R. Davidge [290]. Hopes were expressed that the Committee would 'discover that regional planning, now so well established as an idea, can be brought into action to the general advantage of the country and of the employment of labour.' [291] But the Committee, created while the Labour Government was in power, was to suffer from changing political fortunes, and met on only five occasions before producing an Interim Report in July 1931. In this, the Committee expressed its reservations about existing regional reports as a basis for future action. These reports (a product of local authority cooperation) covered only one-fifth of England and Wales; they were unable to embrace re-development schemes for built-up areas; they were largely advisory and at an interim stage; and they did not address the question of public works as such. The Committee therefore felt unable to offer definite proposals for development. But the garden city lobby secured the important statement that the Committee was 'much attracted by the possibilities offered by the development of satellite towns', with the recommendation that this merited further consideration [292]. As shown already, it was left to the Marley Committee to pursue this latter source of interest, with regional planning still awaiting more comprehensive attention.

NORTH AND SOUTH

As well as the 'movement outwards', with a ring of new development surrounding the old, another great divide opened up – that between North and South. As the old industrial areas fell into a decline, the South (and particularly Greater London) prospered through the location of new activities. Starting from a concern for the problems of growth, rather than of decline, the Association was increasingly drawn into a wider debate about national policies and planning in general. The concept of 'decentralization' itself assumed a broader significance.

'The Middle Way'

> 'Planning' is forced upon us . . . not for idealistic reasons but because the old mechanism which served us when markets were expanding naturally and spontaneously is no longer adequate when the tendency is in the opposite direction. (Harold Macmillan, quoted in Marwick, 1964, p. 287)

Between 1918 and 1939 British society experienced radical changes – in the pattern of its industries, in the balance of political power, and in the everyday lives of its people. At the heart of it all was the evidence and effects of fundamental changes occurring in the economic base. The old industries, which had served Britain well enough in expanding world markets through to 1914, fared less successfully in the face of a failure to attract fresh investment at a time of stronger competition from overseas, and in the context of an international depression within this period. At the same time, the problems of the old industries were, to some extent, balanced (in national terms) by the rise of new sources of economic activity – generally, though, in different parts of the country to the areas of decline. Taken together, these amounted to fundamental changes, affecting, at the grand scale, Britain's place in the world, and, at the local scale, the welfare of individuals and communities. The quotation above from Macmillan, calling for 'planning' in the widest sense, reflects a growing consensus that a 'middle way' – avoiding the extremes of either *laisser faire* or a full command economy (exemplified by the Soviet Union in the 1930s) – had to be found to deal with the crisis of change [293].

While the specific priorities of the GCTPA overlapped only partially with the agenda of this wider debate (to do with all aspects of political and economic planning), the general interests of the Association undoubtedly benefited from the gradual emergence of a planning consensus. Moreover, the main area of overlap, namely, that of regional planning, was in itself of central importance, not only to the work of the Association but also in terms of providing a testing ground for the wider cause of planning. For it was in the regions that the full impact of decline and growth was felt, and where some of the first tentative attempts to resolve the resultant problems were applied. It has to be acknowledged that the Association was (at least initially) more directly concerned with the problems associated with growth, as opposed to decline [294]. But the two dimensions of the regional problem were inter-related, and, inevitably (as events show) a concern with one leads, in turn, to a broader national debate.

Although the most severe problems were not to be experienced until the depression years of the early 1930s, there was already, shortly after the end of the First World War, sufficient evidence of the depth of change that was underway [295]. After a shortlived boom, the most vulnerable sectors of the economy were quickly exposed; differential rates and distribution of unemployment marked out the declining areas with a telling accuracy. In overall terms, between 1921 and the first months of 1940, there were never less than a million people out of work. By the winter of 1921–1922 the number of unemployed had increased to two million, and, although there was a moderate recovery during the rest of the 1920s, the international shockwaves that followed the Wall Street Crash of 1929 exposed the crumbling foundations of the old system. From 1931 to 1935 there were consistently more than two million unemployed, rising to a peak of nearly three million in the winter of 1932–1933.

What was especially marked about this was its regional distribution. It was the areas with the traditional industries that took the brunt of the impact. Thus, at the end of the 1920s, one in four shipbuilders, one in five coalminers and iron and steel workers, and one in seven cotton workers were out of work. Moreover, far from being temporary figures, in each of these industries there had been a comparable fall in the total number employed as compared with the period before 1914 [296]. Because these traditional sectors of the economy were in all cases located around the coalfields, it resulted in a clear regional pattern of decline. In what were known initially as the 'depressed areas' (a term subsequently modified to 'special areas')

[297] unemployment was highest, but so, too, were the 'knock-on' effects in terms of family poverty, poor health and high mortality rates, and community decline. Poverty was nothing new to such areas, but, with the old economic base undermined, and young men, especially, leaving in search of work elsewhere, the pattern of community life was irrevocably changed. The Second World War and its aftermath, which brought further displacement to the old pattern, simply reinforced changes that were already underway in the 1930s.

The starkness of decline in the depressed areas was sharpened by the evidence of change in a different sense elsewhere. Industrial investment – desperately needed to counter the obsolescence and decay in the traditional factories and mines – was drawn, instead, to new sources of economic activity. The manufacture of electrical goods, motor cars and aircraft, furniture and other items for the home, and canned foods for the multiple stores, signalled a different pattern of industrial growth. What is more, the new industries flourished, not in the areas where they were needed most – matching decline with fresh opportunities for employment – but in areas nearest to the largest markets. Of these, it was Greater London, with its suburban industrial estates and factories along the arterials, that attracted a disproportionate share of growth. Freed by the expanding electricity grid from the grip of the coalfields and from the all-pervading smoke and grime, white-painted factories surrounded by hedges and trees offered a striking symbol of the new economic landscape.

The North-South divide that opened up was quickly observed, although the political consensus for most of this period was to do little to reverse 'natural' trends. When J. B. Priestley made his 'English Journey' in 1933, at the height of the depression, it was this divide that struck him most forcibly – contrasting the 'nineteenth century' England with the 'new', but also questioning why it had been allowed to happen, and what could be done about it:

> It was all very puzzling. Was Jarrow still in England or not? Had we exiled Lancashire and the North-east coast? Were we no longer on speaking terms with cotton weavers and miners and platers and riveters? Why had nothing been done about these decaying towns and their workless people? Was everybody waiting for a miracle to happen? . . . Why has there been no plan for these areas, these people? [298]

Why, indeed, had there been no plan? One reason was that the political party that identified most closely with a planned approach failed to gain sufficient power to mount a sustained process of public intervention. Two shortlived Labour Administrations, in 1924 and

L. I. H. E.

THE BECK LIBRARY

WOOLTON RD., LIVERPOOL, L16 8ND

between 1929 and 1931, were both dependent on the support of a Liberal minority, and when, in 1931, drastic measures were called for to deal with the economic crisis, the Labour Prime Minister opted instead for a coalition. Following a General Election in October 1931, this was to mean a National Government with a large Conservative majority remaining in power for the rest of the 1930s.

Apart from a political resistance to planning, there is also evidence of an inherent public mistrust of State power. The title of a book published in 1936, *Modern Government as a Busybody on Other Men's Matters*, expressed a popular enough sentiment in British life, nourished on a combination of a long tradition of viewing the market as the natural mediator of events, coupled with lingering fears amongst the middle classes (generated by the Bolshevik Revolution in 1917, and stimulated in the 1930s by evidence of Russian authoritarianism) that planning and revolutionary change were one and the same thing [299]. Interestingly, there is evidence that bureaucrats themselves were amongst those who most opposed further intervention. Illustrating this resistance, a note in 1937, explaining why the recommendations of the Marley Committee (as published in 1935) had not been taken up, offered the following comments:

> The notion of telling industry that it must go here, and must not go there, is appallingly formidable; and no central Board could hope to make a good job of it . . . However, even if one assumes a Board of super-men . . . there are still two formidable obstacles to this 'national planning'. One is our system of local government, and the other our system of private property . . .' [300]

With or without the lead of Labour, however, and in the face of a deep-rooted resistance to intervention, the fact is that, in practice as well as in theory, the case for planning gained ground. On practical grounds, planning had already, of course, gained more than a foothold before the interwar period. Progressing in fits and starts, the State, through local as well as central government, had been drawn into a widening net of reformist activities from at least the middle of the past century, and this proved to be a continuing trend. Writing at the end of the interwar period, Graves and Hodge point to a more recent growth of agricultural marketing boards and public utility services as examples of a marked extension in the range of State activity, concluding that the 'gradual tendency towards socialisation was inescapable.' [301]

Moreover, although the natural preference of the coalition National Government was to resist intervention unless forced to do so, to some extent events after 1931 did in fact force the pace. Decline in the regions, especially, required some form of political response

[302]. The sight of hunger marchers in the centre of London, and the fear of worse if matters were allowed to get out of hand, was enough to prick the national conscience, if not to bring about a radical rethink. One of the first measures, the Unemployment Act of 1934 (which changed the administrative basis for unemployment relief) was widely considered to be inadequate, and its passing was accompanied by a critical debate calling for a more specific approach [303]. Under growing pressure, Neville Chamberlain (as Chancellor of the Exchequer) appointed a team of investigators to report on the 'depressed areas'. Although there was a considerable body of resistance, within the Government and amongst the Civil Service, to the idea of pursuing this route towards regional intervention, once the process was started it developed something of a life of its own. Noting that 'there would be great disappointment unless something tangible was done' [304], Chamberlain then used the reports from his investigators as grounds for new legislation, passed at the end of 1934 as the Special Areas Act. Designed to encourage measures for the economic development and social improvement of the depressed areas, but equipped with limited powers and with meagre resources, the direct impact of the legislation was not impressive. The outgoing Commissioner for Special Areas in England and Wales (an industrialist, P. M. Stewart) urged a second experiment, and, with some reluctance, the Government passed an Amendment Act in 1937, remembered mainly for the trading estates that were established as an outcome.

Of more lasting significance for future planning, the unresolved problems of the distribution of industry (highlighted by Stewart's critical reports) led directly to the formation of a Royal Commission in July 1937, charged with the task of reporting on the national situation and recommending possible courses of action [305]. As events were to prove, the Royal Commission was a landmark in the State's drift towards a more interventionist role. In turn, the regional issue proved to be something of a bait, luring the State even further along a path that it had never consciously chosen to follow. At first, the response to regional unemployment had been to ignore it as a problem apart from that of the general state of the economy; then, through a series of half-hearted measures, the approach was to marginalize it as a localized, territorial issue. But even half-hearted measures kept the issue on the public agenda, with the result that 'once the depressed areas became a national problem it was seen they could not be relieved without a national plan . . .' [306]

The foundations of planning, however, are based not only on pragmatism – on an immediate response to events – but also on a more considered approach. Particularly in the 1930s, an influential body of opinion gathered around the idea that market forces were no longer enough (if ever they were) to deal with the complexities of modern government [307]. In addition to extremist calls for fundamental changes in the British political and economic structure [308], there emerged an important body of 'middle opinion' [309]. This latter development was, in turn, derived from a variety of sources – from within the ranks of the Conservative Party as well as other parties [310], from industry and banking, from liberal-minded academics and civil servants, from pacifists and others in search of a more stable world order, and from the world of science [311]. Organizations such as Political and Economic Planning, the National Peace Council and the League of Nations Union, the Council for Action for Peace and Reconstruction, and the Next Five Years Group were some of the foci around which the idea of planning gathered strength [312]. Although their immediate impact on events was minimal, they contributed to a more favourable climate of opinion within which groups such as the GCTPA were to benefit.

In fact, the Association gained from events in two ways. In direct terms, the regional issue was one that was central to its own objectives, so that as the issue climbed the political agenda the Association's own level of political involvement and public visibility increased. At the same time, the Association gained from the wider legitimacy accorded to the idea of planning in general. Particularly in the two or three years before the outbreak of the Second World War, the role of the Association was not only enhanced by the drift of events, but, also, it was able to make its own contribution. After forty years of experience in arguing for a more rational distribution of settlement, the Association could now enjoy the advantage of making its case in a national forum. The Association (like the State itself) had been drawn into the process by the regional issue, and now it found itself favourably placed within a current that was to sweep in a continuous flow from the debate of the late 1930s, towards the collectivist era of the middle 1940s [313].

Countering the Drift

Unemployment, transference and decentralisation . . . Much depends on what meaning is put into these words by those who have to administer the policy. If it means bringing young miners from the Rhondda to Hackney, or from Durham to Slough, in scores, hundreds, or even thousands, and immersing the migrants in the London Region – it is hardly worth doing. Indeed, apart from a policy of transference, movement is taking place from North to South and is leading to centralisation in London, which is dangerous. (Editorial, *GCTP*, Vol. XIX, No. 3, March 1929, p. 50)

A leader article in the Association's journal in March 1929 – on unemployment, transference and decentralization – seems to be the first attempt to relate a longstanding policy of urban decentralization to uneven rates of development in different regions, with the consequent shifts in population that were already apparent. The article (an attempt to explain 'our philosophy') reveals, as much as anything, the conceptual leap that was involved in moving from an *intra* to *inter* regional level of explanation, but it concludes with a positive enough suggestion: '. . . of all remedial measures we look to town and regional planning to provide a new physico-industrial structure for our country, which shall exhibit, in full power, the principle of Decentralisation.' [314] In the following year, the Association produced a book (an edited collection of papers), *Decentralisation of Population and Industry*, in which evolving ideas on these issues were further developed [315]. Although there is little apparent appreciation of the causes of regional change, a chapter on 'National Planning and Decentralisation' signals the beginnings of a shift in thinking towards what was to become a major plank in the Association's policy later in the 1930s. National planning (it was explained elsewhere) might simply be conceived of as the 'coordination in the elements of the physico-economic structure of the country . . . an extension of regional and town-planning . . .' [316]

In spite of the gravity of the national economic crisis in the early 1930s, the clear impression from the Association's records is that any talk of regional and national planning is still largely within a traditional and restricted concern for the physical environment. The drift to the South was simply adding to the perennial problem of metropolitan growth. Moreover, although the Chelmsford Committee had a brief to examine ways in which regional planning might contribute to the relief of unemployment, it proved to be a body of meagre influence, overtaken by events [317]. Throughout the first half of the 1930s, the Association's interest and influence on the regional question (which, in effect, economic events had cast as a national question) remained negligible. There is a sense in which the Association's policy was in the hands of 'yesterday's men' [318], seemingly incapable of instituting a new approach from within. By way of contrast, in the second half of the 1930s both external and internal factors conspired to restructure what had become jaded and outmoded policies, at variance with changing economic circumstances in the country at large. The year 1936 marks a real turning point in this respect.

Externally, political debate about the differential plight of the regions finally breached the walls of the Association, while, internally, the arrival of Frederic Osborn as Honorary Secretary brought the degree of analytical and campaigning ability that was required to connect traditional priorities with the new situation [319]. As an indication of a changing context, an editorial in June 1936 (reporting on a debate in Parliament in March of that year) led with the heading, 'The Location of Industry'. A year in advance of the formation of the Barlow Committee, the Member for East Middlesbrough is reported as calling for a complete survey of the nation's industries to be undertaken without delay: 'It is becoming essential that the Government should take definite action and I am therefore proposing that the Government should appoint a commission . . .' There was much in the debate of interest to the Association, though in a letter to *The Times*, the cautious Secretary, A. T. Pike, wondered whether the Government would wish to go quite as far as the Member for East Middlesbrough was suggesting [320]. The Association, in distancing itself from a more interventionist approach, was not yet in the vanguard of a regional planning lobby (its own priority remaining the building of more garden cities as a contribution to the problems of growth, if not of decline).

However, in the following year, 1937, events were to force the pace of change, and, with Osborn now clearly in control of policy, the Association was in a position to adopt a more affirmative line. It was Osborn's constant contention that the contradiction between decline in some parts of the country and excessive growth in the London region could only be resolved through the introduction of effective planning machinery. The key to any rational change lay in a policy for the siting of industry, and that, in turn, depended on 'at least a broad outline of a national plan.' [321] The point had been passed where the location of industry could be left to free market forces, although Osborn was not advocating total control either:

What we stand for . . . is the control of the size of towns, and equally the perservation of the countryside from scattered and ribbon building, through the guidance of the location of factories and business premises under a national plan . . . Compulsion of particular industries to go to dictated locations is no essential element of this idea. Certain towns and agricultural districts generally would be barred except under special permit. Certain other towns and areas, as well as the new satellite towns and garden cities, would be the subject of support by definite inducement to industrial or business settlement. Between these extremes there could still be many districts among which firms would make their own choice [322].

Osborn was thinking ahead of what was then being done in practice. The Special Areas Policy was inherently a one-sided approach, and even though the Commissioner for England and Wales had proposed putting London 'out of bounds' for most new industries, while at the same time offering inducements to locate in the Special Areas, the Association despaired 'for any indication that the Government has as yet grasped the necessity for national planning.' [323]

Within a few months, however, as one of his first acts on succeeding Stanely Baldwin as Prime Minister, Neville Chamberlain established a Royal Commission to enquire into the location of industry [324]. The Association drew satisfaction from the fact that Chamberlain was retaining a close interest in issues for which they were themselves campaigning, and that the brief was wide enough to embrace all areas (as opposed to confining attention to the Special Areas). It hoped that the 'mere appointment of the Commission is a proof that the days of laisser-faire which have caused the present chaos are numbered.' [325]

Referring to the problem that faced them as the 'greatest of all the problems of modern civilisation', the Chairman of the Commission, Sir Montague Barlow, urged on his members that issues of immense national importance were involved [326]. The Royal Commission on the Geographical Distribution of the Industrial Population first sat in October 1937, and proceeded over the coming months to take

" We have Letchworth and Welwyn Garden Cities both growing in health, wealth, and population. Are we going to stop there ? . . . . if we could multiply them largely we should be providing an ideal solution to that most difficult problem of our overcrowded industrial towns."—Mr. Neville Chamberlain, Prime Minister, who has been a consistent advocate of Garden Cities

When the Barlow Commission was established in 1937, the Prime Minister, Neville Chamberlain, was already familiar with the garden city campaign.

Sir Montague Barlow, who later became a member of the Town and Country Planning Association.

evidence from a wide range of Government and other bodies. For the Association (and, in particular, through Osborn) this long-awaited sign of political awareness, coupled with the attention given to the work of the Commission in the press, offered an exceptional opportunity for a campaign to arouse public opinion on what the Association now regarded as an overwhelming case for national planning. The 'great and the good' were invited to lend their support to the campaign – not mere ciphers this time, prepared to stamp the Association's efforts with a seal of respectability, but effective politicians who might well play a part in translating the new ideas into official policy. Significantly, as events proved, Clement Attlee led the way with a statement endorsing the work of the Association, and calling for 'a national organisation to say where particular industries are to be located, where the land is to be kept free for residential development, and where there are to be parks and open spaces.' [327] He was supported by other prominent Labour politicians, notably, Arthur Greenwood and John Parker, the latter of whom pointed to 'the negative powers of the present regional committees working in isolation and each planning almost competitively for a vast population which should never be allowed to drift into its areas at all . . .' [328] Liberal politicians, active preservationists, and the old campaigner, Seebohm Rowntree added their names to the planning lobby.

The Association was encouraged by what it saw as an awakening of public opinion to these issues, though it warned that much work had yet to be done before the wheels of national planning would really begin to turn [329]. Towards this end of national planning, at two hearings in May and June 1938, the Association submitted its own evidence to the Royal Commission. Contained in a forty-three page document (prepared by Osborn) the statement took the form of a closely-argued case, probably the most important document for the movement since Howard's original book on garden cities [330]. Conceptually, the thinking behind it was far in advance of the self-justifying utterances of the 1920s and early 1930s, when Letchworth and Welwyn were cited as arguments in themselves for more garden cities. Any doubts about the role of the State were finally expunged, and the whole thrust of the Association's case was for a new framework of planning machinery to enable the wholesale changes that were needed.

In its submission, the Association laid the ground with a review of the garden city idea and experience to date. It followed this by setting out the 'facts' of centralization, explaining as well as describing centripetal forces in Britain. Having established the situation as it then was, a detailed argument was presented, enumerating the various disadvantages of concentration. Resultant high densities, a lowering of housing standards, higher costs of housing, long and unnecessary journeys and traffic congestion, a shortage of play space, separation from the countryside, damage to health, and other disadvantages including the danger from hostile aircraft (a timely issue that was beginning to attract more attention than some of the more traditional arguments) were all cited as reasons to oppose the continued growth of larger cities. The Association then went on to point to the inadequacy of existing town and country planning legislation to deal with these problems: '. . . local and regional Planning Schemes cannot deal with the problem of agglomeration nor adequately with its converse of scattered development.' [331]

The problem, then, was what to do about it all. Of its recommendations, the first proposal was for the institution of national planning, starting with the formation of a National Planning Board to designate areas which should be 'out of bounds' for fresh housing and industrial development, and areas where growth should be encouraged. It was explained that these extreme categories of designation would form the first elements of a national development plan. In the first place, a National Planning Board might be an offshoot of the Ministry of Health, 'though it may be foreseen that the natural line of evolution is towards a separate Ministry for Planning.' [332] A second major

THE DRIFT OF INDUSTRY TO THE SOUTH

The Royal Commission that is now studying this question
has given but scant attention to one of the
outstanding factors which has made

LETCHWORTH THE MOST ATTRACTIVE
INDUSTRIAL CENTRE IN THE SOUTH

ITS HEALTHINESS AND CLEANLINESS ! LOOK AT
THE HEALTH STATISTICS FOR 1936 !

BIRTH RATE		DEATH RATE	INFANTILE MORTALITY RATE
LETCHWORTH	.. **12·7**	**8·2**	**32·**
Average for England and Wales	.. 14·0	12·0	59·

Healthy Workers mean less wastage and more efficient work. Locate your
works at Letchworth, the town that is healthier than a health resort.

First Garden City, Ltd.   ESTATE OFFICE, LETCHWORTH, HERTS.
And Algoa House, 41, Moorfields, London, E.C.2
Telephone : METropolitan 4874

The hearings of the Barlow Commission provided an opportunity for
renewed publicity and campaigning.

proposal was for another central body to be established, this one to be
responsible for building garden cities and satellite towns, and for the
development of existing small towns. These two major proposals
were supplemented by additional recommendations for what was
regarded as 'a stiffening of standards' in respect of statutory planning
bye-laws [333], for the administration of housing and other public
services to be related to the new national planning bodies, and for a
London Regional Authority to deal with the special problems of the
capital.

Taken together, it was an important statement, not simply as a sign
of the Association's thinking, but also (in terms of what was proposed) as a sign of things to come. 'One of the ablest and most
devastating political documents of recent years' is how Osborn's work
was described by the General Secretary of Political and Economic
Planning [334]. Osborn himself was more modest about its qualities,
referring to it as 'some scientific-looking evidence', [335] and confessing that the real reason that it had an influence on the findings of
the Commission had less to do with the cogency of the arguments as
such, and more to do with some behind-the-scenes lobbying. I
worked very hard on the doorstep and behind the arras of that
Commission', [336] Osborn explained, with Abercrombie (a member
of the Commission, as well as being a longstanding member of the
Association) emerging as a crucial contact.

'For example, when he was a member of the Barlow Royal Commission I redrafted for him some of the key paragraphs of the majority report and drafted some of his own minority report – but it was all very "hush-hush" . . .' [337] Tellingly, one reason why it was all so 'hush-hush' was that Osborn wanted to keep his ideas clear of the ring of fanaticism that many people still attached to the garden city movement. The inference is that had it been widely known at the time that Barlow's thinking was being so directly influenced by the Association, the credibility of the whole exercise might have suffered [338]. In fact, Barlow himself publicly acknowledged his interest in the Association's ideas by becoming a member [339].

It was not until 1940 that the Commission's Report was published, and the impact this had can best be discussed in relation to the wider setting of wartime planning. At least by 1938, however, the Association had planted the seeds of new ideas on more fertile ground than it had been able to do in successive attempts with various committees in previous years. Its style of campaigning was changing, and, in particular, the 'insider' role of influencing and persuading key figures in the policy-making chain was to characterize some of the Association's most important work in the future.

THE CAMPAIGN REVIEWED

The long campaign of the interwar years falls into two phases. Until the second half of the 1930s the Association remained very largely a garden city (and satellite town) movement, led by the 'old guard'. From 1936 the leadership and style changed, with a more effective campaign, directed towards national planning as the basis for achieving the Association's own goals. By the eve of the Second World War, the Association had secured an influential place in a growing lobby for more planning.

Managing the Campaign

Our Association took up town planning with the greatest ardour, followed housing, not only with zeal but with critical understanding, and in the last days discovered in regional planning a movement of great power. We gave evidence before the Royal Commission on Local Government, on Traffic and on Squares, and sat on the Unhealthy Areas Committee beside Mr Chamberlain himself.

Hundreds of lectures – it must be almost thousands in twenty-five years – have been given from this office: books, literature – including this Journal – have circulated all over the world. The

International Federation is our daughter, and in every country we have friends.

Without boasting, then, let our members and readers ask what has been the value of our work and influence since the days of our foundation . . . (Editorial, *GCTP*, Vol. XIX, No. 1, January 1929, p. 4)

In answer to the above questions, journal readers would undoubtedly have endorsed the tone of the editorial. A more critical response, with the benefit of hindsight, is that, once the excitement of the immediate postwar years had subsided, the Association went through a long period of relative ineffectuality. It remained active in terms of its traditional range of activities, but these years are marked by a tendency to be reactive rather than proactive. It responded to events (submitting evidence to numerous committees, and defending the integrity of the garden city idea), as opposed to initiating anything new. It is only towards the end of the interwar period, with new officers and a more receptive climate of political opinion, that the Association adopted a more assertive role.

Illustrating the changing style and fortunes of the Association, reports in the late 1920s and early 1930s consistently draw attention to precarious finances and sluggish membership numbers. Thus, the President in 1928 described it as 'little less than a scandal that an Association with our record and prestige cannot attract a subscription list of more than £755 in a financial year; and that considerably enlarged by unusually large subscriptions from a few individual members.' [340] On balance, the Association was holding its own, but it was not making the kind of progress that might have been expected at this stage in its development. As if to rationalize the situation, it was at one time suggested that numbers were, perhaps, not the most important thing at all. Instead, it was claimed that 'our Association must be valued on account of its influence rather than a large membership and an overflowing treasury. Influence is exerted in many directions both by criticism and constructive ideas . . .' [341] To follow this line of argument, the Association (reflecting its own shifting priorities towards the public sector as the source of future garden city building) tried to attract more corporate members from local authorities, as well as individual councillors and officers. Within a few years some progress on this front could be recorded [342], and municipal membership was to remain a feature of the Association in the future.

When the President of the Association said that he thought that 1927 had been 'a satisfactory year, not a sensational year' [343] he was providing an apt description of the years on either side as well. The fact is, however, that, although it was not a sensational period, it was far from being inactive. Speakers, for instance, continued to address various audiences in all parts of the country. Typically, annual reports told of an increase in the demand for lectures, as did the following note, under the heading, 'Methods of Propaganda':

A series of lectures was given by Captain Reiss in Devonshire, and the Secretary has given a special series in the South of England on matters dealing with the preservation of amenities by the preparation of Town-Planning Schemes. The majority of lectures have dealt with Town-Planning and Satellite Towns, and in many cases have been asked for by organisations preparatory to making representations to the Local Authority for the preparation of a scheme. They have been illustrated with slides, films and diagrams. Conferences have been attended and addresses given and no opportunity has been missed to bring to the forefront the policy of Decentralisation [344].

The journal continued to offer a consistent mouthpiece for the Association's policies and views on current issues. Until 1937 the Editor was William L. Hare, a resident of Letchworth and dogged champion of the founding ideals, a careful craftsman producing a professional magazine rather than a colourful campaigner. Numerous editorials reminded readers of the virtues of the only two garden cities in a world that had yet to follow their way. Faced with a financial crisis, and in an attempt to boost circulation figures, the price for a copy of the journal (with ten editions produced in a year) was reduced from one shilling to six pence.

Hare's style of journalism was not, however, likely to attract a popular readership, and, as an alternative way of coping with the deficit, the journal was reduced (as from November 1932) to a quarterly production, under the new title of *Town and Country Planning*. The change of title was designed to reflect the Association's interest in the broader scope of town and country planning legislation, but Hare assured his readers that a new name and format 'will not obscure the old foundation upon which the Garden Cities and Town Planning Association stands.' [345]

One aspect of the Association's work, which attracted little external publicity, but which was nevertheless regarded within the organization as an important practical contribution towards the fulfilment of their ideals, was the support given to Public Utility Companies. Although none of these companies was responsible for promoting a garden city, it remained a belief of the Association that the work of such companies (which enjoyed access to public loans) was worth supporting. The Association offered general advice to numerous companies (and to individuals proposing to form a company), and a separate organization, the English Housing and Town-Planning Trust Ltd., registered at the same address as the Association, provided more detailed legal and technical guidance. Conferences were sponsored by the Association, and at various times representations were made to the Ministry of Health to promote the role of Public Utility Companies [346].

More generally, the Association continued to campaign for better housing, but it also claimed to be 'the chief organisation for advocating and advising on matters dealing with town-planning . . .' [347] As such, it is interesting to see how the network of links with other organizations widened, particularly to take account of the growing countryside preservation lobby. It was said that '. . . much of the work of pointing the way to the preservation of amenities and ordered growth has fallen upon the office', [348] and while that may have been true enough in itself, it was also true that the Association was in touch with other preservationist and general amenity organizations. In 1929, for instance, the Association was represented at and contributed exhibition material for conferences organized by the Council for the Preservation of Rural England, the Advisory Council on the Preservation of Ancient Cottages, the New Health Society, the Royal Society for Arts, and the Countryside Footpaths Preservation Committee. Additionally, the Association maintained regular contact with the main housing reform organizations, with professional associations such as the TPI and RIBA, and with a wide variety of altruistic groups, including the Mothers Union, National Council of Social Service and the National Playing Fields Association.

As well as working with other groups that shared at least some of the Association's ideals, there was also a continuing attempt to avoid political partisanship and to attract all-party support. With the aim of evoking fresh public support, an article was published, 'Garden Cities: An All-Party Programme', consisting largely of quotes made at different times by politicians from different parties [349]. Statements made at different times by Neville Chamberlain and Lloyd George were included, as was the resolution at the Nottingham Conference of the Labour Party in 1918, with its declaration of support for garden cities. The Labour Party was a natural ally in respect of its commitment to State intervention and planning generally, but the Association still met resistance within the Party from those who saw garden cities as being a middle-class irrelevance. Confronting this issue head-on, the Association invited the Secretary of the Amalgamated Union of Building Trade Workers to address its Annual Meeting in February 1928. The Secretary, George Hicks, said that his remarks were made 'from the workman's standpoint'. As such, his words proved to be challenging. Although he knew better than many of his audience how vital it was to improve living and working conditions, he confessed that garden city developments to date:

> . . . filled me with considerable concern. I may be wrong, but I seem to detect in this movement towards garden cities, not so much a movement of the people, as a movement of a certain class of people – a certain section of the middle class. Garden cities are becoming, as it were, a practical ideal of bourgeois villadom . . . I am not in favour of establishing little town paradises, while the most hideous aspects of life in our big industrial centres remain untouched . . . [350]

While the work of the Association could undoubtedly appeal to a wide spectrum of political thought, there were still (as the comments of Hicks illustrate) important potential allies to be convinced.

At a more domestic level, the work of the Association was temporarily affected by a change of address in 1935, from its offices at Gray's Inn (where it had been since 1911) to new premises at 13, Suffolk Street, Pall Mall. Hare chose to lead with an editorial bidding farewell to their cloistered existence (noting, only too correctly, that it had 'given our movement part of its atmosphere') [351]. The greater significance of the move was that the Suffolk Street address also housed other organizations – the Housing Centre, the Under Forty Club, the Mansion House Council on Housing, and the Federation of Housing Societies – although there is no evidence that this new union had any obvious effect on policy. However, another change at that time that undoubtedly did have an impact on policy was the resignation of the Secretary, A. T. Pike, at the end of 1936. This, in itself, encouraged the Association to review its work, with the result that W. L. Hare left as well [352]. It was decided to combine the posts of Secretary and Editor, and Gilbert McAllister (from a field of 150 applicants) was appointed to do the two jobs. The fact that this new appointment followed, by a few months, the arrival of Frederic Osborn (after his spell at Welwyn) as Honorary Secretary of the Association, led immediately to a dramatic period of revitalization [353].

The very first journal edition under the new management was a sign of things to come [354]. McAllister introduced a photograph to the front cover, and on the inside cover he adopted a new, hard-hitting propagandist style. A full page black and white line drawing by Arthur Wragg depicted a street scene of working-class deprivation, with the caption 'While the Chaffinch Sings on the Orchard Bough . . .' Title headings appeared in a large, bold type, and the first item was an article (subsequently produced as a leaflet) by Frederic Osborn, 'Planning is Possible: The missing link in National

Policy.' Osborn and McAllister proved to be an effective partnership at a crucial period in the Association's history.

In his new role, it was Osborn who lost no time in convincing the Executive that the policy of the Association was in need of a complete redraft. As a result, in 1937 a new statement of policy was issued, more in tune with the issues of the day:

1.   To urge the necessity of an immediate check to the growth of London and other overgrown towns, coupled with a definite policy of decentralisation of industry, business and population into new towns of the garden city type and into existing towns of moderate size.

2.   To fix in the public mind, as the pattern for future urban development, the Garden City or Satellite Town – by which is meant a planned town, limited in size but large enough to provide a modern economic, social and civic life, designed both to live and work in, and surrounded by a permanent country belt.

3.   To show how such towns can be created by public authorities or public utility companies, and the financial and planning import- ance of ownership of the whole town site and country belt, and where the owner is a public utility company, of a limit on profits as a corollary of the site monopoly.

4.   In particular, to urge the building of satellite towns, with country belts, by London and other great cities.

5.   To encourage the improvement of existing small and moderate-sized towns in the direction of the Association's ideals, through statutory planning and by local effort.

6.   To advocate national planning as essential to complete the structure of statutory town and country planning. And especially, as part of national planning, control of the size of towns and of major movements of population by means of guidance of the location of industry and by other extensions of the planning method.

7.   To point out that high flats and tenements, and other develop- ments that increase or maintain high density in congested areas, while they seem to be forced on large towns by existing conditions, accentuate rather than solve the problems of slums and transport, while providing an environment entirely unsuited to family life.

" While the Chaffinch Sings on the Orchard Bough . . . "   Arthur Wragg

LOOK—THE SUN !   By Arthur Wragg

As these illustrations show, McAllister's editorship introduced a sharper campaigning style to the journal.

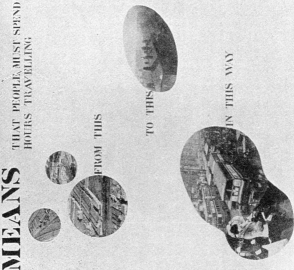

CENTRALIZATION MEANS

THAT PEOPLE MUST SPEND HOURS TRAVELLING

FROM THIS

TO THIS

IN THIS WAY

LONDONERS SPEND £40,000,000 A YEAR IN LOCAL FARES ONE TENTH OF LONDONERS LIVE BY CARTING OTHERS ABOUT

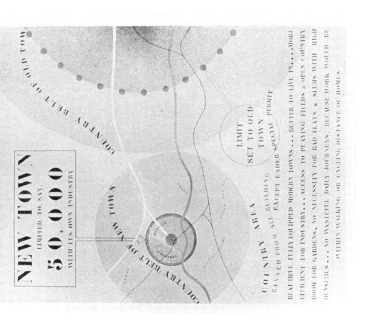

DECENTRALIZATION

NEW TOWN

LIMITED TO, SAY,

50,000

WITH ITS OWN INDUSTRY

COUNTRY BELT OF OLD TOWN

COUNTRY BELT OF NEW TOWN

LIMIT SET TO OLD TOWN

COUNTRY AREA

BANNED FROM ALL BUILDING EXCEPT UNDER SPECIAL PERMIT

BEAUTIFUL FULLY EQUIPPED MODERN TOWNS . . . BETTER TO LIVE IN . . . MORE EFFICIENT FOR INDUSTRY . . . ACCESS TO PLAYING FIELDS & OPEN COUNTRY ROOM FOR GARDENS. NO NECESSITY FOR BAD FLATS & SLUMS WITH HIGH DENSITIES . . . NO WASTEFUL DAILY JOURNEYS, BECAUSE WORK WOULD BE WITHIN WALKING OR CYCLING DISTANCE OF HOMES.

A corner of the Letchworth section of the Exhibition

SATELLITE TOWNS EXHIBITION

Press and Public Take Lively Interest

DECENTRALISATION MEANS

REAL HOMES FOR FAMILIES

WITHIN WALKING DISTANCE OF PLEASANT WORK PLACES

AND OF

PLAYING FIELDS & COUNTRYSIDE

Posters and view from the GTCPA's exhibition, 1937 (see p. 210).

8.   To oppose 'ribbon' or scattered development as spoiling the open countryside and to encourage group development with well-equipped community centres and adequate recreation spaces.

9.   To work out and advocate such details of technique and finance of national territorial planning as are necessary to give the fullest effect to the Association's aims [355].

Already, by 1938, there were definite signs that the new approach was reaping rewards. 'It would be an exaggeration to say that the Garden Cities and Town Planning Association has gone from strength to strength during the past few months, but it is no exaggeration to say that the Association in that period has made an increasingly stronger impact on public and official opinion.' [356] To support the claim, there was evidence of a growing demand for the journal and for the Association's list of publications (including a new series of pamphlets), the formation of a Scottish Branch and a London Planning Group, and a healthy surge of new members [357]. Membership rates for individuals remained at one guinea, although larger subscriptions were always invited. Amongst the new recruits the journal listed many distinguished names, including politicians on both sides of both Houses, local councillors, town planners and lawyers, as well as a welcome number of young people. The Central Council of the Women's Co-operative Guild and the Cambridge Branch of the Council for the Preservation of Rural England joined as corporate bodies.

An exhibition, 'one of the most important propaganda ventures undertaken by the Garden Cities and Town Planning Association' [358], was held in 1937 to promote a policy for satellite towns and decentralization. The latter was shown to be not simply a question of planned overspill, but also of restrictions on new industrial growth in the conurbation. Later in 1937, the journal carried a special feature, giving an opportunity for eminent women to lend their support to the movement [359]. But as well as spreading the ideas of the Association to a wider audience, it also continued to attach importance to fostering, within its own ranks, the support of the 'great and the good'. One such instance was a dinner in November 1938 at the Grosvenor House Hotel in honour of Sir Raymond Unwin, attended by the Minister of Health, and leading names in the housing and planning reform movement. It was an ideal platform for Osborn (in moving a toast to the Chairman of the Association) to impress upon his distinguished audience what the Association now stood for:

Distinguished gathering in honour of Sir Raymond Unwin, 1939.

To clarify and popularise the idea of towns of limited size on a background of unspoiled country; to relate this idea to the ever-growing power of Town and Country Planning, and to press for the national machinery and policy that will take us out of the present state of groping and muddle into real planning – these are the immediate tasks of the Association [360].

The message was no longer that of a nostalgic look back to Letchworth and Welwyn, as an argument in itself for more garden cities. Osborn made it clear that the 'immediate task of the Association' now had to do with lobbying at all levels for the introduction of a national system of planning. Only within such a framework, constructed by the State, could the aims of the Association be achieved.

'In Memoriam'

He was one of those heroic simpletons who do big things whilst our prominent wordlings are explaining why they are Utopian and impossible. (G. B. Shaw on Howard, in a letter to Howard's son, 25th May 1928, *Howard Papers*, Folio 22)

Shaw's letter above was written in response to an appeal for a memorial donation, shortly after Howard's death on the 1st May, 1928. His description of Howard as an 'heroic simpleton' was a fitting obituary for someone so modest and unassuming, yet who has also had a major impact on the course of twentieth-century housing and development. What is more (though only Shaw could use a word like 'simpleton' without offence) the sense of his comments reflected a remarkable consensus of views. Howard, it appears, was universally loved and respected for his sincerity and self-effacing ways, coupled with his relentless pursuit of social improvement.

From both within and beyond the ranks of the Association, obituaries were written, generous in their praise for Howard's contribution to humanity. As a national figure, his death (only a year after he was awarded a Knighthood) attracted a wide press coverage, with headings and claims that would have challenged his own natural humility: 'A Real Benefactor' (*Morning Post*), 'The Father of Town Planning' (*Northern Evening Despatch*), 'A Social Inventor' (*The Spectator*), and 'Father of Garden Cities' (*Estates Gazette*) typify the response [361]. By comparison, though, the loss recorded from within the Association was at times sycophantic as well as extravagant. 'The imperious hand of Death has removed from our presence the father and founder of the garden city movement . . . it is possible to come directly to the secret of his power. It was an open secret, revealed in his beautiful features, his vibrant manly voice, his electric hand-grip, his humour and irresistible persuasiveness. It was not his book or ideas that prevailed over men; it was Ebenezer Howard himself.' [362] More succinctly, the President of the Association at that time, Cecil Harmsworth, later described Howard quite simply (and appropriately) as a 'practical idealist.' [363]

There could be no doubt that Howard was a key figure in the early history of the movement, but any assessment of his contribution is better taken from the views of critics more detached from the emotion and immediacy of his death [364]. Writing in 1945, Lewis Mumford, an influential admirer of the garden city movement, saw in Howard qualities which no society could afford to lose: 'Heaven help England when the non-conformist streak that Howard represented, with a sort of quaker gentleness and humility, disappears.' [365] Osborn, who worked with Howard (but who also developed his own distinctive style), attributed 'Howard's extraordinary achievements and influence to his single-mindedness, the human sympathy that caused him to fasten his attention on a disregarded social issue, his inventiveness, his power of concentration, and his persuasiveness as a writer and speaker. Underlying all this was a simple earnestness apparent to all, whether or not they realised these other qualities.' [366] Undoubtedly, Howard worked hard throughout the life of the Association – 'an indefatigable worker who bent with slavelike devotion to the task of promoting his own ideas' [367] – and, as his remaining correspondence reveals, he was dogged in his attempts to persuade others to support the cause. Cecil Harmsworth recalled how Howard had so impressed Lord Northcliffe in this way that the latter had despatched young Harmsworth to the offices of the Association, 'with instructions to occupy as much space as I liked in the *Daily Mail* reporting the progress that had been made in the development of Letchworth.' [368]

Howard's contribution was acknowledged, but also it seemed to the Association that his death signalled the end of an era. Along with the death of Ralph Neville in 1918, the vital links with the pioneering days had been broken. The reality is, however, that changes were already underway. Howard, himself, had for some years ceased to play a leadership role. A diminutive figure, with a bushy moustache and shabbily conventional dress, from a family in trade and himself working in lowly-paid clerical posts as a stenographer with an insatiable fascination for inventing things, he might almost have been one of the creations of his contemporary, H. G. Wells. Somehow, Howard seemed to belong more to the Edwardian world in which he spread the garden city idea than to the world of his later years. He remained an individualist, a pragmatic anarchist, who (although he was realistic enough to understand the drift of things in the 1920s) showed little enthusiasm for a campaign for State sponsorship as the primary source of new garden cities. He remained loyal to the Association until his death, though he had taken little interest in policy-making since his practical involvement in Welwyn. It was not, then, so much in the sense of a political as that of a spiritual leader that Howard's passing was mourned.

For all the terms of endearment that followed his death, the fact is that the Association had, almost from its inception, pushed Howard aside from the front line of policy-making, rightly (as it happens) allowing him to get on with the propagandist work that he could do best. The first instance came when Neville and the industrialists pruned out Howard's more far-reaching social idealisms, and cast the movement in a mould in which fellow philanthropists could feel at ease [369]. Howard had no personal desire to retain the leadership of the organization, and appears to have been happy enough to accept an evangelistic role, touring the country and communicating his 'overwhelming sense of earnestness, an absolute conviction that he had discovered "the peaceful path of real reform".' [370] Howard was also rather brushed aside by the professionals who progressively gained more influence within the organization, 'completing the suppression of the radical content of Howard's ideas that Neville and his fellow businessmen had initiated.' [371] The relative loss of influence of Howard is something that had upset Barry Parker in the early days of the Association, recalling that 'Howard was so gentle and peaceable, I used, when at the offices of the Garden City Association in London, to resent the way Thomas Adams seemed to domineer over him.' [372]

Any talk of dissent, however, came later. The immediate task of the Association in 1928 was to pay a fitting tribute to its founder, and to carry his work forward. An International Memorial Committee was formed, and a funding appeal was launched to enable the purchase of commemorative tablets to be placed in London, Letchworth and Welwyn, and for a research and education trust to spread the ideas for which he stood [373]. It was an occasion for the 'great and the good' to come forward, and for associated organizations to add their names to the appeal [374]. The Association thrived on publicity and contacts, and, while Howard's death was lamented, it was also an opportunity to make progress with the garden city campaign, 'for the occasion had called forth for him a chorus of public praise which will become a fruitful legacy for those who are left to continue his work.' [375]

Preparing for War

That this Conference of the Garden Cities and Town Planning Association, being of the opinion that great waste and damage is being done to national life, and many chances of real progress are being lost for want of a guiding authority, requests the Executive to take steps which will unite all the interests involved in the proper use of the land: in order to press on the Government the desirability of establishing, at the earliest possible moment, an authority to co-ordinate and control the rapid changes which are taking place. (Resolution unanimously agreed by delegates, Cardiff, May 1939)

Only weeks before the outbreak of the Second World War, the Association (its terminology already tainted by the language of war) sought to assemble a Planning Front for a domestic campaign [376]. Osborn contended that there were 'almost innumerable commandoes that . . . ought to constitute the natural and noble army of planners.' [377] The basis for this new initiative was a combination of a growing groundswell of public concern in the late 1930s (particularly to do with the loss of open land to development), coupled with a sense of urgency generated by the imminence of war (a product, especially, of the indiscriminate process of evacuation that was already taking place, and of the strategic vulnerability of concentration). What is important to stress is that an effective lobby was already being marshalled before the end of 1939, and that it was not simply the exigencies of war over the next six years which created (as if from nowhere) an irresistible clamour for planning.

The Association took a leadership role in trying to rally support behind a planning campaign based on seven sets of principles and aims. At the head of the list was a call for central machinery to enable

TOWN & COUNTRY PLANNING

January-March, 1939

national planning to get underway. In turn, the Association high-lighted a need to maintain a distinction between town and country in all new development; the protection of good agricultural land and attractive areas of the environment; a basic layout of houses and gardens within towns, and wide country belts around them; the channelling of new development to existing small towns and planned settlements; the restriction (through a system of licences) of new businesses in congested towns and undeveloped rural areas; and a scheme for compensation and betterment [378].

Osborn claimed that these ideas already enjoyed 'a universal and insistent consensus of opinion.' [379] The ideals of the Planning Front (as this approach was termed) would draw in organizations with a wide range of interests – including 'the Council for the Preservation of Rural England, the Playing Fields Association and all urban sports organisations and rambling societies, all housing organisations, allot-ment societies, parks and gardens societies, town amenity groups, civil defence groups, Councils of Social Service and other believers in community life, agricultural and horticultural organisations, plan-ning and highway authorities, and transport societies, besides the professional planners.' [380] If the claim was extravagant and unsus-tainable, it does at least illustrate that the Association was assuming a role far wider than that of a narrow garden city movement. The cause of planning embraced a wider alliance of interests, and it is this alliance that Osborn was active in trying to cement.

The advent of war undoubtedly assisted in this task. From as early as 1938 there was evidence of an unplanned movement of firms and individuals away from congested centres, the threat of air attacks was an issue of growing concern, and thought also needed to be given to the optimum pattern of distribution of armaments production for the war effort. From all this 'a new realism was born.' [381] But if the prospect of war was a spur to planning, its occurrence (from Septem-ber 1939) also imposed new and obvious constraints. The initial reaction of the Association, however, was to stand firm. It declared its determination 'to keep alive – and alert – during the war' [382]. As far as circumstances would allow, it was intended to continue with regular committee meetings, and to enable members to keep in touch, with plans for weekend conferences, day schools and planning lunches. The journal was to continue to be published, its role being not just that of a link between members, but also that of a forum for discussion for the many organizations interested in an immediate campaign for national planning. Underlying its commitment to remain in business was a belief that there would be a great deal of work to be done, not least of all to seek to 'prepare schemes whereby the aftermath of this war will deal more kindly with the aspirations of town-planning than "reconstruction" did after 1914–1918.' [383]

A similar story of 'business as usual' was reported from other units in the planning campaign. The TPI, the RIBA, the NHTPC, and the CPRE all made plans to keep more than a watching brief on events [384]. There was anxiety that controls should not be relaxed during wartime, and the NHTPC even hoped that some fresh housebuilding might be allowed. 'Business as usual' was all, in a way, reminiscent of the early days of the 1914–1918 War, though this time there was (at least in some quarters) an added sense of urgency that the drive towards planning that had gathered momentum before the war should not now be curtailed. Osborn himself was a pacifist, but he, as much as anyone, recognized that in this latter respect some good, might well be gleaned from the war. What would have been just 'commonsense' in times of peace had become, instead, 'a plain necessity'. The case for national planning, he argued (and with him the Association concurred), had become irresistible [385].

NOTES

Business as Usual

1. This view is cited in Cherry (1974*b*), p. 70, based on material in Johnson (1968). It refers to a statement issued in August 1914.
2. Editorial, *GCTP* (NS), Vol. IV, No. 11, November 1914, p. 239.
3. *GCTP* (NS), Vol. V, No. 7, July 1915, p. 128. While priding itself on continuing circulation, the Association also appealed for more subscribers.
4. *GCTP* (NS), Vol. V, No. 8, August 1915, p. 148.
5. GCTPA Annual Report for 1916.
6. Marwick (1965), p. 39.
7. 'Progress at Letchworth' was a regular item in the Annual Reports in this Period. In spite of the general reduction in building activity, the population of Letchworth continued to increase (to about 14,000 by 1915, partly as a result of the temporary influx of Belgian refugees

and because of the mobilization of Letchworth factories for wartime industries).

8. GCTPA Annual Report for 1913.
9. *GCTP* (NS), Vol. VII, No. 1, January 1917, p. 4. A later note in the journal (*GCTP* (NS), Vol. VI, No. 7, October 1916, p. 120) illustrates the misuse of the term through the example of a new cattle market in which the booths for the auctioneers were described as being arranged on garden city lines.
10. This information is extracted from the Annual Reports for 1914 and 1917, but is not available each year to provide a continuous record and source of comparison.
11. GCTPA Annual Report for 1915. Copies of the Memorandum and Articles of Association (dated January 1917) are available in the TCPA archives. It is interesting to note tht the signatories to these documents were Cecil Harmsworth, MP, Lord Salisbury, Ralph Neville (Judge of the High Court), John E. Champney (Shipowner), W. R. Davidge (Surveyor), Warwick H. Draper (Barrister), Ebenezer Howard (Shorthand Writer), Frederick Litchfield (Occupation not specified), R. O. Moon (Physician), Herbert Warren (Solicitor).
12. Cecil Harmsworth, the younger brother of Lord Northcliffe and Lord Rothermere, was to be a Liberal MP from 1906 to 1922 (with Ministerial status from 1915 to 1922). As well as his commitment to the garden city movement, he was also a President of the Commons, Footpaths and Open Spaces Preservation Society.
13. GCTPA Annual Report for 1916.
14. *Ibid.* Harmsworth also observed that 'in the ten years that I have been in the House of Commons I have rarely heard a Labour member addressing himself to such a subject as that which interests us.'
15. *GCTP* (NS), Vol. VI, No. 6, August, 1916, p. 97.
16. *GCTP* (NS), Vol. IV, No. 11, November 1914, p. 240.

Reconstruction

17. The stages in the evolution of the Reconstruction Committee, from its inception in 1916 (under the Chairmanship of the Prime Minister) to its status as a fully-fledged Ministry of Reconstruction are carefully documented in Johnson (1968). A broader treatment of increasing State intervention in this period is provided by Hurwitz (1949). For shorter but helpful observations on reconstruction see Marwick (1965) and Stevenson (1984).
18. Johnson (1968), p. 2.
19. Stevenson (1984), p. 89. Swenarton (1981), chapter 4, provides compelling evidence of this link between a sense of political insecurity and a growing call for social reform. See also Johnson (1968).
20. Johnson (1968), pp. 220–221, speaks of an influential body of 'reconstructionists' – individuals 'joined by shared convictions; they achieved a remarkable identity on program; they shared a broad humanism of outlook which precluded any definition of

reconstruction in narrowly commercial terms.' Their number included Seebohm Rowntree and Raymond Unwin, both with GCTPA connections, and two other prominent planning and housing reformers, Patrick Geddes and Henry Aldridge. The second Reconstruction Committee also included active Fabians, notably, Beatrice Webb and Thomas Jones, in their membership. Webb saw the prospect of 'practical schemes of reform' an attractive one: see MacKenzie and MacKenzie (1984), p. 275.

21. War Cabinet, 1917, in Marwick (1965), p. 239.
22. The social reforms of the 1906 Liberal Administration are a strong case in point. Writers on reconstruction are, in fact, at pains to point to threads of continuity that could be woven into the new fabric. *Laisser faire* had long been eroded and, to that extent, points of contact can be found with earlier reforms.
23. Rodney Barker, in Stevenson (1984), p. 91.
24. Extract from original brief of the Reconstruction Committee, in Johnson (1968), p. 10.
25. Johnson (1968), p. 13.
26. This particular analysis is derived from the 'Local Government Board Memorandum on Housing and the War', 19th June 1916, in Johnson (1968), pp. 20–21. The Local Government Board's position was generally considered to be cautious and conservative. More general evidence of housing forecasts is provided in Swenarton (1981), pp. 66–67.
27. The work of the Housing Panel of the Second Reconstruction Committee is recorded in Johnson (1968), chapter 4.
28. From Addison's *Diary*, in Johnson (1968), p. 95.
29. From an article in *New Statesman*, 23rd March 1918, in Johnson (1968), pp. 114–115.
30. Board of Agriculture (1916).
31. The Right Hon. The Earl of Selbourne, President of the Board of Agriculture, speaking at the Annual Meeting of the GCTPA, March 1916.
32. *Ibid.* An earlier article of Ewart Culpin (*GCTP* (NS), Vol. VI, No. 2, February 1916, pp. 21–24) introduced the scheme under the heading of 'State Garden Villages' and noted that whole pages of the Departmental Report 'might have been culled from our propagandist literature'.
33. 'Report of the GCTPA on the Report of the Departmental Committee on Land Settlement for Discharged Sailors and Soldiers', 1916, in *GCTP* (NS), Vol. VI, No. 3, April 1916, pp. 46–53.
34. *GCTP* (NS), Vol. VI, No. 4, May 1916, pp. 78–79.
35. *Ibid*, p. 78.
36. Two letters to *The Times* are reproduced in *GCTP* (NS), Vol. VI, No. 6, August 1916, pp. 114–116. This extract is from the first, printed on the first day of the Committee stage of the Bill to convert the proposal into legislation. It was noted in the report accompanying the letters that there had 'hardly been a single voice raised in the House of Commons in support of the proposal'.

37. Organizations represented at the Round Table Conference were the Central Chamber of Agriculture, the Agricultural Land Organisation Society, the Farmers' Club, the Rural Housing Association, the National Land and Home League, the Housing Organisation Society, the National Housing and Town Planning Council, the Cooperative Tenants' Housing Council and the Garden Cities and Town Planning Association.
38. GCTPA Annual Report for 1915.
39. J. A. Lovat-Fraser, 'Housing after the War', *GCTP* (NS), Vol. VI, No. 3, April 1916, pp. 41–43.
40. *GCTP* (NS), Vol. VI, No. 7, October 1916, pp. 118–119.
41. This is in contrast to the situation immediately before the war, when Swenarton (1981), p. 47, suggests that the then Government was hoping to channel financial assistance through Public Utility Societies in preference to local authorities.
42. Address by Cecil Harmsworth to the Annual Meeting of the GCTPA, 22nd March 1916.
43. The extent to which garden city ideas of design are incorporated in the Well Hall and Gretna estates is analysed by Swenarton (1981), chapter 3. He cites two further articles on this theme – Culpin (1917) and Pepper and Swenarton (1978). In the former article, Culpin refers to Well Hall as 'A community which . . . is, from the architectural standpoint, without equal in the world.'
44. This is the interpretation of Johnson (1968), based on a reading of the GCTPA Minute Books for this period. See also Swenarton (1981), p. 70, who includes an interesting note of a meeting in December 1916 called by the then President of the Local Government Board, to seek the views of the GCTPA on the housing question. Separate meetings were held with the NHTPC, representatives of the private sector, and the Workmen's National Housing Council.
45. Johnson (1968), p. 66.
46. Johnson (1968), pp. 231–232.
47. Purdom (1917). These were 'revolutionary times', concluded Purdom (p. 20), and the garden city idea was presented as 'a structural idea for the development of the great social organism of England' (p. 21). In Purdom (1951), p. 60, the author explains that he wrote the pamphlet while serving in the army, and that it had no influence, 'except upon Howard, who hitherto discouraged and seeing no future for the idea, was excited into activity'.
48. Purdom (1951), p. 61. It is worth adding that Purdom's commitment to a 'purist' approach had been revealed some years earlier in his work (1913), *The Garden City*.
49. It is interesting to see how the terminology changes in this period. Although there is to be specific reference to Welwyn Garden City, from about 1918 the campaigns for new settlements are invariably couched in terms of 'new towns', 'satellite towns' and 'satellite cities'. Osborn's book *New Towns after the War* is significant in this respect.
50. In a letter to Lewis Mumford, dated 27th September 1968 (Hughes, 1971, pp. 447–448), Osborn explains the unusual background to the

book. Osborn chose anonymity as he was an absentee from the army, but (while acknowledging the formative influence of Purdom on his own ideas) concludes that this publication was 'as much a book by one author as any book can be'. The book was published under the imprint of Dent, but it was financed personally by Purdom.

51. Osborn (1918), p. 55.

52. Hebbert (1981), p. 179, shows that even before the publication of Osborn's book he had obtained a unanimous resolution at the Labour Party Conference in Nottingham in January 1918, supporting a new towns programme as a key component for postwar housing policy. Although much was made of this resolution in subsequent GCTPA propaganda, Osborn later confessed that it was an uncontested, 'and therefore nominal resolution . . . which the Executive could ignore'. (Hughes, 1971, p. 162).

53. Some details of negotiations between the GCTPA and the NGCC are contained in the Association's General Minute Book, 1913–1918.

54. GCTPA General Minute Book, 1913–1918.

55. Purdom (1951), p. 61. It was a strange post for someone who disclaimed any taste for propaganda, but Purdom thought that to accept the offer would be seen as tangible evidence of friendship with the Association. This was clearly a time for healing rifts.

56. A leading light in this movement was W. R. Hughes (see Hughes, 1919). Significantly, T. Alwyn Lloyd was one of the directors – a friend of the garden city movement, and also an active supporter of the NHTPC.

57. Hughes (1919), p. 15.

58. A short note on the activities of this group is included in *GCTP*, Vol. XIV, No. 2, February 1924, p. 43.

Internationalism

59. IGCTPA, First Annual Report, 1915, p. 22. It was also pointed out that only on the very day that war was declared did the last batch of foreign visitors (in England for the First International Conference) depart for countries that were then 'ranged on different sides in the death struggle which is taking place somewhere along the French frontier'.

60. *Ibid.*

61. Purdom (1951), p. 62.

62. IGCTPA Report, 1915–1916. This was a combined report for the two years.

63. The Statement of Accounts for 1917 shows annual receipts totalling only £139.8.5.

64. IGCTPA Report, 1915–1916.

65. IGCTPA Report, 1917. Reference was also made to a visit to Britain by a representative of the American Council of National Defense, who returned with a recommendation for the adoption of garden city housing.

66. *GCTP* (NS), Vol. IV, No. 11, November 1914, p. 242.

67. A full programme of lectures given between September and December 1914 is listed in *GCTP* (NS), Vol. IV, No. 11, November 1914, pp. 242–243.
68. Reports of the Australasian tour are included in the Annual Reports of the International Association, 1915 and 1915–1916.
69. Ewart G. Culpin, 'The Reconstruction of Belgium', *GCTP* (NS), Vol. V, No. 5, May 1915, p. 87.
70. The following organizations were represented on the committee:
    The Belgian Ministry of Agriculture
    The Belgian Commission on Sites of Monuments
    The Belgian Official Committee
    The Royal Institute of British Architects
    The Surveyors' Institution
    The Town Planning Institute
    The Institute of Municipal and County Engineers
    The International Union of Towns
    The International Garden Cities and Town Planning Association
    The National Housing and Town Planning Council
    Co-partnership Tenants' Housing Council
    The Garden Cities and Town Planning Associations of Great
        Britain, Belgium, France, Holland, Poland, Russia and Spain.
71. *GCTP* (NS) Vol. V, No. 4, April 1915.
72. Ewart G. Culpin, 'The Reconstruction of Belgium', *GCTP* (NS), Vol. V, No. 5, May 1915, p. 91. It is not clear whether the idea for an international garden city should be attributed to Culpin or to Ebenezer Howard, who elsewhere (*GCTP* (NS), Vol. V, No. 7, July 1915, p. 129) is acknowledged for his idea of a 'memorial city' for Belgium.

War and Peace

73. As a contemporary, Neville Chamberlain wrote of this period: 'Many people have been sceptical about the suggestion that there was to be a new England, and many others have never intended that it should be very different from the old, if they could help it.' Quoted in McElwee (1962), p. 57.
74. The detailed recommendations for reconstruction are most adequately dealt with in Johnson (1968). See also Hurwitz (1949), chapter XVIII, and Mowat (1955), chapter 1.
75. Bolshevik activities and intentions in Britain are dealt with in general references on the post-1917 period. See, for instance, Johnson (1968), Mowat (1955), and Branson (1975).
76. Johnson (1968), chapter 12.
77. Dawson (1917), p. 7.
78. Hurwitz (1949), chapter XVIII. It is not just wars which generate millennialism, argues Hurwitz, but times of trouble generally.
79. House of Lords Debate, 33, 5s, 7–8, in Hurwitz (1949), p. 292.
80. Beatrice Webb's diary entry, 17th November 1918. See MacKenzie and MacKenzie (1984), p. 324.

81. T. E. Lawrence (1939), *Letters*, New York, p. 262, quoted in Hurwitz (1949), p. 293.
82. J. M. Keynes, quoted in Hurwitz (1949), p. 294.
83. See, for instance: Mowat (1955), p. 14. The term arose from the location of Lloyd George's secretariat during the war in the garden of 10 Downing Street. The use of the term 'garden suburb' was, incidentally, an example of the misuse against which the GCTPA constantly railed.
84. Hurwitz (1949), p. 25.
85. The campaign, and the Government's response, is more fully described in Mowat (1955), pp. 130–131.
86. Material on this whole period, from 1918 through to 1924, has been gleaned from Branson (1975), Glynn and Oxborrow (1976), Graves and Hodge (1971), Hurwitz (1949), Johnson (1968), McElwee (1962), Marwick (1965), Mowat (1955), Seaman (1970), and Stevenson (1984).

Paradise Postponed: Homes Unfit for Heroes

87. Cited in Swenarton (1981), p. 79, from a speech by Lloyd George reported in *The Times* 13th November 1918. Swenarton provides an excellent analysis of the whole 'homes fit for heroes' debate, explaining the policy initiative in terms of an 'insurance against revolution' (the latter being the sense of a phrase used by the Parliamentary Secretary to the Local Government Board in April 1919: 'the money we are going to spend on housing is an insurance against Bolshevism and Revolution.').
88. 'Report of the Committee appointed by the President of the Local Government Board and the Secretary for Scotland to consider questions of building construction in connection with the provision of dwellings for the working class in England and Wales, and Scotland, and report upon methods of securing economy and despatch in the provision of such dwellings', PP 1918, Cd. 9191, vii. Chaired by Sir John Tudor Walters, the report was subsequently endorsed through a manual for local authorities on estate design: Local Government Board, *Manual on the Preparation of State-Aided Housing Schemes*, 1919. See Swenarton (1981), chapter 5. Garden city enthusiasts welcomed the fact that the report recommended building houses with gardens in a syle familiar to their earlier campaigns, but house design in itself did not mean that the new houses would be built in garden cities. The approach was, therefore, to satisfy garden suburb rather than garden city proponents.
89. Jackson (1985), chapter 5. Not only did Unwin influence the recommendations of the report, but he was also in close association with Seebohm Rowntree and Christopher Addison in the war years.
90. It would be easy to exaggerate the extent to which housing reform and social disorder can be related, but it is clear from the Parliamentary debate at the time that politicians (who would not

otherwise have favoured radical housing reform) saw this relationship clearly. See Swenarton (1981), pp. 77–87.

91. Bowley (1945), p. 271, records that 170,100 houses were built with Addison subsidies between 1919 and 1928. Although new schemes were not permitted after 1921, houses already in the pipeline were allowed to be completed. As for the quality of the Addison houses, Burnett (1978), p. 226, includes some observations on consumer satisfaction – including the results of an enquiry by the Women's Committee of the GCTPA.

92. Bowley (1945), p. 271.

93. See, especially, Bowley (1945), Burnett (1978), Merrett (1979), Orbach (1977) and Swenarton (1981). I am also indebted to Professor E. C. Penning-Rowsell for a copy of his unpublished paper, 'The development of urban housing: interpretations of the role of the state, 1918–1933', Middlesex Polytechnic.

94. *GCTP*, Vol. IX, No. 1, January 1919, p. 1.

95. 'A National Housing Policy', a Memorandum submitted by the GCTPA to the President of the Local Government Board, 20th February 1919.

96. *GCTP*, Vol. IX, No. 2, February 1919, p. 21.

97. Swenarton (1981), pp. 77–81, records the Cabinet's discussions in this period, including Lloyd George's warning to his Cabinet on 3rd March 1919 that Britain could only hold out against Bolshevism 'if the people were given a sense of confidence'. The cost of reform, he argued, was of little consequence 'compared to the stability of the State'.

98. *GCTP*, Vol. IX, No. 4, April 1919, pp. 61–62.

99. *GCTP*, Vol. IX, No. 12, December 1919, p. 222.

100. The Housing (Additional Powers) Act was passed in December 1919, primarily to extend subsidy provisions to private housebuilders, and to allow local authorities to curb 'luxury' building in their areas where this interfered with their own plans. As an incidental provision, Clause 9 enabled land to be acquired for garden cities. But, contended the Association (*ibid*, p. 223), the mere acquisition of land was not enough, and, by linking it with garden suburbs and garden villages, all it would do would be to add confusion to the public mind.

101. *GCTP*, Vol. XI, No. 8, August 1921, p. 177.

102. GCTPA Annual Report for 1917.

103. Local reports on the National Campaign were regularly included in the Association's journal. These particular examples are from the middle of 1919, when public opinion was gathering momentum. See *GCTP*, Vol. IX, No. 8, August 1919, pp. 159–160, and *GCTP*, Vol. IX, No. 9, September 1919, pp. 177–179.

104. See, for instance, *GCTP*, Vol. XI, No. 3, March 1921, pp. 55–57; April 1921, pp. 79–81; May 1921, pp. 107–110; June 1921, pp. 131–133; July 1921, pp. 155–160.

105. *GCTP*, Vol. XIII, No. 5, May 1923, p. 59.

Garden Cities and Satellite Towns

106. The new policy was adopted at the Annual Meeting of the GCTPA, February 1920.
107. The case for garden cities at this time is illustrated by the following articles in the Association's journal: C. B. Purdom, 'The Garden City Principle', *GCTP*, Vol. IX, No. 7, June 1919, pp. 104–105, and July 1919, pp. 123–127; R. Unwin, 'New Problems in Town Planning', *GCTP*, Vol. X, No. 5, May 1920, pp. 108–113; and a closely-argued case for interventionism by F. J. Osborn, under the pseudonym of E. Ormiston, 'The Public Control of the Location of Towns', *GCTP*, Vol. IX, No. 2, February 1919, pp. 23–30. At the Annual Meeting of the GCTPA in March 1921, G. B. Shaw delivered a speech, entitled 'Why Garden Cities should be supported' (an interesting speech but, in fact, not really living up to its title).
108. Swenarton (1981), pp. 63–64, shows, for instance, that Adshead was critical of the picturesque house designs at Letchworth.
109. Prof. S. D. Adshead, 'Town Planning and Reconstruction', Presidential address to the Town Planning Institute, 1919.
110. 'A Sign of the Times', *GCTP*, Vol. IX, No. 2, February 1919, p. 22.
111. W. Loftus Hare, 'Politics and Garden Cities', *GCTP*, Vol. X, No. 12, December 1920, pp. 234–236.
112. The main procedural change was that it now became possible for local authorities to authorize the preparation of a scheme through their own formal resolution, rather than having to get the prior approval of the Ministry of Health. It remained a cumbersome procedure, however, and (although the measure was passed in 1919) it was not until 1923 that local authorities with a population of 20,000 or more were formally required to prepare schemes for their extensions. See Cherry (1974*b*), pp. 82–85.
113. *GCTP*, Vol. IX, No. 4, April 1919, p. 62. The comment, at that stage, was on the town planning provisions of the Bill.
114. *GCTP*, Vol. IX, No. 12, December 1919, p. 223.
115. The definition, with the approval of the Executive, was included in the GCTPA Annual Report for 1919.
116. There is a lengthy discussion on the meaning and use of the term 'satellite town' in Purdom (1949), Part I.
117. Report of a Parliamentary Question and Answer, 19th May 1920, in *GCTP*, Vol. X, No. 6, June 1920, p. 136.
118. The proposal was to amend the Government's Housing Bill, 1920. See *GCTP*, Vol. XI, No. 1, January 1921, p. 2.
119. *GCTP*, Vol. XI, No. 7, July 1921, p. 153.
120. *Ibid.* Also see 'The New Housing Bill', *GCTP*, Vol. X, No. 5, May 1921, pp. 112–113. The Bill was subsequently enacted as the Housing Act, 1921.
121. *GCTP*, Vol. XI, No. 12, December 1921, pp. 267–269.
122. GCTPA Annual Report for 1920.
123. See the 'Chamberlain Committee' (1920 and 1921), Vernon and Mansergh (1940), p. 249 and Cherry (1980*b*).

124. See Osborn (1946*a*), p. 52, and Cherry (1980*b*), p. 168.
125. Cherry (1980*b*), p. 168.
126. 'A Memorandum by the Garden Cities and Town Planning Association for the consideration of the Local Authorities represented at the Greater London Housing Conference called by the London County Council on October 30th, 1918.' The Memorandum was prepared by a sub-committee consisting of W. R. Davidge, H. V. Lanchester, Cuthbert Brown, Warwick Draper and C. B. Purdom.
127. A report of the conference (including Purdom's diagrams of satellite towns around London) is included in *GCTP*, Vol. X, No. 5, May 1920, pp. 93–107.
128. *Ibid*, pp. 101 and 105.

The Second Garden City

129. From a conversation between Osborn and Howard, in Osborn (1970), p. 8.
130. *Ibid*, p. 9. This account is borne out in Purdom (1951), pp. 64–65, complete with details as to the relative merits of the Red Lion as opposed to the Old Bull.
131. Correspondence between Ebenezer Howard and Lord Salisbury, Howard Papers, Folio 22.
132. In one sense, that was undoubtedly a coincidence. But it should be noted that the immediate postwar period was one of unprecedented land transactions, with many large estates on the market. As late as 1922, *The Times* monitored continuing sales under the heading, 'England changing hands', as cited in Mowat (1955), p. 203.
133. Purdom (1951), p. 66, recalls that the main contributions were from J. R. Farquharson (£2,000), Franklin Thomasson (£1,000), G. C. Blane (£1,000), and H. B. Harris (£500). Osborn's recollection (1970), p. 10, is rather different as to details though he agrees that Farquharson, an industrialist, was the main contributor.
134. Purdom's version (1951), pp. 67–68, is that both he and Osborn urged Howard 'to say nothing until the way in which to tackle Salisbury had been decided upon,' whereupon Howard gave a speech (duly reported in the Press) claiming that Salisbury had agreed to sell his land. Salisbury was apparently furious, 'and said he would have nothing further to do with him or his hare-brained scheme.'
135. A letter to Farquharson (dated 10th January 1927) reflects the importance of Farquharson's contribution. '. . . there would have been comparatively little to go upon had not you and I had that conversation in the Board Room of First Garden City when you agreed to make your contribution two thousand pounds and not one thousand only – a fact which helped me there and then to get one thousand from Thomasson and a loan to myself of five hundred pounds from Harris, repaid out of moneys afterwards raised, and later in the day a further five hundred from Blane . . . You and I are,

I am sure, convinced that there was a beneficial power behind us.' See Macfadyen (1970), pp. 121–122.

136. Details of the Welwyn proposal (including comparable schemes to date) are contained in the 'Memorandum for Lord Salisbury on the proposed Second Garden City near Welwyn, Herts', Howard Papers, Folio 22.
137. Osborn (1970), p. 13.
138. Purdom (1951), p. 70.
139. Osborn (1970), p. 14.
140. A full record of the development is contained in a variety of sources. For instance, see Purdom (1949).
141. Macfadyen (1970), p. 121.
142. From 'Statement of the Provisional Board of Second Garden City', 1919, in Osborn (1946a), p. 48.
143. From the first report on Welwyn in the Association's journal, *GCTP*, Vol. IX, No. 9, September 1919, p. 171.
144. From 'Statement of the Provisional Board of Second Garden City', 1919, in Osborn (1946a), p. 48.
145. *GCTP*, Vol. IX, No. 10, October 1919, p. 186.
146. Purdom (1951), p. 71.
147. GCTPA Annual Report for 1920.
148. GCTPA Annual Report for 1921.

Organization and Finance

149. *GCTP*, Vol. X, No. 3, March 1920, p. 64.
150. 'A Note by the Hon. Treasurer', in *GCTP*, Vol. XI, No. 1, January 1921, p. 28.
151. Membership numbers are not regularly reported, but estimates can be made on the basis of subscription income. Thus, the Cash Statement for 1922 shows a subscription income of £625 17s 6d, at a time when the minimum subscription was 21s. A similar membership total can be estimated in the next few years.
152. GCTPA Annual Reports for 1918, 1919 and 1920.
153. 'A Note by the Hon. Treasurer', in GCTP Vol. XI, No. 1, January 1921, p. 28.
154. GCTPA Annual Report for 1923.
155. GCTPA Annual Report for 1922.
156. Purdom (1951), p. 61.
157. *Ibid*. Additionally, in a note in the Osborn Papers (on some ideas for a history of the TCPA, dated March 1974), Osborn blames Culpin for opening the floodgates to garden suburbs. 'There is no doubt that Culpin has a considerable place in the history of the Association. But he should not be credited as a force for the essential garden city idea.'
158. This, at least, is the view of Purdom, who knew Reiss well. As to whether it was Purdom alone who recruited Reiss, the latter had a slightly different recollection, recalling a deputation of three members of the Association (Reiss, n.d.), pp. 11–12. He had already decided that he would devote himself to housing and welcomed the

invitation. For a note on Reiss's friendship with Rowntree, see Briggs (1961), p. 65.

159. Purdom (1951), p. 62.
160. *GCTP*, Vol. XIV, No. 12, December 1924, p. 267. The Executive, 'with a staff always too small to do everything we should like to do', took this as another opportunity to reorganize the diminished staff team.
161. Amongst those who appeared in the obituary columns were the Rt. Hon. Earl Brassey (a Vice President and Director of First Garden City Ltd.), Canon Scott Hoiland (a Vice President), Mr J. F. Roxburgh (a Member of Council) – all reported in 1919; Fred Litchfield ('one of the old brigade of the Association') in 1923; and Aneurin Williams (a leading member of the Association from the outset) in 1924.
162. 'The Late Hon. Mr Justice Neville', *GCTP*, Vol. IX, No. 1, January 1919, pp. 4–6.
163. Continuing in the same mould, Neville's successor as Chairman was Cecil Harmsworth. Like Neville he was a prominent Liberal, in Harmsworth's case with a background in industry and a career in politics. Harmsworth could offer both money and contacts, and when he resigned the Chairmanship in 1919 he was immediately offered the Presidency of the Association.
164. From a new feature in the journal, 'Our Window in Gray's Inn', which endeavoured to give readers a picture of what went on in the Association's offices. The first of these appeared in *GCTP*, Vol. XI, No. 2, February 1924, pp. 42–43.
165. *Ibid*, p. 42.
166. 'Our Window in Gray's Inn', *GCTP*, Vol. XI, No. 6, June 1924, p. 134.
167. Notes on the February conference are included in the journal *GCTP*, Vol. X, No. 1, January 1920, p. 20, and *GCTP*, Vol. X, No. 3, March 1920, p. 65. The speaker for the final session ('The Need for Women on Housing Committees') was Miss Browning, who was subsequently appointed to the Association to administer the new Women's Section.
168. The following organizations attended the Association's offices: Women's House Property Managers' Association, Standing Joint Committee of Women's Industrial Organisations, Metropolitan Public Gardens Association, National League for Health Maternity and Child Welfare, Women's Village Councils' Federation, National Council of Women, Women's Local Government Society, Women's Municipal Reform Association, Women's Freedom League, Women's Sanitary Inspectors' and Health Visitors' Association, Women's International League, Conservative Women's Reform Association, Rural Housing Association, Baby Week Council, and Mothers' Union.
169. GCTPA Annual Report for 1920. It is interesting to note that the list of societies which affiliated is not exactly the same as the attendance list at the May conference. Some, like the Conservative Women's

Reform Association, appear to have had second thoughts, while others, like the Fabian Society Women's Group, were not present in May but decided to affiliate.
170. An outline profile of what the Women's Section did is gained from brief notes in *GCTP* in 1920 and 1921. There are no substantive articles on this theme.
171. *GCTP*, Vol. XIII, No. 2, February 1923.
172. GCTPA Minute Book, 14th May 1920 to 29th July 1924.
173. See, especially, *GCTP*, Vol. X, No. 12, December 1920, p. 247.
174. GCTPA Annual Report for 1919. Lectures were given to the following women's organizations – Schools for Mothers, the Women's Guild of the Co-operative Society, Women's Liberal Association, Women's Institutes, and the National Council of Women.

Politics and Propaganda

175. Howard Papers, Folio, 25, letter from Howard, 30th January 1923.
176. *Ibid*, letter from Astor, 16th February 1921.
177. *Ibid*, letter from Cadbury, 8th February 1923.
178. *Ibid*, letter from Wedgwood Benn, 11th May 1920.
179. Howard Papers, Folio 22, letter from Shaw, 21st July 1921.
180. Howard Papers, Folio 25, letter from Wells, undated.
181. W. F. Hare, 'Politics and Garden Cities', *GCTP*, Vol. X, No. 12, December 1920, p. 234.
182. In a book review of Hughes (1919), *GCTP*, Vol. X, No. 2, February 1920, p. 35.
183. Purdom, speaking to the London Labour Party, *GCTP*, Vol. X, No. 5, May 1920, p. 99.
184. 'Garden Cities and National Housing Policy', *GCTP*, Vol. XIV, No. 3, March 1924, p. 50. In offering examples of Tory support, the Association might also have cited the case of Sir Theodore Chambers, Chairman of Second Garden City Ltd.
185. *GCTP*, Vol. XI, No. 1, January 1921, p. 28.
186. GCTPA Annual Report for 1919. Additionally, a catalogue of slides is reproduced in the journal in 1924, explaining that sets of about fifty could be hired by members at a cost of five shillings.
187. 'Our Liberty', *GCTP*, Vol. X, No. 7, July 1921, p. 167.
188. 'A Review of some British Journals', *GCTP* Vol. XI, No. 6, June 1921. Other journals included in this review were *The Architect* (criticized for adopting a belligerent stance towards building workers), *The Architects' Journal* (in contrast with *The Architect*, 'more seriously disposed to solve difficult problems by their study than by the easy heroics of the last ditch', though taken to task for neglecting town planning issues in its columns), *The Builder* (with no clear line on 'the politics of building'), *The British Builder* ('more stylish in production and less bulky than its contemporaries'), and *The Journal of British Architects* (continuing 'its dignified career').
189. Perhaps it was this evangelizing that deterred the editors of *Town*

Planning Review from responding to a proposal (10th November 1920) by the Association to amalgamate the two publications. The Association was clearly in an expansive mood for there was also a proposal (13th May 1921) to seek 'closer working arrangements with the Town Planning Institute.' (GCTPA Minute Book, 14th May 1920 to 29th July 1924)

190. In these years, the journal carried regular advertisements and reports on events at the Annual Ideal Home Exhibitions.
191. *GCTP*, Vol. IX, No. 4, April 1919, pp. 78–79.
192. *GCTP*, Vol. XI, No. 3, March 1921, p. 54.
193. GCTPA Leaflet No. 1, 1923, sold at a penny each.
194. GCTPA Annual Report for 1921.

Overseas Relations

195. A report of this conference is included in *GCTP*, Vol. IX, No. 12, December 1919, pp. 239–240. The delegation from England included Ebenezer Howard, Raymond Unwin, Barry Parker, Henry Aldridge and C. B. Purdom.
196. *Ibid*, p. 240.
197. Purdom (1951) recalls that Associated Newspapers (which had for long had an interest in garden cities through the Harmsworths) offered every facility without seeking to interfere with the proceedings.
198. 'The Revival of the International Association', *GCTP*, Vol. X, No. 3, March 1920, p. 45.
199. Culpin and Purdom met their old acquaintances, Bernhard Kampffmeyer and Adolf Otto, and 'a very pleasant time was spent.' (*GCTP*, Vol. X, No. 7, July 1920, p. 164).
200. Purdom (1951), p. 62.
201. *Ibid*, p. 63. The Organizing Secretary was Harry Chapman, who had until then been the GCPTA's Librarian. Purdom's indictment was based on the fact that Chapman 'loved only England, and in England Essex, and in Essex only the countryside, its beer and roast beef, and cricket.' But he concedes that Chapman did a good job mastering French and German to make himself more efficient, staying in the post until he was dismissed in 1936.
202. *Ibid*, p. 64.
203. The Association's journal continued to report the business of the International Association as well as other overseas events and contacts. In addition to news coverage during the 1920s the journal also included more reflective articles on international topics.

'The Movement Outwards'

204. Williams-Ellis (1975), p. 20.
205. *GCTP*, Vol. XVIII, No. 6, July 1928, p. 158. The 'Movement Southwards' is considered in the sections, 'The Middle Way' and 'Countering the Drift'.

206. See, for instance, the work of Hall (1969) and Hall *et al.* (1973) and Jackson (1973).
207. C. E. M. Joad, in a symposium of views, *TCP*, Vol. VI, No. 22, March 1938, p. 29.
208. A general context for the dual role of the State and the private sector is provided in Mowat (1955), Graves and Hodge (1971), Branson and Heinemann (1971), and Stevenson (1984). Specific housing texts of value to this debate are Bowley (1945), Burnett (1978), Jackson (1973) and Oliver *et al.* (1981).
209. The figure of 800,000 houses is derived from Bowley (1945), p. 271.
210. 'Dunroamin' is used by Oliver *et al.* (1981), p. 11, to describe the world of the 'semi'.
211. Bowley (1945), p. 271.
212. *Ibid.*
213. An enquiry into people's homes, conducted by Mass Observation, cited in Burnett (1978), p. 232.
214. Priestley (1984), first published in 1934.
215. *Ibid*, p. 300.
216. Ibid, pp. 301, 303.
217. Osborn (1938), p. 6.
218. Examples are given in the following section. Oliver *et al.* (1981), p. 90, and Jackson (1973), pp. 128–129, show how developers used 'attractive names' as a selling technique. As the latter points out, 'developers intuitively sought to evoke the old suburban daydream of *Rus in Urbe.*'
219. Williams-Ellis (1975), p. 187.
220. Evidence of this emerging consensus for State action is provided in Williams-Ellis (1938); and in various articles and editorials in the journal at that time.
221. *TCP*, Vol. VII, No. 29, December 1939, p. 139.

An Antidote to Sprawl

222. Chamberlain's Unhealthy Areas Committee has already been described. See also Cherry (1980*b*) on the role of Chamberlain. It is interesting to note that in 1929 Chamberlain was asked to be President of the Association, but he declined on the grounds that he could render more service to the garden city movement in a private capacity. (GCTPA Minute Book, 8th February 1929 to 13th October 1933)
223. F. J. Osborn, 'Much Housing and No More Garden Cities: An accusation of failure', *GCTP*, Vol. XVI, No. 8, October 1926, pp. 194–196.
224. *GCTP*, Vol. XV, No 7, July 1925, p. 155.
225. Hardy and Ward (1984), pp. 71–91. Neville went so far as to advertise Peacehaven in these terms on the back of London tram tickets.
226. To develop the thoughts behind this contention I am most grateful to

John Gold, Oxford Polytechnic, who has discussed with me his own research on the modernist movement in Britain.

227. Sharp (1932), p. 143. In his attack on garden city principles, Sharp even laid the blame for Peacehaven at the door of the Association. Later in the 1930s, Thomas Sharp used the columns of the *Architectural Review* to pursue his attack on the garden city.

228. 'A Challenge to Garden Cities', *TCP*, Vol. 1, No. 2, February 1933, pp. 45–46. See also Thomas Adams, 'The Garden City Under Fire', *TCP*, Vol. 1, No. 4, August 1933, pp. 124–127.

229. From the *RIBA Journal* 1932, quoted in Stansfield (1981).

230. Hebbert (1981) p. 184. Interestingly, as early as April 1925, speaking at the Association's Annual Dinner, Neville Chamberlain had deplored the prospect of 'barrack-like flats or tenements' as an 'abomination'. It is also worth noting that in the late 1930s the *Architectural Review* pursued the modernist theme with vigour, one of the articles most at odds with the Association's ideals being Le Corbusier's 'The Vertical Garden City', Vol. LXXIX, January–June – the title being a complete contradiction of terms.

231. Report in *GCTP*, Vol. XV, No. 8, August 1925, p. 185 and p. 207.

232. *GCTP*, Vol. XXII, No. 1, January 1932, p. 3.

233. *GCTP*, Vol. XIX, No. 9, November 1929, p. 250.

234. Simon and Simon (1935), p. 19.

235. The letter to *The Times* was signed by the President of the British Legion and others. The two booklets were Kirk (1933) and one authored by Ex-Service Man J47485 (1933), who was, in fact, the architect, A. Trystan Edwards.

236. 'One Hundred New Towns', *TCP*, Vol. II, No. 7, June 1934, pp. 81–82.

237. This has already been referred to in the context of a debate on this issue in successive editions of *TPR*, Vol. 4, Nos. 2, 3 and 4, 1913–1914.

238. Trystan Edwards (1933), p. 36.

239. *GCTP*, Vol. XIX, No. 2, February 1929, p. 25.

240. 'Garden Cities in Relation to the National Housing Policy and Regional-Planning', Memorandum from the Council of the GCTPA to the Minister of Health, submitted on 18th October 1929.

241. This Memorandum was first aired at the Annual Conference of the National Housing and Town Planning Council in November 1930, an occasion chosen because of the attendance of a large number of local authority representatives.

242. The Chelmsford Committee is considered in the following section, in connection with the growth of regional planning.

243. From the terms of reference of the Committee, in Marley Committee (1935).

244. Apart from Chambers and Unwin, the rest of the committee were Lord Marley (Chairman), Mr R. Bell, Mr J. C. Burleigh, Sir Ernest Clark, Alderman Rose Davies, Mr J. Chuter Ede, MP, Mr C. Gerald Eve, Mr T. Peirson Frank, Alderman W. T. Jackson, Mr J. Norval, Mr P. J. Pybus, and Sir William Whyte.

245. Papers on the Marley Committee are filed in PRO: HLG/52/724–741.
246. PRO: HLG/52/724.
247. *Ibid*. T. Alwyn Lloyd did, in fact, have an opportunity to present his views to the Committee, as he made representations on behalf of the Town Planning Institute.
248. *Ibid*. The rejected nominee was Sir Edgar Bonham Carter, who, like Alwyn Lloyd, appeared before the Committee, in this case to represent the views of Letchworth.
249. *GCTP*, Vol. XXI, No. 8, September–October 1931, p. 195.
250. *Ibid*.
251. PRO: HLG/52/741.
252. GCTPA, 'Proposals for the Building of Garden Cities', n.d.
253. *TCP*, Vol. III, No. 11, June 1935, p. 80.
254. *Ibid*, pp. 83–85.
255. Although the new Act retained provision (Clause 35) to enable the building of garden cities, and went some way to improve on the existing situation, the powers remained permissive and the Act itself was greeted 'with a large measure of disappointment.' 'The Bill and the Act', *GCTP*, Vol. XXII, No. 5, August–September 1932, pp. 117–118. For a general assessment of the Act, see Ward (1974).
256. PRO: HLG/52/741, note from Mr Francis, 18.1.35.
257. PRO: HLG/52/741, Sir Arthur Robinson, in a handwritten addition to Mr Francis's note, 18.1.35.
258. PRO: HLG/52/741, note from Sir Arthur Robinson to the Minister, 29.1.35.
259. These two pamphlets, 'The Practicability of Garden Cities' and 'Health and Garden Cities', were part of a series which in 1939 also included two pamphlets by Osborn, 'Planning is Possible' and 'The Planning of Greater London'.

The Emergence of Regional Planning

260. Although in the immediate postwar period housing emerged as an important source of regional interest, it should be acknowledged that during the war the production of munitions, and proposals under the Electricity Act, had been organized on a regional basis.
261. The South Wales Regional Survey Committee was established, with Sir W. H. Seager as Chairman, in February 1920. It reported in September 1920. In fact, as Cherry (1974*b*, p. 87) shows, a Joint Committee for the South Yorkshire coalfield predates the South Wales survey, but the latter is recognized as the first major study. See Cherry (1974*b*), pp. 87–88, and 'A National Housing Policy (III)', *GCTP*, Vol. XI, No. 5, May 1921, pp. 107–111.
262. *GCTP*, Vol. XI, No. 5, May 1921, p. 111.
263. 'The Provincial Government Areas of England', *GCTP*, Vol. X, No. 9, September 1921, p. 214.
264. The Ministry of Health's proposals were published in its own shortlived journal, *Housing* (22nd November 1920), and discussed in *GCTP* 'A National Housing Policy (IV)', Vol. XI, No. 7, July 1921.

The Association preferred to refer to the subdivisions as 'regions' and 'sub-regions', rather than the Ministry's terminology, 'divisions' for the larger areas and 'regions' for the smaller.

265. See Fawcett (1919).
266. See Cole (1921).
267. 'A Memorandum by the Garden Cities and Town Planning Association', submitted to the Greater London Housing Conference (called by the London County Council) 30th October 1918.
268. *GCTP*, Vol. XII, No. 1, January 1922, p. 2.
269. *GCTP*, Vol. XIV, No. 4, April 1924, p. 70, reported a statement by the then Minister of Labour, Tom Shaw, warning that the removal of factories would add to the difficulties of London boys and girls in finding work. In an editorial note, it was argued that a planned process of decentralization would result in gains all round.
270. 'Regional Planning Conference at Manchester', two reports (before and after the conference), in *GCTP*, Vol. X, No. 5, May 1920, p. 116, and No. 6, June 1920, p. 140.
271. *GCTP*, Vol. XVI, No. 12, December 1925, p. 306. The Association's position on this was expressed in the form of evidence to the Royal Commission on Local Government in 1925. It was pointed out that large cities were experiencing difficulties in building beyond their boundaries, and were precluded from establishing satisfactory garden cities. A small Departmental Committee was recommended to seek a solution.
272. GCTPA Annual Report for 1928.
273. See, for instance, 'Regional Planning Reports', a summary of reports to date, in *GCTP*, Vol. XVI, No. 12, December 1925, pp. 306–308.
274. GCTPA Annual Report for 1930. Although names are not mentioned in this particular note, the Association will be referring to the likes of Professor Abercrombie, W. R. Davidge and Professor Adshead, all of whom were active in preparing regional reports.
275. *GCTP*, Vol. XIII, No. 10, October 1923, p. 173.
276. In an editorial, addressed to the Labour Government of the day: *GCTP*, Vol. XIV, No. 9, September 1924, p. 185.
277. *Ibid.*
278. 'The Idea of a National Plan', *GCTP*, Vol. XIX, No. 4, April 1929, p. 79.
279. R. L. Reiss, 'Regional Planning in relation to Garden Cities and Satellite Towns', *GCTP*, Vol. XVII, No. 6, July 1927, pp. 169–171.
280. R. Unwin, 'Garden Cities and Regional Planning', *GCTP*, Vol. XXII, No. 1, January 1932, pp. 7–8.
281. Some references to the direct involvement of the GCTPA in this lobby have already been cited in this section. Neville Chamberlain's role on the Unhealthy Areas Committee (1921) is also significant as a link. So, too, is Unwin's membership and the work of the London Society (1919), and his contribution to Webb (1921), in the form of an essay, 'Some Thoughts on the Development of London', pp. 177–192. Another important source of support was the London County Council, which in 1924 resolved to examine whether to move

towards the establishment 'of garden cities (alternatively known as satellite towns or new industrial centres) on the general lines of Letchworth and Welwyn garden cities.' (*GCTP*, Vol. XVI, No. 4, April 1926, p. 75). See also Miller (1989*a*).

282. Chairman's Address to the Annual General Meeting of the GCTPA, 24th February 1928.
283. Cherry (1974*b*), p. 97, based on a report in the *JTPI*, Vol. XII, No. 6, 1926, pp. 147–148.
284. Miller (1989*a*), pp. 23–24, provides information about the composition of the Committee.
285. Greater London Regional Planning Committee (1929, 1931, 1933).
286. Greater London Regional Planning Committee (1931, and included in appendix to Final Report, 1933, p. 109).
287. The full title of the Chelmsford Committee was the Departmental Committee on Regional Development. See Chelmsford Committee (1931).
288. *GCTP*, Vol. XXI, No. 2, February 1931, pp. 27–28. A distinction is made between advisory and executive committees. A Joint Executive Committee is endowed with the power of itself preparing a joint statutory scheme on behalf of its constituent members, while a Joint Advisory Committee is limited to preparing plans and proposals to be recommended to its constituent members for their individual adoption. The advantage of joint executive action was seen to be that it increased the prospect of organized arrangements for carrying out the features of a concerted plan of joint rather than local benefit.
289. GCTPA submission to Marley Committee, p. 8.
290. The other members were Lord Chelmsford (Chairman), Mr H. Alexander, Sir Ernest Clark, Mr A. Dryland, Sir George Etherton, Mr W. J. Hadfield, Mr F. W. Hunt, Mr J. Norval and Mr J. H. Rothwell.
291. *GCTP*, Vol. XXI, No. 2, February 1931, p. 27.
292. Chelmsford Committee (1931).

'The Middle Way'

293. Harold Macmillan wrote two books in the 1930s on this theme – *Reconstruction: a plea for a national policy* (1933) and *The Middle Way* (1938). This theme is pursued at the end of this section.
294. Cherry (1974) shows how, more generally, there was 'little professional comment on the social problems of unemployment and economic depression' (p. 109), although Osborn presented a paper, 'Industry and Planning', to the TPI in July 1932.
295. Helpful sources on these general trends in employment and occupational changes include Stevenson (1984), chapter 10, Mowat (1955), chapter 8, and Branson and Heinemann (1971), chapters 1–5.
296. Stevenson (1984), p. 269.
297. The change in terminology came when the Depressed Areas Bill (November 1934) was amended in its passage through the House of Lords. Hannington (1937) contends that, in spite of the official

change, such areas continued to be known as 'depressed' 'distressed' and 'derelict' areas.

298. Priestley (1984), p. 307.
299. Graves and Hodge (1971), p. 258, describe this antibureaucratic tendency. The book cited was by Sir Ernest Benn, and other examples are given pursuing a similar theme.
300. Note (dated 3.2.37) in Ministry of Health file, PRO: HLG/52/741.
301. Graves and Hodge (1971).
302. In addition to general texts on the 1930s, a valuable source on the emergence of regional policy is Parsons (1986). On the political imperative for intervention see, especially, pp. 11–23.
303. Parsons (1986), pp. 12–13, points to a series of articles and correspondence in *The Times*, calling for something more to be done about the 'places without a future'.
304. Chamberlain, quoted in Parsons (1986), p. 14.
305. A fuller consideration of this Royal Commission (on the Geographical Distribution of the Industrial Population) is given in the following section of this chapter.
306. Mowat (1955), p. 463.
307. As contemporary writers, Graves and Hodge (1971), chapter 15, provide valuable insights into the sources of a new planning lobby. Subsequently, Marwick (1964) and Smith (1979) offer important sources on the growth of an influential consensus for planning in this period.
308. The Communist Party, for instance, failed to attract a membership of more than 18,000, but it gained localized influence in militant industrial areas, such as South Wales, and amongst middle-class students.
309. The term 'middle opinion' is used by Marwick (1964) to describe the emerging area of agreement, in contrast to the areas of conflict and disagreement in the 1930s.
310. Conservative politicians include Harold Macmillan and Duncan Sandys, the latter of whom was particularly sympathetic to the aims of the Association in the 1950s. Within the Labour Party, the National Labour Committee (composed of Labour supporters of the National Government) 'served as a central point around which the exponents of the ideas of political agreement could cohere' (Marwick, 1964, p. 289).
311. Amongst the many influential individuals who committed themselves to the idea of planning was J. M. Keynes, whose *General Theory of Employment, Interest and Money* was published in 1936, and which was to provide a vital source of ideas for economic planning after 1945. In turn, leading members of the Association joined some of the new groups established to promote a planned approach. Raymond Unwin was a member of Political and Economic Planning, and Seebohm Rowntree was a leading light in the Next Five Years Group.
312. Each of these groups is described in Marwick (1964).
313. Marwick (1964) concludes that the collectivism of the post-war era owes its origins to the intellectual foundations laid in the 1930s.

Countering the Drift

314. 'Unemployment, Transference and Decentralisation', *GCTP*, Vol. XIX, No. 3, March 1929, pp. 49–51.
315. Warren and Davidge (1930), chapter 7.
316. 'The Idea of a National Plan', an editorial in *GCTP*, Vol. XIX, No. 4, April 1929. This editorial has the hand of Davidge (who wrote the chapter on national planning in his book with Herbert Warren (1930)).
317. The Chelmsford Committee has already been considered in this chapter in the context of intra-regional planning.
318. The Association's book of 1930 was written largely by members who had been active before 1914. Warren and Davidge were the editors, with chapters contributed, for instance, by Unwin, Pepler, Loftus Hare, Parker and Adams. The fact that members had been active over a long period is not in itself an indictment, but there is certainly little evidence of fresh ideas to match a new situation.
319. As early as 1932, Osborn had addressed town planners on the importance of the location of industry, and the further development of his ideas was published in a leaflet for The New Fabian Research Bureau in 1934, 'Transport, Town Development and Territorial Planning of Industry'. In the latter, the importance that Osborn is consistently to attach to getting the right machinery for planning is reflected in his proposal for a National Industrial and Commercial Siting Board, charged with the duty of guiding the location of new manufacturing businesses and industrial and commercial developments throughout the country.
320. Letter to *The Times*, reprinted in 'The Location of Industry', *TCP*, Vol. IV, No. 15, June 1936, pp. 79–81.
321. From an important statement of the Association's new approach: F. J. Osborn, 'Planning is Possible: The missing link in national policy', *TCP*, Vol. V, No. 18, March 1937, pp. 39–42.
322. *Ibid*. In this context, Osborn goes on to propose the establishment of a National Industrial Siting Board.
323. 'A Critical Commentary', *TCP*, Vol. V, No. 18, March 1937, p. 62.
324. The full terms of reference of the Royal Commission were threefold:

'To enquire into the causes which have influenced the present geographical distribution of the industrial population of Great Britain and the probable direction of any change in that distribution in the future; to consider what social, economic or strategical disadvantages arise from the concentration of industries or of the industrial population in large towns or in particular areas of the country; and to report what remedial measures if any should be taken in the national interest.' Barlow Report (1940), pp. vii–viii.

325. 'The Royal Commission', *TCP*, Vol. V, No. 20, September 1937, p. 115.
326. As reported in *TCP*, Vol. VI, No. 21, December 1937, p. 3.

327. From a symposium of views, *TCP*, Vol. VI, No. 22, March 1938, pp. 25–30.
328. *Ibid*.
329. 'Public Opinion and Planning', *TCP*, Vol. VI, No. 23, July–September 1938, p. 89.
330. The evidence for the Association was prepared by Osborn and submitted by Cecil Harmsworth (as Chairman of the Council) on 5th May and 15th June, 1938. See GCTPA (1938).
331. GCTPA (1938), p. 31.
332. *Ibid*, p. 36.
333. *Ibid*, pp. 40–41. This 'stiffening of standards' included proposals for compensation and betterment.
334. The Association's evidence was reviewed by Max Nicholson, General Secretary of PEP (Political and Economic Planning), in *TCP*, Vol. VI, No. 23, July–September 1938, pp. 92–93. There was, in fact, mutual appreciation between the two organizations, both of which were campaigning for more planning. Thus, in *TCP*, Vol. VII, No. 27, July–September 1939, pp. 103–105, Osborn wrote a favourable review of PEP's own publication (1939).
335. Osborn, in Hughes (1971), p. 62.
336. *Ibid*, p. 17.
337. *Ibid*, p. 271. Osborn also acknowledged the support of another member of the Commission, Mrs W. L. Hichens, who kept both Osborn and Abercrombie 'hard at this underground work.'
338. *Ibid*, p. 17. In assessing the role of the Association at this time, see also Osborn (1938), Hall (1969) chapter 2, and Hebbert (1981).
339. Letter to Osborn, 28th July 1939 (Osborn Papers).

Managing the Campaign

340. President's address to the Annual Meeting of the GCTPA, February 1928. Subscriptions rates were at that time still a guinea per annum.
341. Editorial, *GCTP*, Vol. XVI, No. 3, March 1926, p. 49.
342. By 1939, for instance, the Annual Report for that year shows that about 130 local authorities and regional planning committees had become members or subscribers to the journal.
343. President's address to the Annual Meeting of the GCTPA, February 1928.
344. Annual Report of the GCTPA for 1928.
345. Editorial, *TCP*, Vol. 1, No. 1, November 1932, p. 5.
346. An important example is that of a Statement of Evidence submitted to the Ministry of Health's Departmental Committee on Housing, as reported in *TCP*, Vol. 1, No. 3, May 1933, pp. 80–81. The Association's work for Public Utility Companies is also recorded in the Annual Reports.
347. Annual Report of the GCTPA for 1929.
348. *Ibid*.
349. *GCTPA*, Vol. XVII, No. 6, July 1928, pp. 157–160.

350. A copy of the speech as a whole is included in *GCTP*, Vol. XVIII, No. 3, March 1928, pp. 61–63.
351. 'Farewell to Grays Inn', *TCP*, Vol. III, No. 1, December 1934, p. 1.
352. Hare's dismissal was a bitter episode in the Association's history. He responded with a Memorandum to the Executive Committee (n.d.), performing 'the very unpleasant task' of citing evidence of his maltreatment – 'a catalogue of illegalities, carried out despite my insistent protest, reveal the administration to be unworthy of confidence, and if they are continued, will bring the Association to disaster.' It is clear that Osborn was the main source of Hare's wrath. (Osborn Papers).
353. Osborn was responsible for the general work of the Association, with McAllister answerable to him.
354. *TCP*, Vol. V, No. 18, March 1937.
355. 'New Statement of Policy', published for the first time in *TCP*, Vol. V, No. 19, June 1937, p. 110.
356. *TCP*, Vol. VI, No. 22, 1938, p. 35.
357. Osborn later (in June 1946) claimed that from 1936 he had restricted membership to people 'in express agreement with our policy' (Hughes, 1971, p. 126). But that is an odd statement that cannot be reconciled with membership appeals at the time, which invite new members to join the campaign but which do not insist on a declaration of agreement. It seems more likely that he was referring simply to members of the Executive.
358. *TCP*, Vol. V, No. 19, June 1937, p. 89.
359. 'Famous Women Demand Planning', *TCP*, Vol. V, No. 20, September 1937, pp. 129–135. In addition to a feature article by Rose Simpson, General Secretary of the English Women's Co-operative Guild, there were contributions by Dame Sybil Thorndike, Margaret Cole, Cicely Hamilton, Naomi Mitchison, Marjorie Gullan, Lady Pentland, Katharine Bruce Glasier, Dame Elizabeth Cadbury, Pearl Binder, Ellen Wilkinson, MP, Margaret Yates and Caroline Haslett.
360. *TCP*, Vol. VII, No. 26, January–March, 1939, p. 46.

'In Memoriam'

361. A record of obituaries is included in *GCTP*, Vol. XVII, No. 5, May–June 1928, pp. 109–112.
362. Editorial, *GCTP*, Vol. XVIII, No. 5, May–June 1928, p. 101.
363. Harmsworth (1936), p. 2.
364. Unfortunately, it appears that most of Howard's papers were destroyed by his wife after his death, making a definitive biography difficult to achieve. The main secondary sources on Howard are Macfadyen (1970), Harmsworth (1936), Osborn (1946*a*), Osborn (1950), Moss-Eccardt (1973), Fishman (1977) and Beevers (1988).
365. Mumford, in Hughes (1971), p. 106.
366. Osborn (1946*b*), p. 234.
367. Although Fishman (1977), p. 25, is describing Howard's early work, the description is consistent with his later efforts.

368. Harmsworth (1936), p. 2.
369. Fishman (1977), chapter 5, explains this process, showing how an absence of working-class support left Howard dependent on business interests.
370. *Ibid*, p. 25.
371. *Ibid*, p. 80.
372. Barry Parker, writing to Frederic Osborn, in Buder (1969), p. 398.
373. Funds so collected later became a source of controversy. A proposal to create a Howard Memorial Medal to honour distinguished members of the planning movement was bitterly opposed by Purdom, who thought that 'the "planning movement" does not yet justify it . . . I can see no other effect of the existence of the medal at the present time than to help to perpetuate the unreality of town planning in this country.' (Ebenezer Howard National Memorial Committee, Minute Book, Osborn Papers).
374. A full list of signatories to the appeal is shown in *GCTP*, Vol. XVIII, No. 10, December 1928, p. 272, with additional signatories in *GCTP*, Vol. XIX, No. 2, February 1929, p. 39.
375. Editorial, *GCTP*, Vol. XVIII, No. 5, May–June 1928, p. 101.

Preparing for War

376. The term 'Planning Front' is first used in an editorial (under that heading) in *TCP*, Vol. VII, No. 27, July–September 1939, pp. 95–98. The ideas behind it were expounded at the conference organized by the Association at Cardiff in May 1939.
377. Report of GCTPA Cardiff Conference, 1939, in *TCP*, Vol. VII, No. 27, July–September 1939, p. 114.
378. Editorial on the Planning Front, *TCP*, Vol. VII, No. 27, July–September, 1939, pp. 95–96.
379. *Ibid*, p. 97.
380. *Ibid*, p. 98.
381. *Ibid*, p. 96.
382. A report of a special meeting of the Executive, in *TCP*, Vol. VII, No. 28, December 1939, p. 158.
383. *Ibid*.
384. 'The Planning World in Wartime', *TCP*, Vol. VII, No. 28, December 1939, pp. 159–160.
385. 'The War and Planning Nemesis', *TCP*, Vol. VII, No. 28, December 1939, pp. 139–140.

5

CORRIDORS OF POWER
1939–1946

Whether or not the abnormal conditions of warfare have the effect of accelerating trends that are already under way, or whether they lead society along new paths, the fact is that wars are invariably a source of change. This was certainly the case in Britain in 1945. The six-year war – apart from the changes brought about during the war itself – left the country in a mood for radical change. In particular, there was a will to replace the failed policies of the 1930s, with their associations of unemployment and related inequalities, with a bold new approach to offer hope and brighter prospects for all. The 'People's War' would lead, in turn, to the 'People's Peace'.

The Town and Country Planning Association (renamed in 1941) was actively involved in the whole process, during the war and after. In part, it was once again simply caught up in wider trends beyond its own making, but this time (unlike the interwar period) moving towards ends for which it had itself long campaigned. And, in part, it sought to make its own running, ensuring that reforms were not delayed and that they were right in detail as well as in principle. Arguably, for the first time in its existence, the political context was receptive to the Association's demands. Doors hitherto locked, now swung open, and the Association found itself (at times somewhat mystified, if not daunted, by its new position) in the corridors of power, with a real opportunity to influence policy.

The opportunity was not wasted, and while power proved to be far more elusive than the mere opening of doors might have suggested, the new planning policies that emerged were broadly consistent with the Association's own aims. Lower densities within the cities, green belts and new towns were all to feature in the postwar plans. By 1946 – with the passing of the New Towns Act – the first phase of the Association's campaign (that had started in pursuance of garden cities in 1899) was over. It had certainly not achieved all that it had wanted and there was still work to be done, but the aims of the Association in the future and the nature of its work would no longer be the same.

VISION OF JERUSALEM

Long before the prospect of victory, let alone peace, was even assured, reconstruction took its place on the political agenda. In turn, to town and country planning was attributed an important role in future plans for society as a whole. Within this context, the TCPA sought both to ensure that adequate planning machinery was in place to do the job, and that policies were formulated in good time and with the 'right' ends.

War and Reconstruction

The whole nation is at present under the most intense physical and spiritual stress, having bent itself to a struggle which must be bitter and hard and may be long. On the civil population that stress is infinitely greater than it was in the First World War. Yet the public attitude towards thinking and planning ahead is altogether more favourable than it was at a similar phase of that war. In 1915 any discussion of the problems of social rehabilitation, let alone social progress, in the unforeseeable future, would have been regarded as a diversion from the war effort. Not until the third or fourth year was such discussion generally considered tolerable. Not until victory seemed in sight were the first steps taken towards reconstruction. (F.J. Osborn, in *TCP*, Vol. VIII, No. 32, December 1940, p. 65)

Osborn's observation that thoughts of reconstruction arose at a much earlier stage in the Second World War than in the 1914–1918 conflict was borne out by events. Already, barely twelve months after the onset of war, plans were being laid for Britain at peace; indeed, in some cases, this process had already started before the outbreak of war [1].

Partly, it can be asserted that the prompt start was due to the groundwork that had already been laid in the 1930s, and that what was done after 1939 was little more than a reinforcement and acceleration of existing trends – hastening 'progress along the old grooves.' [2] The idea of planning, for instance, had been carefully propagated in the previous decade, and like a plant ready for the rain, it flourished in the exceptional climate of wartime. Reconstruction was rooted in an implicit acceptance of more planning, bearing fruit in a wide range of social, economic and physical fields. As the wartime historian, Paul Addison, notes, the ground had already been well prepared by groups like the Garden Cities and Town Planning Association (the Town and Country Planning Association after 1941), and the agenda was already set:

> Professional bodies like the Town and Country Planning Association, centre pressure-groups like Political and Economic Planning and the Next Five Years Group, advisory committees like those of Spens and Barlow, the school of Keynsian economists, the social investigators of poverty and malnutrition like Rowntree and Boyd Orr – these were the architects of reconstruction and consensus. Perhaps true power resides not with the occupants of high office, but with the people who define the agenda for them [3].

Partly, too, the impetus for reconstruction owes its early start to a discernible drift towards the Left in British politics. This is not to be exaggerated, but the events of May 1940, when Neville Chamberlain's Conservative Administration gave way to a coalition led by Winston Churchill (within which Labour Ministers worked alongside Conservative and Liberal colleagues), proved to be a significant break with the political past. Progressive reconstruction plans were introduced, and the war years saw not only a swing of popular opinion towards Labour, but also the cementing of an all-party consensus in favour of further reforms when the war was over [4]. It was a consensus drawn from 'the whole of the centre of British political life: Cripps and Eden, Herbert Morrison and R. A. Butler, the Liberal Action Group and the Tory reformers, William Beveridge and William Temple, and many influential members of the Fabian Society.' [5]

Progress in achieving some of the specific objectives sought by the Association can best be seen as part of a wider package of reforms that were initiated under the broad rubric of reconstruction. Perhaps physical reconstruction, with its vision of Phoenix arising from the ashes of yesterday's slums, lent itself most easily to the popularization of the whole programme. Amidst the bombed property, the connections were there for all to see: 'It was more than bricks and mortar that collapsed in West Ham on the 7th and 8th of September 1940, it was a local order of society which was found hopelessly wanting, as weak and badly constructed as the single brick walls which fell down at that blast.' [6] The need to rebuild society was as apparent as the need to rebuild the cities.

It is not that enemy bombing was in itself a direct and only cause of wholesale reconstruction, so much as that it provoked popular awareness about a string of related issues. The damage inflicted on British cities 'let in daylight in a double sense. People began to speculate on better things that might be built on the acres of rubble; and from this they went on to speculate how the out-of-date areas left unbombed might be replanned.' [7]

From there it was only a short step to questioning the whole fabric of society for which the war was being fought. Physical reconstruction was, therefore, by no means an isolated issue, and associated changes on parallel economic and social fronts proved to be of fundamental importance to the shape of postwar Britain.

Thus, on the economic front, Keynsianism was introduced as a budgetary technique as early as 1941, opening the way for an unprecedented programme of State intervention and the promise of a future of full employment policies [8]. On the social front, the foundations of postwar policies for social security, family allowances, State education, and a National Health Service had all been laid before 1943. When Sir William Beveridge's report on the future of the social services was published in 1942, with a commitment to abolish 'want' and to provide a comprehensive programme of social security 'from the cradle to the grave', it sold more than 600,000 copies and attracted widespread acclaim [9]. Buoyed up by the tide of optimism following victory at El Alamein (announced a few days before the publication of the report), Beveridge's Plan and the call of 'Beveridge now' reflected the level of popular interest in reconstruction and a growing sense that there could be no going back to the 'bad old days'.

In the middle years of the war, reconstruction issues were eagerly discussed in all sectors of society. The British soldier on active service attended classes on citizenship, organized by the Army Bureau of Current Affairs; while at home listeners tuned in to radio broadcasts that included the voice of Beveridge on the ever-popular 'Brains Trust', answering the 'ordinary man's questions'. Meanwhile, reconstruction issues were fuelled by special editions of *Picture Post*, by cheap and accessible Penguin specials, and by leader articles in *The Times* (far enough to the Left to be described as 'the threepenny edition of the *Daily Worker*'). [10] Pressure groups like the TCPA, advocating the cause of planning, suddenly found that for once they were swimming with rather than against the tide.

Yet, in spite of a growing political realization that the 'People's War' would lead inexorably to a 'People's Peace', the Prime Minister was initially reluctant to lead the way along the reconstruction road. It was conceded that plans would have to be laid for eventual demobilization, and there was merit in countering German propaganda with an optimistic British version of a postwar world. But Churchill was known to be less than enthusiastic to promise too much too soon. Reflecting this view at the top, the first steps towards reconstruction were tentative, and gave little indication of the growing popular will for change. Thus, a War Aims Committee, under the chairmanship of Clement Attlee, lasted for only five months from August to the end of December 1940, when it was disbanded on failing to reach agreement [11].

The next step, with the mantle of reconstruction handed on to another Labour politician of Ministerial rank, Arthur Greenwood, proved to be no more encouraging for the cause of radical change. Greenwood's Cabinet Committee on Reconstruction Problems (established in February 1941) drew up an extensive agenda, embracing every conceivable issue (with a review of the control and acquisition of land by public authorities – raising the possibility of land nationalization – just one item on a long list) [12]. But his committee met on only four occasions over a twelve-month period – a reflection that 'reconstruction had a very low priority in Whitehall in the second winter of the war' [13] – and when it did meet it soon discovered that it could do little to compel action in the various Ministries responsible for new policies. With nothing of consequence achieved, Greenwood was forced to resign his post in March 1942.

After Attlee and Greenwood, it was then the turn of a third Labour Minister, Sir William Jowitt, to take on the job on reconstruction. Although Jowitt's powers and standing were, in fact, somewhat less than those of Attlee and Greenwood, during his term of office (from March 1942 to November 1943) 'public interest in reconstruction grew in leaps and bounds.' [14] Unlike his predecessors, his term of office coincided with a more eventful period, in the sense that significant plans were already beginning to emerge through the various Government Departments. Jowitt's reign was greatly enhanced by the appearance in 1942 of several major reports, notably, the Scott Report on land utilization in rural areas, the Uthwatt Report on compensation and betterment, and the above-mentioned Beveridge Report [15]. Such was the public interest aroused by these publications that the erstwhile reluctant Prime Minister was moved in March 1943 to broadcast his own plans for reconstruction – a four-year programme based on the findings of the much-publicized reports commissioned by his own Government. At the same time, while benefiting from this turn of events, Jowitt suffered from a shift in the balance of power away from his own advisory committee and towards the individual Ministries. Thus, in November 1943 new arrangements were introduced with Lord Woolton installed as Minister of Reconstruction with a full Cabinet place.

In some respects, the appointment of Lord Woolton marks the end of the first phase of the reconstruction debate. A vision of a better Britain was now firmly lodged on the political agenda and, so it seemed, there could be no turning back. There was, in fact, nothing inexorable about events, but at least the tide was now running strongly in favour of reconstruction. Moreover, within this context, 'this was the year in which land use planning began to emerge as a complex story in itself. The broad canvas gave way to a much more detailed picture.' [16] All of which provides an interesting backcloth against which to analyse the specific role of the TCPA. To what extent in the early half of the war did the Association – in the context of a growing surge of public opinion in favour of planning – contribute to the vision of reconstruction that began to take shape on the 'broad canvas'? And, particularly after 1943, how much was it involved in putting together the 'detailed picture' of town and country planning?

Reconstruction Machinery

> The framework of a fine machine was built. But the late Government stopped short of finishing the job. There is the machine, all bright and shining, embodying a big investment of Ministerial and Parliamentary time, but unable to function for lack of a few indispensable parts. (F. J. Osborn, in *TCP*, Vol. XIII, No. 50, Summer 1945, p. 56).

During the war, and in the context of the wider reconstruction debate, the Association sought to advance the cause of planning in two ways – through getting the right machinery to do the job, and then ensuring that it produced the right output. There was, therefore, an administrative and a policy side to the Association's work (as, indeed, there had been for some years before the war too, as evidenced in the submission to the Barlow Committee in 1938).

As the above quote indicates, on the machinery side the Association could take stock at the end of the war in Europe and report notable gains but not a total victory. Moreover, it will become apparent that the Association's aim to progress machinery and policy in tandem proved to be a consistent source of frustration. Any advances in planning came about piecemeal, and while, with the benefit of hindsight, it is tempting to impose an overriding logic on the course of events, that is not (for good reason) necessarily how it was seen at the time.

To look, first, at the machinery of reconstruction, even before the onset of war the Association's view had already been clearly stated. Of seven principles that were intended to unite a proposed Planning Front, one was concerned with the establishment of a central body for national planning, and one with a change in compensation and betterment procedures [17]. The use of the prewar term Planning Front gave way to the less militaristic National Planning Basis, but the machinery goals remained the same [18]. To this end, the Association sought both to foster and articulate public opinion, and to influence politicians and civil servants. And, with the publication of the Barlow Report at the end of January 1940, the Association was provided with its first major wartime opportunity to present its case.

The Report had been eagerly awaited, and its publication was welcomed by the Association as a 'turning-point . . . of worldwide significance . . . We hail the Nine Conclusions of the Report as the first authoritative draft of a Charter of National Planning.' [19] Amongst the nine conclusions so enthusiastically hailed there were important recommendations regarding the most appropriate form of planning machinery. Notably, there was an unequivocal call for immediate national action, and for a Central Authority with powers that would take it beyond the range of existing Government Departments. On the surface, at least, these recommendations closely reflected the essence of the Association's own submission to the Royal Commission in 1938 [20].

In practice, though, the Barlow findings fell short of the Association's hopes. This is evidenced in two ways. At a public level, it was significant that there was dissent amongst the members of the Commission, to the extent that the Report itself revealed unresolved differences of view. As well as what were known as the Majority Proposals (signed by ten Commissioners, including the Chairman), the publication included a Note of Reservation (signed by three of the Majority), a Minority Report (signed by the three remaining Commissioners), and a Dissentient Memorandum on Planning by one of the Minority. Two of the three Minority Commissioners (Professor Abercrombie and Mrs Hichens) were influential members of the Association, and their point that stronger measures were needed to deal with the urgent problems to be addressed coincided with the Association's own policy. In particular, the Central Authority recommended in the Minority proposals should be nothing less than a new Department of State with a Minister of Cabinet rank. The Dissentient Memorandum, the work of Abercrombie, dealt with the details of planning machinery in relation to the location of industry.

At a private level, a sense of disappointment that the Report did not emerge with a stronger set of recommendations is revealed in Osborn's own doubts as to how best to respond. Aware of the Report's limitations, he later confessed that 'when the Report was finally published I was in grave doubts for forty-eight hours whether to damn it as feeble, or to hail it (and interpret it) as a great crossing of the Rubicon, because it could have been otherwise interpreted.' Osborn chose the latter course of action, which 'proved to my relief the right course.' [21]

In September of the same year as the Barlow Report, the Association saw signs of further progress on the planning front. Lord Reith (with his pioneering BBC experience behind him) was appointed as the first Minister of a newly-formed Department of Works and Building [22]. It was widely seen as being an imaginative appointment, with Reith not the sort of person who would be overwhelmed by that part of his brief that addressed the immediate problems of preparing emergency measures to deal with bomb damage, to the exclusion of a wider brief to look at the whole question of reconstruction of town and country planning after the war. 'I welcome the formation of the new Ministry' was the heading of a message from the Chairman of the Association's Executive in the pages of the journal, exhorting Reith to prepare 'a bold and imaginative policy under new auspices.' [23]

Within a month of Reith's appointment, the Association delivered a copy of a Memorandum (addressed to the Prime Minister and for the attention of other interested Ministries), entitled 'Town Planning in relation to the Present Emergency and After-War Reconstruction' [24]. The Memorandum addressed both policy and machinery issues, the latter including a proposal to enhance central planning through the formation of a new Ministry of Building and National Planning. There is also evidence that Osborn was consulted by Reith in the early stages of taking office. Thus, over a weekend in November Osborn responded to a request to map out his thoughts on the future shape of regional planning and, with a rare display of modesty, attached a note to his lengthy paper to tell Reith that 'I had not previously thought out a Regional System, and I feel a certain effrontery in reorganising British local government on paper in a weekend without any consultation.' [25] Osborn followed up his submission with a meeting in Reith's office, and Reith, in turn, spent the first day of February 1941 on a private visit to Welwyn [26].

Amongst the incomplete files and records of correspondence it is impossible to disentangle cause and effect but, whether Reith was influenced by the Association's lobbying or not, his actions on taking office were certainly along the lines advocated by the Association. By February 1941 Reith had secured from the Cabinet a definitive statement that:

(a) The government will be favourably disposed towards the principle of planning, as part of a national policy, and some central planning authority will be required.

(b) In planning the physical reconstruction of town and country, the planning authority will be able to proceed in the light of a positive policy in regard to such matters as agriculture, industrial development and transport.

(c) The central government would arrange for the planning by the central planning authority or other government agency of services and other matters requiring treatment on the broadest national scale. Matters calling for treatment on a regional basis would be planned by a regional authority [27].

The Government's endorsement of Reith's approach was followed by the creation of a Consultative Panel on Physical Reconstruction, where Reith could call on the advice of experts other than his own civil servants. Osborn was given a sight of a provisional list of the proposed Panel, and immediately wrote to the Ministry with his own list of names. The membership, he advised, should be drawn up with the aim of securing the implementation of Barlow's 'Nine Points' [28]. Again, it is impossible to disentangle cause and effect, but the Association could take considerable satisfaction from the fact that of the twenty-one members of the newly-formed Panel, nine (including Osborn) were members of the Association. Two of these nine had been signatories of the Barlow Minority Report, and one was Barlow himself [29]. In terms of potential influence, the interests of the Association were undoubtedly well placed at what can be seen as a critical juncture in planning history. From a position of external lobbying, the case could now be made from within the offices of Government.

It is worth delving a little further into this change in positioning for the Association, much of which was to depend on the influence which Osborn himself could exert. In his own recollections, Osborn clearly has mixed feelings about it all. He was clearly flattered to be able to tell his correspondent, Lewis Mumford, that he had been given a room in the Ministry [30], and elsewhere he describes himself as an 'unpaid Under-Sec' [31]. He conveys an impression that he was Reith's right-hand man, as, for instance, '. . . drafted with Lord R. papers for Cabinet by which R. got acceptance of Barlow Recs.' [32] Helped, no doubt, by the insider information of Panel members, this was also a time of 'much lobbying by Assn. of Lords and Commons.' [33]

At the same time, there is also a strong sense of being overawed and even disappointed by the new situation within the corridors of Whitehall. Reith's domain proved to be 'only a tiny section tucked away in the vast building of the Ministry of Works and Buildings . . . its secretariat and principal officers should have first-class civil servants; at present they are necessarily juniors, and have not constant and direct access to the Minister . . . The official relationship of Lord Reith's Reconstruction Division to the other Ministries dealing with related issues of Reconstruction is remote and does not produce common thinking.' [34] Moreover, some years later Osborn confessed that his relationship with Reith was 'curious . . . in which R. looked down on O. as £5,000 p.a. Chairman to £500 p.a. junior clerk, and up to him as Guru.' [35] And Reith, himself, in his autobiography, later recalled that Osborn (along with Lord Balfour of Burleigh) 'gave a great deal to it' (the Panel), but that 'the credit for what was accomplished was in large measure Vincent's' (the civil servant appointed to serve the Panel) [36].

If the hope had been that opening the doors of Whitehall would somehow reveal the secret of political power – neat and ready to be plundered – this was clearly an illusion. But, for all its limitations, the formation of the Reconstruction Panel was rightly welcomed at the time by the Association. Moreover, the Association could also report on progress in the prospects of new machinery to tackle the old and critical problems of land values. In April 1941 the Expert Committee on Compensation and Betterment (the Uthwatt Committee) published its interim findings [37]. The establishment of this committee had been another of Reith's initiatives, and its interim report was produced within four months. Its recommendations were far-reaching, but while the Government accepted the principles of compensation and betterment as a crucial element (immediately applicable to the problems of reconstruction in the blitzed cities), the Association regretted that 'the most important recommendation', the creation of a Central Planning Authority, had not been accepted [38].

For the rest of 1941 it seemed that the flagship of a Central Planning Authority had become 'becalmed in the Saragasso Sea of Anthony Greenwood's Reconstruction Committee.' [39] It proved, however, to be a temporary lull, and in February 1942 Cabinet approval was given for Reith's proposal to transfer planning powers from the Ministry of Health to a duly strengthened Ministry of Works and Planning. 'This is an important decision,' proclaimed the Association, '. . . the reflection of a unanimous plea for a great forward movement in positive and national planning.' [40]

At the same time, the Association lamented Churchill's decision (within a few days of announcing plans for the establishment of the new Ministry) to dismiss Reith from high office. The Association was correct in its view that Reith had done much in his short term of office to 'set going the thinking and research processes on which the ultimate planning policy will depend.' [41] Reith's departure was undoubtedly a loss, but at least the Association was able to take some consolation from the appointment of a member of its own Executive, Henry Strauss, as Parliamentary Secretary in the new Ministry (headed by an industrialist, Lord Portal) [42].

If personalities were important to the Association, so, too, was the quality of the machinery with which the agents of planning were asked to work, and on this the Association still had its doubts. The new Ministry represented an advance over the old arrangements, but it still fell short of the ideal of a Central Planning Authority with unequivocal power. It was noted that the existence of a separate Ministry of Reconstruction was just one source of ambiguity and potential conflict that could stand in the way of effective planning. 'There is not yet a machine; there are parts lying all over the place.' [43]

Progress was, at best, incremental, and in February 1943 the hybrid Ministry of Works and Planning (with a wide range of only loosely-connected powers) gave way to a separate Ministry of Town and Country Planning. The first Minister was the Labour Politician W. S. Morrison, with Strauss continuing in the role of Parliamentary Secretary. Against a background of lobbying within Government circles for planning powers to be dispersed across the full range of domestic Ministries, the decision to concentrate powers in this way and to elevate the status of the term 'town and country planning' (something that would have been inconceivable even a few years before), was understandably welcomed by the Association: 'a landmark in our campaign – our Battle of Egypt.' [44]

The most immediate task of the new Ministry was to construct the machinery to enable the rebuilding of Britain's bombed cities. The resultant Town and County Planning Act of 1944 had its limitations – 'a tepid affair beside the Uthwatt Report.' [45] Moreover, the Association returned to its old concern that machinery and policy were not being developed together, lamenting the fact that the latest 'machinery proposals' had not been accompanied by 'an inspiring statement of the policy they are intended to implement.' [46] And the Act did not in itself resolve the problem of dividing powers between different Ministries – the main ones, in addition to Town and Country Planning, being the Board of Trade and the Ministries of Works and of Health. At the very least, the Association called for 'adequate coordination' between the four departments [47]. At the same time, the Act was acknowledged as another important advance, strengthening the principle of public control of land use and acknowledging a public claim to permitted increases of land value.

The machinery was, then, at least partly in place, and certainly in very much better shape than at the outset of war. How much the Association contributed to this process, though, is debatable. It was undoubtedly influential in helping to establish the parameters of the exercise, but evidence of contributing to the detailed construction of the machinery is scanty. After the euphoria of 1941, when the Association could loudly voice its views on Reith's Reconstruction Panel, Osborn was soon to discover that a position gained could disappear just as quickly. He subsequently wrote to Morrison to ask what had happened to the Panel (which, since the departure of Reith, was no longer meeting) and to enquire whether there were any plans for the new Ministry to revitalize it. A reply was drafted, explaining that 'the special circumstances surrounding the creation of the Panel have passed', but Morrison (perhaps fearing that this would only encourage further lobbying) decided, instead, that 'it will be better not to send a reply to Mr Osborn at this stage.' [48]

In his authoritative interpretation of the reconstruction process, Cullingworth is, by implication, dismissive of influence from the Association. Instead, he looks in part for an explanation of early progress to the failure of senior ministers (preoccupied with urgent war affairs) to resist the bandwagon for central planning; partly to the diffuse nature of reconstruction planning, with the effect that the machinery of planning was, at best, constructed piecemeal; and, in part, progress is attributed to the single-mindedness of Reith [49]. It is itself worthy of comment that throughout the whole of the first volume of Cullingworth's official history of environmental planning, gleaned from the most detailed of sources, there is not a single mention of the Town and Country Planning Association.

The New Planning

> . . . the policy of Dispersal, Green Belts, and New Towns, already officially accepted, seemed in a fair way to being implemented . . . The seeds of a more enlightened policy have germinated. (TCPA Annual Report for 1945)

By the end of the war, the TCPA could confidently speak of 'the New Planning' [50]. For more than forty years, the Association had sought to propagate the seeds of 'Dispersal, Green Belts and New Towns', and now at last there were signs of growth.

Without attributing cause and effect, the gap between the Association's aims and what came to be official policy narrowed in the wartime years. From 1938, in fact, when evidence was submitted to the Barlow Committee, it had become apparent that the Association was no longer solely a garden city movement. What it sought in terms of policy (though still rooted in garden city principles) now explicitly addressed the regional and metropolitan problems of the day. Throughout the war years, the Association campaigned on this broader front, best illustrated by the five principles of the National Planning Basis that were concerned with policy outcomes rather than machinery:

* The distinction between Town and Country should be maintained in all development, and sporadic building in rural areas discouraged. In particular, good food-growing land, places of special landscape beauty, and areas suitable for national parks or

coastal reservations, should be protected from ordinary building development.

* Good design and layout of buildings and roads should be an object of policy equally with sound construction. Outdoor advertising should be limited to certain approved situations.

* In the rebuilding of urban areas, the density of residential districts should be limited so as to provide a sufficiency of open space for all necessary purposes, including reasonable garden-space for family houses. Wide country belts should be reserved around and between all cities and towns, so that town-dwellers may have access to the countryside.

* New developments required by industrial changes, by decentra-lisation from congested areas, or by the growth of towns up to their planned limits, should be directed to other existing towns, or to new towns carefully sited to meet the needs of industry, agriculture and social amenity. New towns and extending towns should be planned as compact units, scattered or ribbon building being prevented. All developments and redevelopments should be planned and equipped for the encouragement of local community activities.

* As a means of promoting a better national distribution and balance of industry in the regions of Great Britain, the Ministry charged with National Planning should have power (a) to pre-vent, except under licence, the settlement of new industrial undertakings in overgrown and congested towns and in under-developed rural areas, and (b) to offer inducements to industry to settle in suitably selected places. Business firms should retain full freedom of choice among areas where such restriction is not imposed [51].

If these were the main planks of the Association's policy, the avowed task was then to convince others – and particularly a Govern-ment that proved to be reluctant to commit itself to explicit planning policies – that this was the way forward. In its wartime campaign, the Association was assisted by the publication of a series of influential reports and plans which, although not amounting to a coherent policy in themselves, provided a platform from which pressure could be exerted.

Barlow, Uthwatt and Scott offered the basic ingredients for the kind of national policy that the Association was advocating, and in November 1942 the Council agreed a statement to this effect [52].

From Barlow's nine recommendations came what the Association believed should be at the core of a national policy – a recognition of the need to redevelop congested urban areas, coupled with the dispersal of industries and population to enable redevelopment to take place at reasonable densities, and a wider framework of regional policies to bring about a more balanced distribution of economic activity. From Uthwatt the Association welcomed the proposed means by which within the cities local authorities would be able to implement effective redevelopment plans, while outside the built-up areas the State acquisition of development rights would make it possible to secure urban containment and meaningful green belts. Finally, in the case of Scott (in spite of reservations that the protection of the countryside might sometimes be seen to be favouring higher urban densities) the Association drew from the report an endorsement of planned dispersal (as opposed to sprawl) and a goal of rural revitalization that had been enshrined in the Association's doctrine from the days of Howard.

In pressing the Government for the adoption of these reports as a basis for national policy, the Association claimed that it was advocating a consensus view. 'The membership of the Association is representative of the best opinion, not only of technical planners, but of those among the industrialists, sociologists, economists, agriculturists, leaders of organized labour, administration and municipal authorities who have given prolonged attention to all the town and countryside issues related to planning.' [53] The policy that was commended to the Government was 'balanced' and would enjoy wide support, and it was predicted that an early announcement committed to a comprehensive national policy 'would have an electric effect on national enthusiasm.' [54]

An early announcement on policy was not, however, forthcoming. Osborn's belief (on which the Association's statements were based) that the building blocks for a new policy were already in place, and that all the Government had to do was to apply the glue provided by a national consensus, proved to be an illusion. It was, as Michael Hebbert points out, an illusion for two reasons [55]. For one thing, although Osborn had a basis for claiming the existence of a consensus to plan, there was certainly no unanimity as to what should actually be done. Strongly-held differences as to acceptable densities for redevelopment (which Osborn thought should not exceed a maximum of 85 persons per acre); a reluctance on the part of large city authorities to 'export' people and jobs; and a powerful rural lobby which viewed any kind of dispersal (planning or otherwise) with distaste, all showed the difficulty in arriving at a clear overall policy [56]. A second impediment to rapid progress was the continuing division of Ministerial responsibilities for planning within the Government. As noted in the previous section, although planning powers as such were (at least from February 1943) brought under one roof, the Ministry of Health continued to be responsible for housing, the Board of Trade took a leading role regarding industrial location, and the Ministry of Works controlled the building process. Against this kind of political and administrative background, the idea of a single, coherent policy remained well-intentioned but naive.

Evidence of the false optimism on which the Association's claims were based is illustrated with a decision by the Ministry of Health in March 1943 to press ahead with a one-year housing programme in advance of any agreement on the course of overall planning. The Association, fearing a repeat of the post-1918 situation, was incensed, and quickly issued a policy statement pointing out that to build in advance of planning would be to throw away an opportunity that had been carefully nurtured; 'there is a grave danger that the widespread hopes aroused by the "Blitz" and two years of national discussion will be disappointed, and that the 1919–39 course of development will be resumed.' [57] Privately, Osborn wrote to Mumford at that time, reporting that the 'immediate planning situation is bad' but that he still had 'a great deal of hope for a Decentralisation policy, which is just practicable in this country.' [58]

In the short term, this hope for a decentralization policy suffered a further setback with the publication later in 1943 of the County of London Plan – '. . . a profound disappointment. It talks the language of "decentralisation" and plans to slow up the process as much as possible.' [59] The Association complained that the plan for the capital (another of Reith's initiatives) had fallen short in terms of housing standards, it failed to address adequately the vital question of industrial relocation, and it dealt only with a part of London [60]. Osborn blamed Abercrombie for losing 'the chance of a century', and himself for not sitting 'on his doorstep at County Hall as I did on Barlow's doorstep during the sittings of the Commission . . .' [61] But in terms of the postwar influence of the plan, Osborn's criticism has itself been dismissed as being 'rather trivial' [62].

The fact was that progress was being made, but not as quickly nor as comprehensively as the fundamentalists would have wished to see. Policy did not suddenly appear as a perfect apparition, but it evolved piecemeal and always somewhat less than perfect. Thus, by 1944 the Association could welcome the Government's acceptance (four years after publication) of the main ideas of the Barlow Report, while at the same time expressing criticisms of the Board of Trade's narrow interpretation of industrial location policy [63]. There was also in that year the White Paper on Control of Land Use, an acceptance in part of the Uthwatt proposals, and also the clearest and most comprehensive statement yet on the direction of national planning [64]. Yet the

Association lamented that these documents (together with the 1944 Town and Country Planning Bill) 'still do not present the nation with a clear and positive planning policy.' [65]

The dilemma in formulating a comprehensive approach is most clearly analysed by Parsons, who points to a central problem as being the effective separation of the crucial industrial location powers from the rest of planning [66]. Far from being a consensual evolution from the recommendations of Barlow and prewar opinion, industrial location policy is seen largely as a product of the contingencies and administrative experience of wartime (when central industrial planning was essential to ensure war supplies); of the relative influence of key politicians at the Board of Trade; and of a general tendency to treat industrial location as an 'economic issue'. As a result of all these factors, the war, 'more effectively than could have been possible in peace time, enabled the integrated planning model to be separated into two distinct realms; physical planning and economic management.' [67] This separation was duly sealed in the 1945 Distribution of Industry Act, under the administrative control of the Board of Trade. It marked a fundamental setback for the Association, which, while welcoming the new powers that could be used to influence the location of industry, had always anticipated a more integrated approach. There is a sense in which the Association had naively played the 'three card trick', and had lost the 'lady' – devoting all its attention and energies to monitoring events at the Planning Ministry, while one of its key cards was being played elsewhere.

If the loss of industrial location policy was a setback, it was hard, however, to take issue with the very real progress inherent in Abercrombie's Greater London Plan [68]. That, in many ways, represented the very quintessence of all the Association had striven for. The promise of containment of urban sprawl and a policy of planned dispersal, complete with new settlements, was beyond contention. Here was the essential doctrine, first set out in Howard's gospel of 1899, proposed for the metropolis itself; the eternal conflict between Good and Evil could at last be resolved. In determining the outcome, Osborn was sure of the Association's part. Abercrombie had wavered at the time of the County of London Plan, but just in time he had been shown the light:

The difference between Abercrombie's first and second London Plans is at least partly due to our criticisms of the first. Great efforts were made to induce him to resign from the Town and Country Planning Association and to fasten on to me the disrepute of a wrecker of planning; but I knew that Abercrombie was unhappy about his compromise with the leaders of the LCC, who wanted no dispersal at all; and I maintained a strategy of critical encouragement, which succeeded just when I had begun to doubt whether I had been mistaken in refraining from an all-out attack [69].

By the end of the war, the cause of planning policy had come a long way. Even the Association was prepared to concede that, 'Decongestion and Dispersal is the key-note of national planning policy.' [70] But it was a qualified concession. The Association remained concerned that emergency housing needs would pre-empt proper planning, legislation for compensation and betterment had still to be passed, and the Board of Trade seemed intent on trying to solve local employment problems in a national and regional vacuum. The potential was there to bring the various parts together, but the Association had its doubts about the power of the Planning Ministry to do this. Important gains had been made, but, as the following comment illustrates, there was still a strong sense of unease as to whether the package would continue to hold. '"Everybody" is talking Dispersal, Satellite Towns, Green Belts, Location of Industry, etc, (everybody, that is, except the much larger everybody, who is still talking Housing, as in 1919).' [71] The spectre of dashed hopes after the First World War still haunted the minds of those who had failed to build Jerusalem then.

PROPAGANDA AND POLITICS

The public interest aroused by the prospect of reconstruction brought to the Association new members and a level of political support that had been rare in its history. In response, the Association employed a wide range of propagandist techniques to advance the cause, and helped to form an influential network of policy-makers. Alliances were formed with other organizations, and sources of opposition were challenged.

Managing in Wartime

A WORD TO MEMBERS. After the War much of Britain will be rebuilt. Shall this be done on the old lines, or can we do it in such a way as to give living space for all and the physical framework for a higher state of civilisation? A great opportunity opens before us, and members are asked to help the Association now, both by financial contributions and by personal work. (TCPA Annual General Report for 1942)

The war was a time for action. Sensing that the political tide was at last flowing in the direction of planning, the Association was intent to take full advantage of an historic opportunity – 'the opportunity for which the Association had waited for 42 years has come.' [72] With an almost chiliastic intensity, the forgers of Association policy were not to be deterred by the mere distractions of a World War. Indeed, it was not simply a question of 'business as usual' (as in the First World War), but rather of business with a vengeance to ensure that this time the opportunity did not slip away.

A new confidence is apparent in the way the Association presented its case. Far less, now, an outsider group advocating a minority cause, the Association claimed for itself a leadership role in the wider campaign – 'the foremost town-planning association' [73] and 'the only authoritative society concerned with education and propaganda for town and country planning.' [74] The fortunes of the organization improved during the war, but behind the rhetoric of leadership its resources remained pitifully small.

In staffing terms, the Association started its wartime campaign with a staff of just one, the Assistant Secretary, Miss Baldwin. As the pace of activity was increased, Miss Baldwin was joined by Mrs McAllister, who dealt with public relations as well as editing the journal, and in 1942 by a new Organising Secretary, Miss Clarke. Meanwhile, the Association continued to rely on a team of voluntary workers to assist the full-time staff. Osborn, of course, was centrally involved in everything that went on, but even his role was part-time. As he confessed to Lewis Mumford 'I'm making munitions most of most days in my home town and sweating away at the problems of legislation and administration of national planning in the evenings and in half-days at the embryo Ministry of Planning in London . . .' [75]

Although the Library was left at its London address, and the Executive Committee continued to meet there, an early decision was taken to move the office to 10 Parkway, Welwyn Garden City. The arrangement, largely to suit the working arrangements of Osborn, aroused some amusement as an example of unplanned decentralization. 'Even the offices of the Garden Cities Association had fled to Welwyn,' observed W. A. Robson, in a lecture at the London School of Economics [76]. In fact, the Association returned before the end of the war, in May 1944, to two suites of offices at 27 King Street, Covent Garden. It was a mark of the status of the organization at the time that the new offices were subsequently opened by the Minister of Town and Country Planning, W. S. Morrison.

As the war progressed, and public interest in planning issues heightened, the membership position followed a similar pattern of growth to that of staffing and accommodation. At the end of 1939, the total membership subscriptions (which were still one guinea per person) amount to £580. By 1942 this figure had nearly doubled to a new total of £1,112, with an even greater rate of growth in the following year, when 668 new members joined (including local authorities and private businesses). Progress was maintained for the rest of the war (in spite of 'interference with activities by flying bombs' [77], which slowed down the rate of growth in 1944) with a membership in 1945 exceeding 2,000 (including 300 local authorities), contributing subscriptions totalling nearly £3,000 [78].

Only at the time of the Letchworth campaign and in the post-1918 'homes for heroes' euphoria had the membership numbers been of this order. Undoubtedly, the Association would dearly have loved to have enjoyed a consistently large support (if only for the financial security which this might have brought), but with the rewriting of history a virtue was made of small numbers. The Association had not 'hitherto sought a large popular membership . . . but most of the people engaged in planning, architecture, local and national government, and in sociology who are active in planning thought and propaganda are members.' [79] At the same time, while small numbers might be equated with elitism, the fact is that the flood of new members drawn in by the reconstruction debate was warmly encouraged. Each edition of the journal listed the names of new members, and asked for their active support and additional donations where possible. A large, popular membership was now seen to be important to the success of the campaign, as well as a more traditional membership of influence.

Osborn (who became Chairman of the Executive in 1944 as well as continuing as Honorary Secretary) was determined, however, that a larger membership should not lead to any diffusion of aims [80]. And on the aims of the Association he was absolutely clear. The war campaign was to be fought on the platform of the National Planning Basis, adopted by the Council of the Association in January 1941 [81]. In this were contained the immediate policy objectives for the Association (considered in terms of machinery and content aims in the previous two sections), all directed towards the creation of a new system of town and country planning to come into full being with the ending of the war. There were other bodies which could be counted on to campaign on particular issues that were consistent with the aims of the National Planning Basis, but none, it was claimed, that adopted such a comprehensive approach [82].

In asserting its own leadership, and in reflecting the policy changes that had been introduced, an important event was the decision to change the name of the organization from Garden Cities and Town Planning Association to Town and Country Planning Association. Just as the decision in 1909 to replace the original title of the Association had signalled the adoption of a broader role, so, too, did the 1941 decision mark the final abandonment of garden city objectives *per se* and a bid for planning leadership in the reconstruction campaign. Although the changes seem to have aroused little in the way of controversy, the issues were carefully weighed up in a confidential note to members in February 1941 [83].

On the one hand, it was contended that the present name limited the Association's membership and scope of influence. The first reason was that the idea of garden cities (which was embodied in the title) still attracted a bad press, being 'connected in many people's minds with bad speculative building, and with cranks, sandals, "longhair" etc.' [84] It was thought that amongst two groups in particular – intellectuals who were drawn to the idea of planning, but not necessarily to garden cities; and countryside preservationists who confused garden cities with indiscriminate sprawl – the terminology was particularly obstructive to gaining new members. Other reasons for a change were that the Association was often confused with the commercial publicity of Letchworth and Welwyn; the existing title did not show an equal concern for the interests of the countryside; the confusion of the term 'garden cities' with garden suburbs; and the obscuring of broader motives behind the single issue of garden cities.

To set against the reasons for a change, it was recognized that there was some merit in retaining the old title. The Association had, after all, won an international reputation on the basis of its adherence to garden city principles. To abandon that part of its title might imply a loss of faith 'in Howard's essential idea just when it is nearest to official and public acceptance.' [85] Moreover, if the term had become widely used by speculators and suburb builders that could itself be seen as a sign of the authority of the term; the association of the organization with gardens was a source of popular support, in view of a widespread preference for houses with gardens; and the essentials of the garden city ideas were as vital and applicable as ever.

On balance, though, the case for the new title was considered to be irresistible. The Barlow Report, it was argued, had established the garden city idea as an integral part of the new planning orthodoxy, so that the campaign for acceptance of the principle had already been won. Additionally, if the Association was to attract a larger membership it was essential that it should shake off any hint of sectional interests in the sense of being seen as a narrow garden city body. Members could, in any case, be assured that garden city principles would not be abandoned, if only because the leading figures in the Association would continue to be closely associated with the progress of garden cities. Finally, if the Association was serious about adopting a broad leadership role, the proposed change of title would simply bring it into line with the titles of town and country planning legislation that had been on the statute books since 1925.

The membership was clearly in tune with the reasoning in the note that had been sent to them, and 'by a large majority' [86] a vote was recorded at the Annual Meeting on the 14th March 1941 to adopt the new title, Town and Country Planning Association.

Ways and Means

> Mr Goddard Watts suggested that although public opinion is in favour of planning, surveys show that in the main the public are cynical, and do not believe that much effective planning will be done after the war. This was discussed in relation to the Association's propaganda. (Minutes of TCPA Informal Sub-Committee on Propaganda, 21st January 1942)

Mr Goddard Watts (representing the Building Industries) was a member of the sub-committee of the Association which became known as the Education Propaganda Committee [87]. His observation that there was still a long way to go if public support was to be sustained was itself a reason for the establishment of a special committee to add to the Association's efforts. The committee made its own limited contribution to the campaign, but it is likely that its main value was in bringing into the fold representatives of the press and industry [88]. The fact is that, in practical terms, by 1942 the Association was already involved in a wide range of activities to publicize its aims and to win the support of leading thinkers and decision-makers, along with the constituents of 'public opinion'.

It was a period of intense activity, and the propagandist methods of the Association took a variety of forms. One source of influence (which had proved to be effective before, as for instance at the time of the campaign for the first garden city) was the use of conferences to draw in the leading thinkers of the day. Throughout the war, conferences were held on the major policy issues that the Association believed would underpin the structure of a new planning system.

The first of these, in Febraury 1940, was held in London to get agreement between the main bodies concerned with planning as to the shape of a postwar planning policy [89]. Representatives from the RIBA, TPI, CPRE and the National Trust were amongst those who could find enough common ground in what was later publicized as the National Planning Basis.

Plans for a residential conference at Oxford in June 1940 to discuss the Barlow Report had to be cancelled because of the war situation, but the conference was rearranged for March 1941. The idea of taking key figures away from the immediacy of the war effort in order to discuss the good that might come from it all, and then of publishing the outcome, proved to be an effective formula. Thus, at Oxford, 181 participants met over a three-day period at Lady Margaret Hall, 'at a time when interest in the problems of planning is growing in ever-increasing volume.' [90] As well as the Association's own stalwarts, the gathering included representatives from national and local politics, academia, the professions and industry. Patrick Abercrombie, Montague Barlow, G. D. H. Cole, John Dower, C. B. Fawcett, A. L. Hobhouse, William Holford, G. L. Pepler, Rt. Hon. Lord Justice Scott, Lewis Silkin, Sir Ernest Simon, Dudley Stamp and Sir George Stapledon were amongst the distinguished and influential gathering [91]. There was an intensity and sense of urgency about the proceedings, with no time wasted on courtesies and ceremonies [92].

If the proceedings proved to be typical of the conferences that followed, so, too, was the outcome (published, as were the others, in book form) [93]. Inevitably, perhaps, with such a range of participants, the outcome was clearly not as conclusive as Osborn would have wished. Instead of an unequivocal endorsement of the main Barlow recommendations, 'some of the pieces of the jig-saw came out and waltzed joyfully all over the area of the puzzle.' [94] Osborn had to confess that the event had not achieved its original intention to consolidate the way forward. But in bringing together key actors in the unfolding planning drama the conference had its own considerable value, and was to be followed by comparable events, on Industry and Rural Life (held at Cambridge in 1942), on Country Towns (at the Royal Empire Society in London in 1943), on Ways and Means of Rebuilding (also in London in 1943), and on The New Planning (in London in 1944).

These wartime conferences were landmarks in their own way, if only in addressing the differences of view that existed. There may have been a consensus about planning as a general principle (to which the Association contributed), but by no means the same degree of consensus about the details. As a series, in bringing together the various parties and in mapping out the postwar planning agenda, the conferences were impressive. And it is as a series that Armytage thinks they should be judged, accrediting to Osborn the organization of the 'most significant, if not the most important, conferences of the century on this subject.' [95]

Divergent thoughts about reconstruction were poured into a ferment of discussion, and Osborn was ceaseless in his efforts to bring together the various parties to seek a blend of agreement, while at the same time opening it all up to a wider public at home and in the forces overseas. Indeed, it was only when 'the common man and woman came into the planning discussion, (that) commonsense came too.' [96] Given the level of public interest, the problem, within the Association, was one of how best, with the limited resources available, to contribute most effectively to the debate. As Osborn confessed to Barlow, 'under present conditions, when the whole country is

ON JOY'S RETURNING MORN!

GET READY FOR THE GOOD LIFE

TWO MINUTES FROM THE TOWN CENTRE

THE PATHWAY TO WELWYN GARDEN CITY WILL AGAIN BE OPEN. THE TOWN, CONCEIVED AND BUILT IN HAPPIER DAYS, WILL BE THERE TO GREET THE SMILING MORN.—"A TOWN DESIGNED FOR HEALTHY LIVING AND INDUSTRY; OF A SIZE THAT MAKES POSSIBLE A FULL MEASURE OF SOCIAL LIFE . . . . ."

LIVE AND WORK IN WELWYN

WELWYN GARDEN CITY LIMITED · WIGMORES NORTH · WELWYN GARDEN CITY

Wartime propaganda took a variety of forms, including raising the spirits with the promise of peacetime.

wanting meetings on the subject this is giving us any number of headaches . . .' [97]

Undoubtedly, the most efficient way of reaching large numbers of people was to take advantage of the growing popularity of BBC radio broadcasts. Often these were presented in terms of debates between exponents of different factions, and Osborn later noted of this period: 'Many broadcasts on planning by TCPA members; some fierce controversies about NT policy, Comp. and Bett., houses v. flats etc.' [98] With the names of Barlow, Uthwatt and Scott widely known and planning issues now a key part of any reconstruction strategy, the BBC felt able in 1943 to involve seventy speakers (including Osborn) in a series of discussions linked together as 'Making Plans'. Such was the level of interest in broadcasting that popular programmes could then be simulated at the Association's own events, in the form, for instance, of Brains Trusts on housing and planning [99].

Another way to cope with limited resources was to encourage local groups to take up the challenge, and to organize their own events. A study syllabus and information bulletins were prepared to assist organizers, and there is evidence of Rotary Clubs, Women's Institutes and schools receiving local speakers. But the production of bulletins was itself an extra call on the Association's staff, and it also 'proved difficult in war-time to find local secretaries and organisers.' [100] Occasionally, however, extra resources were unexpectedly made available to break the deadlock, as when a grant from Cadbury's enabled the shipment through the Red Cross of 2,000 books and pamphlets on planning to prisoners of war in foreign camps [101].

Nearer home, the Association launched a series of lunchtime meetings in London, where members of the public could meet without having to brave the evening blackouts. The first of these was in January 1941, when the Parliamentary Secretary to the Ministry of Works and Building spoke on the role of his Ministry to a lunchtime gathering in the Dome Lounge of Dickins and Jones. The meetings – well attended and widely reported (with an average of twenty-five journalists at each meeting) – were adjudged an 'unqualified success'

Lunchtime meetings were one means of promoting the campaign.

and a welcome 'distraction from immediate war-time cares.' [102] What is more, to ward off any unfair criticism, it was pointed out that the frugal lunches were 'well within the limits of the Ministry of Food's austerity requirements.' [103] As well as the lunchtime meetings there was also a lecture programme organized for the Planning Forum, a section established in 1944 to encourage the participation of younger members of the Association.

Another way in which the Association advanced its cause was through a prodigious output of publications. As well as books arising from the above conferences, these publications included policy statements and memoranda on the main planning developments of the day, the journal (which appeared without a break throughout the war), and a series of booklets under the rubric of *Rebuilding Britain* [104]. From 1941 to 1944 twelve booklets were produced, with authors including Clough Williams-Ellis (who had claimed a place as a leading preservationist with his prewar publication, *Britain and the Beast*), Seebohm Rowntree (still influencing the Association more than forty years after his seminal study of poverty in York at the turn of the century), G. D. H. Cole (immersed in reconstruction work through the Nuffield College Social Reconstruction Survey), and Lewis Mumford (with whom Osborn had recently started a transatlantic exchange of correspondence). Osborn also found the time to edit a series of Year Books, *Planning and Reconstruction*, a remarkable compendium of everything one needed to know about reconstruction [105]. Information ranged from briefings on the latest policy developments to advertisements for efficient geysers and rubber flooring for postwar homes. These books also included regular listings of the Ministries and their officials, the main organizations and key planners with an interest in reconstruction, and sources of books, periodicals and films. They were entirely practical publications at the time, but for the historian of wartime planning their subsequent value as an authoritative source is immense.

The role of the Association in disseminating information on a burgeoning output of planning literature went well beyond the listings in *Planning and Reconstruction*. The Association's own Library continued in business throughout the war at its London office, and one of the tasks of the hard-pressed custodian of the collection was to undertake a survey of planning literature in 600 large public libraries throughout the country, and to produce a Town Planning Bibliography for the National Book Council. As well as noting which libraries had acquired copies of the Association's own publications, the Librarian was pleased to report some progressive approaches to the topic. Bristol was picked out for special mention, on account of a special booklet, 'Rebuilding Britain', listing seventeen pages of books and periodicals [106].

Films and exhibitions also offered opportunities to spread the message. In response to a request by the Housing Centre to cooperate in a conference and exhibition especially arranged at the request of the National Women's Organisations, the Association prepared its own six-screen exhibition, 'The Countryside in National Planning'. At the end of May 1942, the screens were erected alongside displays prepared by the Electrical Association for Women and the Women's Gas Council (the latter carrying the assuring message for the Association that 85 per cent of the women of Poplar wanted separate family houses with gardens in preference to flats) [107]. The Association was also keen to publicize and arrange showings of 'When We Build Again', the film sponsored by Cadbury's to educate the public in the benefits of planning. Of particular interest to the Association was the proposal for a satellite town to accommodate displaced uses from the overcrowded city. The fact that the satellite town was designed by Thomas Sharp (who favoured higher densities than did the garden city enthusiasts) was not allowed to weaken the Association's support for the essential message of planned overspill [108]. In 1943 an exhibition of the same name was prepared jointly by the Association with Cadbury's. Designed primarily 'to interest the layman' it was first shown at Heal's in Tottenham Court Road, with Sir William

Wartime exhibitions attracted leading politicians and planners – including Sir William Beveridge at the exhibition, 'When We Build Again' (1943).

Professor Patrick Abercrombie at one of the TCPA's wartime exhibitions.

Beveridge performing the opening ceremony. From there it was taken on tour, complete with models and usually with a showing of the film as well.

In all its propagandist activity, it would have been easy to have lost sight of some very real problems that still existed. For a start, the Association was by no means the only organization with a message to get across, and there were other organizations at work with very different, and conflicting, aims (considered more fully in the next section). Additionally, there were prudent warnings that the public was not necessarily as excited or as cognisant about planning as the propagandists might have hoped.

Compared with housing, with its obvious connections with the lives of ordinary people, there was the view that 'popular planning still stands at the garden gate.' [109] Moreover, in terms of tactics, there was a word of warning about the value of exhibitions. Too often, it was claimed, the 'invasion of museums and galleries, village institutes and company showrooms by exhibitions . . . barely touch the ordinary general public, and without this sympathetic support national schemes will be of little avail.' [110] These were warnings for propagandists that have continued to this day to hold meaning.

Consensus and Conflict

> I learned myself of the thoroughness with which he was scanning the horizon for indications of support at the time. I was 17 and had been printing on the kitchen table a tiny magazine which commended the TCPA's National Planning Basis, the document for which the Association was striving to gain widespread support from other organisations. Osborn noted this sign of the times in his Planning Commentary and wrote to encourage me. (Colin Ward, 1974*a*, p. 15)

The strength of a pressure group is derived, in part, from the networks of support it is able to extend, and, as Colin Ward's above anecdote illustrates, small organizations were important to the Association as well as large. Enlisting allies from all quarters to back the National Planning Basis was an important aim in the early years of the war, and there was enough common ground to attract organizations with potentially competing interests (explored later in this section), such as the RIBA and CPRE.

The TPI was an obvious ally in the cause of promoting the idea of planning, and this common cause was certainly not harmed by a continuing pattern of overlapping memberships between the two organizations (a pattern more apparent in the early years of the Institute, but still in evidence in this period). Thus, the President of the Institute in 1939 was W. Harding Thompson, who, in addition to that post, was also a member of the Association's Executive. His Presidential address echoed the Association's call for a Central Planning Authority, and offered the thought that 'the State could initiate a scheme for planned decentralisation in peacetime.' [111] A policy memorandum from the Institute to the Prime Minister in October 1940 endorsed the need for a national approach to reconstruction, drawing attention to the findings of the Barlow Report [112].

As well as working with professional bodies, the Association was also quick to support other attempts to promote the cause of planning. One such attempt was the work of the 1940 Council, an organization set up in February 1940 under the Chairmanship of Lord Balfour of Burleigh (a Conservative landowner and a Council member of the TPI) [113], with the aim of planning the country's resources on a rational basis. A leader in *The Times* in October 1940 welcomed the formation of the Council, lending support to the view that it was certainly not too early to be thinking about reconstruction [114]. It was an all-party organization, with a Conservative Chairman presiding over a Council that included Labour politicians, the Liberal, Seebohm Rowntree, and the Communist Dean of Canterbury.

Members of the Association on the Council included Osborn, Abercrombie and Barlow (the last-named of whom had been so impressed with the Association's evidence to his Committee that he not only joined the Association but subsequently became a member of its Council and a Vice President). As well as the Association, the TPI, RIBA, CPRE and NCSS were also represented. The Council was instrumental in securing the formation of a parliamentary reconstruction group, and was well represented on Reith's Reconstruction Panel [115].

The 1940 Council was a focal point for lobbying efforts, but, characteristically, the reconstruction network was composed of groups for which planning was a means to more specific ends. Thus, the *Planning and Reconstruction Year Book* in 1945 could list nearly 250 organizations defined as being interested in planning and reconstruction. These included many organizations with a secondary interest in this – such as the British Commercial Gas Association, the National Association of Lift Makers, and the Women's Engineering Society. But there were also bodies with a very direct interest, such as the Association for Planning and Reconstruction (a London-based centre for research), the Nuffield College Social Reconstruction Survey (which conducted research, largely for the Government, on reconstruction issues), and the Bournville-based West Midland Group on Post-War Reconstruction and Planning [116].

On the political front, the Association was concerned to see progress in all three parties. In spite of its 'apolitical' stance as an organization, Osborn and other TCPA members carried the campaign into the discussions of the Labour Party Reconstruction Committee. There were thirteen sub-committees, and that concerned with planning was chaired by Lewis Silkin, who Osborn recalls 'was then against TCPA policy and favoured flats in London.' With some satisfaction, though, Osborn also notes that all the other members of the committee sided with his own 'anti-flats' view [116]. Sensing, perhaps, that Osborn was getting too carried away by one party, Barlow offered a gentle but (with hindsight) remarkably perceptive piece of advice:

I have no doubt you can get many cheers at Labour meetings for land nationalisation, but you do not allow enough for the greater power at the poll represented by the small commercant, industrialist and shopkeeper, the sort of man and woman who are the backbone of the co-op movement, in Lancashire and the industrial north . . . as I always told my Labour friends they will not secure a real majority at any rate for a good many years to come, unless they can carry the man with small savings with them [117].

The Association, though, could also draw support from the other parties. Both the Liberals and Conservatives had their own reconstruction committees, with the former dating from the autumn of 1940 and including amongst its members the tireless Seebohm Rowntree, a veteran from the First World War reconstruction campaign. Less was expected of the Conservatives when it came to planning, but Osborn was surprised and pleased to find that of the three parties it was the Conservatives who produced the policy statement which expressed 'most clearly the policy which advanced town and country planners have evolved in the last few years.' [118]

These were heady days, with support to be found in all quarters, and for the busy advocates it may have seemed that a consensus for the kind of planning expounded by the Association was all but universal. In fact, if there was a consensus in the making, it remained thinly veneered, with a real danger of fractures along various seams. The 'high density' architects, the powerful metropolitan lobbies, and rural preservationists each represented different sources of conflict. Of these, it was perhaps with the advocates of high-density developments that differences were most sharply exposed.

Since 1936 it had been the Association's policy to oppose high flats and tenements, and other developments which maintained or led to increases in densities, and this approach was endorsed in the National Planning Basis. It was a policy which reflected a growing concern over the influences of the modernist school of architecture in the 1930s (as developed, for instance, in the pages of the *Architectural Review*), and the specific proposals of groups like the MARS Group with their futurist vision of urban life [119]. During the war years the Association lost no opportunity to oppose not simply high-density redevelopment proposals, but, particularly, the most abhorrent manifestation of high densities, the block of flats. The RIBA, for instance, attracted criticism for contemplating 'entirely unacceptable densities' in its own plans for the postwar rebuilding of London, which would have called for a high proportion of flat dwellings [120]. To support its position, the Association called on the views of all and everyone with a dislike of flats – like Florence White of the Spinsters' Pension Association, who warned that 'it would be a great pity if, because of their particular circumstances, a section of women had no choice but to accept a mode of living they were not in favour with, just because flats were the simplest solution of their housing problem.' [121]

In its vigil against high densities, the Association also had to contend with the 'middle density' lobby, including some of the old garden city opponents. Amongst these were Trystan Edwards (still trying to win support for the Hundred New Towns Association), Thomas Sharp, Geoffrey Boumphrey and Professor Adshead [122]. Additionally, there was always the danger of lapses amongst the Association's own believers, like Professor Abercrombie, who disappointed Osborn with his plan for the redevelopment of inner London [123].

Moreover, outside the circle of architectural idealists, the Association also sought to counter the arguments of a powerful metropolitan lobby. Lewis Silkin (with whom Osborn crossed swords on the Labour Party's reconstruction committee) attended the Association's 1941 Oxford Conference on behalf of the LCC, and spoke of the difficulties of any proposed decentralization in London [124]. He put forward the view that high densities should not necessarily be looked upon as an evil, and, indeed, Londoners had been shown to prefer living in flats close to their work, as opposed to cottages in the suburbs. A similar rift opened at the Association's 1943 London Conference on housing and employment, when Paul Cadbury (speaking as Chairman of the Housing Panel of the Birmingham Public Works Committee) responded to a paper by Osborn by saying that he thought that some high-density building was inevitable. It was unrealistic, he argued, to expect that a large city's population (currently, in the case of Birmingham, living at a density of 250 persons per acre) could be rehoused at ten houses to the acre [125].

If there were threats to consensus from within the cities there was no less a problem from the shires. A postwar strategy of planned overspill would gain from a rural-based acceptance of the idea if not the details. The Scott Report could have offered an appropriate formula – and indeed, went some way towards doing so in its advocacy of urban containment, though the report was not without the odd offending paragraph [126]. Osborn wrote privately to Barlow to say how disappointed he was with the Report. 'It should have been a clear step forward; instead of which, here we are all perplexed as to whether we must tactically bless it in general and curse it in private, or curse it altogether.' [127] The Association (as with the other wartime reports, none of which matched up to its own exacting standards) chose the former response, and won from Lord Justice Scott a request to all members of his Committee that they should write to assure the Association that they were not, in fact, opposed to new towns [128]. Although the exercise did not fully resolve the matter [129], the distinguished judge was at least persuaded to join the ranks of the Association's Vice Presidents. A semblance of consensus was, therefore, restored.

BRITAIN IN 1945

The ending of the war and the election of a Labour Government with a landslide majority heightened the sense of euphoria and expectation for the creation of a 'brave new world'. In all this, the Association was determined to see new towns built as shining citadels in the new Britain, and updated its theoretical statements in support of the concept. More than that, it was actively involved in the Governmental process of formulating policy, which, within a year of the ending of the war, had led to new towns legislation.

Brave New World

The world opening before us was not a pale imitation of one we had lost, but a lucky dip of extraordinary things we had never seen before. If, later, we seemed to snarl with baffled rage at the disillusionment and apathy of our elders, perhaps this is why. They treated it as a dreary mess; they forgot that for us it could have been a brave new world. (Susan Cooper, in Sisson and French, 1964, p. 57)

Susan Cooper's view of Britain from a child's perspective has a wider significance. 'It could have been a brave new world' offers a fitting epitaph for the hopes and disappointment of the immediate postwar years.

The war in Europe ended on the 7th May 1945, and later that month the Government was dissolved. The wartime coalition had done its job, and in June the electorate went to the polls, with Churchill (and most of the pundits) confident of a Conservative victory [130]. Instead, when the results were announced on the 26th July 1945 they recorded a Labour landslide, with a majority Government comprising 393 Labour MPs. Whether or not this was British socialism's 'one great historic moment' [131] is debatable, but it was undoubtedly a moment of great significance – a swing to the Left on such a scale offering, so it seemed, a mandate for social revolution.

What is more, the Election result itself may have come as a surprise, but the idea of progressive social reform (as indicated in the previous sections of this chapter) had already been widely accepted. More than that, in the closing stages of the war, various measures had been introduced that could later provide a practical basis for postwar policy. Social insurance, economic policy and employment, industrial location, education, health and town and country planning all have legislative and policy origins in the period before the end of the war. When Clement Attlee formed his new Cabinet, there were great expectations that what had been done so far would prove to be only the start. At the polls a majority of the population had effectively called for a rejection of the past, and for a forward march into a brave new world [132].

Attlee was not an obvious revolutionary, but only a few years before the outbreak of war he had written in unequivocal terms that the root cause of society's problems lay in the private ownership of the means of life, and that the remedy lay in public ownership [133]. The way forward seemed to be clear enough, and, indeed, on the face of it, a revolution of sorts was started. The first King's Speech of the new Government promised the nationalization of the Bank of England, the coal industry and civil aviation, the establishment of a national health service and increased social security; and to this list was added in later years the nationalization of the railways, electricity, gas and steel, and important changes in town and country planning. Between 1945 and 1951 the role of the State changed in three ways, all of which endorsed the importance of planning in the postwar world. At the macro-economic level, Keynsian principles of a managed economy were fully incorporated; in terms of the State's ability to control production and distribution, key sectors of the economy were nationalized; and, on the social front, the pillars of the Welfare State were raised. Although these changes were not to amount to a revolution, the world of postwar Britain was beginning to look very different to that of the past.

The TCPA viewed these unfolding events with what might be described as qualified optimism – acknowledging progress in gaining acceptance for the wider cause of planning, but worrying, first, as to whether the Government would act quickly and decisively enough to stop housing policy dictating terms (as it had done in 1918), and, subsequently (when legislation was, in fact, forthcoming) questioning the details. In the first place, with the war over, planners were immediately warned against complacency: 'There is no V-Day yet for the planners; not even a D-Day.' [134] Taking stock in the summer of 1945, the Association could note the advance of 'Dispersal Planning', while at the same time listing what still needed to be done. What is interesting to note is an implicit belief in the existence of a political consensus on most planning issues. There was

little doubt that, whatever party is in power, the Government will have every intention of pursuing the Dispersal Policy worked out by their all-party predecessors. Most of the needed powers are there already, and the further powers needed ought not to be contentious – except in the matter of compensation and betterment [135].

In the event, the Association was right, and the immediate postwar years were marked by new legislation and policies that were central to its own long-standing objectives. For all the Association's faith in the other parties, a Labour Government was the most likely to press ahead with new measures, and the Association was not to be disappointed. Piece by piece, the building blocks of a new planning system were set into place. The Distribution of Industry Act, 1945, had been passed shortly before the dissolution of the Coalition Government, and (for all the Association's reservations about 'taking work to the workers', rather than adopting a more comprehensive approach) [136] was to set the pattern for postwar regional policy for the next fifteen years. To this was added the 1946 New Towns Act (integral to the whole of the Association's being, and considered in the next section), the 1947 Town and Country Planning Act and the 1949 National Parks and Access to the Countryside Act.

It was, without doubt, an impressive advance for planning. And yet, the association had its reservations – partly to do with the details of legislation, and with the mediocre calibre of some of the politicians and civil servants who had the job of putting it into practice [137]. But, also, the specific advances in town and country planning have to be seen in the context of a wider programme that proved to be less radical than it first promised, and in the context of a Government that was very soon to lose its political shine. Ralph Miliband is one who has analysed the post-1945 programme in terms of the modernization of capitalism, rather than as a strategy to undermine it [138]. Thus, from a Marxist viewpoint, the 'radical measures' of the Attlee Government can, alternatively, be seen as a means to better regulate the economy, to strengthen key industries and services, and to serve the reproduction of labour. Subsequent writers have argued that the so-called advances in town and country planning fall into these same categories [139]. While the TCPA was not itself arguing in these terms, it shared with others a growing unease that the Golden City under construction was not, after all, Jerusalem. Moreover, ideological doubts were reinforced by a very rapid decline in the Government's fortunes. Within a year, the country was in the grip of shortages and associated doubts as to whether bureaucratic planning was, after all, the best way forward. The severe winter of 1947 added to the troubles of the Government and fuelled the doubts of the nation. In a short space of time, heady talk of social reconstruction gave way to pragmatism and survival.

New measures continued to be passed, but, while subsequent writers acknowledge the achievements, it is also as the 'age of austerity' that this period of early hope is sadly recalled [140].

'New Towns after the War'

> We have to think after this war, as we ought to have thought after the last, not merely of a housing programme, but of a town-building programme. And we must begin the reorganisation of our industrial and social system by the establishment of new towns as soon as possible after the termination of the war. (Osborn, 1942*b*, pp. 51–52)

If austerity proved to be a dominant theme later in the 1940s, there is no doubt (as already demonstrated in the context of the wartime reconstruction debate) that hope flourished in the early half of the decade. It was in the hope that the ideas contained in his original 1918 book, *New Towns after the War*, might fare better after the Second World War that Osborn was encouraged to try again. Osborn could find many parallels between the two periods, but a major difference, he asserted, was that in 1942 (when the new issue was published) people had become 'planning conscious', and 'a new symbiosis' had evolved from the hitherto detached cells of planning thought [141].

A brief look at the case presented for new towns – still at the very heart of the Association's being – can offer a theoretical context for the legislative and practical changes that were shortly to follow. Together with two subsequent publications (considered later in this section), the links with Howard's original concept of garden cities were both strengthened and refined, and the idea of new towns was connected to other developments in town and country planning.

An obvious source of continuity is that Osborn believed that the basic case he had advanced twenty-four years previously (and that itself modelled on Howard's book some twenty years before that) remained sound – so much so, that he was able to leave 'the little book of 1918 much as it was . . .' [142] In the tradition of a whole genre of political and religious tracts, Osborn offers first a vision of Heaven, prior to a depiction of earthly problems and remedy for salvation. With the ending of the war, the nation would be presented with an opportunity for 'a more imaginative and scientific policy than has ever been attempted.' [143] Unlike in 1918, this time the opportunity could not be squandered. With the prospects of redemption, what follows 'is a suggestion for a national plan' [144].

But first the horrors of the existing situation had to be reaffirmed. Very much in the mould of Howard, the problem was defined in terms of the 'disease' of city and country, and of the unsatisfactory relationship between the two. The city was condemned for continuing to sap the health and vitality of its unwilling captives, the view being that it remained 'beyond all question that the great city has been inimical to life and health . . . Considered historically, its drain upon the racial life has been comparable with that of war.' [145] Likewise, country life lacked vitality, its inhabitants socially as well as economically impoverished, a backwater to the nation's life. Revitalization would depend on tackling the problems of town and country together, but far from that happening, the experience of the interwar years had only worsened the situation. The big cities had simply become larger, and for most of this period little thought had been given to the overall distribution of population.

So what was the solution? It was, of course, a programme for a new generation of garden cities, complete with many of the essential qualities originally advocated by Howard – including corporate ownership, a population in each case of between 30,000 and 50,000, a balance of activities, and a generous agricultural belt. What is more, practical lessons could be drawn from the only two garden cities to date, Letchworth and Welwyn. For all the reasons, there

was no escape from the logic of the situation. An intelligent policy for Great Britain must include the creation of new small towns on the garden city formula, and the application of the lessons learnt to the existing small towns [146].

One essential difference with the original doctrine of Howard, however, concerned the role of the State. Osborn had already, in 1918, heralded a more important role for the State, only to be outflanked by Howard with the formation of Welwyn by private initiative – with the result that 'The four New Townsmen, who set out to persuade Britain to build one hundred new towns, found instead that for a large part of their lives they were to participate in the building of one new town.' [147] But this time there could be no compromise. Central organization was now considered to be essential, though it was not envisaged that the Government would itself be the building agency. In return for its involvement, the State would benefit from a quickening of the democratic life of the whole national community. And, more than that, with what a Marxist would later see as the real rationale for postwar new towns, the programme would assist in the wholesale restructuring of British industry that was (as the events of the 1930s had revealed) long overdue [148]. Osborn, himself, was certainly not arguing from a Marxist standpoint, but his analysis of the fundamental changes that lay ahead is fuel to the argument that new towns finally came about less because of an underlying idealism and more because they had an important role to play in the postwar economy. As such, Osborn's analysis is worth quoting in full:

During the first ten years or so after this war we shall have to build a vast number of houses, largely with the aid of national funds. Their erection will coincide with a period of reconstruction in which our manufacturing, agricultural, educational, and public health methods will come under review. Wide changes will occur. The reorganisation of home and foreign trade, the deliberate encouragement of agriculture and certain other basic industries, the impetus to scientific discovery, and the reaccommodation of pre-war businesses, will necessitate the establishment of many new factories, and the development of new plans, new processes, and new kinds of skills. Practically a fresh urban equipment will have to be produced on a colossal scale – houses, roads, factories, all the plant and machinery of industrial life. What is more obvious than to place much of this equipment in new towns designed to secure not only efficiency but the health and happiness of the workers and their families [149]?

Such was the logic of the case that, with the growing prospects of some kind of planned overspill in the postwar period, Osborn decided it was timely to republish the original gospel according to Howard [150]. It was, in any case, an opportunity for Osborn, together with Lewis Mumford, the American sociologist and author, to introduce the volume with their own prefatory remarks [151]. Osborn used the opportunity to review the progress that had been made since the book was first published in 1898. He brought events right up to date, concluding with the view that it had to be remembered that 'in reading this book we are studying a blue-print nearly fifty years old. What is astonishing is not that it had faded on the edges, but that its centre remains so clear and bright.' [152] In turn, Mumford set the ideas within a wider historical and comparative canvas, observing that, technologically, the whole idea of dispersal was by then a more practical possibility than it had ever been before [153].

At the same time, Osborn was encouraged to go beyond the reissue of *Garden Cities of Tomorrow*, and to produce his own garden city panacea. The idea had been in gestation for some years (delayed, as he complained to Mumford, as a result of his many other activities) [154], and was finally published in 1946 under the title of *Green-Belt Cities*. It was concerned with the whole question of the size of towns and the disposition of towns in relation to the countryside, of which there was 'no social issue more important.' [155] Inevitably, it covered old ground reaffirming the essential principles attached to garden cities, and offering reasons as to why things had gone so badly wrong in the interwar years. It followed a familiar (and largely uncritical) path across the pioneer country of Letchworth and Welwyn, looking for lessons and pointing to the many features that could be emulated. The real value of the book, though, came with the very specific guidelines for what he called a 'national policy for dispersal' [156]. It was a timely call and, to the extent that it was applied to the actual conditions in Britain in the mid-1940s (as opposed to the reissue of Howard's book, which really amounted to a reaffirmation of principles), the main ideas are worth summarizing.

Firstly, the national policy for dispersal was just that – a strategy to relocate as many as five million people throughout the country. In such a vast undertaking, the Ministry of Town and Country Planning (as the Central Planning Authority) would have a key role to play, though it was emphasized that regional and local authorities would be better placed to decide on the details of relocation. It was seen to be preferable to distribute the new towns fairly evenly across the country, and (to counter the opposition of preservationists) it was calculated that the total programme would not consume more than 1 per cent of existing farmland and woodland. For each new town the old figures of 30,000 and 50,000 were retained as acceptable population limits, and various criteria were suggested for the selection of sites – including the continuing ties of industries to be relocated; the benefits a new town would bring to the rural reception area; the feasibility of providing basic services; and the potential of the site to contribute to a sense of community [157].

Perhaps of even more topicality were the suggestions for the promotion and finance of new towns. Recalling the difficulties (and good fortune) that had surrounded the assembly of land at both Letchworth and Welwyn, Osborn was adamant that compulsory purchase had to be an essential part of the process, whatever the developing agency. Although there was already some statutory provision for the purchase of land for new settlements, a new Act would be desirable for an exercise on the scale proposed. Compared with Howard, Osborn laid more stress on the role of the State (as he had done since 1918), but, in the best traditions of the Association (with its interest in local and voluntary initiatives) he could also see a role for other agencies. Thus, as well as State corporations, promoting agencies might include local authorities, private enterprise (including estate companies, landowners, building societies and construction firms), and cooperatives and limited dividend associations. Likewise, capital would be attracted from both the public and private sectors. Once underway, the towns would best be owned and managed by some kind of trust acting in the interests of the residents – having the freedom of action of private enterprise, but with a limit on profits [158]. Finally, in addition to advice on the overall strategy, and on the administrative structure, Osborn drew again on the detailed experience of Letchworth and Welwyn to suggest how 'to get the communities going' [159].

What is interesting in relation to what were still hypothetical suggestions – and to what might have been recorded as simply another garden city tract – is that while Osborn was correcting his proofs he learnt of the formation by the Government of a New Towns Committee. Overnight, as it were, ideas of this sort, based on actual experience, assumed a new topicality. It was immediately obvious to Osborn, as to others, that British planning was about to enter a new phase, and there is something of the tiredness and relief of an old campaigner in his comment that the 'long period of debate seems to be drawing to its close, and the period of action to be setting in.' [160] Events were drawing Osborn, no less than the Association, towards a notable watershed. The first stage in the long march was nearly over.

Official Utopias

New towns did not figure conspicuously in the competition of party programmes during the post-war General Election of 1945. As in 1918, the major accent was on promises of maximum speed in building houses . . . Party managers could see few votes in a strong emphasis on dispersal. The TCPA therefore felt by no means confident that the combination of central flat-building and a great suburban explosion would not be repeated, whichever party won the election. (Osborn and Whittick, 1977, p. 53)

Given the speed with which events unfolded after 1946, it is worth recalling that the prospects for new towns at the end of the war were by no means as bright as one might have expected. With the passing of the 1944 Town and Country Planning Act, the urgency for additional measures seemed to disappear, leaving Osborn 'in the doldrums' and wondering how the Association could 'get into the breeze again.' [161] Fresh winds proved to be closer than he thought, however, for in October 1945 (just two months after assuming office) the new Minister of Town and Country Planning, Lewis Silkin, announced a departmental committee under the chairmanship of Lord Reith to:

consider the general questions of the establishment, development, organisation and administration that will arise in the promotion of new towns in furtherance of a policy of planned decentralisation from congested urban areas; and in accordance therewith to suggest guiding principles on which such towns should be established and developed as self-contained and balanced communities for work and living [162].

Less than ten months later (on the 1st August 1946) the New Towns Act had entered the statute book. It was, on any account, a remarkably brief period within which to enact a measure that had hitherto – as the evidence of the interwar period shows – been considered to be too radical (in the sense of enhancing the role of central planning and direction, and of interfering with private property rights), and the fact that the Act was passed with all-party support adds to the conundrum. Why was the measure brought forward at all, why was it then dealt with so expeditiously, and what, in all this, was the role of the TCPA?

Undoubtedly, part of the explanation lies in what had taken place before the decision to appoint the Reith Committee. In preparing the ground, there was the long campaign of the Association from the end of the last century, culminating in the favourable disposition of the wartime planning reports and the winning of a consensus amongst an influential network of policy-makers (considered earlier in this chapter). But there was also a more immediate impact on the emergence of policy at the end of the war, which had more to do with 'behind-the-scenes' activities in terms of advising and influencing civil servants and politicians on some of the specifics of a future new towns policy. Two instances can be cited.

One instance of this type of 'insider' work is that of the informal advice offered to a committee that had been set up in January 1944 within the Ministry of Town and Country Planning (with representatives from the Ministry of Health) under the chairmanship of the chief technical adviser, G. L. Pepler [163]. The committee had the task of making proposals as to what administrative and legislative arrangements would be needed for the development of 'satellite or new towns'. Pepler had, in fact, been quietly working on this issue since 1942 – 'known to Osborn only through hints dropped by Abercrombie and Pepler over lunch in London clubs' [164] – and it may be significant that the formation of the committee follows some advocacy from Osborn. Thus, on the 30th August, 1943, Osborn wrote to the then Minister, W. S. Morrison, suggesting the formation of a small, expert committee to study and report on the actual methods by which new towns could be created, and putting forward his own name as someone who could take an active part in its work [165]. It was Pepler who advised the Minister that Osborn should be told that 'the problems he refers to are all under consideration', and that he might like to contribute an 'unofficial report' [166]. Osborn did not respond immediately, but midway through the work of the Pepler Committee, in May 1944, he submitted a twenty-eight page Memorandum, 'Creation of New Towns' (a forerunner of the proposals contained in *Green-Belt Cities*) [167]. The Pepler Report was completed in August 1944, and discussions continued amongst Ministry officials at least until December of that year. An attempt to get the full proposals incorporated in the Town and Country Planning Bill (then under consideration) was rejected on the grounds that the Bill had already progressed too far to take on anything as complex as the new town clauses (although some minor amendments were made to ease the way for local authority development outside its own area). The significance of the Pepler Report is that when Reith came to do his job in 1946 he was able to rest his own proposals on a solid base of groundwork. How far the Association had influenced the report is debatable, but it could, at least, record Pepler's longstanding membership of the Association, the fact that Osborn had suggested the formation of a committee just four months before this was done, and the submission of a lengthy memorandum at a crucial stage in the committee's deliberations.

A second instance of the Association's 'behind-the-scenes' work at this time had to do with the 'conversion' of Lewis Silkin. It has to be recalled that Silkin, wearing his LCC hat in the war years, had looked to high-density redevelopment rather than overspill. A turning point came with the completion of Abercrombie's Greater London Plan at the end of 1944, with its recommendations for a massive programme of planned overspill, including the relocation of nearly half a million people in ten new towns (with suggested sites). Silkin had by then (after lengthy debates within the Labour Party Reconstruction Committee, and with some pressure from senior party politicians) [168] conceded a modest acceptance of the possibility of a few new towns, and Osborn had remained on amicable terms with him despite their initial differences. Thus, Osborn felt well-placed to suggest to Silkin that they should set up a joint study group of TCPA and LCC members to consider how Abercrombie's overspill proposals might be put into practice. 'Silkin cordially agreed, and some progress was made with nominations' [169] before the end of the war and the General Election put an end to this immediate development. What is significant, though, is the good relations that had been fostered. So much so that when Silkin was appointed as Minister of Town and Country Planning, Osborn claims that 'almost his first action' was to see the files of correspondence with the TCPA and to appoint the Reith Committee [170]. Even allowing for a personal distortion of history, the evidence supports the notion that Silkin's own position had moved a long way from his uncompromising advocacy of high-density redevelopment, and that (if only through attending some of the wartime conferences organized by the TCPA) he was in no doubt about the strength and objectives of the new towns lobby. It could certainly have done no harm to have had a Minister of this disposition in post at this particular juncture [171].

Nor, indeed, did it do any harm to have W. S. Morrison in post before Silkin. The extent to which he was influenced by the TCPA is far from clear [172], but the fact remains that his own role was an important link in the emergence of a new towns policy. It was Morrison who had set up the Pepler Committee, and who (with the findings of that body) subsequently, in May 1945, urged the Minister of Reconstruction, Lord Woolton, to support an experimental new town at Stevenage. The issue had become urgent, he argued, in the light of the Abercrombie proposals for Greater London, and the need for a very extensive housing programme. Woolton stalled, and Morrison came back in July with more detailed arguments (largely based on the findings of the Pepler Report). Before a decision was forthcoming, Morrison had to make way in August for Silkin. It was an inconclusive point at which to leave, but he endowed his successor with a valuable legacy of reports and a widening awareness of new towns in Government circles [173].

The TCPA's luck held when Lord Reith took on the job of chairing the New Towns Committee established by Silkin. Reith was far too much of an individualist to be a member of the TCPA, but he had drawn on the advice of those members of the Association who had sat on his earlier Reconstruction Panel. Thus, on his new appointment, there was some satisfaction on both sides. Reith, for his part, acknowledged as 'most useful' a list of people whom Osborn thought might be on the new committee [174]; while the Association waxed lyrical in the journal – 'Beveridge, Barlow, Scott, Uthwatt . . . The name Reith completes the quintet which is designed to produce new harmonies of social life and physical environment.' [175]

Letters were sent from Reith at the end of September 1945, inviting membership of the committee, and Osborn was one of the recipients. It was a relatively small committee, with nine members from England and Wales, and two from Scotland, and the Association had done well not only to secure Osborn's inclusion but also that of W. H. Gaunt, a former estate manager of First Garden City Ltd. Another member, John Watson, was a member of the Association who had argued for new towns in the Conservative Party wartime reconstruction committee [176]. There were also two co-opted members, one of whom, A. W. Kenyon, had been a former resident architect planner at Welwyn. Of the related professions, the RIBA was represented by its President, Percy Thomas, but the TPI was left out. Once on the committee, Osborn clearly played an active role, sitting on both sub-committees (Constructional and Financial Problems, and Planning, Executive and Administrative Problems) and contributing to special study groups on social and welfare facilities, entertainment, and shops [177]. Moreover, although Reith himself wrote most of the reports, he was assisted through some 'long night sessions with FJO.' [178] Osborn was also to take some credit for healing a potential rift within the committee, and contributing to a unanimous report [179].

Subsequent generations of planners have marvelled at the speed with which the committee completed its task, and that with which the Government responded. From the date of its first meeting, it was only four months until the publication in January 1946 of a first interim report, recommending a government-sponsored corporation as the most suitable form of agency. This was followed in April by a second interim report, concerned with the powers needed to acquire land and ownership arrangements when the town had been developed. In turn, the final report was published in July, with 'ideas and guidance for those who will have the responsibility for creating new towns.' [180] A certainty of implementation underpinned the whole exercise, and it is telling that the final report followed rather than preceded Parliamentary debate on the Bill. Given the speed of the exercise, it is interesting to note that two of the main participants had thought it would take less time. Osborn had rather taunted Reith before the committee's formation, saying that he was 'rather shocked at the thought of the committee taking as long as nine months. My idea was that it could (be done) in a couple of months . . .' [181] Suitably goaded, Reith responded that Osborn had written as if he had expected that '*I* (Reith) thought it would take 9 months. I mentioned to you privately that Mr Silkin had given this estimate, but I should be both surprised and sorry if a committee of which I was chairman took anything like this time . . .' [182]

The fact is that the job could be done quickly (if not quickly enough for some) because of the careful groundwork that had been laid in the war years [183], and because the Bill had a remarkably easy run through the legislative channels. It was given Parliamentary time much earlier than had been expected, and then enjoyed all-party support [184]. There are various explanations for this – including the sympathetic treatment at the hands of Herbert Morrison, who had Government responsibility for organizing the queue of proposed legislation; the space created by the abandonment at that stage of legislation to deal with compensation and betterment; the earlier winning of all-party support for new towns as a sensible way of dealing with the postwar housing problem; and the political skills of the Minister, Lewis Silkin. In the last resort, without the commitment of the Minister, the legislation would have foundered [185].

For the Association, the passing of the 1946 Act amounted to an immense triumph. The cause of garden cities, albeit now with a new name, had been advanced from its origins within the covers of a cheap book with a readership of late-Victorian 'cranks', to the status of an Act of Parliament with the prospect of a programme for the immediate implementation of new towns in various parts of the country. Inevitably, perhaps, some valued principles had been lost along the way, and even in the last stages, in the deliberations of the Reith Committee and at the hands of the Minister, cherished ideals were sacrificed for a wider cause. Garden city pioneers were particularly sad to see the loss of opportunity for future development to be other than by State development corporations, and the failure of legislation to safeguard increases in land value for the residents. These were fundamental components of the original garden city scheme which Osborn had, in vain, attempted to see incorporated in the legislation [186]. For C. B. Purdom, the new Act spelt the end of the garden city idea [187], while the Chairman of Welwyn Garden City Ltd., viewed events with 'much misgiving', not least of all because of the exclusion of private enterprise [188].

But, overall, the policy objectives of the Association had, in large measure, been achieved; planned overspill had become official policy, and that, in a note of quiet satisfaction, 'certainly looks like some success for the TCP Association's campaign . . .' [189] More than that, Osborn later reflected that it was his own personal role that had been crucial in securing this end:

I think (after the most crucial examination and continual re-examination of the facts) that I personally have been a decisive factor in the evolution of the new towns policy and that this evolution is extremely important historically. I mean no less than without my fanatical conviction and persistent work in writing, lecturing and especially lobbying, the New Towns Act of 1946 would not have come about, at any rate in that period. (Nor would it have come about without the concentration on the matter for a time by Silkin, an extraordinarily dynamic, even ruthless politician. But he did it under my influence, and for him it was a political episode rather than a passionate conviction, and he has since lost much of his interest in it.) [190]

This is an important claim, that will be evaluated in the final chapter, in the context of other influences on the emergence of policy. In the meantime, it is appropriate to note that the passing of the New Towns Act marked the ending of the first phase of the Association's activities. The campaign for planned overspill had been won; now the task was to ensure that the policy was carried out to the best of everyone's ability. With the unique experience of its members in building new communities, the Association was well placed to take a leading role in the next phase, just as it had done to date. Finding itself in the centre of the stage was a 'bewildering moment' [191], but there was a role to play that was no less important than that of the past. It was the Minister, Lewis Silkin, who defined what was different, and what the Association now had to do. In the past, he said, the Association had concentrated on propaganda, but it was no longer necessary to preach for remedies that had now been adopted.

Instead, the Association could acknowledge 'the triumph of passing from the propaganda stage to the stage of action.' [192] Propaganda would continue to be an important part of the Association's activities in the years ahead (more, in fact, than Silkin appears to have envisaged) but so, too, would a close involvement in some of the practical details of new town building. Osborn's 'real anxiety as to what the new towns will be like' [193] is a key to the new agenda.

NOTES

War and Reconstruction

1. For instance, Political and Economic Planning, the prewar group that had been formed to press for more government planning, had already (before war was declared) set up a Post-War Aims Group. Within a week of the outbreak of the war, PEP issued a paper on war aims. See Stevenson (1984), pp. 451–452.
2. Calder (1971), p. 20.
3. Addison (1977), p. 182.
4. Addison (1977), p. 13. In the rest of his book, Addison explores how and why this swing to reform occurred, and why, in the event, it implied only very modest change in society itself.
5. Calder (1971), pp. 614–615.
6. Doreen Idle, *War over West Ham* (1943), in Barker (1978), p. 256.
7. Osborn (1946*b*), p. 52.
8. Stevenson (1984), pp. 447–448.
9. Addison (1977), pp. 217–218. In spite of its populist appeal, however, the report was at first met with resistance by a majority of Conservative politicians.
10. A view ascribed to a right wing MP, in Calder (1971), p. 338.
11. Cullingworth (1975), p. 5.
12. *Ibid*, pp. 12–13.
13. Addison (1977), p. 167.
14. Cullingworth (1975), p. 19.
15. An accessible summary of the Scott and Uthwatt Reports was provided in a Penguin Special by Young (1943). The Nuffield College Social Reconstruction Survey (1943) also produced its own summary of the major planning reports (Barlow, Uthwatt and Scott).
16. Cullingworth (1975), p. 1.

Reconstruction Machinery

17. The first discussion of the Planning Front appeared in *TCP*, Vol. VII, No. 27, July–September 1939, pp. 95–98.
18. 'The Seven Point Planning Policy', *TCP*, Vol. VIII. No. 30, April 1940, pp. 31–34. 'With the exception of the word "shirt", no word is more discredited than the word "front".' (Henry Strauss, MP).

19. 'A Charter of Planning', *TCP*, Vol. VIII, No. 30, April 1940, pp. 3–4.
20. GCTPA (1938).
21. Osborn, in a letter to Lewis Mumford, 8th April 1957, in Hughes (1971), pp. 271–272.
22. The Ministry of Works and Buildings was formed from the previous Office of Works.
23. Norman Macfadyen, in *TCP*, Vol. VIII, No. 32, December 1940, p. 75.
24. A copy of this Memorandum is reproduced in *TCP*, Vol. VIII, No. 32, December 1940, pp. 71–74.
25. PRO File HLG/86/16, letter from Osborn to Reith, 17th November 1940.
26. PRO File HLG/86/16.
27. Statement accepted by the Cabinet on 13th February 1941, in Cullingworth (1975), p. 15.
28. PRO File HLG/86/3, letter from Osborn to H. G. Vincent, 20th February 1941.
29. The nine members of the Association on the Panel were Professor Abercrombie, Lord Balfour of Burleigh, Sir Montague Barlow, W. H. Gaunt, Mrs Lionel Hichens, T. Alwyn Lloyd, F. J. Osborn, L. Dudley Stamp and Sir William E. Whyte.
30. Osborn to Mumford, 17th October 1941, in Hughes (1971), p. 18.
31. From what Osborn describes as 'off the cuff' notes on the Association's history, dated 21st March 1974, and sent to David Hall as a contribution to a proposed publication to celebrate the Association's 75th Anniversary.
32. *Ibid*.
33. *Ibid*.
34. 'Strictly Confidential' note to 'certain members' of the Association, 26th December 1941, Osborn Papers.
35. Osborn, 21st March 1974, *op.cit.*
36. Reith (1949), p. 428. The point is reinforced by the fact that in his 531-page autobiography that is the only reference to Osborn, and there is no reference at all to the TCPA as such.
37. Uthwatt Report (1941).
38. 'Uthwatt and After', *TCP*, Vol. IX, No. 35, Autumn 1941, pp. 73–74.
39. Addison (1977), p. 177.
40. 'The Central Planning Authority', *TCP*, Vol. X, No. 37, Spring 1942, p. 1.
41. Osborn and Whittick (1977), p. 46, later conclude that Reith's dismissal 'remains something of a mystery even after a study of his account of the affair in his extraordinarily candid autobiography.'
42. Strauss was a Labour politician who, in addition to his involvement with the TCPA, was an active member of the Society for the Preservation of Ancient Buildings.
43. 'The Planning Situation', *TCP*, Vol. X, No. 38, Summer 1942, p. 39.
44. 'A Victory and a Challenge', *TCP*, Vol. X, No. 40, Winter 1942–43.

45. 'Storm', *TCP*, Vol. XII, No. 46, Summer 1944, p. 55.
46. *Ibid*.
47. 'Town and Country Planning Association's Programme for Immediate Action', *TPR*, Vol. XIII, No. 48, Winter 1944–45, pp. 170–171.
48. Internal Ministry of Town and Country Planning correspondence dated 13.5.43 and 14.5.43, PRO File HLG/86/3.
49. Cullingworth (1975), p. 51.

The New Planning

50. 'The New Planning' was the title of one of the Association's wartime conferences, held in December 1944 after the passing of the Town and Country Planning Act.
51. The National Planning Basis was regularly reprinted in the pages of the journal and in the Association's annual reports in this period.
52. 'Town and Country Planning Policy', a statement authorized by the Council of the TCPA at a meeting on the 14th November 1942.
53. 'The Planning Situation', *TCP*, Vol. X, No. 38, Summer 1942, p. 39.
54. *Ibid*, p. 41.
55. Hebbert (1981), pp. 186–187.
56. Hebbert (1981) cites evidence from the Association's wartime conferences to illustrate the wide differences of view on these issues. These conferences are considered separately in the following section.
57. TCPA Memorandum on Housing and Planning Policy, 19th March 1943.
58. Letter from Osborn to Mumford, 23rd March 1943, in Hughes (1971), p. 35.
59. Letter from Osborn to Mumford, 7th September 1943, in Hughes (1971), pp. 39–40.
60. 'County of London Plan. A statement by the TCPA Executive', reprinted in *TCP*, Vol. XI, No. 42, Summer 1943, pp. 118–121.
61. Letter from Osborn to Mumford, 7th September 1943, in Hughes (1971), pp. 39–40.
62. Cherry (1974*b*), p. 127.
63. 'Town and Country Planning Policy. A statement by the TCPA Executive', reprinted in *TCP*, Vol. XII, No. 46, Summer 1944, pp. 76–81.
64. Cherry (1974*b*), p. 125, regards the White Paper as 'a remarkable affirmation', and the clearest statement before or since on national planning objectives.
65. 'Town and Country Planning Policy', *op.cit*.
66. Parsons (1986), especially chapter 3, 'After Barlow: Distribution of Industry and Full Employment Policy'.
67. *Ibid*, p. 63.
68. Abercrombie (1945). The Greater London Plan was, in fact, completed and publicized in December 1944, but not officially published until 1945.

69. Letter from Osborn to Mumford, 27th December 1945, in Hughes (1971), p. 112.
70. 'Plannning Policy after the Election', *TCP*, Vol. XIII, No. 50, Summer 1945, p. 56–60.
71. Letter from Osborn to Mumford, 3rd September 1945, in Hughes (1971), p. 102.

Managing in Wartime

72. GCTPA Annual Report for 1940, p. 3.
73. *TCP*, Vol. VIII, No. 32, December 1940, p. 91.
74. GCTPA Annual Report for 1940, p. 3. The leadership role of the Association was endorsed (though not with the same unequivocality) by Julian Huxley in a radio broadcast on postwar planning in 1942, when he referred to the Association as 'perhaps the most comprehensive' private organization concerned with physical planning. *The Listener* 28th May 1942 (reprinted in *TCP*, Vol. X, No. 38, Summer 1942, p. 77).
75. Letter from Osborn to Mumford, 17th October 1941, in Hughes (1971), p. 18.
76. *TCP*, Vol. VIII, No. 30, April 1940, p. 33.
77. TCPA Annual Report for 1944, p. 4.
78. Membership and subscription totals are derived from the Annual Reports for the years 1939 to 1946.
79. *TCP*, Vol. X, No. 37, Spring 1942, p. 11.
80. There is no evidence that this policy was (or could be) enforced rigorously, but successive statements in the annual reports for 1943 and 1944 state that new members were asked to signify general agreement with the essentials of policy on joining.
81. All new members, on joining the Association, were required to signify general agreement with the National Planning Basis.
82. This was the message reiterated in successive annual reports and journal editorials in this period, for example 'The Planning Situation', *TCP*, Vol. X, No. 38, Summer 1942, pp. 39–41.
83. 'Name of the Association': Confidential Note to Members, February 1941, Osborn Papers.
84. *Ibid*, p. 1.
85. *Ibid*, p. 1.
86. Notice of the first Meeting of the newly-elected Council of the Association, 24th March 1941.

Ways and Means

87. After an informal meeting of this sub-committee in January 1942 it was decided by the Executive to formalize the status of the committee. The agreed membership in March 1942 was R. S. Forman, S. J. Fay, G. Goddard Watts, Clayton Young, Paul Redmayne, F. J. Osborn, Gilbert McAllister and Elizabeth

McAllister. The minutes of this committee are available for the whole of 1942.

88. R. S. Forman represented the London Press Exchange, G. Goddard Watts the Building Industries, and Clayton Young spoke for Ford Motors Ltd. Paul Redmayne was the Advertising Manager of the Bournville Village Trust.

89. 'The Seven Point Planning Policy', *TCP*, Vol. VIII, No. 30, April 1940, pp. 31–34.

90. Towndrow (1941), p. 5.

91. *Ibid*, pp. 170–173.

92. Osborn reported that even the presentation of the Howard Medal to Barry Parker – an event that normally would have called for a dinner in its own right – was completed in five minutes.

93. A series of books reporting on the conferences was published by Faber and Faber, edited, in turn, by Towndrow (1941), Newbold (1942), Baron (1944), Tyerman (1944) and Bliss (1945).

94. Osborn, in Towndrow (1941), p. 12.

95. Armytage (1961), p. 426.

96. Osborn (1946*a*), p. 52.

97. Osborn to Barlow, 6th November 1942, Osborn Papers.

98. Osborn, 21st March 1974 (see note 31).

99. For instance, a Brains Trust was held at the Conference of the National Women's Organisations in May 1942, with a panel comprising Osborn for the TCPA, the architect Judith Ledeboer of the Ministry of Health, Elizabeth Denby, a housing consultant, and Richard Coppock of the National Federation of Building Trades Operatives.

100. TCPA Annual Report for 1942, p. 5.

101. *Ibid*.

102. *TCP*, Vol. X, No. 37, April 1942, pp. 24–25.

103. *TCP*, Vol. X, No. 38, Summer 1942, p. 66. The subject of lunches seemed to sidetrack the work of the Education Propaganda Committee in 1942, when the minutes show lengthy discussion on the relative merits of a snack lunch at 4s per head at the Arts Theatre, as opposed to a 1s 6d sandwich lunch at the YWCA. The former was preferred, but unsatisfactory accommodation led to correspondence with the British Council, the Royal Empire Society and Gas Industry House as possible alternative venues.

104. The twelve booklets are listed in the Bibliography, with reference to their place in the *Rebuilding Britain* series.

105. Osborn (1942–1944).

106. The work of the Librarian is reported in *TCP*, Vol. X, No. 38, Summer 1942, p. 67, and a copy of the Bristol booklet is available in the TCPA archives.

107. *TCP*, Vol. X, No. 38, Summer 1942, pp. 66–67.

108. It will be recalled that Sharp had attacked garden city principles in the 1930s, and that he, in turn, received a hostile review of his book, *Town and Countryside*, in the pages of the journal.

109. 'Planning Propaganda', an article by Hugh Pilcher on town planning

and public opinion, in *TCP*, Vol. XI, No. 42, Summer 1943, pp. 74, 76.

110. 'Education through Exhibitions', an article by Sylvia Pollak, *ibid*, p. 75.

Consensus and Conflict

111. *JTPI*, Vol. XXVI, No. 1, November–December 1939, p. 3.
112. 'Reconstruction and Development': a Memorandum submitted by the TPI to the Prime Minister, 25th October 1940.
113. Lord Balfour of Burleigh was already known as someone with a public interest in housing and health issues. He had been a Kensington Borough Council councillor since 1924, Chairman of Kensington Housing Trust since 1926, and President of the Royal Sanitary Institute from 1931 to 1941.
114. 'After the War', *The Times*, 10th October 1940.
115. A note on the 1940 Council is included in *TCP*, Vol. IX, No. 34, Summer 1940, p. 69; with a fuller source as PRO File HLG/86/1.
116. Information on the various reconstruction groups is listed in Sections 9 and 10 of the Year Book (1944–1945). In addition to Osborn, TCPA members on the Labour Party committee included Lady Simon of Wythenshaw, the Rev. Charles Jenkinson of Leeds, and Richard Coppock. Seebohm Rowntree carried the Association's case to the Liberal Party committee, and Lord Balfour of Burleigh and John A. F. Watson did the same on the Conservative committee.
117. Letter from Barlow to Osborn, 9th November 1942, Osborn Papers.
118. 'Conservative Party and Planning', *TCP*, Vol. XII, No. 45, April 1944, pp. 32–33.
119. Hebbert (1981), pp. 186–187. As an example of the articles on this theme in the *Architectural Review* in the late 1930s, see Le Corbusier, 'The Vertical Garden City', Vol. LXXIX, January–June.
120. The Association's view, in *TCP*, Vol. XI, No. 42, Summer 1943, p. 68.
121. *TCP*, Vol. X, No. 40, Winter 1942–43, p. 118.
122. Hebbert (1981), p. 187. In relation to the work of Edwards, it is interesting to note that in 1941 the Hundred New Towns Association was trying to enlist support amongst the great and the good. Sir Malcolm Stewart was approached, and wrote to Lord Reith for advice as to whether it was an appropriate organization with which to be associated. Reith advised against, on the basis that it was based on a scheme for decentralization that lacked a practical basis. PRO File HLG/90/3.
123. See, for instance, Hughes (1971), pp. 39–40.
124. Towndrow (1941), pp. 109–110. Lewis Silkin had served as Chairman of the LCC's Housing and Town Planning Committees, and was Chairman of the Housing and Planning Sub-Committee of the Labour Party's Reconstruction Committee between 1941 and 1943.
125. Tyerman (1944), p. 59.
126. The paragraph to which the Association took particular exception

was Para. 202 of the Report, where 'the Committee seem to look lingeringly at the discredited and unpopular expedient of saving space by rehousing urban people in flats.' See 'Barlow, Scott, Uthwatt . . . ?' *TCP*, Vol. X, No. 39, Autumn 1942, pp. 83–85.

127. Letter from Osborn to Barlow, 27th August 1942, Osborn Papers.
128. Osborn 21st March, 1974 (see note 31).
129. *Ibid*. Osborn singles out Sir Dudley Stamp as the *bête noire* in Scott's attempt to pour oil on troubled waters. Stamp 'lapsed, and controversy continued after N.T. Act of 1946.'

Brave New World

130. Anthony Howard, in Sissons and French (1964), p. 18, describes the General Election forecasts as ranking 'among the political howlers of the century.'
131. This is Anthony Howard's view, *op.cit.*, p. 15.
132. It is fair to say that these expectations were composed of fears (amongst the former ruling class) as well as hopes amongst Labour's voters. See Anthony Howard, *op.cit.*
133. Addison (1977), p. 271, quotes from Attlee's book *The Labour Party in Perspective*, published in 1937.
134. 'Planning Policy after the Election: what remains to be done', *TCP*, Vol. XIII, No. 50, Summer 1945, pp. 56–60.
135. *Ibid.*
136. 'Distribution of Industry', *TCP*, Vol. XIII, No. 49, Spring 1945, p. 1.
137. In a letter to Mumford, 27th December 1945, Osborn wrote that, apart from Lewis Silkin and Herbert Morrison, who were in charge at the Ministry of Town and Country Planning, he 'doubted the strength of the personnel in the next layer below the top.' In Hughes (1971), p. 113.
138. Miliband (1969), pp. 106–113.
139. A Marxist critique of town and country planning now has an extensive literature. Historically, it gains momentum in the 1960s, by which time it had become apparent to liberal critics as well as Marxists that the post-1945 system of town and country planning had failed to 'deliver'.
140. Sissons and French (1964) introduce their book, *The Age of Austerity*, with the comment that 'austerity' was a word as current after 1945 as 'affluence' has been since 1958.

'New Towns after the War'

141. Osborn (1942*b*), pp. 12 and 46. The role of the TCPA in bringing about this so-called symbiosis is considered, but Osborn avoids the trap of attributing cause and effect: '. . . it is difficult to judge how far the merging of opinion has been influenced by such efforts, or whether events would not have brought it about in any case.'
142. *Ibid*, p. 14.
143. *Ibid*, p. 17.

144. *Ibid*, p. 22.
145. *Ibid*, p. 28.
146. *Ibid*, p. 51.
147. *Ibid*, p. 11.
148. Mullan (1980), for instance, on pp. 15–17, examines the *raison d'être* of the new towns in these terms. He cites the view of Manuel Castells that new towns were, above all, a response to the urban crisis of the London region.
149. Osborn (1942*b*), p. 38.
150. The publisher, Faber and Faber, clearly had doubts about the venture. Although *Garden Cities of Tomorrow* was a classic of its type, and Osborn was insistent that the time was right for a reissue, the first print run in 1946 was limited to 2,000. Orders exceeded this total before publication, however, and an immediate reprint was made.
151. Osborn's transatlantic correspondence with Mumford dates from 1938, and wartime planning and other developments were closely monitored by the two writers. Osborn approached Mumford to collaborate in a reissue of their mentor's work, initially with a view to publication by 1944. There were hopes that interest would be aroused on both sides of the Atlantic. See Hughes (1971).
152. Osborn, in Howard (1965 edition), p. 25.
153. Mumford, in Howard (1965 edition), p. 38.
154. Letter from Osborn to Mumford, 7th December 1943, where Osborn tells Mumford that he has only spare time for writing and the work of the TCPA. Hughes (1971), p. 45.
155. Osborn (1946*b*), p. 13.
156. Part Three of *Green-Belt Cities* is devoted to proposals for a national policy for dispersal, and the ways and means of achieving it.
157. For the general strategy, and the siting of new towns, see Osborn (1946*b*), pp. 131–148.
158. *Ibid*. On the promotion and finance of new towns, see pp. 148–154.
159. *Ibid*. A section, 'Getting the Communities Going', is included on pp. 154–160.
160. *Ibid*, p. 22.

Official Utopias

161. Letter from Osborn to Mumford, 13th February 1945, in Hughes (1971), p. 76.
162. Terms of reference of the New Towns Committee, October 1945.
163. A full copy of the 'Report of the Interdepartmental Group on Administrative and Legislative Arrangements Needed for the Development of Satellite or New Towns (Pepler Report) 1944' is included in Cullingworth (1979), pp. 592–602.
164. Hebbert (1981), pp. 188–189.
165. Letter from Osborn to W. S. Morrison, 30th August 1943, in PRO File HLG/90/336.

166. Internal memo from Pepler to Morrison, 4th September 1943, in PRO File HLG/90/336.
167. A copy of Osborn's submission is included in PRO File HLG/90/336.
168. According to Osborn (in his notes on the history of the TCPA, 21st March 1974, Osborn Papers) Laski, Shinwell and Morgan Philips met with members of the Silkin Committee, after which there was an emphasis in Labour Party publications on a new towns policy.
169. Osborn, *ibid.*
170. Osborn, *ibid.*
171. In addition to Silkin (regarded as a man of 'mental mobility'), the Association could also note the appointment of Fred Marshall as the Junior Minister in the Department – a politician whom Osborn regarded as a supporter of 'my policy'. See letter from Osborn to Mumford, 14th–17th August 1945, in Hughes (1971), p. 91.
172. Morrison was undoubtedly aware of the Association's priorities when he was at the Ministry, if only through the regular flow of policy memoranda and the publicity surrounding their other activities, though that is not, in itself, evidence that his own views were changed.
173. Cullingworth (1979), pp. 11–12.
174. Note added to letter from Osborn to Reith, 4th September 1945, Osborn Papers.
175. 'New Towns – Better Cities', *TCP*, Vol. XIV, No. 53, Spring 1946, p. 3. It is also interesting to note a letter from Barlow to Reith congratulating the latter on his appointment, and confessing how he had himself attempted 'to get Nuffield College at Oxford to get to work on the question, but their young professors, who live in a curious world of their own, mostly detached from any reality, could not see any importance in it.' PRO File HLG/84/2.
176. In addition to Reith and Osborn, the full membership of the Reith Committee was – Ivor Brown, Editor of *The Observer*; Sir Henry Bunbury, former Controller and Accountant General of the Post Office; L. J. Cadbury, Chairman of Cadbury Bros. Ltd and Chairman of News Chronicle Ltd.; Mrs M. Felton, LCC member of Town Planning Committee; H. W. Gaunt, Chairman of Hertfordshire County Planning Committee; W. H. Morgan, Middlesex County Engineer; Sir Malcolm Stewart, Chairman of London Brick Co. Ltd.; Percy Thomas, President of the RIBA; J. A. F. Watson, member of Central Housing Advisory Committee, Ministry of Health; Sinclair Shaw, Advocate; and Captain J. P. Younger, Convenor of Clackmannan County Council.
177. See PRO File on New Towns Committee, HLG/84/7.
178. Osborn's notes on TCPA history (see note 31).
179. *Ibid.* The issue in question was that of the value of religious bodies in community building, a point pressed by Mrs Felton. 'FJO got her round by drafting a para. in which religious bodies were associated with political bodies as useful for the purpose.'
180. The three reports are detailed in the Bibliography. See Reith Report (1946).

181. Letter from Osborn to Reith, 4th September 1945, Osborn Papers.
182. Letter from Reith to Osborn, 5th September 1945, Osborn Papers.
183. Cullingworth (1979), p. 23, reveals that these preparations extended even to the drafting of legislation in advance of the establishment of the Reith Committee.
184. The main Parliamentary debate is recorded in H. C. Parl. Debates, 1945–46, Vol. 422, 8th May 1946. One of the remarkably few sour notes came from the MP for Dorset South, Viscount Hinchingbrooke, who reminded Silkin (who had introduced his speech with a promise of Utopia) that an earlier Utopian, Thomas More, had lost his head, and that he hoped that the Minister would shortly lose his office.
185. As Cullingworth (1979), p. 26, notes: 'It took all Silkin's skill and determination to steer his proposals through Whitehall and the Cabinet.'
186. Cullingworth (1979), p. 25, shows that in standing committee Silkin rejected amendments to the Bill to enable local authorities and 'authorized associations' to build new towns – both of which Osborn (1946*b*), p. 149, had included in a list of appropriate bodies: 'state corporations, local authorities, urban and rural; private enterprise, including estate companies, groups of landowners, building societies, and great constructional firms; limited dividend associations and co-operative societies.'
187. Purdom (1951), p. 84.
188. Sir Theodore Chambers, in Purdom (1949), p. ix.
189. Letter from Osborn to Mumford, 21st October 1945, in Hughes (1971).
190. Letter from Osborn to Mumford, 16th October 1962, in Hughes (1971), p. 327.
191. Letter from Osborn to Mumford, 20th August 1946, in Hughes (1971).
192. Lewis Silkin, addressing the TCPA Conference, 'Building New Towns', July 1946, Osborn Papers.
193. Letter from Osborn to Mumford, 20th August 1946, in Hughes (1971).

6

EVALUATION

It was a long campaign, and in the previous pages evidence from nearly half a century has been gathered. This evidence now provides a basis from which to draw some conclusions – about the general shape of the campaign, about the capacity of a pressure group to influence government policy, and about the place of the garden city movement in modern planning.

LOOKING BACK

> An ideal is as necessary to the reformer as the established fact is to the conservative . . . A progressive movement must have an ideal, and an ethical ideal for the future must be in so far abstract as it is not yet realised and embedded in social institutions. (L. T. Hobhouse, 1898, quoted in Freeden, 1978, p. 252)

The pursuance of an ideal (as Hobhouse notes in a general sense in the above quote, dating from the same year as the publication of *To-morrow*) is at the heart of it all, the source of any reforming campaign. In the case of the Association's history, whatever judgement is reached as to effectiveness and influence, the evidence is unambiguous in terms of continuity and commitment to a cause. The very fact of longevity is itself evidence of this. From 1899 to 1946 (and then beyond that) the Association pursued its ends as a voluntary group, its members fired by altruism rather than material gain, as committed to the worth of the organization at the end of this period as were the pioneers at the start. In one sense, then, it is hoped that the findings have demonstrated the purposiveness of the organization, and the motive force of high ideals.

But, as well as simply providing a record of commitment to a cause, there are valuable analytical lessons that can be drawn from the whole episode. In organizational terms, the history of the Association is a case study of a twentieth-century pressure group at work. From the evidence of its long campaign, some generalizations can be made about a number of key elements that have characterized the means and ends of the campaign – notably, the question of aims, the financial basis and internal organization, propagandist methods employed to promote the cause, aspects of membership, and leadership issues [1]. While generalizations are drawn specifically from the evidence of the Association, they can all illustrate wider aspects of pressure group politics in this period.

Aims

Driven though the Association always was by ideals, it is significant that the actual aims at the end of the period were not the same as those at the outset. Indeed, the aims were frequently modified, and were, in due course, substantially changed.

The original aims were simple enough – to promote Howard's ideas, and to initiate the first garden city. Successive amendments in the Association's first ten years widened the brief to encourage collaboration with other organizations, to embrace related garden suburb and garden village developments, and to promote town planning in general. A further change in 1920 directed the Association's priorities explicitly towards the postwar housing programme, attempting to secure some influence on an expanded building programme. Conceptually, though, it was not until the second half of the 1930s (reinforced in the National Planning Basis of 1941) that the aims were restructured to place the Association in the forefront of a lobby for national planning. Garden cities remained on the agenda, but the whole thrust of the organization had been redirected towards wider aims and with the State (rather than private enterprise and voluntary agencies) as the source of reform. The Association had come a long way from Howard's rationalist belief that progress could be secured through the example of demonstration projects.

So, too, had the Association moved a long way from the radicalism of Howard's early aspirations, with their promise of common land ownership and, beyond that, 'a glorious and peaceful revolution.' [2] A recent biography of Howard lends weight to the thesis that the history of the garden city movement is a history of the dilution of an idea that was conceived originally as 'a master key' to unlock the gates to a whole new form of society [3]. Even before *To-morrow* was published, some of the sharper elements had been removed to make the scheme more palatable to a cross-section of British society [4]. Subsequently, the arrival of Ralph Neville at the turn of the century and the incorporation of the Association within a network of Liberal businessmen and politicians; the constraints imposed by the need for financial viability in the two garden cities; and, later, the price to be paid for a place in the outer circles of government (as advisers and members of official committees in the 1930s and 1940s) led the movement further from its original ideals.

A lesson that might be drawn from this is that political survival may sometimes have to be bought at the price of adaptation. The record shows that the Association made sacrifices from the outset to widen its base of support, and to increase the chances of putting at least some of its ideas into practice. It responded pragmatically to constraints and opportunities, but, seen with the benefit of hindsight, the response is not without some overall coherence – reflecting quite closely the changing material context in which the pressure group operated. The world in 1946 (especially with the promise of the State as a source of social improvement) was a very different world to that of the politically threatening 1890s, when revolution might have flared up from any one of a number of sources. And the passing of nearly half a century had seen far-reaching changes to the social, economic and geographical map of Britain, transforming the context in which the Association's priorities were determined.

Against this background, it is one thing to decry the abandonment of sacred principles, but the fact is that, had the Association tied itself rigidly to its original aims, it is unlikely that it would still have been listened to by the 1940s. As it was, its aims were, by then, closely in accord with a wider lobby for planning, and at least the opportunity was open to influence events. A general conclusion is that an original gospel may sometimes have to be rewritten in the interest of achieving anything at all.

Finance and Organization

In some respects, the way in which the Association was financed and organized changed far less than other aspects of its campaign. The pioneers of the Association, who might have found difficulty in comprehending the issues faced by their successors in the 1940s, would at least have found plenty that was familiar in the internal workings of the organization.

It has, for a start, never been a wealthy organization. Consistently, the Association has had to rely on subscriptions and donations (with the latter exceeding the former only at times of exceptional national interest in the issues promoted by the Association, as, for instance, in the early 1940s). And, although the annual subscription was soon raised beyond the level of the 'democratic shilling' (which Howard had vainly hoped would attract a large body of working-class members), it never exceeded a guinea in the period in question. It enjoyed some philanthropic support (Cadbury, Lever, Rowntree and Harmsworth being amongst its sponsors), but such support – critical though it was when the two garden city companies were formed – was spasmodic and never a basis for long-term planning.

A limited and uncertain budget was an obvious constraint on what the Association could do, and, not least of all, on its ability to recruit full-time staff. Typically, the office was staffed by a handful of dedicated officers (perhaps only one or two on a full-time basis, with the rest working part-time and voluntarily), writing out receipts, answering an endless stream of enquiries, searching the newspapers for even the merest signs of support, organizing lecture programmes and conferences, and producing literature and exhibition material to carry the message to all parts of the world. This pattern and organization of activities changed little over the years. On particular occasions (as, for instance, after the First World War, in the euphoria of 'homes for heroes') it was possible to recruit extra staff, but the partial abandonment of the housing programme was enough to see a quick return to prewar staffing levels.

Also largely unchanged over the years was the Association's committee structure. From its inception, it operated through a dual structure of a Council (with about fifty members) to determine policy and a smaller Executive (supported by special subcommittees) to put it into practice. At no time in this period of the Association's history – even though at the time of its formation the committee structure was an object of criticism [5] – was this pattern radically altered.

In general terms, one might observe that a pressure group treads a fine line between a structure that seeks to be democratic but, in involving a large number of members, runs the risk of becoming too bureaucratic; or a structure that closes out those many outsiders who can keep an organization in touch with external events and offer influence in wider political circles. In the case of the Association, it is probably true to say that the form of organization worked well enough when there were strong leaders in post, but that at other times (most of the 1920s, for instance) the committee structure did little to focus priorities. One has to conclude that the Association's committees were, at best, a supplementary source of power rather than a mainspring for action.

Propagandist Methods

Less static than the form of organization were the means by which the Association communicated its message. In the pre-1914 era, it relied on a wide range of those methods that were technically available at the time. Public lectures, penny tracts, a regular journal, conferences, drawing room discussions, political lobbies, international tours, letters to the press, overlapping memberships with professional bodies, a long list of vice presidents and recruitment of the 'great and the good' to the cause, exhibitions, slide shows and special books. It belonged to a noble tradition of radical causes that relied on reason and persuasion, rather than the more provocative tactics of the likes of suffragettes and trade unionists who resorted (in the same period) to street demonstrations and strikes.

Over the years, the Association did not materially deviate from this tradition – holding to the belief that reason and persuasion would eventually win the day – though individual methods changed, largely as a response to new technology. In the post-1918 'homes for heroes' campaign, the Association could boast the use of films to show bemused audiences the wonders of the garden city (a source of communication that proved to be important in the Second World War too). In the 1940s (as well as films) the Association was also able to capitalize on the popularity of radio broadcasts, reaching a far wider audience that it had been able to do before.

Technology apart, the personal lobbying of key figures – to lend respectability to the cause, to attract donations, and to win political influence – was important to the Association throughout its history. Particularly from the late 1930s, this was a considered strategy rather than a general sweep of the field; Frederic Osborn sought to shape the decisions of various key figures in the planning world. He was able to reap the benefits of nearly two decades of careful lobbying of Neville Chamberlain, he saw the importance of keeping in close touch with members of the Barlow Committee (not least of all with Professor Abercrombie, and, subsequently, with Montague Barlow himself), he cast a role for himself as an adviser to Lord Reith, and his work in drawing Lewis Silkin away from the traditional priorities of a metropolitan lobby cannot be overstated.

In contrast with Osborn's strategy of political lobbying, the earlier record suggests that methods were employed in a less structured way, and with no apparent attempt to evaluate the effectiveness of one method as opposed to another. As an instance, the practice of undertaking strenuous lecture tours around the institutes and civic associations in the years before 1914 was laudable in itself, but one might conjecture as to whether or not it was the most fruitful use of limited resources.

At a more general level, it can be concluded that pressure groups have a wide choice of propagandist methods at their disposal, and that the Association's history offers a useful case study of a twentieth-century group at work. It might also be concluded that the selection of those methods that will be most effective at a particular time will be crucial to the success of a campaign, and that, in the case of the Association, the record of doing this well is mixed.

Membership

Two aspects of membership are of particular interest, one to do with numbers over time and the other with composition. As far as numbers are concerned, a pressure group may aspire either to mass recruitment or to a 'cadre' approach. Whatever the utopian aspirations of Howard, the record shows that the Association was never to attract the kind of following that would have represented a political force in its own right. Instead, for most of its history, the Association was to rely on a membership list totalled in hundreds rather than thousands.

Relative totals and changes over time are illustrated on p. 300. It can be seen that, from its inception in 1899, the profile is marked by three peaks – in 1903–1904 (at the time of publicity attached to the launch of the first garden city), when the membership totals about 2,500; immediately after the First World War (amidst the 'homes for heroes' euphoria), when the figure reaches about 1,800; and towards the end of the Second World War (when hopes were high for reconstruction), with a sharp rise to about 2,300. These three peaks are clearly related to events of national significance, only the first of which was of the Association's own making.

Equally, it can be seen how difficult it was to sustain a large membership, with, on each occasion, numbers dropping away quite rapidly to a 'hard core' of devoted followers. For most of the interwar period, the Association survived with a total that at times dropped below 500, before Barlow and the lively reconstruction debate revived flagging numbers. Thus, at no time (not even when, in relative terms, its membership figures were healthy) could the Association use the argument that it enjoyed a mass following. Instead, its propagandist strength had to be derived from other sources. In this respect, it would be helpful to know more about the social composition of the membership, and of the influence and contacts that individuals could offer the Association. Sadly, however, the paucity of the membership records makes it impossible to be definitive about the backgrounds of those who joined. Nevertheless, some deductions can be made.

From what one can derive from the general records, the initial membership would have been of people (mainly men) not unlike Howard; non-conformist, lower middle-class radicals of modest means, attracted to the idea of 'commonsense socialism' in preference to parallel political strategies in the 1890s that carried with them a threat of violence or centralist doctrine. Howard's was an easy philosophy with which to live, and the new commonwealth beckoned [6].

The evidence suggests that, with the arrival of Ralph Neville, these well-meaning idealists were rather pushed into the background, in

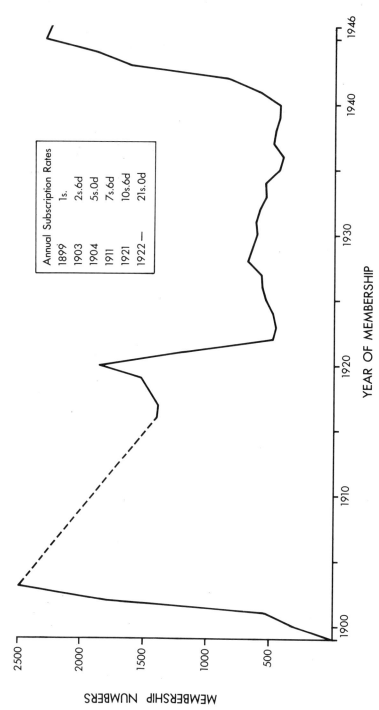

YEAR OF MEMBERSHIP

Annual Subscription Rates	
1899	1s.
1903	2s.6d
1904	5s.0d
1911	7s.6d
1921	10s.6d
1922 —	21s.0d

MEMBERSHIP NUMBERS

Membership numbers calculated annually on the basis of the accounts for the preceding year. Where precise numbers of members are not specified these have

been calculated on the basis of $\dfrac{\text{the total sum received for subscriptions} - 20\%}{\text{minimum individual subscription rate}}$ (the 20% representing a notional deduction to take account of subscriptions above

the recommended minimum). Where neither membership numbers nor the accounts are available, the trend has been extrapolated and is shown by a dotted line.

Changing membership totals, 1899–1946, reflecting wider patterns of interest in planning.

favour of a new breed of fellow professionals and businessmen, recruited to lend the Association the hard edge that it lacked in its first years. Talk of socialism (even in the muted form used by Howard) gave way to what was ostensibly a 'non-political' stance, but one which was, in effect, a position that fitted neatly into a 'New Liberalism' mould. Liberal politicians were well represented amongst its Edwardian members.

Subsequently, the 'homes for heroes' campaign unleashed not simply the Liberal impulses of Lloyd George, but also a vigorous contribution from the growing Labour Party (which had, in 1918, lent its official support to the idea of garden cities). It is probable that many of the Association's new members, signed up in the crowded meeting halls where housing was discussed, were Labour voters who saw housing as a central plank in the programme of social reform that was promised.

Only the faithful remained loyal to the cause in the barren interwar years, though towards the end of the 1930s there was a campaign to enlist the support of local authorities as corporate members. Beyond that, when new members were enrolled in the early 1940s they would have been attracted by the idea of planning as opposed simply to the idea of the garden city. As such, this would have embraced a broader cross-section of society – intellectuals who had for some years been heralding the end of *laisser faire*, soldiers on active service who received copies of the Association's wartime publications, and a growing pool of those who were to elect a Labour Government to power in 1945.

With so little evidence, it would be rash to offer conclusive comments on the class composition of the membership. There are, however, enough fragments of evidence (for example in the propagandist methods used, letters received, reports of meetings) to lend support to a view that it was, predominantly, a middle-class organization with an educated membership who believed in the power of persuasion, and who could participate in the processes of rational debate. While it might be unfair to conclude that the Association's membership illustrates the view that 'the flaw in the pluralist heaven is that the chorus sings with an upper class accent' [7], there might, at least, be a hint of truth in this.

Leadership

Undoubtedly, of all the factors affecting the Association's history, the role of key figures has proved to be fundamental. Over nearly half a century, there are various personalities who played an important part.

For all their striking differences – the one a 'social inventor', and the other a 'political strategist' – the two 'giants' in the movement were Howard and Osborn. Each, in turn, had a fundamental impact on the course taken by the Association. From Howard the garden city movement derived its basic manifesto, and it is to him that the Association is indebted for his perseverance and almost mystical belief in the truth of the idea. From the platforms of meeting halls, it was Howard who preached the gospel of the garden city with a missionary's fervour, and secured for it a place in the nation's social conscience. Howard's strengths were in evangelizing rather than in organizing; in clinging to the spiritual purity of the idea, rather than in engaging in political machinations. It was his naivety as much as anything else which (in spurning the advice of others who knew better) brought the movement the second garden city. But in other respects his naivety and gentle nature left him ill-equipped to retain a central role in the Association, and for most of this period he was a figurehead rather than an active leader [8].

By contrast, Osborn took over where Howard left off, pouring new life into the garden city idea at the time of the First World War, and changing it in the process. Osborn, a Fabian and member of the Independent Labour Party, was always more sympathetic to the idea of a place for the State in future developments, a predilection that grew over the years. Following his apprenticeship in the pioneer town of Welwyn in the 1920s, the middle 1930s saw Osborn embark on a determined strategy to convert the Association into an organized lobby for a national system of planning. Single-minded like Howard, but more assertive when he had to be, Osborn's skills lay in directing the Association's efforts towards clear goals, and in political lobbying and propagandizing to secure their implementation. Garden cities, as such, slipped down the agenda, but, in turn, in the early 1940s the Association owed to Osborn a level of influence and importance that had eluded it in the bleak interwar years.

If Howard and Osborn were the true leaders, there were others who played critical roles at different times. It is questionable, for instance, as to whether the Association would have survived far into the present century (let alone whether it would have seen the foundation of Letchworth), had it not been for the guiding hand of Ralph Neville. But his was also a heavy hand, and the price to pay for his leadership was the dilution of Howard's more far-reaching ideals [9].

In its pioneer days, the Association was also moulded in the hands of a series of able administrators, Thomas Adams, Ewart Culpin and C. B. Purdom. The first of these, Thomas Adams, helped to set the organization on a national footing (and it was during his tenure as Secretary that the membership total reached a level not attained again in the period under study). Quite apart from his subsequent contribution to the early development of Letchworth, the Association gained (as with others) from his growing stature over the years as a planner of international esteem.

When Adams moved on to other things, the vacuum was filled by Ewart Culpin, who added to the growing national reputation an international dimension (not least of all in his role as a founder member of the IGCTPA). But for some of the purists, Culpin, who embraced garden suburbs and general planning goals within the orbit of the organization, was beyond the pale. Osborn, for instance, refused to acknowledge Culpin as a key figure in the garden city movement on account of his treachery in allowing the essential garden city idea to be 'submerged in the fashion for open housing estates and garden suburbs.' [10]

In contrast, C. B. Purdom, who succeeded Culpin as Secretary of the GCTPA in the early 1920s, was a garden city purist. Though enormously able, he found himself powerless to stem the oncoming tide of suburban development, and quickly retreated to the sanctuary of Welwyn. There he worked alongside Osborn and others who might, otherwise, have been turning their energies to the national cause rather than risking obscurity in a second demonstration project. This tension between the goals of specific projects and a wider campaign is at the heart of many of the Association's problems in its first thirty years or so.

There were others, too, to whom the Association owed a debt. As professional architects and town planners, Raymond Unwin and Patrick Abercrombie embraced the cause of garden cities, but not to the exclusion of related forms of development. As with Adams, their own professional progress as international figures served also to enhance, by association, the reputation of the garden city movement itself. The influence of Unwin, with his deep understanding of the social meaning of garden city architecture, was particularly influential, though his attachment to garden suburbs drew him away from the heart of the movement.

As well as the officers and professionals, there were others who, like Neville, lent their worldly experience and sponsorship to a worthy cause. R. L. Reiss worked unstintingly in pursuance of better housing, striking up a useful bond with another major figure in the housing reform movement, and a longstanding friend of the Association, Seebohm Rowntree. Additionally, both Lord Harmsworth and Sir Theodore Chambers (the latter devoting most of his time to Welwyn), provided the Association with valuable political and financial links.

Equally, it must be said that there were times when the leadership was lacking. With the departure of Culpin and then Purdom in the early 1920s, it is hard to find much that is positive in the leadership of the organization until the arrival of Osborn (and the able Gilbert McAllister) in 1936. The best that can be said of those middle interwar years is that the efforts that were expended enabled the Association to survive.

As a more general conclusion, it might be conjectured that the fortunes of pressure groups are heavily dependent on strong leadership, whether this takes the form of charismatic figures or of a team approach. Equally, groups are susceptible to the appropriation of their essential ideas by new leaders who, for one reason or another, see merit in redirecting priorities. There are elements of each of these styles and processes in the Association's own history, with important implications for the survival of the initial garden city ideal.

MAKING POLICY

> The structural properties of social systems are both medium and outcome of the practices that constitute those systems . . . structure is both enabling and constraining. (Giddens, 1982, pp. 36–37)

In contrast to the last section, which looked at inputs to the process of pressure group politics, this section and the next turn to outputs. How effective, it is asked, was the Association in achieving what it set out to do?

There are two aspects to be considered – the first is to stand back from the substantive issues surrounding the garden city movement, and to assess, in conceptual terms, the effectiveness of the Association as a pressure group; and the second aspect (leading from the first) is to conclude on whether or not nearly a half century of campaigning affected the course of planning history.

To take the first of these considerations of output, an assessment of a pressure group's effectiveness can be measured against various criteria. Thus, one source of assessment is to relate what is actually achieved to its initial and evolving goals. In the case of the Association, did it, for instance, fulfil the promise of disseminating the ideas of Howard, and of stimulating the building of garden cities based on these ideas? Was the New Towns Act the embodiment of these aims and the fulfilment of a long campaign, or was it a rebuttal of the basic principles of the garden city movement? Important though these questions are, they have, to some extent, been answered in the preceding text, and will, in any case, be returned to in the following section. The short answer is that progress was made on a number of fronts, though what was actually achieved on the ground fell some way short of the Association's underlying hopes and aspirations.

But (important though the above is as an issue in its own right) there is a more telling question (raised in the first chapter) that needs first to be answered; it is a general question surrounding the very nature of pressure group politics, and one that can now be explored, using the evidence of the Association's history. Quite simply, are pressure groups a political irrelevance, powerless in the face of weightier forces; or can they affect the course of events, and, particularly, the course of policy? The question is posed in an extreme form (a caricature of Marxist and pluralist explanations which neither would adopt without refinement), but it serves as a basis for an analysis that uses the helpful concepts of 'structure' and 'agency'. Each can be considered in turn, prior to examining inter-relationships between the two as a more satisfactory source of explanation. The above quote by Anthony Giddens provides a useful pointer towards the conclusion of the argument.

Structure

A structural explanation will look to 'macro' forces in society as the primary source of change. The basic workings and imperatives of a capitalist economy, the dictates of international trade, the fundamental constraints of class and ideology, and the hegemony of a particular culture will all be starting points in a structural analysis. It follows from this that individuals and organizations are simply passive agents, with little or no power to influence events – a view that is forcefully expressed by Louis Althusser, in that 'the structure of the relations of production determines the places and functions occupied and adopted by the agents of production, who are never anything more than the occupants of their places . . .' [11]

Thus, in a structuralist context, pressure groups might be seen as being either 'meaningless because they are monopolized by the capitalists' [12], or as being incorporated to serve the ends of the capitalist system. In this latter sense, two possible roles can be cast. One is where the actions of a pressure group are directed to serve the accumulation process, helping (normally, in an unintended way) to make capitalism more efficient; and the other role is one of helping to strengthen the legitimacy and social control functions of the State [13].

This is a serious critique of the role of pressure groups, and, consequently, of their potential to promote their cause and to influence the making of policy. In the case of the Association, acceptance of the thrust of this critique would lead to a clear conclusion that its work has been, at best, ineffectual, and, at worst, misguided. Whether such a view is valid or not depends, in turn, on the evidence of structural constraints on the campaign in the period from 1899.

A strong conclusion that has emerged from the evidence is that the progress of the Association does indeed appear to be closely related

to the incidence of wider events and processes. Without repeating the
substance of the evidence, a number of examples can be cited:

* There was the basic contradiction between some of the ideas
  inherent in Howard's original proposal (for instance, the need
  to raise large amounts of capital in the open market, while acknowledging the financial risks and dividend limitation that was
  involved) [14].

* The urgency of the 'housing question' (in the 1890s and in the
  pre-1914 period), that provided a context for interest in the formation of Letchworth and the growth of a wider planning lobby,
  cannot be divorced from wider concerns about internal and
  external security and a need to create a healthier environment for
  the country's working and fighting force.

* The shortlived boost to the Association's campaign that came in
  the years around the end of the First World War was also underpinned by political uncertainties and a determination to buttress
  (through better housing and other reforms) the walls of capitalism
  against the new forces of Bolshevism.

* No less significant, but in a negative sense, the lack of progress in
  the 1920s was not simply a product of inept leadership within the
  Association in this period, but was, more significantly, a product of
  a hostile political climate, in which *laisser faire* was still being
  advocated as the correct basis for economic and social government.

* Conversely, in the 1930s, the collapse of the world economy, and
  the structural problems of British industry, heralded the start of a
  new approach, with interventionism to supersede *laisser faire* as
  the essential basis for action. The resurgence of the Association
  after 1936, now carrying the banner of planning as opposed to,
  simply, that of garden cities, has to be seen in the context of these
  wider developments.

* A final example can be drawn from the early 1940s, when the
  Association was centrally involved in the seminal reconstruction
  debate – fired by a variety of motives, not least of which a need to
  modernize industry and prevent a return to the damaging conditions of the 1930s – that led, after the war, to a substantial
  redrawing of the social, economic and political map of Britain.

The above examples are sufficient to reinforce the important
conclusion that the Association's history has been inseparably bound

up with wider events. Looking at the period overall, the achievements of the Association are but a part of a general advance in
housing and planning reforms that are, in turn, a product of structural
changes. The decline of Britain's traditional industries, the country's
changing place in the world market, and the threat to capitalism from
opposing political ideologies have all had a fundamental influence on
the pattern of reformism in this century. Likewise, the changing
balance of social classes, the rise in disposable incomes amongst all
classes, a changing settlement geography, and new social tastes and
aspirations have all had a basic impact on the process of reform.

Structural factors are clearly important, but not necessarily the
only source of explanation. To point to a relationship between
structural forces and the specific actions of the Association is neither
to explain it as solely a question of cause and effect, nor to preclude
the possibility of an active response to imposed conditions. Structure,
as the above quote of Giddens illustrates, can be enabling as well as
constraining; and the role of a pressure group need not be as negative
as an extreme structuralist view would suggest.

Agency

Just as structural explanations address 'macro' issues, so it can be said
that agency explanations focus on the 'micro' level. The concept of
agency is one that rests on the importance of individuals and groups as
a major source of influence and change. In turn, there is a basic
pluralist presumption of liberal democratic principles, where everyone has access to the political process and where governments are
responsive to reasonable demands. There is also a presumption that
everyone is equipped to participate in the process, either as individuals or through the machinery of formal groups. It is in this latter
context that pressure groups are able to articulate and champion
particular sets of interests; they are key agents in the political process.

Certainly, the Association's history yields fruitful evidence of
agency factors at work. Apart from the very existence of the Association, the record of its activities is replete with examples that stress an
agency source of influence:

* There was, for instance, the charismatic approach of Howard
  himself, preaching the gospel of the garden city from the public
  platform, calling for true believers to come forward.

* In addition to Howard, the annals of the Association stress the
  work of other garden city pioneers as key figures in the movement.
  The likes of Adams, Unwin, Abercrombie and Osborn have
  already been acknowledged in the previous section. Of these,

Osborn carries the greatest weight, and it has been shown that he, himself, had no doubts about his own ability to influence policy-makers.

* There is also abundant evidence of the Association's self-acknowledgement, as, for example, in seeing its role as critical to the passing of the first town planning legislation in 1909, and, again, in frequent references to its ascribed place as the leading town planning and housing pressure group of its day.

* The wide range of propagandist methods employed by the Association (not least of all being the formation of two garden cities as demonstration projects) is also evidence of the trust put in the political process and in the power of reason to bring about change.

* Finally, of particular significance, one must cite the example of the New Towns Act, which was explained within the Association, not only as a product of its own persistent lobbying, but actually as an outcome of the personal influence of Osborn.

This is all compelling evidence in itself. But, as with the structural explanation, this evidence alone is not proof of cause and effect. In the case of agency factors, assessing their importance can be assisted by the application of a number of related concepts to explain the decision-making process. These concepts are, in turn, lodged within a pluralist framework of explanation, and it will remain to reconcile the competing claims of the structuralist arguments.

Following the work of John Kingdon [15], the thesis is that pressure groups, while not necessarily being directly responsible for a particular policy decision, may have an important role in creating an awareness of the issues and in 'softening up' politicians and others. It is a role which is directed towards creating a favourable political environment, so that decision-makers are primed and receptive to the issue in question.

In questioning how it is that some ideas surface onto a political agenda and others do not, Kingdon uses the concept of a 'policy community' of politicians, administrators and specialists. Within these communities, ideas float around in the same way that molecules floated around in what biologists called 'the primeval soup', before life came into being:

Many ideas are possible, much as many molecules would be possible. Ideas become prominent and then fade. There is a long process of 'softening up' . . . Ideas confront one another (much as molecules bumped into one another) and combine with one another in various ways . . . While many ideas float around in this policy primeval soup, the ones that last, as in a natural selection system, meet some criteria. Some ideas survive and prosper; some proposals are taken more seriously than others [16].

The garden city idea 'survived and prospered', although it changed in various ways along its evolutionary path. To continue Kingdon's reasoning, this should not be seen as a free-floating process. Pressure groups play their part, and within these are 'policy entrepreneurs' – people who work tirelessly in pursuit of a particular cause, and who await the opportunity to secure enactment. Eventually, a 'policy window' will open, and 'policy entrepreneurs must be prepared, their pet proposals at the ready, their special problem well-documented, lest the opportunity pass them by.' [17]

It is an interesting argument, consistent with the Association's history in so many respects. Once the garden city idea was formed, it was consistently advocated in competition with competing ideas about the future of settlements. The persistence of its advocacy led to a very high level of awareness amongst policy-makers, and when opportunities arose, the Association was well-placed to press home its case. The continuity of the campaign ensured that the idea of the garden city would not somehow float away, and key individuals (notably, Osborn) emerged to play the role of the 'policy entrepreneur'.

The problem with this argument is that it leaves unanswered one crucial question. Why is it that 'policy windows' are opened at particular times, creating opportunities for implementation? If this were to be purely a product of rational argument and persuasion, it would not account for the fact that they are opened at some times and not others. An agency form of explanation, putting stress on the organizational capacity of a pressure group and the skills of key individuals, clearly goes some way towards locating the influence of the Association, but it does not, on its own, provide a complete answer. For this it is necessary to reconcile the competing claims of the two perspectives, structure and agency.

Levels of Influence

The conclusion to emerge is that both structure and agency hold clues as to the role of the Association, the one apparently minimizing its contribution and the other enhancing it. In theoretical terms, to polarize the two perspectives is itself questionable. This is the essence of the work of Anthony Giddens, who advances the idea of 'structuration' as an expression of the continuing inter-relationships between the two: '. . . the settings and circumstances within which action

occurs do not come out of thin air; they themselves have to
be explained within the very same logical framework as that in
which whatever action described and "understood" has also to be
explained.' [18]

In the case of the Association it is concluded that an explanation of
its effectiveness as a pressure group will call on both structural and
agency arguments, recognizing a critical interplay between the two.
Thus:

* It is to structure that one must look to account for the time and form
  in which the garden city idea was deemed to be politically acceptable. In other words, at certain times the garden city idea (pruned
  of its more radical pretensions) features on the political agenda,
  and it is to the conjunction of wider events that one must look to
  explain this process.

* Likewise, agency factors have a role to play, and it is these that can
  explain the promotion of the garden city idea, as opposed to
  alternative theories of development. When (as a result of structural
  factors) the policy window was opened, the Association was in a
  position to ease its own policy into place.

Osborn was correct in attributing to himself (and to decades of
previous campaigning by others) a critical role in bringing about the
1946 New Towns Act, but it was only a partial truth. The fact that the
State sanctified the doctrine of the garden city at that time rests on
the force of wider circumstances as well.

SHAPING PLANNING HISTORY

> One should never be excessively realistic in humane plans. There
> are always too many difficulties and only a small percentage of aims
> may be attained. (Ebenezer Howard, quoted in Beevers, 1988,
> p. 184)

The previous section was designed to map out the sphere of influence
of the Association, showing how much might be attributable to its
own actions and how much has been due to wider circumstances.
Although boundaries were delineated, it was concluded that the
scope available to the Association to promote its cause was still quite
extensive.

This latter conclusion is certainly the view of an important body of
professional opinion, which attributes to the Association a key role in
helping to shape the planning system that emerged in the first half of
this century. The remainder of this section will first acknowledge this

view, before concluding with a qualified endorsement along the lines that the Association was influential, though not necessarily to the extent that has often been claimed.

It is uncommon to find a planning history text that fails to pay tribute to the garden city movement as a major source of influence on the development of modern planning thought and practice [19]. The underlying strength of the ideas on which the Association has campaigned has been variously accounted for in terms of the simplicity of the concept, the inherent potential for social improvement, the political acceptability of garden cities in the context of an increase in reformist measures, and the sheer 'Englishness' and cultural compatibility of the whole notion of the garden city [20]. Undoubtedly, the Association played an important (and often misread) part in articulating an ideal of houses with gardens, located at low densities beyond the old metropolitan boundaries, as a basic building block in the 'anti-urban' utopia [21]. In turn, anti-urbanism (a current of thought that flows from an earlier period, but which is given new form by the garden city and other ideas in this century) has proved to be a powerful source of imagery, integral to the pattern of twentieth-century planning thought and development [22].

Against this backcloth of anti-urbanism, one line of reasoning has been to explain the emergence of modern town planning in terms of an evolutionary logic, impelled by the force of the garden city movement. Thus, a classic exposition in these terms is that of Lewis Mumford, who (in a rebuttal of garden city critics) sees a progression from Howard's original scheme through to the adoption by the State of a programme of new towns:

In the first generation of its existence, Howard's 'impractical' proposals succeeded in bringing about the establishment of two Garden Cities, Letchworth and Welwyn; and both of these communities, starting as private enterprises, with limited prospects of gain, not merely survived indifference and opposition, but have affected the pattern of housing and city-building in many areas, from Scotland to India. It was the success of these ideas that led Sir Anthony Montague Barlow's parliamentary committee to recommend the industrial decentralization in garden cities as a remedy for the increasing congestion of London; and this led in turn to the New Towns Act of 1946, which projected a ring of New Towns around London and in various parts of England [23].

The idea of a progression of reformism has been endorsed by Peter Hall, who sees in the planning reports of the early 1940s the inspiration of Howard; particularly, he attributes the inheritance of the important notion that the planner has a responsibility to 'try to shape

L. I. H. E.

THE BECK LIBRARY

WOOLTON RD., LIVERPOOL, L16 8ND

the life of the community through physical arrangements.' [24] In later works, Hall recognizes that the influence of the garden city movement was by no means confined to national boundaries [25]; a view shared by Cherry, in the statement that 'this particularly British contribution to world planning was to flower in the new towns of post-war years.' [26]

While the work of the Association is not necessarily synonymous with the garden city movement (with the later years, especially, seeing a widening gap between the ideas it campaigned for and the original concept of the garden city), the role of the pressure group has correctly been acknowledged by planning historians as a key factor in the emergence of modern planning. Gordon Cherry, for instance, sees the Association as having from the start 'a very great influence on the planning movement.' [27] Likewise, looking particularly at the interwar period, Eric Reade contends that 'one of the strongest influences on what I have called this "mainstream" source of inter-war planning ideas was the Garden Cities and Town Planning Association.' [28] Particularly fulsome in his praise is Donald Foley, who has written (in 1962) that:

> As a social movement town planning has been promoted and guided for over sixty years by the Town and Country Planning Association . . . Overall, the garden city movement has been amazingly effective, and its active leaders must be credited with energetic and imaginative enterprise . . . through live experiments and persistent propagandizing, the Association has had a major impact on government policy and on the substantive doctrine pursued by British town planning [29].

In acknowledging the influence of the Association, it is not inconsistent to single out the particular contribution of key individuals who were instrumental in promoting the movement. Hall, for example, considers that Howard has been 'the most important single character' in the history of modern planning ideas and influence [30]. More specifically, in writing on new towns, Aldridge starts with the claim that:

> it was the tenacity and even eccentricity of two men that transformed, over the course of nearly fifty years, an inventor's obsession into a major piece of public policy. Ebenezer Howard had the idea; F. J. Osborn had the dedication, the political acumen and the longevity to keep it on the public agenda until new towns were enshrined in legislation [31].

Others, too, might be mentioned, and it is interesting to note that in a volume of pioneers in British planning, no less than seven of the eight pioneers 'adjudged to have made a unique contribution to British town planning this century' held office of some sort (elected or appointed) within the Association [32].

In various ways, then, the Association is widely acknowledged as a key actor on the twentieth-century planning stage; a conclusion that is broadly consistent with the evidence presented in the previous chapters. However, while it played an important part, it was not necessarily the star role it sometimes appeared to cast for itself. Indeed, a consistent theme in preceding chapters has been that, important though the Association was at various junctures, its role is often overstated. To balance this latter interpretation, a number of reservations can be made.

Firstly, there is the important argument expressed in the previous section, namely, that the Association's history cannot be explained in isolation from its structural context. It remains a sobering conclusion to conjecture that the general growth of State intervention in the first half of the twentieth century (not simply in the field of town and country planning, but across a broad sweep of social reforms) might have occurred in any case, with or without the accompanying work of pressure groups. This is not to deny a role in shaping what emerged, but it is to question whether the likes of the Association had any part in activating the process in the first place.

Secondly, while the Association was active throughout this period, it was by no means the only group that was lobbying for better housing and a more effective system of planning; nor were its own champions the only key figures in the planning movement. The National Housing and Town Planning Council and the Town Planning Institute are but two bodies that have made their own distinctive contribution to the shape of modern planning. Likewise, there is no shortage of examples of professionals, civil servants and politicians who were either not wholly committed to the garden city movement or were in some cases (like Thomas Sharp and Trystan Edwards) vehemently opposed, but who, nevertheless, played their own part in the emerging system.

Finally, in attributing credit to the Association for contributing to radical changes, not only to the planning system but, no less, to what has actually been built, a number of strands in the argument are sometimes confused. For a start, the garden city idea itself has been frequently and persistently conflated in the eyes of critics with the garden suburb and general suburban movement, if not with the even wider idea of 'anti-urbanism'. The kind of claim that suggests that if 'the garden city concept could be measured it would probably directly involve tens of millions of people' [33], needs, therefore, to be looked at very closely. It was part of, but by no means the whole of, this broader process.

Even if one were to accept a close link between garden cities and garden suburbs (and there are certainly grounds, for instance through the joint work of Raymond Unwin in both types of scheme, to take this view), there is strong evidence to show that Howard's scheme was by no means the start of it all. Apart from evidence of a long period of 'ideological preparation' [34], the last quarter of the nineteenth century could already boast the completion of a number of carefully-conceived garden suburbs and garden villages. Houses with gardens, a vernacular style of architecture, and a form of community planning were already gaining popular support, well before the establishment of Letchworth as a new model of settlement. In many respects, the first garden city was a culmination of ideas rather than the start of something new. A romantic version of suburbanization was likely to occur in any case, with or without the efforts of a pressure group.

And, as an added note of reservation, the claim that there is an unbroken path from *To-morrow* to the New Towns Act overlooks the fact that, all along the way, various elements of the original scheme were discarded. What eventually emerged as the fulfilment of a long campaign, was in some ways a testimony to its relative failure. It was not a garden city utopia that was to be enshrined in legislation, and certainly not the 'cooperative commonwealth' to which Howard originally aspired.

So, overall, the record stands as one of mixed achievement. It is concluded that the Association has made a distinctive contribution to the development of modern planning. But it is also concluded that this has to be seen in the context of associated ideas, key figures and institutions, and underlying economic, social and political processes. In the end, the Association's specific contribution might perhaps be likened to a single theme in a decorative pattern, albeit a theme of conspicuous intensity.

NOTES

A Record of the Association

1. This classification of key elements is derived from the importance attached to these characteristics in the foregoing chapters. The classification accords closely to that formulated by Ball and Millard (1986), who consider the nature and characteristics of pressure groups in terms of aims and objectives, organization, group membership, and the assets or resources of the group in relation to government.
2. From Howard's original manuscript, 'The Master Key', in Beevers (1988), p. 43.
3. See Beevers (1988). The thesis is one that has already been pursued in Buder (1969) and Fishman (1977), but Beevers adds new evidence and

insights, not least of all some revealing correspondence from G. B. Shaw to Howard and Neville.

4. For instance, the garden city was originally to have been named 'Unionsville', but that, suggests Beevers (1988), p. 54, might have 'conjured up a picture of some raw railroad town on the American prairie.'

5. G. B. Shaw, for instance, described the structure (with its plethora of committees) as one that might have been designed to provide a platform for 'cranks' with all kinds of 'irrelevant obsessions'. See Beevers (1988), p. 80.

6. Both Fishman (1977) and Beevers (1988) lend support to this view.

7. The view of E. Schattschneider, 1960, cited in Dunleavy and O'Leary (1987), p. 159.

8. Beevers (1988) provides convincing evidence, not only of Howard's managerial weaknesses, but also of a persistent lack of personal confidence.

9. Neville's uncompromising treatment of Howard is well illustrated in correspondence quoted in Beevers (1988), p. 88, where Howard is admonished for deterring would-be Letchworth investors with his continued public warnings of the financial risks involved.

10. Osborn, in a note (on the history of the TCPA) to David Hall, 21st March 1974. Osborn Papers.

Effectiveness as a Pressure Group

11. Louis Althusser, 1976, quoted in Walton and Himmelweit (1986), p. 32.

12. Dunleavy and O'Leary (1987), p. 223.

13. The 'accumulation' and 'legitimation' argument is reviewed, for instance, in Dunleavy and O'Leary (1987), chapter 5.

14. Beevers (1988), chapter 6, cites some hitherto unpublished letters from G. B. Shaw to shed fresh light on this issue. Shaw was consistently doubtful that capitalists could be persuaded to invest in the project as Howard had conceived it.

15. Kingdon (1984).

16. *Ibid*, p. 123.

17. *Ibid*, p. 173.

18. Giddens (1984), p. 360.

Influence on Planning History

19. An interesting exception is J. B. Cullingworth, who, in his text on town and country planning in Britain (1985), and in his official history of new towns policy, carries barely more than a passing reference to the work of the Association. It has to be recognized, however, that Cullingworth is dealing with official sources.

20. Beevers (1988) adds to an existing view that the garden city fitted comfortably into a specifically English mould of culture. It is an appealing argument, but it leaves unanswered the reasons for its

popularity in other countries, such as Germany.

21. The garden city idea was not, in fact, 'anti-urban', but was popularly
    seen to be so. The erroneous labelling is typified by Petersen (1968) in
    the view that 'Garden City Planning, based on the postulate that urban
    problems are insoluble within the framework of the metropolis, in
    effect denotes anti-city planning' (p. 160).
22. See, for instance, Glass (1955).
23. Mumford (1966), p. 594.
24. Hall *et al.* (1973), Vol. 1, p. 111.
25. Hall, P. (1984 and 1988).
26. Cherry (1970), p. 33.
27. Cherry (1974*a*), p. 36.
28. Reade (1987), p. 44.
29. Foley (1962), pp. 10, 16.
30. Hall (1988), p. 87.
31. Aldridge (1979), p. 1.
32. Cherry (1981*a*), p. 9.
33. Batchelor (1969), p. 200.
34. Petersen (1968), p. 160.

APPENDIX

Main events from the Formation of the Garden City Association to the New Towns Act

1899	Formation of Garden City Association.
1902	Re-publication of *To-morrow* as *Garden Cities of Tomorrow*.
1902	Formation of First Garden City Pioneer Company Ltd.
1903	Purchase of estate at Letchworth.
1903	Formation of First Garden City Company Ltd. (First Garden City Pioneer Company Ltd. wound up).
1904	Start of publication of regular Association journal, *The Garden City*.
1908	Change of journal name to *Garden Cities and Town Planning*.
1909	Change of Association's name to Garden Cities and Town Planning Association.
1913	Formation of International Garden Cities and Town Planning Association.
1917	Registration of the British Garden Cities and Town Planning Association (Incorporated).
1917	Formation of National Garden Cities Committee.
1918	Incorporation of NGCC with GCTPA.
1919	GCTPA National Housing Campaign.
1919	Purchase of land for Welwyn Garden City.
1919	Formation of Second Garden City Ltd.
1922	Change of IGCTPA name to International Garden Cities and Town Planning Federation.
1928	Death of Ebenezer Howard.
1929	Change of IGCTPF name to International Federation for Housing and Town Planning.
1932	GCTPA submission to Marley Committee.
1932	Change of journal name to *Town and Country Planning*.
1936	Introduction of new management structure and policy aims.
1938	GCTPA submission to Barlow Committee.
1939	GCTPA organization of Planning Front as national lobby.
1940	Publication of Barlow Report.
1941	Agreement of National Planning Basis as statement of aims.
1941	Change of Association's name to Town and Country Planning Association.

1941–44 TCPA Reconstruction Conferences and publication of series, *Rebuilding Britain*.
1945 Representation on Reith Committee.
1946 New Towns Act.

BIBLIOGRAPHY

SPECIAL COLLECTIONS

Town and Country Planning Association (London): the records of the Association have provided the richest source of primary material. Two catalogues exist – Martin Stott (1978) 'Material in the archives of the Town and Country Planning Association', and Phillippa Bassett (1980) 'A list of the historical records of the Town and Country Planning Association', Centre for Urban and Regional Planning Studies, University of Birmingham and Institute of Agricultural History, University of Reading. A particularly valuable source is the Association's journal, published as *The Garden City* from 1904 to 1908, *Garden Cities and Town Planning* from 1908 to 1932, and *Town and Country Planning* from 1932. In addition to the journal, the collection contains minute books, correspondence, press cuttings, illustrations and ephemera. These (and extracts from the Association's journal) are separately referenced in the notes in the foregoing text.

Garden City Museum (Letchworth): a varied collection of press cuttings, leaflets, journals, articles and books on the origins of the garden city movement in general, and of Letchworth in particular.

Howard Papers (Hertford): a limited but helpful collection of Howard's records, stored in the Hertfordshire Record Office.

John Johnson Collection of Printed Ephemera (Oxford): includes a variety of early twentieth-century pamphlets of the garden city movement and other housing campaign records.

National Housing and Town Planning Council (London): an unclassified collection, but with the early minute books intact.

Osborn Papers (Welwyn Garden City): a voluminous collection of papers, including some of the minute books of the Association. Of particular interest is the personal correspondence with leading politicians and planners of the day. The collection is now catalogued; see Eserin and Hughes (1990).

Royal Institute of British Architects (London): a guide to the very extensive records of the Institute has been edited by Angela Mace, *The RIBA: A guide to its archive and history*, Mansell: London, 1986. Selected references have been used, particularly for the period before 1914.

Royal Town Planning Institute (London): early records of the Institute, together with copies of the first editions of the *Journal of the Town Planning Institute*.

JOURNALS

Journal sets consulted (as opposed to individual journal references) were as follows:

Architectural Review
The City
The Garden City
Garden Cities and Town Planning
The Housing Journal
The Housing Reformer
Journal of the Town Planning Institute
Town and Country Planning
Town Planning Review

Journal abbreviations used in the referencing system are as follows:

AJ   (Architects Journal)
AR   (Architectural Review)
GC   (The Garden City)
GCTP   (Garden Cities and Town Planning)
IJURR (International Journal of Urban and Regional Research)
JAIA   (Journal of the American Institute of Architects)
JAIP   (Journal of the American Institute of Planners)
JTPI   (Journal of the Town Planning Institute)
PHB   (Planning History Bulletin)
PP   (Planning Perspectives)
TCP   (Town and Country Planning)
TPR   (Town Planning Review)

BOOKS AND ARTICLES

Abercrombie, P. (1933) *Town and Country Planning*. London: Thornton Butterworth.
Abercrombie, P. and Forshaw, J. H. (1943) *County of London Plan 1943*. London: Macmillan.
Abercrombie, P. (1945) *Greater London Plan 1944*. London: HMSO.
Adams, T. (1905) *Garden City and Agriculture: How to solve the problem of rural depopulation*. London: Simpkin, Marshall, Hamilton, Kent.
Adams, T. (ed.) (1906) *Housing in Town and Country*. London: Garden City Association.
Adams, T. *et al.* (1932) *Recent Advances in Town Planning*. London: J. and A. Churchill.
Addison, P. (1977) *The Road to 1945: British politics and the Second World War*. London: Quartet.
Adshead, S. D. (1941) *A New England*. London: Muller.
Aldridge, H. R. (1915) *The Case for Town Planning*. London: NHTPC.

Aldridge, M. (1979) *The British New Towns: A programme without a policy*. London: Routledge and Kegan Paul.

Ashworth, W. (1954) *The Genesis of Modern British Town Planning: A study in economic and social history of the nineteenth and twentieth centuries*. London: Routledge and Kegan Paul.

Armytage, W. H. G. (1961) *Heavens Below: Utopian experiments in England, 1560–1960*. London: Routledge and Kegan Paul.

Baker, A. G. (1970) Housing Reform: The early years. An account of the origins of the National Housing and Town Planning Council. London: NHTPC.

Ball, A. R. and Millard, F. (1986) *Pressure Politics in Industrial Societies: A comparative introduction*. London: Macmillan.

Barker, T. (ed.) (1978) *The Long March of Everyman, 1750–1960*. Harmondsworth: Penguin.

Barlow Committee (1940) *Report of the Royal Commission on the Distribution of the Industrial Population*. (Cmd 6153) London: HMSO.

Barnett, H. (1918) *Canon Barnett: His Life, Work and Friends* (Vols. 1 and 2). London: John Murray.

Baron, S. (ed.) (1944) *Country Towns in the Future England*. London: Faber and Faber.

Batchelor, P. (1969) The origins of the Garden City concept of urban form. *Journal of the Society of Architectural Historians*, Vol. 28, No. 3, pp. 184–200.

Beevers, R. (1988) *The Garden City Utopia: A critical biography of Ebenezer Howard*. London: Macmillan.

Benn, E. J. P. (1936) *Modern Government as a Busybody in Other Men's Matters*. London: Allen and Unwin.

Beveridge, W. (1944) *Full Employment in a Free Society*. London: Allen and Unwin.

Birchall, J. (1987) *Building Communities: The cooperative way*. London: Routledge.

Blatchford, T., 'Nunquam' (1893) *Merrie England*. London: Clarion. (Reprinted by Journeyman Press, 1976).

Bliss, B. (ed.) (1945) *The New Planning*. London: Faber and Faber.

Board of Agriculture (1916) *Final Report of the Departmental Committee to consider the settlement or employment on the land of discharged sailors and soldiers*. (Cd 8181, 8277) London: HMSO.

Booth, W. (1890) *In Darkest England and the Way Out*. London: Salvation Army.

Bournville Village Trust (1941) *When We Build Again*. London: Allen and Unwin.

Bournville Village Trust (1955) *The Bournville Village Trust, 1900–1955*. Bournville: Bournville Village Trust.

Bonham-Carter, Sir E. (1950) Planning and development of Letchworth Garden City. *TPR*, Vol. 21, No. 4, pp. 362–376.

Booth, C. (ed.) (1889–1902) *Life and Labour of the People in London*. London: Macmillan.

Bowley, M. (1945) *Housing and the State, 1919–1945*. London: Allen and Unwin.

Bowman, S. E. (ed.) (1962) *Edward Bellamy Abroad*. New York: Twayne Publishers.

Bradley, I. C. (1987) *Enlightened Entrepreneurs*. London: Weidenfeld and Nicolson.

Branson, N. and Heinemann, M. (1971) *Britain in the Nineteen Thirties*. London: Weidenfeld and Nicolson.

Branson, N. (1975) *Britain in the Nineteen Twenties*. London: Weidenfeld and Nicolson.

Briggs, A. (1961) *Social Thought and Social Action: A study of the work of Seebohm Rowntree, 1871–1954*. London: Longman.

Briggs, A. (1968) *Victorian Cities*. Harmondsworth: Penguin.

Bruce, M. (1966) *The Coming of the Welfare State*. London: Batsford.

Buder, S. (1969) Ebenezer Howard: The genesis of a town planning movement. *JAIP*, Vol. 35, pp. 390–398.

Bullock, E. H. (1944) *Planning Tomorrow's Britain*. London: Muller.

Bullock, N. (1987) Plans for post-war housing in the UK: the case for mixed development and the flat. *PP*, Vol. 2, No. 1, pp. 71–98.

Burnett, J. (1978) *A Social History of Housing, 1815–1970*. Newton Abbott: David and Charles.

Busby, R. J. (1976) *The Book of Welwyn: The story of the five villages and the garden city*. Chesham: Barracuda Books.

Calder, A. (1971) *The People's War: Britain 1939–1945*. London: Panther.

Calder, P. R. (1941) *Start Planning Now: A policy for reconstruction*. London: Kegan Paul.

Canovan, M. (1977) *G. K. Chesterton: Radical Populist*. New York: Harcourt Brace Jovanovich.

Chamberlain Committee (1920 and 1921) *Principles to be followed in dealing with Unhealthy Areas*. Interim Report, 1920; Second and Final Report, 1921. London: Ministry of Health.

Chelmsford Committee (1931) *Interim Report of the Departmental Committee on Regional Development*, Ministry of Health. (Cmd 3915) London: HMSO.

Cherry, G. E. (1970) *Town Planning in its Social Context*. London: Leonard Hill.

Cherry, G. E. (1972) *Town Planning in its Social Context*. London: Leonard Hill.

Cherry, G. E. (1974a) The Housing, Town Planning, etc. Act, 1919. *The Planner*, Vol. 60, No. 5, pp. 681–684.

Cherry, G. E. (1974b) *The Evolution of British Town Planning*. Leighton Buzzard: Leonard Hill.

Cherry, G. E. (1975) Factors in the Origins of Town Planning in Britain: The example of Birmingham, 1905–1914. CURS Working Paper No. 36, Birmingham University.

Cherry, G. E. (ed.) (1980a) *Shaping an Urban World: Planning in the Twentieth Century*. London: Mansell.

Cherry, G. E. (1980b) The place of Neville Chamberlain in British Town Planning, in Cherry (ed.) (1980a), pp. 161–179.

Cherry, G. E. (ed.) (1981a) *Pioneers in British Planning*. London: Architectural Press.

Cherry, G. E. (1981*b*) 'George Pepler, 1882–1959', in Cherry, G. E. (ed.) (1981*a*), pp. 131–149.

Cherry, G. E. (1988) *Cities and Plans: The shaping of urban Britain in the nineteenth and twentieth centuries*. London: Arnold.

Cole, G. D. H. (1921) *The Future of Local Government*. London: Cassell.

Cole, G. D. H. (1945) *Building and Planning*. London: Cassell.

Colls, R. and Dodd, P. (eds) (1986) *Englishness, Politics and Culture 1880–1920*. London: Croom Helm.

Creese, W. L. (1966) *The Search for Environment: The garden city, before and after*. New Haven: Yale University Press.

Cullingworth, J. B. (1975) *Environmental Planning 1939–1969, Vol. I Reconstruction and Land Use, 1939–1947*. London: HMSO.

Cullingworth, J. B. (1979) *Environmental Planning 1939–1969, Vol. III New Towns Policy*. London: HMSO.

Cullingworth, J. B. (1985) *Town and Country Planning in Britain*, 9th ed. London: Allen and Unwin.

Culpin, E. G. (ed.) (1910) *The Practical Application of Town Planning Powers*. London: P. S. King and Co.

Culpin, E. G. (1913) *The Garden City Movement Up-to-date*. London: GCTPA.

Culpin, E. G. (1917) The remarkable application of town-planning principles to the War-time necessities of England. *JAIA*, Vol. 4, No. 4.

Dangerfield, G. (1966) *The Strange Death of Liberal England*. London: Macgibbon and Kee.

Darley, G. (1975) *Villages of Vision*. London: Architectural Press.

Dawson, W. (ed.) (1917) *After-war Problems*. London: Allen and Unwin.

Day, M. G. and Garstang, K. (1975) Socialist theories and Sir Raymond Unwin. *TCP*, Vol. 43, pp. 346–349.

Day, M. G. (1981) The contribution of Sir Raymond Unwin and R. Barry Parker to the development of site planning theory and practice, c. 1890–1918, in Sutcliffe, A. (ed.) (1981*a*).

Deakin, D. (ed.) (1989) *Wythenshawe: The story of a garden city*. Chichester: Phillimore.

Delaney, F. (1985): *Betjeman Country*. London: Paladin.

Dix, G. (1981) Patrick Abercrombie, 1879–1957, in Cherry, G. E. (ed.) (1981*a*), pp. 103–130.

Donnelly, Desmond (1949) The Town and Country Planning Association. *TCP*, Vol. 17, No. 65, pp. 13–18.

Douglas, R. (1976) *Land, People and Politics: A history of the land question in the United Kingdom, 1878–1952*. London: Allison and Busby.

Dunleavy, P. and O'Leary, B. (1987) *Theories of the State: The politics of liberal democracy*. London: Macmillan.

Eden, W. A. (1947) Ebenezer Howard and the Garden City Movement. *TPR*, Vol. XIX, pp. 123–143.

Edwards, A. Trystan (written under the pseudonym of Ex-Service Man J47485) (1933) *A Hundred New Towns for Britain*. London: Simkin Marshall.

Elliott, P. (1972) *The Sociology of the Professions*. London: Macmillan.

Eserin, A. and Hughes, M. (eds.) (1990) *The Sir Frederic Osborn Archive: A descriptive catalogue.* Hertford: Hertfordshire County Council.

Evans, H. (ed.) (1972) *New Towns: The British Experience.* London: Charles Knight.

Fawcett, C. B. (1919) *Provinces of England: A study of some geographical aspects of devolution.* London: Williams and Norgate.

Fishman, R. (1977) *Urban Utopias in the Twentieth Century.* New York: Basic Books.

Foley, D. L. (1962) Idea and Influence: The Town and Country Planning Association. *JAIP*, Vol. XXVIII, pp. 10–17.

Fraser, D. (1984) *The Evolution of the British Welfare State.* London: Macmillan.

Freeden, M. (1978) *The New Liberalism: An ideology of social reform.* Oxford: Clarendon Press.

Freestone, R. (1986) Exporting the Garden City: Metropolitan images in Australia, 1900–1930. *PP*, Vol. 1, pp. 61–84.

Freestone, R. (1989) *Model Communities: The Garden City Movement in Australia.* Melbourne: Nelson.

Gardiner, A. G. (1923) *Life of George Cadbury.* London: Cassell.

Garside, P. L. (1988) 'Unhealthy Areas': Town planning, eugenics and the slums, 1890–1945. *PP*, Vol. 3, No. 1, pp. 24–46.

Gaskell, S. M. (1981) The suburb salubrious: Town planning in practice, in Sutcliffe A. (ed.) (1981*a*).

Gaskell, S. M. (1987) *Model Housing: From the Great Exhibition to the Festival of Britain.* London: Mansell.

GCA (1908) *Town Planning: In theory and practice.* London.

GCTPA (n.d., *c.* 1925) *Labour Saving in Small Houses: Being the report of an inquiry made by a sub-committee of the Women's Section of the GCTPA.* London: King.

GCTPA (n.d., *c.* 1932) *Proposals for the Building of Garden Cities: Evidence presented by the GCTPA to the Government Committee on Garden Cities.* London: GCTPA.

GCTPA (1938) *Royal Commission on the Geographical Distribution of the Industrial Population: Evidence of the GCTPA.* London: GCTPA.

Giddens, A. (1982) *Profiles and Critiques in Social Theory.* London: Macmillan.

Giddens, A. (1984) *The Constitution of Society: Outline of the theory of structuration.* Berkeley and Los Angeles: University of California Press.

Gillie, B. (1979) Landmarks in the history of British town and country planning, 1909–1939. *PHB*, Vol. 2, No. 1, pp. 5–11.

Glass, R. (1955) Urban Sociology in Great Britain, reprinted, pp. 47–73, in Pahl, R. E. (ed.) *Readings in Urban Sociology.* Oxford: Pergamon, 1968.

Glynn, S. and Oxborrow, J. (1976) *Interwar Britain: A social and economic history.* London: Allen and Unwin.

Gough, I. (1979) *The Political Economy of the Welfare State.* London: Macmillan.

Gould, P. (1988) *Early Green Politics: Back to nature, Back to the land, and Socialism in Britain, 1880–1900.* Brighton: Harvester Press.

Graves, R. and Hodge, A. (1971, first published 1940) *The Long Weekend: A social history of Great Britain, 1918–1939*. Harmondsworth: Penguin.

Greater London Regional Planning Committee (1929, 1931, 1933) *First Report* (1929); *Interim Reports: Decentralisation and Open Spaces* (1931); *Second Report* (1933). London: Knapp Drewett.

Hague, C. (1984) *The Development of Planning Thought: A critical perspective*. London: Hutchinson.

Hall, J. E. D. (1974) *Labour's First Year*. Harmondsworth: Penguin.

Hall, P. (1969) *London 2000*, 2nd ed. London: Faber and Faber.

Hall, P., Gracey. H., Drewett, R. and Thomas, R. (1973) *The Containment of Urban England* (Vols. 1 & 2). London: Allen and Unwin.

Hall, P. (1974) *Urban and Regional Planning*. Harmondsworth: Penguin.

Hall, P. (1984) Metropolis 1890–1940: Challenges and Responses, in Sutcliffe, A. (ed.) (1984).

Hall, P. (1988) *Cities of Tomorrow: An intellectual history of urban planning and design in the twentieth century*. Oxford: Basil Blackwell.

Hall, S. (1984) The rise of the representative/interventionist state, 1880s–1920s, pp. 7–49, in McLennan, G., Held, D. and Hall, S. (eds.) *State and Society in Contemporary Britain: A critical introduction*. Cambridge: Polity Press.

Halliday, R. J. (1968) The Sociological Movement, the Sociological Society and the genesis of academic sociology in Britain. *Sociological Review* (NS), Vol. 16, No. 3, pp. 377–398.

Halsey, A. J. (1986) *Change in British Society*, 3rd ed. Oxford: Oxford University Press.

Hannington, W. (1937) *The Problem of the Distressed Areas*. London: Gollancz.

Hardy, D. (1979) *Alternative Communities in Nineteenth Century England*. London: Longman.

Hardy, D. and Ward, C. (1984) *Arcadia for All: The legacy of a makeshift landscape*. London: Mansell.

Hardy, D. (1991) *From New Towns to Green Politics: Campaigning for town and country planning, 1946–1990*. London: E. and F. N. Spon.

Harmsworth, C. B. (1936) *Some Reflections on Sir Ebenezer Howard and his Movement*. London: GCTPA.

Harris, G. M. (1906) *The Garden City Movement*. London: GCA.

Harrison, M. (1981) Housing and town planning in Manchester before 1914, in Sutcliffe, A. (ed.) (1981*a*).

Harrison, M. (1989) The 1901 Garden City Association conference at Bournville. Paper presented at the Fourth International Planning Conference, Bournville.

Hawtree, M. (1981) The emergence of the town planning profession, in Sutcliffe, A. (ed.) (1981*a*).

Hayden, D. (1981) *The Grand Domestic Revoluion: A history of feminist designs for American homes, neighbourhoods and cities*. Cambridge (Mass): MIT Press.

Hebbert, M. (1980) *The Inner City Problem in Historical Context*. London: Social Science Research Council.

Hebbert, M. (1981) Frederic Osborn, 1885–1978, In Cherry, G. E. (ed.) (1981*a*).

Hobsbawm, E. J. (1969) *Industry and Empire*. Harmondsworth: Penguin.

Hopkinson, T. (ed.) (1970) *Picture Post 1938–50*. Harmondsworth: Penguin.

Horsfall, T. C. (1904) *The Improvement of the Dwellings and Surroundings of the People: the example of Germany*. Manchester: Manchester University Press.

Howard, E. (1898) *To-morrow: a peaceful path to real reform*. London: Swann Sonnenschein. Revised and republished as *Garden Cities of Tomorrow* in 1902, Swann Sonnenschein. Republished in 1946 with prefaces by F. J. Osborn and L. Mumford as *Garden Cities of Tomorrow*, London: Faber and Faber; and in 1965 with a new foreword by F. J. Osborn.

Hughes, M. R. (ed.) (1971) *The Letters of Lewis Mumford and Frederic Osborn*. Bath: Adams and Dart.

Hughes, W. R. (ed.) (1919) *New Town: a proposal in agricultural, industrial, educational, civic and social reconstruction*. London: Dent.

Hulse, J. W. (1970) *Revolutionists in London: A study of five unorthodox socialists*. Oxford: Clarendon Press.

The Hundred New Towns Association (1938) *The Hundred New Towns Association: Formation, progress and future policy*. London: HNTA.

Hurwitz, S. J. (1949) *State Intervention in Great Britain: A study of economic control and social response, 1914–1919*. London: Frank Cass.

Inter-Departmental Committee on Physical Deterioration (1904) *Report of the Inter-Departmental Committee on Physical Deterioration*. (Cd 2175) London: HMSO.

Jackson, A. A. (1973) *Semi-detached London: Suburban development, life and transport, 1900–1939*. London: Allen and Unwin.

Jackson, F. (1985) *Sir Raymond Unwin: Architect, planner and visionary*. London: Zwemmer.

Joad, C. E. M. (ed.) (1934) *Manifesto: Being the book of the federation of progressive societies and individuals*. London: Allen and Unwin.

Johnson, P. B. (1968) *Land Fit for Heroes: The planning of British reconstruction, 1916–1919*. Chicago: The University of Chicago Press.

Jones, G. (1986) *Social Hygiene in Twentieth Century Britain*. London: Croom Helm.

Keable, G. (1946) *Towns for Tomorrow*. London: SCM Press.

Keable, G. (1963) *To-morrow Slowly Comes*. London: TCPA.

Keating, P. (ed.) (1976) *Into Unknown England, 1966–1913*. Glasgow: Fontana.

King, A. D. (1980) Exporting planning: the colonial and neo-colonial experience. In Cherry, G. E. (ed.) (1980*a*).

Kingdon, J. W. (1984) *Agendas, Alternatives and Public Policies*. Boston, Mass: Little Brown.

Kirk, P. T. R. Rev. (1933) *New Towns for Old*. Industrial Christian Fellowship.

Le Corbusier (1936) The vertical garden city. *AR*, Vol. LXXIX, January–June, pp. 9–10.

Lever, W. H. (1927) *Viscount Leverhulme, by his Son*. Boston: Houghton Mifflin.

Levinson, D. L. (1975) British Pressure Groups: Three Case Studies. Unpublished BA Thesis, Harvard College.

London Society (1919) *Development Plan of Greater London: Prepared during the Great War, 1914–1918*. London, 1919.

Lowe, P. and Goyder, J. (1983) *Environmental Groups in Politics*. London: Allen and Unwin.

Macfadyen, N. (1927) 'The Need for New Towns', reprint of paper to Manchester Statistical Society, 9th March 1927. London: John Heywood.

Macfadyen, N. (1970, first published 1933) *Sir Ebenezer Howard and the Town Planning Movement*. Manchester: Manchester University Press.

MacKenzie, N. and MacKenzie, J. (eds.) (1983) *The Diary of Beatrice Webb. Volume Two 1892–1905: All the Good Things of Life*. London: Virago.

MacKenzie, N. and MacKenzie, J. (eds.) (1984) *The Diary of Beatrice Webb. Volume Three 1905–1924: The Power to Alter Things*. London: Virago.

Macmillan, H. (1933) *Reconstruction: A plea for national policy*. London: Macmillan.

Macmillan, H. (1938) *The Middle Way: A Study of the problem of economic and social progress in a free and democratic society*. London: Macmillan.

McAllister, G. and McAllister, E. G. (1941) *Town and Country Planning: A study of physical environment. The prelude to post-war reconstruction*. London: Faber and Faber.

McAllister, G. and McAllister, E. G. (eds.) (1945) *Homes, Towns and Countryside: A practical plan for Britain*. London: Batsford.

McDougall, G. (1979) The State, Capital and Land: The history of town planning revisited. *IJURR*, Vol. 3, pp. 361–380.

McElwee, W. (1962) *Britain's Locust Years, 1918–1940*. London: Faber and Faber.

Mansbridge, J. (1942) *Here Comes Tomorrow*. London: Dent.

Marley Committee (1935) *Garden Cities and Satellite Towns: Report of Departmental Committee*. Ministry of Health. London: HMSO.

Marsh, J. (1982) *Back to the Land: The pastoral impulse in Victorian England from 1880 to 1914*. London: Quartet.

Marshall, P. (1962) A British Sensation, in Bowman, S. E., (ed.) *Edward Bellamy Abroad*. New York: Twayne Publishers.

Marshall, T. H. (1965) *Social Policy in the Twentieth Century*. London: Hutchinson.

Marwick, A. (1964) Middle Opinion in the Thirties: Planning progress and political agreement. *English Historical Review*, Vol. LXXIX, No. 311, pp. 285–298.

Marwick, A. (1965) *The Deluge: British society and the World War*. London: Bodley Head.

Marwick, A. (1976*a*) *The Home Front: The British and the Second World War*. London: Thames and Hudson.

Marwick, A. (1976*b*) People's War and Top People's Peace? British Society and the Second World War, in Sked, A. and Cook, C. (eds.) *Crisis and Controversy: Essays in Honour of A. J. P. Taylor*. London: Macmillan.

Mass Observation (1943) *An Enquiry into People's Housing*. London: John Murray.

Masterman, C. F.G. (ed.) (1901) *The Heart of Empire*. London: T. F. Unwin.

Masterman, C. F.G., Hodgson, W. B. *et al*. (1907) *To Colonise England: a plea for a policy*. London: T. Fisher Unwin.

Masterman, C. F.G. (1909) *The Condition of England*. London: Methuen.

Meller H. (1990) *Patrick Geddes: Social Evolutionist and City Planner*. London: Routledge.

Merrett, S. (1979) *State Housing in Britain*. London: Routledge and Kegan Paul.

Miliband, R. (1969) *The State in Capitalist Society: An analysis of the Western system of power*. London: Weidenfeld and Nicolson.

Miller, M. (1979) Garden city influence on the evolution of housing policy. *Local Government Studies*, Vol. 5, No. 6, pp. 5–22.

Miller, M. (1981) Raymond Unwin, 1863–1940, in Cherry, G. E. (ed.) (1981*a*).

Miller, M. (1986) A Revaluation of the Garden City. Report of a colloquium held at Delft, March 1986. *PHB*, Vol. 8, No. 2, pp. 8–11.

Miller, M. (1989*a*) The elusive green background: Raymond Unwin and the Greater London Regional Plan. *PP*, Vol. 4, No. 1, pp. 15–44.

Miller, M. (1989*b*): *Letchworth: The first garden city*. Chichester: Phillimore.

Minett, M. J. (1974) The Housing, Town Planning, etc. Act, 1909. *The Planner*, Vol. 60, No. 5, pp. 676–680.

Mitchell, E. (1967) *The Plan that Pleased*. London: TCPA.

Ministry of Town and Country Planning (1944): *The Control of Land Use*. (Cmd 6537) London: HMSO.

Morris, A. E. J. (1971) From Garden Cities to New Towns. *Official Architecture and Planning*. Vol. 34, No. 12, pp. 922–925.

Morris, A. J. A. (1974) *Edwardian Radicalism 1900–1914*. London: Routledge and Kegan Paul.

Morris, W. (1890) *News from Nowhere*. London, first published in serial form in *Commonweal* (January–October 1890).

Morton, A. L. (1978) *The English Utopia*. London: Lawrence and Wishart.

Moss-Eccardt, J. (1973) *Ebenezer Howard: An illustrated life of Sir Ebenezer Howard, 1850–1928*. Tring: Shire Publications.

Mowat, C. L. (1955) *Britain between the Wars, 1918–1940*. London: Methuen.

Mullan, B. (1980) *Stevenage Ltd: Aspects of planning and politics of Stevenage New Town, 1945–78*. London: Routledge and Kegan Paul.

Mumford, L. (1943) *The Social Foundations of Post-War Building*, Rebuilding Britain Series, No. 9. London: Faber and Faber.

Mumford, L. (1944) *The Plan for London County*, Rebuilding Britain Series, No. 12, London: Faber and Faber.

Mumford, Lewis (1961) *The City in History*. New York: Harcourt Brace.

Mumford, Lewis (1966) *The City in History*. Harmondsworth: Pelican.

National Council for Social Service (1943) *The Size and Structure of a Town*. London: Allen and Unwin.

National Council for Social Service (1944) *Dispersal: An enquiry into the advantages and feasibility of the permanent settlement out of London and other great cities of office, clerical and administrative staffs*. London: Oxford University Press.

Nettleford, J. S. (1910) *Practical Housing*. Letchworth: T. Fisher Unwin and Garden City Press.

Nettleford, J. S. (1914) *Practical Town Planning*. London: St Catherine Press.

Neville, R. (n.d.) *Some Papers and Addresses on Social Questions*. London: Spottiswood, Ballantyne.

Newbold, H. B. (ed.) (1942) *Industry and Rural Life*. London: Faber and Faber.

New Townsmen (1918) *New Towns after the War*. London: Dent.

NHTPC (1910) *1900–1910: A Record of 10 Years' Work for Housing and Town Planning Reform*. Leicester: NHTPC.

Nuffield College Social Reconstruction Survey (1943) *Britain's Town and Country Pattern*, Rebuilding Britain Series, No. 2. London: Faber and Faber.

Oliver, P. *et al.* (1981) *Dunroamin: The suburban semi and its enemies*. London: Barrie and Jenkins.

Onslow Committee (1925, 1928, 1929) *Royal Commission on Local Government: First Interim Report* (Cmd 2506). London: HMSO, 1925; *Second Interim Report* (Cmd 3213). London: HMSO, 1928; *Final Report* (Cmd 3436). London: HMSO, 1929.

Orbach, L. (1977) *Homes for Heroes: A study of the evolution of British public housing, 1915–1921*. London: Seeley.

Osborn, F. J. (1932) Industry and Planning. *JTPI*, Vol. XVII, No. 7, pp. 229–242.

Osborn, F. J. (1934) *Transport, Town Development and Territorial Planning of Industry*. London: The New Fabian Research Bureau.

Osborn, F. J. (1938*a*) *The Planning of Greater London*. London: GCTPA.

Osborn, F. J. (n.d., *c*.1938) *Planning is Possible: The missing link in national policy*. London: GCTPA.

Osborn, F. J. (1938*b*) The problem of the great city: A Royal Commission at work. *Political Quarterly*, Vol. IX, No. 3, pp. 408–420.

Osborn, F. J. (ed.) (1940–44) *Rebuilding Britain*. London: Faber and Faber.

Osborn, F. J. (1941) *Overture to Planning*, Rebuilding Britain Series, No. 1. London: Faber and Faber.

Osborn, F. J. (1942*a*) *The Land and Planning*, Rebuilding Britain Series, No. 7. London: Faber and Faber.

Osborn, F. J. (1942*b*) *New Towns after the War*. London: Dent.

Osborn, F. J. (ed.) (1942–45) *Planning and Reconstruction*. London: Todd.

Osborn, F. J. (1942*c*) *Planning and the Countryside*. (Incorporates TCPA Memorandum to Lord Justice Scott's Committee on Development in Rural Areas, January 1942), Rebuilding Britain Series, No. 8. London: Faber and Faber.

Osborn, F. J. (1943) *Making Plans*. London: Todd.

Osborn, F. J. (1946*a*) The Garden City Movement: Reaffirmation of the validity of Ebenezer Howard's idea. *Landscape Architecture*. Vol. 36, No. 2, pp. 43–54.

Osborn, F. J. (1946*b*) *Green-Belt Cities: The British contribution*. London: Faber and Faber.

Osborn, F. J. (1950) Sir Ebenezer Howard: the evolution of his ideas. *TPR*, Vol, 21, pp. 221–235.

Osborn, F. J. (1959) *Can Man Plan? and other verses*. London: Harrap.

Osborn, F. J. and Whittick, A. (1977) *The New Towns: Their origins, achievements and progress*, 3rd ed. London: Leonard Hill.

Osborn, F. J. (1970) *Genesis of Welwyn Garden City: Some Jubilee memories*. London: TCPA.

Osborn, F. J. (1971) The history of Howard's 'social cities'. *TCP*, Vol. 39, No. 12, pp. 539–545.

Parsons, D. W. (1986) *The Political Economy of British Regional Policy*. London: Croom Helm.

Pearson, L. (1988) *The Architectural and Social History of Cooperative Living*. London: Macmillan.

Pease, E. R. (1963) *The History of the Fabian Society*. London: Cass.

Pepler, G. L. (1931) Twenty-one years of town planning in England and Wales. *JTPI*, Vol. XVII, No. 3, pp. 49–72.

Pepler, G. L. (1949) Forty years of statutory planning. *TPR*, Vol. 20, No. 2, pp. 130–108.

Pepper, S. (1978) The garden city legacy. *AR*, Vol. 163, No. 976, pp. 321–324.

Pepper, S. and Swenarton, M. (1978) Home Front: garden suburbs for munitions workers, 1815–1918. *AR*, Vol. CLXIII, No. 976, pp. 366–375.

Petersen, W. (1968) The ideological origins of Britain's new towns. *JAIP*, Vol. 34, pp. 160–170.

Pleydell-Bouverie, M. (1944) *Daily Mail Book of Post-War Homes*. London: Daily Mail.

Political and Economic Planning (1939) *Report on the Location of Industry: A survey of present trends in Great Britain affecting industrial location and regional development, with proposals for future policy*. London: PEP.

Priestley, J. B. (1984, first published 1934) *English Journey*. London: Heinemann.

Pumphrey, R. (1941) *Industry and Town Planning*, Rebuilding Britain Series, No. 6. London: Faber and Faber.

Purdom, C. B. (1913) *The Garden City: a study in the development of a modern town*. London: Dent.

Purdom, C. B. (1917) *The Garden City after the War*. Letchworth.

Purdom, C. B. (ed.) (1921) *Town Theory and Practice*. London: Benn.

Purdom, C. B. (1942) *Britain's Cities Tomorrow: Notes for everyman on a great theme*. London: King, Littlewood and King.

Purdom, C. B. (1945) *How should we rebuild London?* London: Dent.

Purdom, C. B. (1949, first published 1925) *The Building of Satellite Towns*. London: Dent.

Purdom, C. B. (1951) *Life Over Again*. London: Dent.

Purdom, C. B. (1963) *The Letchworth Achievement*. London: Dent.

Read, D. (1972) *Edwardian England, 1901–15: Society and politics*. London: Harrap.

Reade, E. (1987) *British Town and Country Planning*. Milton Keynes: Open University Press.

Rees, G. and Lambert, J. (1985) *Cities in Crisis: The political economy of urban development in postwar Britain*. London: Arnold.

Reiss, C. (n.d.) *R.L. Reiss: A memoir*. Welwyn.

Reiss, R. L. (1918, revised 1919) *The Home I Want*. London: Hodder and Stoughton.

Reith Committee (1946*a*) *Interim Report of the New Towns Committee*. (Cmd 6759). London: HMSO.

Reith Committee (1946*b*) *Second Interim Report of the New Towns Committee* (Cmd 6794). London: HMSO.

Reith Committee (1946*c*) *Final Report of the New Towns Committee*. (Cmd 6876). London: HMSO.

Reith, J. C. W. (1949) *Into the Wind*. London: Hodder and Stoughton.

Relph, E. (1987) *The Modern Urban Landscape*. London: Croom Helm.

Reynolds, J. P. (1952) Thomas Coglan Horsfall and the town planning movement in England. *TPR*, Vol. 23, pp. 52–60.

Richmond, A. C. (1945) *Land Settlement and Town Planning*, Rebuilding Britain Series, No. 11. London: Faber and Faber.

Robson, W. A. (1941) *The War and the Planning Outlook*, Rebuilding Britain Series, No. 4. London: Faber and Faber.

Rockey, J. R. (1977) The Ideal City and Model Town in English Utopian Thought, 1849–1902. Unpublished Ph.D. thesis, University of Oxford.

Rodwin, L. (1956) *The British New Towns Policy: Problems and implications*. Cambridge, Mass: Harvard University Press.

Rowntree, B. S. (1901) *Poverty: a study of town life*. London: Macmillan.

Roweis, S. T. (1981) Urban planning in early and late capitalist societies: outline of a theoretical perspective', pp. 159–177, in Dear, M. and Scott, A. J. (eds.) *Urbanisation and Urban Planning in Capitalist Society*. London: Methuen.

Rowland, P. (1968) *The Last Liberal Government: The promised land, 1905–1910*. London: Barrie and Rockliff.

Rowntree, S. (1944) *Portrait of a City's Housing*, Rebuilding Britain Series, No. 13. London: Faber and Faber.

Scott Committee (1942) *Committee on Land Utilization in Rural Areas: Report* (Cmd. 6378). London: HMSO.

Seager Committee (1920) *South Wales Regional Survey Committee* (Ministry of Health). London: HMSO.

Seaman, L. C. B. (1970) *Life in Britain between the Wars*. London: Batsford.

Searle, G. R. (1971) *The Quest for National Efficiency*. Oxford: Basil Blackwell.

Sennett, A. R. (1905) *Garden Cities in Theory and Practice* (Vols. 1 and 2). London: Bemrose.

Sharp, T. (1932) *Town and Countryside: Some aspects of urban and regional development*. London: Oxford University Press.

Sharp, T. (1936) Universal suburbia. *AR*, Vol. LXXIX, January–June, pp. 115–120.

Simon, E., Sir, and Simon, Lady (1935) *Wythenshawe*. London: Longmans, Green.

Simon, E. D. (1945) *Rebuilding Britain: A Twenty Year Plan*. London: Gollancz.

Simpson, M. (1985) *Thomas Adams and the Modern Planning Movement: Britain, Canada and the United States, 1900–1940*. London: Mansell.

Simpson, R. (n.d., c.1938) *The Practicability of Garden Cities: A plea for planned industry*. London: GCTPA.

Sissons, M. and French, P. (eds.) (1964) *Age of Austerity 1945–1951*. Harmondsworth: Penguin.

Sked, A. and Cook, C. (1979) *Post-war Britain: A political history*. Harmondsworth: Penguin.

Smets, M. (1987) Belgium reconstruction after World War I: a transition from civic art to urban planning. *PP*, Vol. 2, No. 1, pp. 1–26.

Smith, T. (1979) *The Politics of the Corporate Economy*. Oxford: Martin Robertson.

Smith, H. L. (ed.) (1987) *War and Social Change: British Society in the Second World War*. Manchester: Manchester University Press.

Stansfield, K. (1981) Thomas Sharp, 1901–1978, in Cherry, G. E. (ed.) (1981*a*), pp. 150–176.

Stevenson, J. and Cook, C. (1977) *The Slump: Society and politics during the Depression*. London: Cape.

Stevenson, J. (1984) *British Society 1914–45*. Harmondsworth: Penguin.

Stranz, W. (1973) *George Cadbury*. Aylesbury: Shire Publications.

Stuart, C. (ed.) (1975) *The Reith Diaries*. London: Collins.

Sutcliffe, A. (ed.) (1980) *The Rise of Modern Urban Planning, 1800–1914*. London: Mansell.

Sutcliffe, A. (ed.) (1981*a*): *British Town Planning: The Formative Years*. Leicester: Leicester University Press.

Sutcliffe, A. (1981*b*) *Towards the Planned City: Germany, Britain, the United States and France, 1780–1914*. Oxford: Basil Blackwell.

Sutcliffe, A. (1981*c*): *The History of Urban and Regional Planning: An annotated bibliography*. London: Mansell.

Sutcliffe, A. (ed.) (1984) *Metropolis 1890–1940*. London: Mansell.

Sutcliffe, A. (1989) The garden city movement and its role in British town planning before 1914. Paper presented at the Fourth International Planning Conference, Bournville.

Swenarton, M. (1981) *Homes Fit for Heroes: The politics and architecture of early state housing in Britain*. London: Heinemann.

Swenarton, M. (1985) Sellier and Unwin. *PHB*, Vol. 7, No. 2, pp. 50–57.

Tanner, M. F. (1987) Sir Dudley Stamp 1898–1966. *PHB* Vol. 9, No. 2, pp. 30–35.

Tarn, J. N. (1973) *Five Per Cent Philanthropy: An account of housing in urban areas between 1840 and 1914*. Cambridge: Cambridge University Press.

The 1940 Council (1942) *Ground Plan for Britain*. London.

Towndrow, F. E. (ed.) (1941) *Rebuilding Britain*. London: Faber and Faber.

Tyerman, D. (ed.) (1944) *Ways and Means of Rebuilding*. London: Faber and Faber.

Unwin, R. (1909) *Town Planning in Practice*. Letchworth: T. Fisher Unwin.

Unwin, R. (1912) *Nothing Gained by Overcrowding: How the garden city type of development may benefit both owner and occupier*. London: GCTPA.

Uthwatt Committee (1941) *Expert Committee on Compensation and Betterment: Interim Report* (Cmd 6291). London: HMSO.

Uthwatt Committee (1942) *Expert Committee on Compensation and Betterment; Final Report* (Cmd 6386). London: HMSO.

Vernon, R. V. and Mansergh, N. (eds.) (1940) *Advisory Bodies: A study of their uses in relation to Central Government, 1919–1939*. London: Allen and Unwin.

Walker, H. J. (1987) The Outdoor Movement in England and Wales, 1900–1939. Unpublished Ph.D. Thesis, University of Sussex.

Walton, T. and Himmelweit, S. (1986) The Individual in Society, pp. 7–43, in *Models of Man and Social Science* (D102, Unit 31). Milton Keynes: The Open University.

Ward, C. (1974*a*) *Say it Again, Ben! An evocation of the first seventy-five years of the Town and Country Planning Association*. London: TCPA.

Ward, S. V. (1974) The Town and Country Planning Act, 1932. *The Planner*, Vol. 60, No. 5, pp. 685–689.

Ward, S. V. (1988) *The Geography of Interwar Britain: The State and uneven development*. London: Routledge.

Warren, H. and Davidge, W. R. (1930) *Decentralisation of Population and Industry: A new principle in town planning*. London: King.

Webb, Sir Aston (ed.) (1921) *London of the Future: by the London Society*. London: Duttons.

Whittick, A. (1943) *Civic Design and the Home*. Rebuilding Britain Series, No. 10, London: Faber and Faber.

Whittick, A. (1987) *FJO – Practical Idealist: A biography of Sir Frederic Osborn*. London: TCPA.

Williams-Ellis, C. (ed.) (1938) *Britain and the Beast*. London: Dent.

Williams-Ellis, C. (1941) *Plan for Living*, Rebuilding Britain Series, No. 5. London: Faber and Faber.

Williams-Ellis, C. (1975, first published 1928) *England and the Octopus*. Glasgow: Blackie.

Williamson, D. B. (1948) *New Beginnings and New Towns*. London: TCPA.

Young, G. M. (1943) *Country and Town: A summary of the Scott and Uthwatt Reports*. Harmondsworth: Penguin.

Young, T. (1980) The Eugenics Movement and the Eugenics Idea in Britain, 1900–1914. Unpublished Ph.D. thesis, University of London.

PLANNING PERSPECTIVES

An International Journal of
Planning, History and the Environment.

EDITORS: **Professor G. Cherry**   **Professor A. Sutcliffe**
University of Birmingham, UK   University of Leicester, UK

Planning Perspectives reflects the interest of those concerned with the planning of the environment as well as those who seek to provide explanations for the origins and consequences of planning ideas, methods and activities.

The Journal's scope is international, linking the past with the present and the future on a worldwide basis and thus tracing the development and transfer of different planning practices.

Planning Perspectives brings together a variety of disciplines which combine to produce a fuller understanding of the complex factors which influence planning. These include academic disciplines such as historical sociology and geography, and economic, social and political history, as well as the more applied fields of public health, housing, construction, architecture and town planning.

An important feature of **Planning Perspectives** is its substantial book review section. This allows a wide-ranging and critical appraisal of the broad area of current international planning research.

For further information, a free sample copy of **Planning Perspectives** or subscription enquiries, write to
     Journals Promotion Dept.
     E & FN Spon
     2–6 Boundary Row
     London, SE1 8HN, UK
OR
     Journals Promotion Dept.
     E & FN Spon
     29 West 35th Street
     New York, NY10001-2291, USA

E & FN SPON
An Imprint of Chapman & Hall

INDEX

175781

MARYLAND LIBRARY   BECK LIBRARY
Tel. 737 3530   737 3511

Telephone renewals can only
be accepted after 4.30 p.m.

This book is

8